American Casebook Series
Hornbook Series and Basic Legal Texts
Nutshell Series

of

WEST PUBLISHING COMPANY
P.O. Box 64526
St. Paul, Minnesota 55164–0526

ACCOUNTING

Faris' Accounting and Law in a Nutshell, 377 pages, 1984 (Text)

Fiflis, Kripke and Foster's Teaching Materials on Accounting for Business Lawyers, 3rd Ed., 838 pages, 1984 (Casebook)

Siegel and Siegel's Accounting and Financial Disclosure: A Guide to Basic Concepts, 259 pages, 1983 (Text)

ADMINISTRATIVE LAW

Davis' Cases, Text and Problems on Administrative Law, 6th Ed., 683 pages, 1977 (Casebook)

Gellhorn and Boyer's Administrative Law and Process in a Nutshell, 2nd Ed., 445 pages, 1981 (Text)

Mashaw and Merrill's Cases and Materials on Administrative Law–The American Public Law System, 2nd Ed., 976 pages, 1985 (Casebook)

Robinson, Gellhorn and Bruff's The Administrative Process, 3rd Ed., 978 pages, 1986 (Casebook)

ADMIRALTY

Healy and Sharpe's Cases and Materials on Admiralty, 2nd Ed., 876 pages, 1986 (Casebook)

Maraist's Admiralty in a Nutshell, about 362 pages, 1988 (Text)

Schoenbaum's Hornbook on Admiralty and Maritime Law, Student Ed., 692 pages, 1987 (Text)

Sohn and Gustafson's Law of the Sea in a Nutshell, 264 pages, 1984 (Text)

AGENCY—PARTNERSHIP

Fessler's Alternatives to Incorporation for Persons in Quest of Profit, 2nd Ed., 326 pages, 1986 (Casebook)

AGENCY—PARTNERSHIP—Cont'd

Henn's Cases and Materials on Agency, Partnership and Other Unincorporated Business Enterprises, 2nd Ed., 733 pages, 1985 (Casebook)

Reuschlein and Gregory's Hornbook on the Law of Agency and Partnership, 625 pages, 1979, with 1981 pocket part (Text)

Selected Corporation and Partnership Statutes and Forms, 621 pages, 1987

Steffen and Kerr's Cases and Materials on Agency-Partnership, 4th Ed., 859 pages, 1980 (Casebook)

Steffen's Agency-Partnership in a Nutshell, 364 pages, 1977 (Text)

AGRICULTURAL LAW

Meyer, Pedersen, Thorson and Davidson's Agricultural Law: Cases and Materials, 931 pages, 1985 (Casebook)

ALTERNATIVE DISPUTE RESOLUTION

Kanowitz' Cases and Materials on Alternative Dispute Resolution, 1024 pages, 1986 (Casebook)

Riskin and Westbrook's Dispute Resolution and Lawyers, 223 pages, 1987 (Coursebook)

Riskin and Westbrook's Dispute Resolution and Lawyers, Abridged Ed., 223 pages, 1988 (Coursebook)

Teple and Moberly's Arbitration and Conflict Resolution, (The Labor Law Group), 614 pages, 1979 (Casebook)

AMERICAN INDIAN LAW

Canby's American Indian Law in a Nutshell, 288 pages, 1981 (Text)

Getches and Wilkinson's Cases on Federal Indian Law, 2nd Ed., 880 pages, 1986 (Casebook)

List current as of January, 1988

T7202—1g

LAW SCHOOL PUBLICATIONS—Continued

ANTITRUST LAW

Gellhorn's Antitrust Law and Economics in a Nutshell, 3rd Ed., 472 pages, 1986 (Text)

Gifford and Raskind's Cases and Materials on Antitrust, 694 pages, 1983 with 1985 Supplement (Casebook)

Hovenkamp's Hornbook on Economics and Federal Antitrust Law, Student Ed., 414 pages, 1985 (Text)

Oppenheim, Weston and McCarthy's Cases and Comments on Federal Antitrust Laws, 4th Ed., 1168 pages, 1981 with 1985 Supplement (Casebook)

Posner and Easterbrook's Cases and Economic Notes on Antitrust, 2nd Ed., 1077 pages, 1981, with 1984-85 Supplement (Casebook)

Sullivan's Hornbook of the Law of Antitrust, 886 pages, 1977 (Text)

See also Regulated Industries, Trade Regulation

ART LAW

DuBoff's Art Law in a Nutshell, 335 pages, 1984 (Text)

BANKING LAW

Lovett's Banking and Financial Institutions in a Nutshell, 409 pages, 1984 (Text)

Symons and White's Teaching Materials on Banking Law, 2nd Ed., 993 pages, 1984, with 1987 Supplement (Casebook)

BUSINESS PLANNING

Painter's Problems and Materials in Business Planning, 2nd Ed., 1008 pages, 1984 with 1987 Supplement (Casebook)

Selected Securities and Business Planning Statutes, Rules and Forms, about 475 pages, 1987

CIVIL PROCEDURE

American Bar Association Section of Litigation—Reading on Adversarial Justice: The American Approach to Adjudication, edited by Landsman, about 204 pages, 1988 (Coursebook)

Casad's Res Judicata in a Nutshell, 310 pages, 1976 (text)

Cound, Friedenthal, Miller and Sexton's Cases and Materials on Civil Procedure, 4th Ed., 1202 pages, 1985 with 1987 Supplement (Casebook)

Ehrenzweig, Louisell and Hazard's Jurisdiction in a Nutshell, 4th Ed., 232 pages, 1980 (Text)

Federal Rules of Civil-Appellate Procedure—West Law School Edition, 596 pages, 1987

Friedenthal, Kane and Miller's Hornbook on Civil Procedure, 876 pages, 1985 (Text)

Kane's Civil Procedure in a Nutshell, 2nd Ed., 306 pages, 1986 (Text)

CIVIL PROCEDURE—Cont'd

Koffler and Reppy's Hornbook on Common Law Pleading, 663 pages, 1969 (Text)

Marcus and Sherman's Complex Litigation—Cases and Materials on Advanced Civil Procedure, 846 pages, 1985 (Casebook)

Park's Computer-Aided Exercises on Civil Procedure, 2nd Ed., 167 pages, 1983 (Coursebook)

Siegel's Hornbook on New York Practice, 1011 pages, 1978 with 1987 Pocket Part (Text)

See also Federal Jurisdiction and Procedure

CIVIL RIGHTS

Abernathy's Cases and Materials on Civil Rights, 660 pages, 1980 (Casebook)

Cohen's Cases on the Law of Deprivation of Liberty: A Study in Social Control, 755 pages, 1980 (Casebook)

Lockhart, Kamisar, Choper and Shiffrin's Cases on Constitutional Rights and Liberties, 6th Ed., 1266 pages, 1986 with 1987 Supplement (Casebook)—reprint from Lockhart, et al. Cases on Constitutional Law, 6th Ed., 1986

Vieira's Civil Rights in a Nutshell, 279 pages, 1978 (Text)

COMMERCIAL LAW

Bailey's Secured Transactions in a Nutshell, 2nd Ed., 391 pages, 1981 (Text)

Epstein, Henning and Nickles' Basic Uniform Commercial Code Teaching Materials, 3rd Ed., about 720 pages, 1988 (Casebook)

Henson's Hornbook on Secured Transactions Under the U.C.C., 2nd Ed., 504 pages, 1979 with 1979 P.P. (Text)

Murray's Commercial Law, Problems and Materials, 366 pages, 1975 (Coursebook)

Nickles, Matheson and Dolan's Materials for Understanding Credit and Payment Systems, 923 pages, 1987 (Casebook)

Nordstrom, Murray and Clovis' Problems and Materials on Sales, 515 pages, 1982 (Casebook)

Nordstrom, Murray and Clovis' Problems and Materials on Secured Transactions, 594 pages, 1987 (Casebook)

Selected Commercial Statutes, 1527 pages, 1987

Speidel, Summers and White's Teaching Materials on Commercial Law, 4th Ed., 1448 pages, 1987 (Casebook)

Speidel, Summers and White's Commercial Paper: Teaching Materials, 4th Ed., about 578 pages, 1987 (Casebook)—reprint from Speidel, et al. Commercial Law, 4th Ed.

Speidel, Summers and White's Sales: Teaching Materials, 4th Ed., 804 pages, 1987 (Casebook)—reprint from Speidel, et al. Commercial Law, 4th Ed.

LAW SCHOOL PUBLICATIONS—Continued

COMMERCIAL LAW—Cont'd

Speidel, Summers and White's Secured Transactions—Teaching Materials, 4th Ed., 485 pages, 1987 (Casebook)—reprint from Speidel, et al. Commercial Law, 4th Ed.

Stockton's Sales in a Nutshell, 2nd Ed., 370 pages, 1981 (Text)

Stone's Uniform Commercial Code in a Nutshell, 2nd Ed., 516 pages, 1984 (Text)

Uniform Commercial Code, Official Text with Comments, 994 pages, 1978

UCC Article 9, Reprint from 1962 Code, 128 pages, 1976

UCC Article 9, 1972 Amendments, 304 pages, 1978

Weber and Speidel's Commercial Paper in a Nutshell, 3rd Ed., 404 pages, 1982 (Text)

White and Summers' Hornbook on the Uniform Commercial Code, 3rd Ed., 1988 (Text)

COMMUNITY PROPERTY

Mennell and Boykoff's Community Property in a Nutshell, about 475 pages, 1988 (Text)

Verrall and Bird's Cases and Materials on California Community Property, 4th Ed., 549 pages, 1983 (Casebook)

COMPARATIVE LAW

Barton, Gibbs, Li and Merryman's Law in Radically Different Cultures, 960 pages, 1983 (Casebook)

Glendon, Gordon and Osakive's Comparative Legal Traditions: Text, Materials and Cases on the Civil Law, Common Law, and Socialist Law Traditions, 1091 pages, 1985 (Casebook)

Glendon, Gordon, and Osakwe's Comparative Legal Traditions in a Nutshell, 402 pages, 1982 (Text)

Langbein's Comparative Criminal Procedure: Germany, 172 pages, 1977 (Casebook)

COMPUTERS AND LAW

Maggs and Sprowl's Computer Applications in the Law, 316 pages, 1987 (Coursebook)

Mason's An Introduction to the Use of Computers in Law, about 275 pages, 1988 (Text)

CONFLICT OF LAWS

Cramton, Currie and Kay's Cases-Comments-Questions on Conflict of Laws, 4th Ed., 876 pages, 1987 (Casebook)

Scoles and Hay's Hornbook on Conflict of Laws, Student Ed., 1085 pages, 1982 with 1986 P.P. (Text)

Scoles and Weintraub's Cases and Materials on Conflict of Laws, 2nd Ed., 966 pages, 1972, with 1978 Supplement (Casebook)

CONFLICT OF LAWS—Cont'd

Siegel's Conflicts in a Nutshell, 469 pages, 1982 (Text)

CONSTITUTIONAL LAW

Barron and Dienes' Constitutional Law in a Nutshell, 389 pages, 1986 (Text)

Engdahl's Constitutional Federalism in a Nutshell, 2nd Ed., 411 pages, 1987 (Text)

Lockhart, Kamisar, Choper and Shiffrin's Cases-Comments-Questions on Constitutional Law, 6th Ed., 1601 pages, 1986 with 1987 Supplement (Casebook)

Lockhart, Kamisar, Choper and Shiffrin's Cases-Comments-Questions on the American Constitution, 6th Ed., 1260 pages, 1986 with 1987 Supplement (Casebook)—abridgment of Lockhart, et al. Cases on Constitutional Law, 6th Ed., 1986

Manning's The Law of Church-State Relations in a Nutshell, 305 pages, 1981 (Text)

Miller's Presidential Power in a Nutshell, 328 pages, 1977 (Text)

Nowak, Rotunda and Young's Hornbook on Constitutional Law, 3rd Ed., Student Ed., 1191 pages, 1986 (Text)

Rotunda's Modern Constitutional Law: Cases and Notes, 2nd Ed., 1004 pages, 1985, with 1987 Supplement (Casebook)

Williams' Constitutional Analysis in a Nutshell, 388 pages, 1979 (Text)

See also Civil Rights, Foreign Relations and National Security Law

CONSUMER LAW

Epstein and Nickles' Consumer Law in a Nutshell, 2nd Ed., 418 pages, 1981 (Text)

Selected Commercial Statutes, 1527 pages, 1987

Spanogle and Rohner's Cases and Materials on Consumer Law, 693 pages, 1979, with 1982 Supplement (Casebook)

See also Commercial Law

CONTRACTS

Calamari & Perillo's Cases and Problems on Contracts, 1061 pages, 1978 (Casebook)

Calamari and Perillo's Hornbook on Contracts, 3rd Ed., 904 pages, 1987 (Text)

Corbin's Text on Contracts, One Volume Student Edition, 1224 pages, 1952 (Text)

Fessler and Loiseaux's Cases and Materials on Contracts, 837 pages, 1982 (Casebook)

Friedman's Contract Remedies in a Nutshell, 323 pages, 1981 (Text)

Fuller and Eisenberg's Cases on Basic Contract Law, 4th Ed., 1203 pages, 1981 (Casebook)

Hamilton, Rau and Weintraub's Cases and Materials on Contracts, 830 pages, 1984 (Casebook)

LAW SCHOOL PUBLICATIONS—Continued

CONTRACTS—Cont'd

Jackson and Bollinger's Cases on Contract Law in Modern Society, 2nd Ed., 1329 pages, 1980 (Casebook)

Keyes' Government Contracts in a Nutshell, 423 pages, 1979 (Text)

Schaber and Rohwer's Contracts in a Nutshell, 2nd Ed., 425 pages, 1984 (Text)

Summers and Hillman's Contract and Related Obligation: Theory, Doctrine and Practice, 1074 pages, 1987 (Casebook)

COPYRIGHT

See Patent and Copyright Law

CORPORATE FINANCE

Hamilton's Cases and Materials on Corporate Finance, 895 pages, 1984 with 1986 Supplement (Casebook)

CORPORATIONS

Hamilton's Cases on Corporations—Including Partnerships and Limited Partnerships, 3rd Ed., 1213 pages, 1986 with 1986 Statutory Supplement (Casebook)

Hamilton's Law of Corporations in a Nutshell, 2nd Ed., 515 pages, 1987 (Text)

Henn's Teaching Materials on Corporations, 2nd Ed., 1204 pages, 1986 (Casebook)

Henn and Alexander's Hornbook on Corporations, 3rd Ed., Student Ed., 1371 pages, 1983 with 1986 P.P. (Text)

Jennings and Buxbaum's Cases and Materials on Corporations, 5th Ed., 1180 pages, 1979 (Casebook)

Selected Corporation and Partnership Statutes, Regulations and Forms, 621 pages, 1987

Solomon, Schwartz' and Bauman's Materials and Problems on Corporations: Law and Policy, 2nd Ed., about 900 pages, 1988 (Casebook)

CORRECTIONS

Krantz's Cases and Materials on the Law of Corrections and Prisoners' Rights, 3rd Ed., 855 pages, 1986 with 1988 Supplement (Casebook)

Krantz's Law of Corrections and Prisoners' Rights in a Nutshell, 2nd Ed., 386 pages, 1983 (Text)

Popper's Post-Conviction Remedies in a Nutshell, 360 pages, 1978 (Text)

Robbins' Cases and Materials on Post Conviction Remedies, 506 pages, 1982 (Casebook)

CREDITOR'S RIGHTS

Bankruptcy Code, Rules and Forms, Law School Ed., 792 pages, 1988

Epstein's Debtor-Creditor Law in a Nutshell, 3rd Ed., 383 pages, 1986 (Text)

CREDITOR'S RIGHTS—Cont'd

Epstein, Landers and Nickles' Debtors and Creditors: Cases and Materials, 3rd Ed., 1059 pages, 1987 (Casebook)

LoPucki's Player's Manual for the Debtor-Creditor Game, 123 pages, 1985 (Coursebook)

Riesenfeld's Cases and Materials on Creditors' Remedies and Debtors' Protection, 4th Ed., 914 pages, 1987 (Casebook)

White's Bankruptcy and Creditor's Rights: Cases and Materials, 812 pages, 1985, with 1987 Supplement (Casebook)

CRIMINAL LAW AND CRIMINAL PROCEDURE

Abrams', Federal Criminal Law and its Enforcement, 882 pages, 1986 (Casebook)

Carlson's Adjudication of Criminal Justice, Problems and References, 130 pages, 1986 (Casebook)

Dix and Sharlot's Cases and Materials on Criminal Law, 3rd Ed., 846 pages, 1987 (Casebook)

Federal Rules of Criminal Procedure—West Law School Edition, 567 pages, 1987

Grano's Problems in Criminal Procedure, 2nd Ed., 176 pages, 1981 (Problem book)

Israel and LaFave's Criminal Procedure in a Nutshell, 4th Ed., about 500 pages, 1988 (Text)

Johnson's Cases, Materials and Text on Criminal Law, 3rd Ed., 783 pages, 1985 (Casebook)

Johnson's Cases on Criminal Procedure, 859 pages, 1987 (Casebook)

Kamisar, LaFave and Israel's Cases, Comments and Questions on Modern Criminal Procedure, 6th Ed., 1558 pages, 1986 with 1987 Supplement (Casebook)

Kamisar, LaFave and Israel's Cases, Comments and Questions on Basic Criminal Procedure, 6th Ed., 860 pages, 1986 with 1987 Supplement (Casebook)—reprint from Kamisar, et al. Modern Criminal Procedure, 6th ed., 1986

LaFave's Modern Criminal Law: Cases, Comments and Questions, 2nd Ed., about 1000 pages, 1988 (Casebook)

LaFave and Israel's Hornbook on Criminal Procedure, Student Ed., 1142 pages, 1985 with 1987 P.P. (Text)

LaFave and Scott's Hornbook on Criminal Law, 2nd Ed., Student Ed., 918 pages, 1986 (Text)

Langbein's Comparative Criminal Procedure: Germany, 172 pages, 1977 (Casebook)

Loewy's Criminal Law in a Nutshell, 2nd Ed., 321 pages, 1987 (Text)

Saltzburg's American Criminal Procedure, Cases and Commentary, 3rd Ed., about 1200 pages, 1988 (Casebook)

LAW SCHOOL PUBLICATIONS—Continued

CRIMINAL LAW AND CRIMINAL PRO-CEDURE—Cont'd

Uviller's The Processes of Criminal Justice: Investigation and Adjudication, 2nd Ed., 1384 pages, 1979 with 1979 Statutory Supplement and 1986 Update (Casebook)

Uviller's The Processes of Criminal Justice: Adjudication, 2nd Ed., 730 pages, 1979. Soft-cover reprint from Uviller's The Processes of Criminal Justice: Investigation and Adjudication, 2nd Ed. (Casebook)

Uviller's The Processes of Criminal Justice: Investigation, 2nd Ed., 655 pages, 1979. Soft-cover reprint from Uviller's The Processes of Criminal Justice: Investigation and Adjudication, 2nd Ed. (Casebook)

Vorenberg's Cases on Criminal Law and Procedure, 2nd Ed., 1088 pages, 1981 with 1987 Supplement (Casebook)

See also Corrections, Juvenile Justice

DECEDENTS ESTATES

See Trusts and Estates

DOMESTIC RELATIONS

Clark's Cases and Problems on Domestic Relations, 3rd Ed., 1153 pages, 1980 (Casebook)

Clark's Hornbook on Domestic Relations, 2nd Ed., Student Ed., about 1100 pages, 1988 (Text)

Krause's Cases and Materials on Family Law, 2nd Ed., 1221 pages, 1983 with 1986 Supplement (Casebook)

Krause's Family Law in a Nutshell, 2nd Ed., 444 pages, 1986 (Text)

Krauskopf's Cases on Property Division at Marriage Dissolution, 250 pages, 1984 (Casebook)

ECONOMICS, LAW AND

Goetz' Cases and Materials on Law and Economics, 547 pages, 1984 (Casebook)

See also Antitrust, Regulated Industries

EDUCATION LAW

Alexander and Alexander's The Law of Schools, Students and Teachers in a Nutshell, 409 pages, 1984 (Text)

Morris' The Constitution and American Education, 2nd Ed., 992 pages, 1980 (Casebook)

EMPLOYMENT DISCRIMINATION

Jones, Murphy and Belton's Cases on Discrimination in Employment, 1116 pages, 1987 (Casebook)

Player's Cases and Materials on Employment Discrimination Law, 2nd Ed., 782 pages, 1984 (Casebook)

EMPLOYMENT DISCRIMINATION—Cont'd

Player's Federal Law of Employment Discrimination in a Nutshell, 2nd Ed., 402 pages, 1981 (Text)

Player's Hornbook on the Law of Employment Discrimination, Student Ed., about 650 pages, 1988 (Text)

See also Women and the Law

ENERGY AND NATURAL RESOURCES LAW

Laitos' Cases and Materials on Natural Resources Law, 938 pages, 1985 (Casebook)

Rodgers' Cases and Materials on Energy and Natural Resources Law, 2nd Ed., 877 pages, 1983 (Casebook)

Selected Environmental Law Statutes, about 654 pages, 1987

Tomain's Energy Law in a Nutshell, 338 pages, 1981 (Text)

See also Environmental Law, Oil and Gas, Water Law

ENVIRONMENTAL LAW

Bonine and McGarity's Cases and Materials on the Law of Environment and Pollution, 1076 pages, 1984 (Casebook)

Findley and Farber's Cases and Materials on Environmental Law, 2nd Ed., 813 pages, 1985 (Casebook)

Findley and Farber's Environmental Law in a Nutshell, 343 pages, 1983 (Text)

Rodgers' Hornbook on Environmental Law, 956 pages, 1977 with 1984 pocket part (Text)

Selected Environmental Law Statutes, 654 pages, 1987

See also Energy Law, Natural Resources Law, Water Law

EQUITY

See Remedies

ESTATES

See Trusts and Estates

ESTATE PLANNING

Kurtz' Cases, Materials and Problems on Family Estate Planning, 853 pages, 1983 (Casebook)

Lynn's Introduction to Estate Planning, in a Nutshell, 3rd Ed., 370 pages, 1983 (Text)

See also Taxation

EVIDENCE

Broun and Meisenholder's Problems in Evidence, 2nd Ed., 304 pages, 1981 (Problem book)

Cleary and Strong's Cases, Materials and Problems on Evidence, 3rd Ed., 1143 pages, 1981 (Casebook)

LAW SCHOOL PUBLICATIONS—Continued

EVIDENCE—Cont'd

Federal Rules of Evidence for United States Courts and Magistrates, 370 pages, 1987

Graham's Federal Rules of Evidence in a Nutshell, 2nd Ed., 473 pages, 1987 (Text)

Kimball's Programmed Materials on Problems in Evidence, 380 pages, 1978 (Problem book)

Lempert and Saltzburg's A Modern Approach to Evidence: Text, Problems, Transcripts and Cases, 2nd Ed., 1232 pages, 1983 (Casebook)

Lilly's Introduction to the Law of Evidence, 2nd Ed., about 600 pages, 1987 (Text)

McCormick, Sutton and Wellborn's Cases and Materials on Evidence, 6th Ed., 1067 pages, 1987 (Casebook)

McCormick's Hornbook on Evidence, 3rd Ed., Student Ed., 1156 pages, 1984 with 1987 P.P. (Text)

Rothstein's Evidence, State and Federal Rules in a Nutshell, 2nd Ed., 514 pages, 1981 (Text)

Saltzburg's Evidence Supplement: Rules, Statutes, Commentary, 245 pages, 1980 (Casebook Supplement)

FEDERAL JURISDICTION AND PROCEDURE

Currie's Cases and Materials on Federal Courts, 3rd Ed., 1042 pages, 1982 with 1985 Supplement (Casebook)

Currie's Federal Jurisdiction in a Nutshell, 2nd Ed., 258 pages, 1981 (Text)

Federal Rules of Civil-Appellate Procedure—West Law School Edition, 596 pages, 1987

Forrester and Moye's Cases and Materials on Federal Jurisdiction and Procedure, 3rd Ed., 917 pages, 1977 with 1985 Supplement (Casebook)

Redish's Cases, Comments and Questions on Federal Courts, 878 pages, 1983 with 1986 Supplement (Casebook)

Vetri and Merrill's Federal Courts, Problems and Materials, 2nd Ed., 232 pages, 1984 (Problem Book)

Wright's Hornbook on Federal Courts, 4th Ed., Student Ed., 870 pages, 1983 (Text)

FOREIGN RELATIONS AND NATIONAL SECURITY LAW

Franck and Glennon's United States Foreign Relations Law: Cases, Materials and Simulations, 941 pages, 1987 (Casebook)

FUTURE INTERESTS

See Trusts and Estates

HEALTH LAW

See Medicine, Law and

IMMIGRATION LAW

Aleinikoff and Martin's Immigration Process and Policy, 1042 pages, 1985, with 1987 Supplement (Casebook)

Weissbrodt's Immigration Law and Procedure in a Nutshell, 345 pages, 1984 (Text)

INDIAN LAW

See American Indian Law

INSURANCE

Dobbyn's Insurance Law in a Nutshell, 281 pages, 1981 (Text)

Keeton's Cases on Basic Insurance Law, 2nd Ed., 1086 pages, 1977

Keeton and Wydiss' Insurance Law, Student Ed., about 1024 pages, 1988 (Text)

Wydiss and Keeton's Case Supplement to Keeton and Wydiss Insurance Law, 425 pages, 1988 (Casebook)

York and Whelan's Cases, Materials and Problems on Insurance Law, 715 pages, 1982, with 1985 Supplement (Casebook)

INTERNATIONAL LAW

Buergenthal and Maier's Public International Law in a Nutshell, 262 pages, 1985 (Text)

Folsom, Gordon and Spanogle's International Business Transactions – a Problem-Oriented Coursebook, 1160 pages, 1986, with Documents Supplement (Casebook)

Henkin, Pugh, Schachter and Smit's Cases and Materials on International Law, 2nd Ed., 1517 pages, 1987 with Documents Supplement (Casebook)

Jackson and Davey's Legal Problems of International Economic Relations, 2nd Ed., 1269 pages, 1986, with Documents Supplement (Casebook)

Kirgis' International Organizations in Their Legal Setting, 1016 pages, 1977, with 1981 Supplement (Casebook)

Weston, Falk and D'Amato's International Law and World Order—A Problem Oriented Coursebook, 1195 pages, 1980, with Documents Supplement (Casebook)

Wilson's International Business Transactions in a Nutshell, 2nd Ed., 476 pages, 1984 (Text)

INTERVIEWING AND COUNSELING

Binder and Price's Interviewing and Counseling, 232 pages, 1977 (Text)

Shaffer and Elkins' Interviewing and Counseling in a Nutshell, 2nd Ed., 487 pages, 1987 (Text)

INTRODUCTION TO LAW STUDY

Dobbyn's So You Want to go to Law School, Revised First Edition, 206 pages, 1976 (Text)

INTRODUCTION TO LAW STUDY—Cont'd

Hegland's Introduction to the Study and Practice of Law in a Nutshell, 418 pages, 1983 (Text)

Kinyon's Introduction to Law Study and Law Examinations in a Nutshell, 389 pages, 1971 (Text)

See also Legal Method and Legal System

JUDICIAL ADMINISTRATION

Nelson's Cases and Materials on Judicial Administration and the Administration of Justice, 1032 pages, 1974 (Casebook)

JURISPRUDENCE

Christie's Text and Readings on Jurisprudence—The Philosophy of Law, 1056 pages, 1973 (Casebook)

JUVENILE JUSTICE

Fox's Cases and Materials on Modern Juvenile Justice, 2nd Ed., 960 pages, 1981 (Casebook)

Fox's Juvenile Courts in a Nutshell, 3rd Ed., 291 pages, 1984 (Text)

LABOR LAW

Atleson, Rabin, Schatzki, Sherman and Silverstein's Collective Bargaining in Private Employment, 2nd Ed., (The Labor Law Group), 856 pages, 1984 (Casebook)

Gorman's Basic Text on Labor Law—Unionization and Collective Bargaining, 914 pages, 1976 (Text)

Grodin, Wollett and Alleyne's Collective Bargaining in Public Employment, 3rd Ed., (the Labor Law Group), 430 pages, 1979 (Casebook)

Leslie's Labor Law in a Nutshell, 2nd Ed., 397 pages, 1986 (Text)

Nolan's Labor Arbitration Law and Practice in a Nutshell, 358 pages, 1979 (Text)

Oberer, Hanslowe, Andersen and Heinsz' Cases and Materials on Labor Law—Collective Bargaining in a Free Society, 3rd Ed., 1163 pages, 1986 with Statutory Supplement (Casebook)

See also Employment Discrimination, Social Legislation

LAND FINANCE

See Real Estate Transactions

LAND USE

Callies and Freilich's Cases and Materials on Land Use, 1233 pages, 1986 (Casebook)

Hagman's Cases on Public Planning and Control of Urban and Land Development, 2nd Ed., 1301 pages, 1980 (Casebook)

LAND USE—Cont'd

Hagman and Juergensmeyer's Hornbook on Urban Planning and Land Development Control Law, 2nd Ed., Student Ed., 680 pages, 1986 (Text)

Wright and Gitelman's Cases and Materials on Land Use, 3rd Ed., 1300 pages, 1982, with 1987 Supplement (Casebook)

Wright and Wright's Land Use in a Nutshell, 2nd Ed., 356 pages, 1985 (Text)

LEGAL HISTORY

Presser and Zainaldin's Cases on Law and American History, 855 pages, 1980 (Casebook)

See also Legal Method and Legal System

LEGAL METHOD AND LEGAL SYSTEM

Aldisert's Readings, Materials and Cases in the Judicial Process, 948 pages, 1976 (Casebook)

Berch and Berch's Introduction to Legal Method and Process, 550 pages, 1985 (Casebook)

Bodenheimer, Oakley and Love's Readings and Cases on an Introduction to the Anglo-American Legal System, 2nd Ed., about 165 pages, 1988 (Casebook)

Davies and Lawry's Institutions and Methods of the Law—Introductory Teaching Materials, 547 pages, 1982 (Casebook)

Dvorkin, Himmelstein and Lesnick's Becoming a Lawyer: A Humanistic Perspective on Legal Education and Professionalism, 211 pages, 1981 (Text)

Greenberg's Judicial Process and Social Change, 666 pages, 1977 (Casebook)

Kelso and Kelso's Studying Law: An Introduction, 587 pages, 1984 (Coursebook)

Kempin's Historical Introduction to Anglo-American Law in a Nutshell, 2nd Ed., 280 pages, 1973 (Text)

Kimball's Historical Introduction to the Legal System, 610 pages, 1966 (Casebook)

Murphy's Cases and Materials on Introduction to Law—Legal Process and Procedure, 772 pages, 1977 (Casebook)

Reynolds' Judicial Process in a Nutshell, 292 pages, 1980 (Text)

See also Legal Research and Writing

LEGAL PROFESSION

Aronson, Devine and Fisch's Problems, Cases and Materials on Professional Responsibility, 745 pages, 1985 (Casebook)

Aronson and Weckstein's Professional Responsibility in a Nutshell, 399 pages, 1980 (Text)

Mellinkoff's The Conscience of a Lawyer, 304 pages, 1973 (Text)

Mellinkoff's Lawyers and the System of Justice, 983 pages, 1976 (Casebook)

LAW SCHOOL PUBLICATIONS—Continued

LEGAL PROFESSION—Cont'd

Pirsig and Kirwin's Cases and Materials on Professional Responsibility, 4th Ed., 603 pages, 1984 (Casebook)

Schwartz and Wydick's Problems in Legal Ethics, 2nd Ed., about 330 pages, 1988 (Casebook)

Selected Statutes, Rules and Standards on the Legal Profession, 449 pages, 1987

Smith's Preventing Legal Malpractice, 142 pages, 1981 (Text)

Wolfram's Hornbook on Modern Legal Ethics, Student Edition, 1120 pages, 1986 (Text)

LEGAL RESEARCH AND WRITING

Child's Materials and Problems on Drafting Legal Documents, about 276 pages, 1988 (Text)

Cohen's Legal Research in a Nutshell, 4th Ed., 450 pages, 1985 (Text)

Cohen and Berring's How to Find the Law, 8th Ed., 790 pages, 1983. Problem book by Foster, Johnson and Kelly available (Casebook)

Cohen and Berring's Finding the Law, 8th Ed., Abridged Ed., 556 pages, 1984 (Casebook)

Dickerson's Materials on Legal Drafting, 425 pages, 1981 (Casebook)

Felsenfeld and Siegel's Writing Contracts in Plain English, 290 pages, 1981 (Text)

Gopen's Writing From a Legal Perspective, 225 pages, 1981 (Text)

Mellinkoff's Legal Writing—Sense and Nonsense, 242 pages, 1982 (Text)

Ray and Ramsfield's Legal Writing: Getting It Right and Getting It Written, 250 pages, 1987 (Text)

Rombauer's Legal Problem Solving—Analysis, Research and Writing, 4th Ed., 424 pages, 1983 (Coursebook)

Squires and Rombauer's Legal Writing in a Nutshell, 294 pages, 1982 (Text)

Statsky's Legal Research and Writing, 3rd Ed., 257 pages, 1986 (Coursebook)

Statsky and Wernet's Case Analysis and Fundamentals of Legal Writing, 2nd Ed., 441 pages, 1984 (Text)

Teply's Programmed Materials on Legal Research and Citation, 2nd Ed., 358 pages, 1986. Student Library Exercises available (Coursebook)

Weihofen's Legal Writing Style, 2nd Ed., 332 pages, 1980 (Text)

LEGISLATION

Davies' Legislative Law and Process in a Nutshell, 2nd Ed., 346 pages, 1986 (Text)

Eskridge and Frickey's Cases on Legislation, 937 pages, 1987 (Casebook)

Nutting and Dickerson's Cases and Materials on Legislation, 5th Ed., 744 pages, 1978 (Casebook)

LEGISLATION—Cont'd

Statsky's Legislative Analysis and Drafting, 2nd Ed., 217 pages, 1984 (Text)

LOCAL GOVERNMENT

McCarthy's Local Government Law in a Nutshell, 2nd Ed., 404 pages, 1983 (Text)

Reynolds' Hornbook on Local Government Law, 860 pages, 1982, with 1987 pocket part (Text)

Valente's Cases and Materials on Local Government Law, 3rd Ed., 1010 pages, 1987 (Casebook)

MASS COMMUNICATION LAW

Gillmor and Barron's Cases and Comment on Mass Communication Law, 4th Ed., 1076 pages, 1984 (Casebook)

Ginsburg's Regulation of Broadcasting: Law and Policy Towards Radio, Television and Cable Communications, 741 pages, 1979, with 1983 Supplement (Casebook)

Zuckman, Gaynes, Carter and Dee Mass Communications Law in a Nutshell, 3rd Ed., 538 pages, 1988 (Text)

MEDICINE, LAW AND

Furrow, Johnson, Jost and Schwartz' Health Law: Cases, Materials and Problems, 1005 pages, 1987 (Casebook)

King's The Law of Medical Malpractice in a Nutshell, 2nd Ed., 342 pages, 1986 (Text)

Shapiro and Spece's Problems, Cases and Materials on Bioethics and Law, 892 pages, 1981 (Casebook)

Sharpe, Fiscina and Head's Cases on Law and Medicine, 882 pages, 1978 (Casebook)

MILITARY LAW

Shanor and Terrell's Military Law in a Nutshell, 378 pages, 1980 (Text)

MORTGAGES

See Real Estate Transactions

NATURAL RESOURCES LAW

See Energy and Natural Resources Law

NEGOTIATION

Edwards and White's Problems, Readings and Materials on the Lawyer as a Negotiator, 484 pages, 1977 (Casebook)

Peck's Cases and Materials on Negotiation, 2nd Ed., (The Labor Law Group), 280 pages, 1980 (Casebook)

Williams' Legal Negotiation and Settlement, 207 pages, 1983 (Coursebook)

OFFICE PRACTICE

Hegland's Trial and Practice Skills in a Nutshell, 346 pages, 1978 (Text)

Strong and Clark's Law Office Management, 424 pages, 1974 (Casebook)

OFFICE PRACTICE—Cont'd

See also Computers and Law, Interviewing and Counseling, Negotiation

OIL AND GAS

Hemingway's Hornbook on Oil and Gas, 2nd Ed., Student Ed., 543 pages, 1983 with 1986 P.P. (Text)

Kuntz, Lowe, Anderson and Smith's Cases and Materials on Oil and Gas Law, 857 pages, 1986, with Forms Manual (Casebook)

Lowe's Oil and Gas Law in a Nutshell, 443 pages, 1983 (Text)

See also Energy and Natural Resources Law

PARTNERSHIP

See Agency—Partnership

PATENT AND COPYRIGHT LAW

Choate, Francis and Collins' Cases and Materials on Patent Law, 3rd Ed., 1009 pages, 1987 (Casebook)

Miller and Davis' Intellectual Property—Patents, Trademarks and Copyright in a Nutshell, 428 pages, 1983 (Text)

Nimmer's Cases on Copyright and Other Aspects of Entertainment Litigation, 3rd Ed., 1025 pages, 1985 (Casebook)

PRODUCTS LIABILITY

Fischer and Powers' Cases and Materials on Products Liability, about 700 pages, 1988 (Casebook)

Noel and Phillips' Cases on Products Liability, 2nd Ed., 821 pages, 1982 (Casebook)

Phillips' Products Liability in a Nutshell, 3rd Ed., about 350 pages, 1988 (Text)

PROPERTY

Bernhardt's Real Property in a Nutshell, 2nd Ed., 448 pages, 1981 (Text)

Boyer's Survey of the Law of Property, 766 pages, 1981 (Text)

Browder, Cunningham and Smith's Cases on Basic Property Law, 4th Ed., 1431 pages, 1984 (Casebook)

Bruce, Ely and Bostick's Cases and Materials on Modern Property Law, 1004 pages, 1984 (Casebook)

Burke's Personal Property in a Nutshell, 322 pages, 1983 (Text)

Cunningham, Stoebuck and Whitman's Hornbook on the Law of Property, Student Ed., 916 pages, 1984, with 1987 P.P. (Text)

Donahue, Kauper and Martin's Cases on Property, 2nd Ed., 1362 pages, 1983 (Casebook)

Hill's Landlord and Tenant Law in a Nutshell, 2nd Ed., 311 pages, 1986 (Text)

Kurtz and Hovenkamp's Cases and Materials on American Property Law, 1296 pages, 1987 (Casebook)

PROPERTY—Cont'd

Moynihan's Introduction to Real Property, 2nd Ed., 239 pages, 1988 (Text)

Uniform Land Transactions Act, Uniform Simplification of Land Transfers Act, Uniform Condominium Act, 1977 Official Text with Comments, 462 pages, 1978

See also Real Estate Transactions, Land Use

PSYCHIATRY, LAW AND

Reisner's Law and the Mental Health System, Civil and Criminal Aspects, 696 pages, 1985, with 1987 Supplement (Casebooks)

REAL ESTATE TRANSACTIONS

Bruce's Real Estate Finance in a Nutshell, 2nd Ed., 262 pages, 1985 (Text)

Maxwell, Riesenfeld, Hetland and Warren's Cases on California Security Transactions in Land, 3rd Ed., 728 pages, 1984 (Casebook)

Nelson and Whitman's Cases on Real Estate Transfer, Finance and Development, 3rd Ed., 1184 pages, 1987 (Casebook)

Nelson and Whitman's Hornbook on Real Estate Finance Law, 2nd Ed., Student Ed., 941 pages, 1985 (Text)

Osborne's Cases and Materials on Secured Transactions, 559 pages, 1967 (Casebook)

REGULATED INDUSTRIES

Gellhorn and Pierce's Regulated Industries in a Nutshell, 2nd Ed., 389 pages, 1987 (Text)

Morgan, Harrison and Verkuil's Cases and Materials on Economic Regulation of Business, 2nd Ed., 666 pages, 1985 (Casebook)

See also Mass Communication Law, Banking Law

REMEDIES

Dobbs' Hornbook on Remedies, 1067 pages, 1973 (Text)

Dobbs' Problems in Remedies, 137 pages, 1974 (Problem book)

Dobbyn's Injunctions in a Nutshell, 264 pages, 1974 (Text)

Friedman's Contract Remedies in a Nutshell, 323 pages, 1981 (Text)

Leavell, Love and Nelson's Cases and Materials on Equitable Remedies and Restitution, 4th Ed., 1111 pages, 1986 (Casebook)

McCormick's Hornbook on Damages, 811 pages, 1935 (Text)

O'Connell's Remedies in a Nutshell, 2nd Ed., 320 pages, 1985 (Text)

York, Bauman and Rendleman's Cases and Materials on Remedies, 4th Ed., 1029 pages, 1985 (Casebook)

LAW SCHOOL PUBLICATIONS—Continued

REVIEW MATERIALS

Ballantine's Problems

Black Letter Series

SECURITIES REGULATION

Hazen's Hornbook on The Law of Securities Regulation, Student Ed., 739 pages, 1985, with 1988 P.P. (Text)

Ratner's Securities Regulation: Materials for a Basic Course, 3rd Ed., 1000 pages, 1986 (Casebook)

Ratner's Securities Regulation in a Nutshell, 3rd Ed., about 335 pages, 1988 (Text)

Selected Securities and Business Planning Statutes, Rules and Forms, 493 pages, 1987

SOCIAL LEGISLATION

Hood and Hardy's Workers' Compensation and Employee Protection Laws in a Nutshell, 274 pages, 1984 (Text)

LaFrance's Welfare Law: Structure and Entitlement in a Nutshell, 455 pages, 1979 (Text)

Malone, Plant and Little's Cases on Workers' Compensation and Employment Rights, 2nd Ed., 951 pages, 1980 (Casebook)

SPORTS LAW

Schubert, Smith and Trentadue's Sports Law, 395 pages, 1986 (Text)

TAXATION

Dodge's Cases and Materials on Federal Income Taxation, 820 pages, 1985 (Casebook)

Dodge's Wills, Trusts and Estate Planning, 700 pages, 1988 (Casebook)

Garbis, Struntz and Rubin's Cases and Materials on Tax Procedure and Tax Fraud, 2nd Ed., 687 pages, 1987 (Casebook)

Gelfand and Salsich's State and Local Taxation and Finance in a Nutshell, 309 pages, 1986 (Text)

Gunn's Cases and Materials on Federal Income Taxation of Individuals, 785 pages, 1981 with 1985 Supplement (Casebook)

Hellerstein and Hellerstein's Cases on State and Local Taxation, 4th Ed., 1041 pages, 1978 with 1982 Supplement (Casebook)

Kahn and Gann's Corporate Taxation and Taxation of Partnerships and Partners, 2nd Ed., 1204 pages, 1985 (Casebook)

Kaplan's Federal Taxation of International Transactions: Principles, Planning and Policy, about 600 pages, 1988 (Casebook)

Kragen and McNulty's Cases and Materials on Federal Income Taxation: Individuals, Corporations, Partnerships, 4th Ed., 1287 pages, 1985 (Casebook)

TAXATION—Cont'd

McNulty's Federal Estate and Gift Taxation in a Nutshell, 3rd Ed., 509 pages, 1983 (Text)

McNulty's Federal Income Taxation of Individuals in a Nutshell, 3rd Ed., 487 pages, 1983 (Text)

Pennell's Cases and Materials on Income Taxation of Trusts, Estates, Grantors and Beneficiaries, 460 pages, 1987 (Casebook)

Posin's Hornbook on Federal Income Taxation of Individuals, Student Ed., 491 pages, 1983 with 1987 pocket part (Text)

Rose and Chommie's Hornbook on Federal Income Taxation, 3rd Ed., about 875 pages, 1988 (Text)

Selected Federal Taxation Statutes and Regulations, 1399 pages, 1988

Solomon and Hesch's Cases on Federal Income Taxation of Individuals, 1068 pages, 1987 (Casebook)

TORTS

Christie's Cases and Materials on the Law of Torts, 1264 pages, 1983 (Casebook)

Dobbs' Torts and Compensation—Personal Accountability and Social Responsibility for Injury, 955 pages, 1985 (Casebook)

Green, Pedrick, Rahl, Thode, Hawkins, Smith, and Treece's Advanced Torts: Injuries to Business, Political and Family Interests, 2nd Ed., 544 pages, 1977 (Casebook)

Keeton, Keeton, Sargentich and Steiner's Cases and Materials on Tort and Accident Law, 1360 pages, 1983 (Casebook)

Kionka's Torts in a Nutshell: Injuries to Persons and Property, 434 pages, 1977 (Text)

Malone's Torts in a Nutshell: Injuries to Family, Social and Trade Relations, 358 pages, 1979 (Text)

Prosser and Keeton's Hornbook on Torts, 5th Ed., Student Ed., 1286 pages, 1984, with 1988 pocket part (Text)

See also Products Liability

TRADE REGULATION

McManis' Unfair Trade Practices in a Nutshell, 444 pages, 1982 (Text)

Oppenheim, Weston, Maggs and Schechter's Cases and Materials on Unfair Trade Practices and Consumer Protection, 4th Ed., 1038 pages, 1983 with 1986 Supplement (Casebook)

See also Antitrust, Regulated Industries

TRIAL AND APPELLATE ADVOCACY

Appellate Advocacy, Handbook of, 2nd Ed., 182 pages, 1986 (Text)

Bergman's Trial Advocacy in a Nutshell, 402 pages, 1979 (Text)

LAW SCHOOL PUBLICATIONS—Continued

DRAFTING LEGAL DOCUMENTS:

MATERIALS AND PROBLEMS

By

Barbara Child
Director of Legal Drafting
University of Florida

AMERICAN CASEBOOK SERIES

WEST PUBLISHING CO.
ST. PAUL, MINN., 1988

COPYRIGHT © 1988 By WEST PUBLISHING CO.
50 West Kellogg Boulevard
P.O. Box 64526
St. Paul, Minnesota 55164–0526

Library of Congress Cataloging-in-Publication Data
Child, Barbara.
  Drafting legal documents: materials and problems/by Barbara Child.
     p.   cm.—American casebook series)
  Bibliography: p.
  Includes index.
  ISBN 0–314–82176–7
  1. Legal composition. I. Title. II. Series.
KF250.C47 1988   88–3204
808'.06634—dc19   CIP

ISBN 0–314–82176–7

     Child—Legal Drafting ACB

For
Christine Anne Child
and
Matthew H. Wikander

May they and their writing thrive.

*

Acknowledgments

To friends, colleagues, and students from one coast to the other, I wish to express my deep thanks for help making my dream of this book come true.

At the University of Florida College of Law, Dean Frank T. Read, Associate Dean Jeffrey Lewis, and the faculty deserve high praise for their commitment to initiating a program in Legal Drafting as a required course for all second-year law students. I am grateful to them for bringing me to Florida to design and direct the program and for encouraging me in my work.

That work has been a joy from the beginning because of the four Legal Drafting instructors who have shared it with me: Lynn McGilvray–Saltzman, Linda Morton, Betsy Ruff, and Anne Rutledge. They have helped me test every idea I have ever had about drafting and about teaching drafting. They have contributed immeasurably to refining the materials in this book, as well as to sustaining the spirit of its author.

A number of other colleagues here have also contributed ideas and materials, and I wish to thank them as well: Gertrude Block, Iris Burke, Mary Ellen Caldwell, Lynne Capehart, Jeffrey Davis, Joseph W. Little, Robert T. Mann, Toni Massaro, Thomas McDonnell, Robert B. Moberly, Don Peters, David T. Smith, Anne L. Spitzer, and Mary P. Twitchell.

Professor Emeritus Mary Ellen Caldwell at University of Florida and Professor Richard Wydick at University of California at Davis gave me thoughtful critiques and suggestions based on earlier drafts, and I am especially grateful to them for their encouragement. Nancy Savage read the manuscript, and I greatly appreciate her editorial comments.

I also wish to thank my student research assistants, Deborah B. Ansbro, Scott Small and Robert Craig Waters. Special thanks go to research assistant Andrea Wiegel, who also helped index the book. My secretary, Geraldine C. Simmons, deserves a medal for her patience as well as her skill.

These are the people who have contributed in immediate, direct ways, but they are not the only ones for me to thank. At appropriate places in the text, I acknowledge numerous contributions of Reed Dickerson, but that is not enough. Most of us who know anything about drafting learned much of what we know, one way or another, from Professor Dickerson. I thank him for all he has taught me, and I thank John Dernbach, Carl Felsenfeld, David Mellinkoff, and Richard Wydick for all their fine teachings.

I thank David W. Duff and Ray Osheroff, who encouraged me to pursue my love of language along with the law; Tom Davis, Bobby L. Smith, and my other friends and colleagues in the Kent State University English Department who encouraged me earlier to pursue the law along with my love of language; and Gerald Cavanaugh, Vikki Ervin, and my other Legal Drafting students at Golden Gate University School of Law who first urged me to write this book.

For their constant interest and support, although from afar, I thank Betty F. Kirschner, Marjorie Raulfs, and Anne Reid; and for the friendly voice at my ear saying always, "Write that book!" I thank Alan Morris.

Barbara Child

Gainesville, Florida
February, 1988

Summary of Contents

*

Table of Contents

*

Table of Cases

The principal cases are in bold type. Cases cited or discussed in the text are roman type. References are to pages. Cases cited in principal cases and within other quoted materials are not included.

*

DRAFTING LEGAL DOCUMENTS:

MATERIALS AND PROBLEMS

*

Chapter 1

LEGAL DRAFTING: A PREVIEW OF THE COURSE

I. COURSE CONTENTS

A. PURPOSE

The purpose of a course in legal drafting is to engage students in the practical drafting experience that will form a major part of their work as lawyers: preparing documents that effectuate clients' intentions while planning to avoid potential legal problems. In law practice, lawyers not only address specific controversies; in addition, they design and redesign documents to make clear to people what their rights and responsibilities are.

As drafters, lawyers assess policy and seek to avoid litigation. They design estates, prepare leases, hammer out settlement agreements, and draft a wide range of other contractual or legislative documents. In an ordinary office practice, a lawyer is likely in the space of a month or a year to draft everything from a purchase and sale agreement to a lease with a purchase option, or from by-laws for a corporation to a proposed local ordinance on some matter of interest to a client. Thus, a legal drafting course focuses on the lawyer's role as planner, problem-solver, and preventer of trouble. Legal drafting has been described as "preventive law" by Reed Dickerson, author of the classic reference tool, *The Fundamentals of Legal Drafting* (2d ed. 1986).

Ironically, although lawyers generally spend more time practicing preventive law than in litigation, many have yet to learn to practice preventive law as skillfully as they practice litigation law.

PEOPLE v. TITLE GUARANTEE AND TRUST CO.
180 A.D. 648, 650–51, 168 N.Y.S. 278, 280–81 (1917).

The "practice of the law," as the term is now commonly used, embraces much more than the conduct of litigation. The greater, more responsible and delicate part of a lawyer's work is in other directions.

1

Drafting instruments creating trusts, formulating contracts, drawing wills and negotiations, all require legal knowledge and power of adaptation of the highest order. Beside these employments, mere skill in trying law-suits, where ready wit and natural resources often prevail against profound knowledge of the law, is a relatively unimportant part of a lawyer's work.

One study estimates that poor drafting and the resulting interpretation problems led to approximately one-fourth of 500 appellate contract cases.[1]

DICKERSON, TOWARD A LEGAL DIALECTIC
61 Ind.L.J. 315, 316–17 (1985–86).*

The legal profession has undergone a profound shift in professional challenges from a preoccupation with litigation to a broader concern that includes an enormous involvement with public and private planning. * * *

Although lawyers are beginning to realize that most new law is legislative rather than judicial, few realize that statutes constitute only a small fraction of the total output of new law. How is most of it being made? Through the delegated legislation we call "administrative rulemaking." Unfortunately much, if not most, of such legal planning is being done by lawyers with inadequate training in the conceptual and architectural disciplines of planning or is being done by laymen.

* * *

In the nonlitigious area of legal planning, which normally culminates in definitive documents whose purpose is to inform rather than persuade, the lawyer is freest to present balanced legal truth. But this calls for an expertise of which legal education provides little and for which case law is largely irrelevant. Certainly, the law's mission is broader that the dispute resolution * * * represented by litigation.

The purpose of a legal drafting course is ultimately to provide students with the expertise to carry out this broader mission.

B. LEGAL DRAFTING DISTINGUISHED FROM LEGAL WRITING IN GENERAL

Some people use the terms "legal drafting" and "legal writing" interchangeably to refer to any writing about law or any writing that lawyers do. Thus one may say that a lawyer "drafts" a brief or a letter to opposing counsel; likewise, a judge "drafts" an opinion. Perhaps those who use "draft" instead of "write" intend to imply that the writing in question is important enough to warrant several revisions, that is, drafts.

However, the term "legal drafting," when used precisely, refers to the "expression in definitive form of a legal right, privilege, function,

---

1. Shepherd, Book Review of Basic Contract Law by Lon L. Fuller, 1 J. Legal Educ. 151, 154 (1948).

* Copyright © 1986 by Reed Dickerson. Reprinted by permission of the author.

duty, status or disposition." [2] The legal documents involved may be public ones such as statutes, ordinances, constitutions, and regulations. One textbook on government processes illustrates how varied are the sources of pronouncements that "make law." In an exercise, the authors ask students to try to name the originating institutions of several unidentified quotations. The documents are subsequently identified as an NLRB opinion, a Presidential executive order, a state highway department directive, a disciplinary rule from the ABA Code of Professional Responsibility, a letter from a U.S. President to a member of the Federal Trade Commission, a resolution of a state legislature, an act of a state legislature, and a state supreme court rule.[3]

Often legislative documents are private ones such as contracts, corporate by-laws, wills, conveyances, and trusts. From the perspective of legal drafting, an Act of Congress and a two-party rental agreement are the same kind of document. "Whether a document is simple or complicated, it creates, when executed, law not only for the parties but those who are bound by or rely on it." [4]

C. CURTIS, IT'S YOUR LAW
42–44 (1954).*

    * * * The Congress in Washington and the legislatures in the state capitals pass laws. The administrative agencies turn out regulations. The courts hand down judicial decisions and opinions. We forget, even the lawyers themselves forget, that it is the lawyers in their offices who make the bulk of our law.

I spent this morning working on a draft of an agreement for the publication of cheap paper-bound books. The signature of an author and a publisher would turn that agreement into law. This afternoon I watched a client execute a codicil to his will. After he had signed I took the pen. I took it, because it was my own. But if it had been his, he might well have given it to me as a governor might give me the quill with which he had signed a statute which I had drafted. For this codicil was none the less a part of our law. This evening I read the announcement in the afternoon paper of a new bond issue. I recognized one which three of my partners had been working on, drawing the mortgage which secured it and the agreement under which it was to be underwritten and sold. This was law for everyone who bought or sold those bonds.

Where two or three, or more, are gathered together in contract, they set up a small momentary sovereignty of their own. There is

2. R. Dickerson, The Fundamentals of Legal Drafting 3 (2d ed. 1986).

3. H. Linde, G. Bunn, F. Paff, and W. Church, Legislative and Administrative Processes 1–4 (2d ed. 1981).

4. Robinson, Drafting—Its Substance and Teaching, 25 J. Legal Educ. 514, 528 (1973).

nothing fanciful about this. A contract is a little code for a special occasion. A lease is a little statute for your tenancy of a house you have neither built nor bought. Partnership articles or the charter and by-laws of a corporation are quite an elaborate code of law for those who are concerned. A corporate mortgage is a piece of legislation for a large and shifting population of bondholders, affecting, it is true, only a part of their lives, but affecting that part as completely as experienced and foresighted lawyers working late into the urban night can make it.
*   *   *

This private legislation has something of a life of its own, irrespective of legislatures and courts. For one thing, most of it looks for its enforcement to that posse of social fears, private prides, and economic pressures which we are likely to call good faith, and which is just as powerful as the expectation of compulsion. And the more the lawyer who drafts a document anticipates enforcement by the law, the more he prevents it; and the more it takes the place of law. For the very purpose of the document is to avoid recourse to the courts.   *   *   *

This is law which the parties make for their own small domain. As a matter of fact, much of it becomes law for others as well, by imitation. An agreement proves satisfactory. It is not copyrighted. Unlike the latest song, you can copy it for free. It may even get into a law book, and acquire the authority of print, or even of precedent. Other lawyers use it, as we all use any device that saves us time, thought, or the burden of unconventionality. Originality is a vice in this branch of literature. Any substantial change would incur responsibility as well as tempt litigation. Finally it becomes as established in our law as a folk song in our literature, and in strictly the same way. A book of legal forms is the legal cousin of an anthology of popular ballads.

All such legislative documents should be distinguished from briefs, memoranda, and letters. In the latter group of documents, lawyers explain their analysis of legal materials and try to persuade someone to think or behave in a certain way. In fact, the study of this kind of writing is largely a study of the strategy of persuasion, complete with attention to effective appeals to emotion.

In contrast, legal drafting is completely free from emotional content or "sales pitch." It is instead descriptive and prescriptive. The drafter has no need to convince anybody of anything. The drafter instead describes a particular world, large or small, and either prescribes future behavior in that world or describes the consequences of anticipated behavior.

Document drafting also differs from memorandum- and brief-writing in that memoranda and briefs usually focus on relatively few points or issues with sometimes extensive text devoted to each one. In document drafting, each sentence has its own separate significance; moreover, the exact wording of each sentence matters to a far greater extent.

Litigation documents such as pleadings and discovery documents have some of the characteristics of each of the other categories. They are intended to persuade and thus are strategic in design. Generally, they do not prescribe but they often do describe. While they are not precisely within the scope of legal drafting, they require at least some of the same skills.

C. FOCUS ON DRAFTING SKILLS

1. *Major Skills*

A legal drafting course focuses on the following major skills:

a. Forming clear concepts of general or abstract materials.

b. Arranging material systematically in whole documents, sections of documents, and individual provisions.

c. Articulating meanings precisely with extraordinary attention to internal consistency and to degrees of generality or particularity.

The lawyer as drafter needs to develop these skills particularly well when dealing with clients in the clients' role as policy makers. "Policy" here refers to any plan or rule that a client wishes to legislate or propose for agreement in a legal document. Thus government legislators are not the only ones who make policy. A landlord makes policy when providing in a lease how security deposits may be used or specifying tenants' duties to maintain the property. Likewise a testator makes policy when providing in a will who the executor will be or who will take the remainder of the estate. In other words, the entire substantive content of every legislative or contractual document is policy.

Many clients have only a rough idea of what they want to accomplish. Others have a detailed, even rigidly formed, idea but little appreciation of its ramifications. The lawyer is often in a better position than the client to anticipate problems of administering or enforcing a policy. The client may ask the lawyer merely to put the client's ideas on paper in "proper legal form." But the process of drafting involves a great deal more than that.

Even though the lawyer cannot ethically take over the client's decision-making rights and responsibilities, the lawyer can and should advise the client and participate in refining policy. For example, a lawyer might have as a client a landlord who wants to incorporate into a lease the policy that tenants cannot have waterbeds. The lawyer preparing to draft the lease has a duty first to discover whether the state has a statute such as the following one.

83.535 Flotation bedding system; restrictions on use.—No landlord may prohibit a tenant from using a flotation bedding system in a dwelling unit, provided the flotation bedding system does not violate applicable building codes. The landlord may require the tenant to carry in the tenant's name flotation insurance as is standard in the industry in an amount deemed reasonable to protect the tenant and owner against personal injury and property damage to the dwelling units. In any case, the policy shall carry a loss payable clause to the owner of the building.

If there is such a statute, the lawyer's next duty is to investigate the applicable building codes and then advise the client about the legislative restrictions. The lawyer should not merely leave out the waterbed provision. Neither should the lawyer go ahead and include a provision for flotation insurance without first consulting the client. At the very least, the client may have something to say about whether to spell out in the lease the amount of insurance that reasonably protects against property damage to the dwelling unit.

In short, lawyers as drafters are obligated to investigate and advise and not to make policy on their own initiative when no one is looking. The most successful drafting occurs when lawyer and client are true collaborators, each contributing particular kinds of expertise and neither viewing their relationship in terms of the power of one over the other. Thus, for successful collaboration, the lawyer must be an investigator and thinker as well as a writer.

a. Investigating Stage

In the investigating stage, the lawyer learns about the client's objectives and the relevant factual and legal background.

b. Thinking Stage

In the thinking stage, the lawyer refines those objectives into concepts and decides how broad or narrow the concepts ought to be as well as how they ought to be arranged. At this stage, the interaction between lawyer and client is critical. If the lawyer has earned the client's confidence and respect, the lawyer can influence policy in major ways and sometimes can serve as an agent for changes of wide-ranging significance.

c. Writing Stage

Finally, in the writing stage the lawyer composes a document that clearly communicates the client's wishes. If this final stage is successful, the lawyer and client together achieve a refined understanding of the original objectives. The drafting process ultimately expresses these refined concepts.[5]

Legal drafting skills are strategic and not simply the technical skills of grammar and word usage. These strategic skills involve not only finding the right word but also producing the right concept, just as the process of writing not only reflects thought but also gives it shape.[6]

---

5. For a more detailed introduction to the discipline of legal drafting and its relationship to both substantive policymaking and communication, see Dickerson, above note 2, at 1–50; R. Dick, Legal Drafting 1– 10 (2d ed. 1985), both in part summarized here.

6. Dickerson, above note 2, at 354.

Thus the study of drafting is not so much about the techniques of manipulating language as it is about the process of shaping solutions to conceptual problems.[7] Of course, bad language habits such as those exemplified in "legalese" can get in the way of the problem-solving process.[8] Moreover, the study of drafting helps students to learn to exercise sound judgment about what works in real situations involving clients with practical problems, concerns, goals, and limits.

One legal educator describes the lawyer as "at once the architect and the builder of human relationships." [9] To do this work, one needs legal training in the use of linguistic tools and conceptual materials "and their capacity to bear loads and withstand stresses." [10] One also needs a working knowledge of human nature and business practices as well as problem-solving skills and effective use of language. All these are necessary for the lawyer to evaluate plans and the documents embodying those plans for appropriate attention to contingencies and avoidance of the risks that ambiguities can cause.[11]

2. *Audience*

A legal drafting course also focuses special attention on the audience of users of legal documents. Legal drafting is uniquely challenging because of its audience.

a. *Drafting for Litigation and To Avoid It*

On the one hand, the lawyer must draft for the trial counsel and judge as potential users; on the other hand, one hopes by good drafting to prevent litigation altogether. The first job, therefore, is to draft documents that communicate clearly to one's own client. This job becomes further complicated when the client is more than one person, as when one drafts a partnership agreement for a set of partners or a trust agreement and companion wills for a husband and wife. In such circumstances, the lawyer needs to be aware of how the joint clients communicate with each other and whether they have a common understanding of the document in question.

b. *Drafting for Users With Different Degrees of Understanding*

A document is likely to be used by people with different degrees of understanding. Some users will fully understand technical terms or legal terms of art. Others will not understand them at all. Furthermore, it is one thing to assess one's own client or clients; it is another to speculate about other parties who will use the document but whose identity may be unknown, to say nothing of the identity of their present or future counsel. Some private documents such as corporate by-laws

---

7. *Id.* at 5–6.

8. Kirk, Legal Drafting: Curing Unexpressive Language, 3 Tex.Tech L.Rev. 23, 24–25 (1971).

9. Cavers, Legal Education and Lawyer-Made Law, 54 W.Va.L.Rev. 177, 180 (1952).

10. *Id.*

11. *Id.*

or sets of regulations have as their audience whole communities of users, who may be as numerous as the users of some public legislation.

c. Drafting for Different Uses

In addition, the lawyer may intend to use a document in a number of ways. For example, the lawyer may draft a lease for an individual who wants to rent one single-family dwelling for one year. That lease will not work for another client who owns an apartment complex. As soon as the lawyer begins to view the lease as a form, the number of possible contingencies increases. If the client owns several apartment complexes, the further increased possible contingencies dictate still more flexibility. If the lawyer specializes in real estate practice and anticipates producing a form lease for use by many clients, the document needs to be even more flexible. At some point the document may not be able to tolerate any further variety. Then it is time to reconceptualize the problems and produce two or three forms instead.

The temptation to produce, and especially to use, standardized forms is great, particularly because these forms are efficient and minimize risk. However, according to one study, wide use of forms has contributed to a new meaning of "contract." This new meaning looks to the parties' reasonable expectations, not necessarily based on the language of the document. This meaning is quite distinct from the traditional one that looked to the document itself as the manifestation of the parties' mutual assent. The implication for the drafting lawyer is significant. Faced with the risk of a court's looking outside the form document and entitling the other party, usually but not always a consumer, to what that party "reasonably expected," the lawyer may decide it is more prudent to reject the form and tailor a document to a particular transaction.[12]

d. Drafting for Users With Different Points of View

Different users of the same document will approach it from different points of view. One may look to it for protection. Another may be chiefly interested in escaping its coverage. One of the drafter's constant challenges is to draft for the "reader in bad faith." The drafter strives to make the meaning so precise that the reader who would prefer another meaning cannot support it.

If a document is one that a court is likely to construe strictly against the drafter—such as a consumer contract—then explicit and precise language is more necessary than in contracts between businesses or in other documents that courts commonly construe by looking at the internal context to resolve any doubtful matters.[13]

---

12. See Slawson, The New Meaning of Contract: The Transformation of Contracts Law by Standard Forms, 46 U.Pa.L.Rev. 21 (1984).

13. Dickerson, above note 2, at 46.

e. *Drafting for Reference Use*

Writers are used to assuming that readers will read what they write straight through, from beginning to end. However, many legal documents are used for reference. The tenant suddenly wants to know what to do when the landlord fails to repair the steps. The dissident stockholder reads up on voting rights and proxies in time for the annual meeting. Thus legal documents require special organization to make individual provisions easy to find and also sometimes easy to amend.[14]

II. PROBLEMS

PROBLEM 1

Below are parts of the domestic violence legislation from three states. If you would like to introduce yourself to some of the issues to be addressed in a legal drafting course, see how you assess these provisions.

1. Are they organized for easy reading?

2. Are they ambiguous as to what behavior is prohibited or whom the statutes protect?

3. Are they internally consistent?

4. Do they sacrifice clarity for economy or vice versa?

5. Finally, how useful would they be as models if you were drafting domestic violence legislation for a state that had none?

State A

§ 273.5 * Corporal injury; infliction by spouse upon his or her spouse or by person cohabiting with person of opposite sex

1   (a) Any person who willfully inflicts upon his or her spouse, or any
2 person who willfully inflicts upon any person of the opposite sex with
3 whom he or she is cohabiting, corporal injury resulting in a traumatic
4 condition, is guilty of a felony * * *.

5   (b) Holding oneself out to be the husband or wife of the person with
6 whom one is cohabiting is not necessary to constitute cohabitation as
7 the term is used in this section.

8   (c) As used in this section, "traumatic condition" means a condition
9 of the body, such as a wound or external or internal injury, whether of
10 a minor or serious nature, caused by a physical force.

* * *

14. See Dick, above note 5, at 8–10; C. Felsenfeld and A. Siegel, Writing Contracts in Plain English 86–91 (1981), both in part summarized here. See also Conard, New Ways to Write Laws, 56 Yale L.J. 458, 469–81 (1947).

* Note: § 273.5 and § 1000.6 are in different chapters of the same code.

§ 1000.6 *   [Application of chapter; Definitions]

*   *   *

1   (d) As used in this chapter "domestic violence" means intentionally
2 or recklessly causing or attempting to cause bodily injury to a family or
3 household member or placing a family or household member in reason-
4 able apprehension of imminent serious bodily injury to himself or
5 herself or another.

6   (e) As used in this chapter "family or household member" means a
7 spouse, former spouse, parent, any other person related by consanguini-
8 ty, or any person who regularly resides or who within the previous six
9 months regularly resided in the household. "Family or household
10 member" does not include a child.

State B

§ 2919.25   [Domestic Violence.]

1   (A) No person shall knowingly cause or attempt to cause physical
2 harm to a family or household member.

3   (B) No person shall recklessly cause serious physical harm to a
4 family or household member.

5   (C) Whoever violates this section is guilty of domestic violence, a
6 misdemeanor of the first degree. If the offender has previously been
7 convicted of a violation of this section, a violation of this section is a
8 felony of the fourth degree.

9   (D) As used in this section and in section 2919.26 of the Revised
10 Code, "family or household member" means a spouse, person living as a
11 spouse, parent, child, or other person related by consanguinity or
12 affinity, who is residing or has resided with the offender.

State C

§ 415.602   Definitions of terms used in §§ 415.601–415.608

1   As used in §§ 415.601–415.608, the term:

2   *   *   *

3   (3) "Domestic violence" means any assault, battery, or criminal
4 sexual conduct by a person against the person's spouse.

5   *   *   *

6   (5) "Spouse" means a person to whom another person is married or
7 a person to whom another person has been married and from whom
8 such other person is now separated or divorced.

PROBLEM 2

     Compare the following groups of sentences. Is one in each group
best as it is? Can you take parts from each to compose a new version

---

* Note: § 273.5 and § 1000.6 are in different chapters of the same code.

that is better than any of these? Explain your choices. What drafting principles emerge?

Group I

1. Tenant shall be fully responsible for insuring his personal property.

2. Tenant will be responsible for insuring his personal belongings and furnishings.

3. Tenant will provide insurance to adequately insure any personal property owned.

Group II

1. No pets are allowed on the premises.

2. The tenant agrees that he will not keep any pets of any kind on the premises.

3. Tenant shall keep no animal, bird, or pet without Landlord's prior written consent.

Group III

1. The landlord's late acceptance of rent will be limited to one month only, and will not imply any subsequent acceptance of late rent.

2. If Tenant fails to pay rent when due, landlord may terminate this agreement. If Landlord accepts rent late any month, it does not entitle Tenant to pay late again.

3. If either the landlord or the tenant breaks a condition of the rental contract and the other does nothing to enforce it, then that particular condition is waived. However, if that condition is broken again by either landlord or tenant, then the party that was harmed may enforce it.

Chapter 2

DRAFTING PLEADINGS

I. PLEADING FORMS

A. OFFICIALLY AUTHORIZED FORMS

The federal and state civil procedure rules make some of the work of drafting pleadings essentially a matter of following formal requirements. Some states have pleading forms approved by the state supreme court or other official body, such as the Florida conversion and replevin complaint forms below.

FORM 1.939

CONVERSION

COMPLAINT

Plaintiff, A. B., sues defendant, C. D., and alleges:

1. This is an action for damages that (insert jurisdictional amount).

2. On or about _____, 19__, defendant converted to his own use (insert description of property converted) that was then the property of plaintiff of the value of $_____.

WHEREFORE plaintiff demands judgment for damages against defendant.

FORM 1.937

REPLEVIN

COMPLAINT

Plaintiff, A. B., sues defendant, C. D., and alleges:

1. This is an action to recover possession of personal property in _____ County, Florida.

2. The description of the property is:

(list property)

To the best of plaintiff's knowledge, information and belief, the value of the property is $_____.

3. Plaintiff is entitled to the possession of the property under a security agreement dated _____, 19__, a copy of the agreement being attached.

4. To plaintiff's best knowledge, information and belief, the property is located at _____.

5. The property is wrongfully detained by defendant. Defendant came into possession of the property by (describe method of possession). To plaintiff's best knowledge, information and belief, defendant detains the property because (give reasons).

6. The property has not been taken for any tax, assessment or fine pursuant to law.

7. The property has not been taken under an execution or attachment against plaintiff's property.

WHEREFORE plaintiff demands judgment for possession of the property.

NOTE: Paragraph 3 must be modified if the right to possession arose in another manner. Allegations and a demand for damages, if appropriate, can be added to the form.

———

Plaintiffs' lawyers are not required to use such approved forms. In fact, they are expected to adapt the forms to the facts in a particular case. On the other hand, some forms address quite specific situations such as a plaintiff burned in a nightclub or a plaintiff injured because a defendant failed to keep a hallway lighted. In any event, lawyers may use court-approved forms with confidence that pleadings based on the forms are legally sufficient under the state's civil procedure rules, assuming, of course, that the drafter inserts appropriate matter in the blanks that call for insertions.

As states begin to operate more fully on the theory that the purpose of pleadings is merely to give notice to the opposing party, pleadings become more fully reduced to a matter of filling out a form. For example, some California Judicial Council forms are standardized to the extent that one form serves as the complaint for the whole range of personal injury, property damage, and wrongful death actions. The lawyer merely chooses which boxes to check and picks which cause-of-action form to attach. Likewise, one form serves for answers in all of those actions. In a state with such forms, the task of drafting pleadings becomes limited to matters of nonroutine complexity. Here is a sampling of California's forms.

WEST'S 1987 ANN.CALIF. CODES JUDICIAL COUNCIL FORMS

14–15, 32–34, 38, 44–45.*

ATTORNEY OR PARTY WITHOUT ATTORNEY (NAME AND ADDRESS): TELEPHONE:	FOR COURT USE ONLY
ATTORNEY FOR (NAME):	

Insert name of court, judicial district or branch court, if any, and post office and street address:

PLAINTIFF:

DEFENDANT:

☐ DOES 1 TO _____

COMPLAINT—Personal Injury, Property Damage, Wrongful Death | CASE NUMBER:

☐ MOTOR VEHICLE   ☐ OTHER (specify):
  ☐ Property Damage   ☐ Wrongful Death
  ☐ Personal Injury   ☐ Other Damages (specify):

1. This pleading, including attachments and exhibits, consists of the following number of pages: _____

2. a. Each plaintiff named above is a competent adult
   ☐ **Except** plaintiff (name):
     ☐ a corporation qualified to do business in California
     ☐ an unincorporated entity (describe):
     ☐ a public entity (describe):
     ☐ a minor   ☐ an adult
        ☐ for whom a guardian or conservator of the estate or a guardian ad litem has been appointed
        ☐ other (specify):
     ☐ other (specify):

   ☐ **Except** plaintiff (name):
     ☐ a corporation qualified to do business in California
     ☐ an unincorporated entity (describe):
     ☐ a public entity (describe):
     ☐ a minor   ☐ an adult
        ☐ for whom a guardian or conservator of the estate or a guardian ad litem has been appointed
        ☐ other (specify):
     ☐ other (specify):

   b. ☐ Plaintiff (name):
        is doing business under the fictitious name of (specify):

        and has complied with the fictitious business name laws.
   c. ☐ Information about additional plaintiffs who are not competent adults is shown in Complaint—
        Attachment 2c.
                              (Continued)

Form Approved by the
Judicial Council of California   **COMPLAINT**—Personal Injury, Property Damage,
Effective January 1, 1982   Wrongful Death
Rule 982.1(1)   CCP 425.12
                                                                                 [E146]

* Reprinted from West's 1987 Annotated   with permission of the West Publishing
California Codes Judicial Council Forms   Company.

SHORT TITLE:	CASE NUMBER:

COMPLAINT—Personal Injury, Property Damage, Wrongful Death   Page two

3. a. Each defendant named above is a natural person
 ☐ **Except** defendant *(name):*   ☐ **Except** defendant *(name):*

        ☐ a business organization, form unknown   ☐ a business organization, form unknown
        ☐ a corporation   ☐ a corporation
        ☐ an unincorporated entity *(describe):*   ☐ an unincorporated entity *(describe):*

        ☐ a public entity *(describe):*   ☐ a public entity *(describe):*

        ☐ other *(specify):*   ☐ other *(specify):*

     ☐ **Except** defendant *(name):*   ☐ **Except** defendant *(name):*

        ☐ a business organization, form unknown   ☐ a business organization, form unknown
        ☐ a corporation   ☐ a corporation
        ☐ an unincorporated entity *(describe):*   ☐ an unincorporated entity *(describe):*

        ☐ a public entity *(describe):*   ☐ a public entity *(describe):*

        ☐ other *(specify):*   ☐ other *(specify):*

   b. The true names and capacities of defendants sued as Does are unknown to plaintiff.

   c. ☐ Information about additional defendants who are not natural persons is contained in Complaint—
        Attachment 3c.
   d. ☐ Defendants who are joined pursuant to Code of Civil Procedure section 382 are *(names):*

4. ☐ Plaintiff is required to comply with a claims statute, **and**
     a. ☐ plaintiff has complied with applicable claims statutes, **or**
     b. ☐ plaintiff is excused from complying because *(specify):*

5. This court is the proper court because
     ☐ at least one defendant now resides in its jurisdictional area.
     ☐ the principal place of business of a corporation or unincorporated association is in its jurisdictional area.
     ☐ injury to person or damage to personal property occurred in its jurisdictional area.
     ☐ other *(specify):*

6. ☐ The following paragraphs of this complaint are alleged on information and belief *(specify paragraph numbers):*

(Continued)   Page two
                                            [E147]

SHORT TITLE:	CASE NUMBER:

COMPLAINT—Personal Injury, Property Damage, Wrongful Death (Continued) Page three

7. ☐ The damages claimed for wrongful death and the relationships of plaintiff to the deceased are
☐ listed in Complaint—Attachment 7 ☐ as follows:

8. Plaintiff has suffered
☐ wage loss
☐ hospital and medical expenses
☐ property damage
☐ other damage *(specify):*

☐ loss of use of property
☐ general damage
☐ loss of earning capacity

9. Relief sought in this complaint is within the jurisdiction of this court.

10. PLAINTIFF PRAYS
For judgment for costs of suit; for such relief as is fair, just, and equitable; and for
☐ compensatory damages
☐ **(Superior Court)** according to proof.

☐ **(Municipal and Justice Court)** in the amount of $_____
☐ other *(specify):*

11. The following causes of action are attached and the statements above apply to each: *(Each complaint must have one or more causes of action attached.)*
☐ Motor Vehicle
☐ General Negligence
☐ Intentional Tort
☐ Products Liability
☐ Premises Liability
☐ Other *(specify):*

· _____
(Type or print name) (Signature of plaintiff or attorney)

Rule 982.1(1) (cont'd)

COMPLAINT— Personal Injury, Property Damage,
Wrongful Death (Continued)

Page three

CCP 425.12
[E148]

SHORT TITLE:	CASE NUMBER:

_____ **CAUSE OF ACTION**—Premises Liability   Page _____
(number)

ATTACHMENT TO ☐ Complaint ☐ Cross-Complaint

(Use a separate cause of action form for each cause of action.)

Prem.L-1. Plaintiff *(name):*
alleges the acts of defendants were the legal (proximate) cause of damages to plaintiff.
On *(date):*   plaintiff was injured on the following premises in the following

fashion *(description of premises and circumstances of injury):*

Prem.L-2. ☐ **Count One—Negligence** The defendants who negligently owned, maintained, managed and operated the described premises were *(names):*

     ☐ Does _____ to _____

Prem.L-3. ☐ **Count Two—Willful Failure to Warn** [Civil Code section 846] The defendant owners who willfully or maliciously failed to guard or warn against a dangerous condition, use, structure, or activity were *(names):*

     ☐ Does _____ to _____
Plaintiff, a recreational user, was ☐ an invited guest ☐ a paying guest.

Prem.L-4. ☐ **Count Three—Dangerous Condition of Public Property** The defendants who owned public property on which a dangerous condition existed were *(names):*

     ☐ Does _____ to _____
a. ☐ The defendant public entity had ☐ actual ☐ constructive notice of the existence of the dangerous condition in sufficient time prior to the injury to have corrected it.
b. ☐ The condition was created by employees of the defendant public entity.

Prem.L-5. a. ☐ **Allegations about Other Defendants** The defendants who were the agents and employees of the other defendants and acted within the scope of the agency were *(names):*

     ☐ Does _____ to _____
b. ☐ The defendants who are liable to plaintiffs for other reasons and the reasons for their liability are ☐ described in attachment Prem.L-5.b ☐ as follows *(names):*

Form Approved by the
Judicial Council of California
Effective January 1, 1982
Rule 982.1(5)   **CAUSE OF ACTION**—Premises Liability   CCP 425.12
[E152]

ATTORNEY OR PARTY WITHOUT ATTORNEY (NAME AND ADDRESS):	TELEPHONE:	FOR COURT USE ONLY
ATTORNEY FOR (NAME):		

Insert name of court, judicial district or branch court, if any, and post office and street address:

PLAINTIFF:

DEFENDANT:

ANSWER—Personal Injury, Property Damage, Wrongful Death ☐ **COMPLAINT OF** *(name):* ☐ **CROSS-COMPLAINT OF** *(name):*	CASE NUMBER:

1. This pleading, including attachments and exhibits, consists of the following number of pages: _____

DEFENDANT OR CROSS-DEFENDANT *(name):*

2. ☐ Generally **denies** each allegation of the **unverified** complaint or cross-complaint.

3. a. ☐ DENIES each allegation of the following numbered paragraphs:

    b. ☐ ADMITS each allegation of the following numbered paragraphs:

    c. ☐ DENIES, ON INFORMATION AND BELIEF, each allegation of the following numbered paragraphs:

    d. ☐ DENIES, BECAUSE OF LACK OF SUFFICIENT INFORMATION OR BELIEF TO ANSWER, each allegation of the following numbered paragraphs:

    e. ☐ ADMITS the following allegations and generally denies all other allegations:

(Continued)

Form Approved by the
Judicial Council of California
Effective January 1, 1982
Rule 982.1(15)

ANSWER—Personal Injury, Property Damage, Wrongful Death

CCP 425.12
[E158]

SHORT TITLE:	CASE NUMBER:

ANSWER—Personal Injury, Property Damage, Wrongful Death　　　　Page two

f. ☐ DENIES the following allegations and admits all other allegations:

g. ☐ Other *(specify):*

AFFIRMATIVELY ALLEGES AS A DEFENSE

4. ☐ The comparative fault of plaintiff or cross-complainant *(name):*
　　　 as follows:

5. ☐ The expiration of the Statute of Limitations as follows:

6. ☐ Other *(specify):*

7. DEFENDANT OR CROSS-DEFENDANT PRAYS
　　For costs of suit and that plaintiff or cross-complainant take nothing.
　　☐ Other *(specify):*

. . . .
(Type or print name)　　　　　　　　　　　(Signature of party or attorney)

Page two
[E159]

ATTORNEY OR PARTY WITHOUT ATTORNEY *(Name and Address)*:	TELEPHONE NO.	FOR COURT USE ONLY
ATTORNEY FOR *(Name)*:		
Insert name of court, name of judicial district, and branch court, if any:		
PLAINTIFF:		
DEFENDANT:		
GENERAL DENIAL		CASE NUMBER:

You MUST use this form for your general denial if the amount asked for in the complaint or the value of the property involved is $1000 or less.

You MAY use this form if:
1. The complaint is not verified, OR
2. The complaint is verified, and the action is subject to the economic litigation procedures of the municipal and justice courts, EXCEPT

You MAY NOT use this form if the complaint is verified and involves a claim for more than $1000 that has been assigned to a third party for collection.

(See Code of Civil Procedure sections 90–100, 431.30, and 431.40.)

1. DEFENDANT *(name)*:
    generally denies each and every allegation of plaintiff's complaint.

2. ☐ DEFENDANT states the following FACTS as separate affirmative defenses to plaintiff's complaint *(attach additional pages if necessary)*:

Date:

. . . .   ▶   _____
(TYPE OR PRINT NAME)   (SIGNATURE OF DEFENDANT OR ATTORNEY)

If you have a claim for damages or other relief against the plaintiff, the law may require you to state your claim in a special pleading called a cross-complaint or you may lose your claim. (See Code of Civil Procedure sections 426.10–426.40.)

The original of this General Denial must be filed with the clerk of this court with proof that a copy was served on each plaintiff's attorney and on each plaintiff not represented by an attorney. *(See the other side for a proof of service.)*

Form Adopted by Rule 982
Judicial Council of California
982(a)(13) [Rev. January 1, 1987]   **GENERAL DENIAL**   CCP 431.30, 431.40

PLAINTIFF *(name)*:	CASE NUMBER:
DEFENDANT *(name)*:	

PROOF OF SERVICE
☐ **Personal Service**   ☐ **Mail**

> A General Denial may be served by anyone at least 18 years of age EXCEPT you or any other party to this legal action. Service is made in one of the following ways:
> (1) Personally delivering a copy to the attorney for the other party or, if no attorney, to the other party.
>   **OR**
> (2) Mailing a copy, postage prepaid, to the last known address of the attorney for the other party or, if no attorney, to the other party.
> Be sure whoever serves the General Denial fills out and signs a proof of service. File the proof of service with the court as soon as the General Denial is served.

1. At the time of service I was at least 18 years of age and not a party to this legal action.

2. I served a copy of the General Denial as follows *(check either a or b)*:

   a. ☐   **Personal service.** I personally delivered the General Denial as follows:
       (1) Name of person served:
       (2) Address where served:

       (3) Date served:
       (4) Time served:

   b. ☐   **Mail.** I deposited the General Denial in the United States mail, in a sealed envelope with postage fully prepaid. The envelope was addressed and mailed as follows:
       (1) Name of person served:
       (2) Address:

       (3) Date of mailing:
       (4) Place of mailing *(city and state)*:
       (5) I am a resident of or employed in the county where the General Denial was mailed.

   c. My residence or business address is *(specify)*:

   d. My phone number is *(specify)*:

I declare under penalty of perjury under the laws of the State of California that the foregoing is true and correct.

Date:

▶

....
(TYPE OR PRINT NAME OF PERSON WHO SERVED THE GENERAL DENIAL)   (SIGNATURE OF PERSON WHO SERVED THE GENERAL DENIAL)

982(a)(13) (Rev. January 1, 1987)   **GENERAL DENIAL**   Page two
       (Proof of Service)

B. PRIVATELY PUBLISHED FORMS

One cannot rely with the same confidence on pleading forms in privately published form books. These are of uneven quality. Many are written in an obsolete style and some are based on obsolete law as well. Although some do provide the basis for legally sufficient pleadings, the attorney using them bears the burden of testing them against the applicable civil rules as well as other statutory and case law.

II. PARTS OF PLEADINGS

In states where no forms dictate, lawyers still need to produce pleadings with all their formal parts intact. The parts of pleadings are illustrated by the line-numbered complaint and answer below. Those pleadings are line-numbered for easy reference here. In some courts all litigation documents are required to be filed on line-numbered paper, which is produced and sold expressly for that purpose.

A. CAPTION

The caption sets forth the name of the court, the identification of the parties, and the kind of pleading that it is (lines 1–8, 87–94).

B. INTRODUCTORY CLAUSE

The introductory clause specifies whose pleading it is and provides a grammatical foundation for the allegations to follow (lines 9–10, 95–96).

C. BODY

The body contains the allegations regarding the circumstances of the case. The body of a complaint is sometimes called the statement of claim (lines 11–54, 62–66). The body of an answer contains both the defendant's responses to the allegations in the complaint and also any affirmative defenses (lines 97–122).

D. DEMAND FOR JUDGMENT AND RELIEF

In some states, this part appears in the complaint but not the answer (lines 55–61, 67–69), although in other states defendant as well as plaintiff formally demands judgment. (See the California answer form above.)

E. SIGNATURE

Address and phone number always accompany the attorney's signature, as well as the designation of which party the attorney represents (lines 70–75, 127–32). If the attorney is acting as a representative of a firm, the firm's name appears as well. Some courts may also require the attorney's Bar license number.

F. VERIFICATION

A verification is a signed declaration by the party verifying that the pleading has been read and is true. It used to be commonly required on all pleadings. Now verification is commonly required only for certain matters, for instance, applications for injunction, appointment of receivers, and temporary relief such as alimony and child support. The sample replevin complaint below is verified because the plaintiff seeks a prejudgment writ without posting bond. In other words, this verification operates as what is sometimes called a "poverty affidavit" (lines 76–86).

G. CERTIFICATE OF SERVICE

All pleadings except initial complaints conclude with a certificate of service, certifying delivery or mailing to opposing counsel on a given date (lines 123–26). There is no certificate of service on an initial complaint because its service is proved by filing a separate form showing that the complaint and summons have been served. Amended complaints, like all other pleadings except initial complaints, conclude with a certificate of service.

1   IN THE _____ COURT OF _____ IN AND FOR _____
2   COUNTY

3 LESLIE WOROB,	
4 Plaintiff,	CIVIL ACTION
5 vs.	Case No.: 86–000–CA
6 JANICE ANDREWS	Division: J
7 Defendant.	

8   COMPLAINT FOR REPLEVIN AND DAMAGES

9   Plaintiff, LESLIE WOROB, sues defendant, JANICE ANDREWS,
10   and alleges:

11   COUNT I

12   1. This is an action to recover possession of personal property in
13   _____ County, _____.

14   2. The description of the property is:

Item	Estimated Value
1 Automobile: 1978 Mercury Cougar	$2,300.00
1 Console Color Television	500.00
1 Stereo and Speakers	150.00
Record and Tape Collection	4,000.00

20   To the best of plaintiff's knowledge, information, and belief, the total
21   value of the property is $6,950.00.

22   3. Plaintiff is the owner of the property, having purchased all of
23   it, and is entitled to possession of it. A copy of certificate of title to the
24   1978 Mercury Cougar automobile is attached as Exhibit "A". Copies of
25   the bills of sale for the console color television set and the stereo and
26   speakers are attached as Exhibits "B" and "C."

27 4. In early October 1985, plaintiff and defendant made an agree-
28 ment for plaintiff to store the property at the home of defendant, and
29 plaintiff delivered the property to defendant's garage for storage.

30 5. In late October 1985, plaintiff and defendant agreed that plain-
31 tiff would live in defendant's home, and plaintiff moved in and paid
32 rent to defendant at the agreed rate of $30.00 per week through
33 December 31, 1985.

34 6. On December 31, 1985, defendant, without provocation and
35 without just cause, refused plaintiff entry to defendant's home and
36 denied plaintiff access to plaintiff's property.

37 7. To plaintiff's best knowledge, information, and belief, the prop-
38 erty is located at defendant's residence at 241 79th Terrace, _____,
39 _____ County, _____.

40 8. Plaintiff has made repeated demands to defendant that she
41 deliver or release the property to plaintiff, but defendant has failed and
42 refuses to comply.

43 9. Defendant wrongfully detains the property, with the intention
44 to sell it to pay for damage defendant wrongly claims plaintiff caused to
45 defendant's home. Defendant expressed this intention to plaintiff in a
46 letter dated March 9, 1986.

47 10. Plaintiff's property has not been taken for a tax, assessment,
48 or fine pursuant to law.

49 11. Plaintiff's property has not been taken under an execution or
50 attachment against the property of the plaintiff.

51 12. While plaintiff has accumulated a certain amount of personal
52 property during her life, much of which is presently in defendant's
53 possession, plaintiff has no liquid assets with which to post bond for a
54 Prejudgment Writ of Replevin as required by _____.

55 WHEREFORE, plaintiff prays that this Court:

56 A. Enter judgment for possession of the property;

57 B. Waive the posting of bond by plaintiff as required by _____;
58 and

59 C. File with the Clerk of Court an order authorizing the issuance
60 of a Prejudgment Writ of Replevin, or, in the alternative;

61 D. Issue defendant an Order to show cause pursuant to _____.

62 ## COUNT II

63 13. This is an action for damages that exceed $5,000.00.

64 14. On or about December 31, 1985, defendant converted to her
65 own use plaintiff's personal property described in paragraph 2 of Count
66 I, of the value of $6,950.00.

WHEREFORE, plaintiff demands judgment for damages against the defendant, costs, and all such other relief as this Court deems proper.

_____

DAVID S. KING
Attorney for Plaintiff
343 E. Main Street

_____, _____

(___) _____

STATE OF _____ ⎤
COUNTY OF _____ ⎦

Before me, the undersigned authority, this day personally appeared LESLIE WOROB, who deposes and says that the allegations contained in the foregoing Complaint are true and correct.

_____

LESLIE WOROB

Sworn to and subscribed before me this _____ day of March, 1986.

_____

Notary Public—State of _____ at Large
My commission expires _____, 19__

_____

IN THE _____ COURT OF _____, IN AND FOR _____
COUNTY, _____

LESLIE WOROB,
   Plaintiff,
vs.
JANICE ANDREWS
   Defendant.
	CIVIL ACTION
	CASE NO.: 86–000–CA
	DIVISION: J

ANSWER

The defendant, JANICE ANDREWS, answers the plaintiff's Complaint, and says:

1. Defendant is without knowledge of paragraph 1.
2. Defendant denies paragraph 2.
3. Defendant denies paragraph 3.
4. Defendant denies paragraph 4.
5. Defendant admits paragraph 5 except as to the rate.

6. Defendant denies paragraph 6.

7. Defendant admits paragraph 7.

8. Defendant denies paragraph 8.

9. Defendant denies paragraph 9.

10. Defendant admits paragraph 10.

11. Defendant admits paragraph 11.

12. Defendant is without knowledge of paragraph 12.

13. Defendant is without knowledge of paragraph 13.

14. Defendant denies paragraph 14.

FIRST AFFIRMATIVE DEFENSE

15. The 1978 Mercury Cougar automobile was tendered as a gift to defendant by plaintiff as evidenced by an open title signed by LESLIE WOROB and a Power of Attorney given to LESLIE WOROB properly witnessed transferring the automobile to defendant JANICE ANDREWS.

SECOND AFFIRMATIVE DEFENSE

16. The color television, stereo and speakers, and record and tape collection were transferred by plaintiff to defendant in satisfaction of debt for monies advanced and loaned and for services including rent provided to LESLIE WOROB while she was living with JANICE ANDREWS in her private home.

CERTIFICATE OF SERVICE

I certify that a true copy of this answer has been furnished to David S. King, Attorney for Plaintiff, 343 E. Main Street, _____, _____, by U.S. Mail on April 14, 19__.

ROBERT ELLIS, P.A.
Attorney for Defendant
797 W. Main Street

_____, _____

(__) _____

III. DRAFTING COMPLAINTS

Even if an approved form is available, the drafter still must tailor the pleading to the particular case at hand. In a complaint, for instance, the drafter must be sure to state a cause of action by including: (A) grounds for the court's jurisdiction, (B) the factual allegations showing entitlement to relief, and (C) the demand for judgment.

A. JURISDICTION

Typically the court's jurisdiction is invoked by a statutory reference or in an action for damages by a simple statement establishing that the amount of damages sought is within the jurisdictional amount for the court in question. For example:

1. "This is an action for damages that do not exceed $2,500."

2. "This is an action for damages that exceed $2,500 but do not exceed $5,000."

3. "This is an action for damages that exceed $5,000."

B. FACTUAL ALLEGATIONS

The drafter's major work is in the body of the pleading. The old common law rules that used to prescribe rigid forms of pleading are now gone.

1. Short and Plain Statements

Typical state rules of civil procedure simply require a "short and plain" statement of the ultimate facts to plead a claim. There are some technical differences between a "cause of action," which is the common phrasing for the right to bring an action in state court, and a "claim for relief," which is the operative term in federal courts.[1] However, in any court, the drafter's contribution to effective pleadings lies mainly in those short and plain statements of facts.

GLASS, PLEADINGS, CH. 12, FLORIDA CIVIL PRACTICE BEFORE TRIAL

305, 317–18 (4th ed. 1983).

A pleading hopelessly enmeshed in a maze of "to-wits, whereases, saids and aforesaids" does little to develop the material issues of law or fact upon which to resolve the controversy. Pleadings do not have to be reduced to the level of a nursery story to ensure clarity, but nevertheless should be couched in language understandable to the opposing party and the trier of fact.

Cases have been dismissed for violations of the rules requiring plain statements.[2] The irate court opinions dismissing the complaints or affirming their dismissal refer most commonly to prolixity and redundancy. Sometimes, however, the dismissed complaints have suffered from additional flaws of argumentative and conclusory paragraphs,[3] evidentiary statements,[4] extraneous matter,[5] and failure

---

1. See Fed.R.Civ.P. 8(a) and (e).

2. See, for example, Gordon v. Green, 602 F.2d 743, 747, cases cited at 746 (5th Cir.1979).

3. See, for example, Benner v. Philadelphia Musical Society, Local 77, of American Federation of Musicians, 32 F.R.D. 197, 198 (E.D.Pa.1963).

4. See, for example, Johnson v. Hunger, 266 F.Supp. 590, 591 (S.D.N.Y.1967).

5. See, for example, Carrigan v. California State Legislature, 263 F.2d 560, 566 (9th Cir.1959), cert. denied 359 U.S. 980, 79 S.Ct. 901 (1959); Silver v. Queen's Hospital, 53 F.R.D. 223 (D.Hawaii 1971).

to make clear whether amended pleadings supersede previous versions or are to be read in conjunction with them.[6] Such dismissals are typically without prejudice. Yet filing an amended complaint is itself an expensive and time-consuming exercise that is not likely to please many plaintiffs.

The movement from traditional common law and code pleadings to contemporary notice pleadings has fostered a preference for drafting pleadings in lay terms with minimal use of legal terms of art and a growing tendency to reject archaic legalese.

BENSON, PLAIN ENGLISH COMES TO COURT
13 Litigation No. 1, 21, 21, 24 (1986).*

Once an instrument of power, legalese no longer carries clout. It is considered a limp club, or worse: a pathetic attempt to display the accoutrements of classy breeding, like wearing a fedora or spats. Once an instrument of meticulous administration of the courts, legalese in court papers today is a symbol of red tape and inefficiency. The judges who know about good writing suspect that beneath your legalese lurks linguistic, and perhaps legal, incompetence.

* * *

[T]he courts have discovered a useful fact. Most lawsuit papers— complaints, answers, motions, notices, and so on—do not need to be complicated at all, because they do not really *say* anything. Rather, they *do* things, and the things they do are routine. These papers amount to what the linguists call speech acts ("performatives," in the linguists' own jargon), which make things happen, rather than communicate their content.

Judges who appreciate good writing are inclined to reward it. A senior partner in a Santa Monica, California, firm tells the results of the firm's having hired an expert in English to edit all papers that leave the office.

FADEM, LEGALESE AS LEGAL DOES: LAWYERS CLEAN UP THEIR ACT
Prosecutor's Brief 14 (Jan.-Feb. 1979).

It is not an uncommon experience for us to appear for motions, have the judge indicate a predisposition to the view expressed by our papers, sit through a colloquy between judge and adversary lawyer, and depart without having said anything but our name for the record and thank you at the end. The days that happens, I know it pays to have an editor.

Getting rid of legalese goes a long way to make pleadings concise and clear. For example, it is sufficient to refer to the plaintiff and

---

6. See, for example, Gordon v. Green, 602 F.2d at 745.

defendant throughout as "plaintiff" and "defendant" or as "Smith" and "Jones." There is no need to refer to "plaintiff Smith" or "Smith, the plaintiff herein," or "Jones, the above-mentioned defendant." If two or more parties have the same last name, first names can serve to distinguish them.

In some instances, it is more helpful to the reader to refer to parties not by their names but by terms that identify their relationship, such as "landlord" and "tenant" or "buyer" and "seller." This system can be established at the first reference to a party by specifying simply "Smith ('seller')." It is not necessary to recite "(hereinafter referred to as 'seller')."

The same principle applies to identifying things, places, and the like. It is sufficient to refer to "the property" or "the lease" without reciting "the hereinabove-described lease" or even "the said lease." If only one lease is involved, "said" does not help identify it. If more than one lease is involved, to avoid potential ambiguity, they ought to be identified as "the 1986 lease" and "the 1987 lease" or "the house lease" and "the apartment lease" or even "lease 1" and "lease 2." [7]

Sometimes it is necessary to keep language that is not entirely plain and simple. If an action is brought under some particular statute, for example, it is crucial to frame the complaint in the exact language prescribed by the statute.

Also, thorough research of the substantive law involved in the case is always essential. While one may learn quickly from form books and rules how to plead jurisdiction and damages, there remains the need to plead facts sufficient to include all of the elements of any given cause of action.

Here is a checklist for drafting factual allegations:

a. Allege ultimate facts to substantiate every element of the claim.

b. Give the defendant the information needed to draft a responsive pleading.

c. If the action is based on a statute, refer to it specifically.

d. Avoid anticipating affirmative defenses.

e. Avoid including any other extraneous matter such as argumentative or evidentiary statements.

f. Do not include any allegations known to be untrue.

---

7. For further discussion of these and other suggestions for how to draft lawsuit papers without legalese, see Alterman, Plain and Accurate Style in Lawsuit Papers, 62 Mich.B.J. 964 (1983). In addition to pleadings, Alterman discusses motions, notices, affidavits, orders, briefs, stipulations, and correspondence. This article has been expanded into a book, Plain and Accurate Style in Court Papers (1987). For outspoken commentary on a variety of stylistic matters applicable to both pleadings and other legal documents, see Trawick, Form as Well as Substance, 49 Fla.B.J. 437 (1975).

2. Pleadings as Discovery Tools

The main thing to remember is that pleadings serve to raise issues for trial. Issues cannot be raised through discovery. Thus each count in a complaint must state a cause of action.

F. COOPER, WRITING IN LAW PRACTICE
183 (1963).

A well-drawn complaint can serve as a method of discovery; an allegation drawn in narrow and precise language may compel an admission from defendant who could deny the charge, had it been made in general terms. By thus requiring the defendant to reveal in his answer exactly what his position is, the issues may be considerably narrowed, resulting in saving of time at the trial and often serving to open the door to advantageous settlement.

It is possible to use pleadings strategically for discovery purposes, choosing language to suggest to opposing counsel that one has a strong case. For example, plaintiffs' counsel can pursue the strategic goal of forcing defendants either to admit something or to deny it in such specific terms as to reveal the theory of their case. Plaintiffs would thus want to avoid the general and vague language that is easy for defendants to deny generally.

According to one theory about pleadings strategy, it is fruitless for plaintiff to strive to trap defendant into admissions because defendant is almost certain to admit only innocuous facts that do not lead to liability. Under this theory, the only thing for a complaint to do is state a cause of action in terms minimally sufficient to survive a motion to dismiss. However, to the extent that the drafter wishes to try using pleadings to strategic advantage, it helps to be adept at some techniques.

a. Precision and Brevity

The idea is not to complicate things or exaggerate them, because those strategies only make the job of proving the client's case harder. Thus it is better to say that defendant "slapped plaintiff in the mouth" than to say that defendant "assaulted, battered, struck, bruised, and wounded plaintiff." Faced with such a list in a complaint, defendant may respond evasively.

b. Objective Words

Whenever possible, the drafter should use objective words. For example, in many states if plaintiff says that defendant physician "acted negligently," that is stating a legal conclusion. In some states, however, alleging that someone was negligent is considered alleging an ultimate fact rather than drawing a legal conclusion. Whether regarded as fact or conclusion, the statement is in subjective language, and thus it is easy for the defendant to deny. It is more difficult to deny if plaintiff specifies that defendant "left a surgical clamp in plaintiff's stomach."

In a state where plaintiff is obligated to mention negligence itself as the ultimate fact, plaintiff might allege in one sentence that the physician did not remove the clamp and in a separate follow-up sentence that the failure constituted negligence. If defendant is pressed to admit the objective allegation, plaintiff is well on the way to substantiating the subjective one as well.

On the other hand, subjective allegations may often stand alone if no more information is available at the time of pleading. Hence, a plaintiff may successfully allege merely that a defendant negligently operated or maintained a motor vehicle so that it collided with plaintiff's motor vehicle.

c. Separate Allegations

If several allegations appear together in the same sentence, it is tempting for the defendant to deny the lot generally. In other words, if plaintiff says that defendant "owned, operated, managed, and controlled" a store, there are four separate allegations. The defendant who only has a 99-year lease may deny the sentence as a whole. Lists of synonyms joined by the conjunction "and" are generally dangerous. Also, the internal inconsistency of "and/or" is worth avoiding.

Defendants are obligated under federal and typical state pleading rules to respond to a pleading "in good faith," denying only those parts of allegations that they intend to deny and admitting the rest. However, sometimes defendants do not abide by this rule, and judges have been reluctant to impose sanctions on them. Thus it is up to the pleader to frame clear, specific allegations in order to prevent an evasive reply.

C. DEMAND FOR JUDGMENT

The demand for judgment for relief may often be as brief as this: "WHEREFORE, Plaintiff demands judgment against Defendant for damages." It is of course possible to add other more specific terms such as the minimal amount of damages demanded or attorney's fees, costs, and interest, depending on the case. It is also possible to pray for different types of relief either cumulatively or alternatively.

IV. DRAFTING RESPONSIVE PLEADINGS IN SHORT AND PLAIN TERMS

A. ADMISSIONS AND DENIALS

An answer responds to every allegation in the complaint by (1) admitting it, (2) denying it, or (3) alleging that the defendant is without knowledge as to it. Alleging lack of knowledge operates as a denial.

Child—Legal Drafting ACB—3

Defendant's counsel is wise to study carefully the phrasing of plaintiff's allegations. Defendant can legitimately deny an allegation phrased so poorly that it seems to say something untrue, and the result of the denial is to suggest that a question of fact exists about something that plaintiff may not have expected to be in dispute.

When drafting an answer, defendant may choose specifically to admit certain allegations, leaving the rest generally denied. Likewise, defendant may specifically deny certain allegations, leaving the rest generally admitted. Relying on general denials or admissions is somewhat dangerous, however. Because of the rule of automatic admission of any allegation not specifically denied, one may be caught in an inadvertent admission. Thus it is preferable to respond to each paragraph in the complaint in numerical order. This system also makes it easier to refer later to the complaint and answer together on any given issue.

Example of recommended sequence:

Defendant, _____, answers the plaintiff's Complaint and says:

1. Defendant admits paragraph 1.
2. Defendant admits paragraph 2.
3. Defendant denies paragraph 3.
4. Defendant is without knowledge of paragraph 4.
5. Defendant admits paragraph 5.
6. Defendant admits the first sentence of paragraph 6, but denies the remainder of paragraph 6.

Example of sequence not recommended:

Defendant, _____, answers the plaintiff's Complaint and says:

1. Defendant admits paragraphs 1, 2, and 5 and the first sentence of paragraph 6.
2. Defendant denies paragraph 3 and all of paragraph 6 except its first sentence.
3. Defendant is without knowledge of paragraph 4.

State rules typically require "short and plain terms" to defend against claims, and the courts take the rules seriously regarding the appropriate language. If a pleading in a case on appeal is verbose and obscures the issues, the court's impatience may even show in the opinion. Here is an example.

PEARSON v. SINDELAR

75 So.2d 295, 296–97 (Fla. 1954).

* * *

Some time after the complaint was filed, defendants made their first appearance in court by filing a pleading listing five numbered defenses. Both in form and in substance, this pleading resembled a collection of affirmative defenses. It set up matter principally in the nature of avoidance. It could have been construed as an answer, in that each defense referred to a paragraph of the complaint and some of the averments therein were denied, but it was virtually impossible to determine from the whole pleading what position the defendants took with regard to the allegations of the complaint. Plaintiff promptly filed a motion to strike on several grounds, but with particular reference to the requirements of Rule 9(c) of the Florida Common Law Rules, 30 F.S.A., then in force [present Rules of Civil Procedure, Rule 1.8(c), F.S.A.]. Before this motion was heard, defendants filed an amended pleading containing six defenses, but subject to the same infirmities possessed by their original pleading. A second motion to strike was filed, and on July 23, 1953, the court ordered the entire pleading stricken, with leave to amend within ten days.

There can be no doubt as to the propriety of this ruling. This was a simple lawsuit on a written contract and presented no extraordinary problems of defensive pleading. The defendants had twice had their attention called to the requirements of Rule 9(c), but their amended pleading was objectionable under this rule and subject to being stricken under Rule 13(f) [present Rule 1.11(f)].

Former Rule 9 of the Florida Common Law Rules [which, with minor changes, is reproduced as Rule 1.8 of the 1954 Florida Rules of Civil Procedure] outlines the way in which an answer containing affirmative defenses or matter in avoidance is to be framed. The availability of affirmative factual material to be pleaded does not relax the requirement of subsection (c) of the rule that the pleader shall state his defenses in "short and simple terms" [or "short and plain terms", as the 1954 Rules provide]. Subsection (f) of both the old rule and the new requires that "each defense other than denials shall be stated in a separate count or defense whenever a separation facilitates the clear presentation of the matter set forth." Reading subsections (c), (d) and (f) together, it becomes apparent that in the ordinary case, such as the one before us, it is the best practice to confine the body of an answer to simple, categorical admissions or denials, in whole or in part, of the allegations of the complaint paragraph by paragraph [under the new rule it is also permissible to state that the pleader is without knowledge of matter alleged, if such is the fact] and to reserve affirmative defenses or matter in avoidance for separate statement, in numbered paragraphs, following the body of the answer. In this way, the issues become clear, the affirmative defenses can readily be examined for sufficiency, and time is conserved both by counsel and the court.

In the case at bar, the first two defensive pleadings filed were prolix, did not meet the substance of the complaint, and thoroughly obscured the issues, if any there were. * * *

* * *

B. AFFIRMATIVE DEFENSES

The answer also includes any affirmative defenses other than those being made appropriately by motion. An affirmative defense does not deny the plaintiff's claim but avoids it by pleading new matter. The same strategic principles that govern drafting factual allegations in a complaint govern drafting affirmative defenses. The idea is to make them hard for a plaintiff to deny.

C. REPLIES

The exclusive purpose of a reply is to *avoid* the affirmative defenses in the answer. There is no need to reply if an answer contains no affirmative defenses. Likewise, there is no need to reply merely to *deny* what is alleged in an affirmative defense. This is because allegations that require no responsive pleading are automatically denied. The difference between *avoiding* and *denying* is that an avoidance pleads some new matter that prevents the affirmative defense from operating effectively, while a denial merely asserts that the allegation in question is not true.

For example, if the defendant presents the affirmative defense of the statute of limitations, the plaintiff need not reply to assert that the statute has not run. That would be superfluous denial. However, if the plaintiff has been absent from the jurisdiction, tolling the statute, then a reply is in order to avoid the affirmative defense by pleading this new matter.

V. PROBLEMS

PROBLEM 1

Assume that the negligence complaint form below is a court-approved form in your state. (If your state has a different court-approved form for slip-and-fall cases, you might work from it for this problem.)

COMPLAINT

1   Plaintiff, A.B., sues defendant, C.D., and alleges:

2   1. This is an action for damages that (insert jurisdictional
3   amount).

4   2. On _____, 19__, defendant was the owner and in posses-
5   sion of a building at _____ in _____, _____, that was used as a
6   (describe use).

7   3. At that time and place plaintiff went on the property to
8   (state purpose).

9   4. Defendant negligently maintained (describe item) on the
10   property by (describe negligence or dangerous condition) so that
11   plaintiff fell on the property.

5. The negligent condition was known to defendant or had existed for a sufficient length of time so that defendant should have known of it.

6. As a result plaintiff was injured in and about his body and extremities, suffered pain therefrom, incurred medical expense in the treatment of the injuries, suffered physical handicap and his working ability was impaired; the injuries are either permanent or continuing in nature and plaintiff will suffer the losses and impairment in the future.

WHEREFORE plaintiff demands judgment for damages against defendant.

Evaluate the preceding slip-and-fall form based on the drafting principles you have learned so far. Then evaluate the following complaint modeled on the form.

COMPLAINT

Plaintiff, _____, sues defendant, _____, and alleges:

1. This is an action for damages.

2. On the _____ day of _____, 19__, defendant was the proprietor of and operated a retail drug store, pharmacy, and variety store at No. _____, _____ Street, in the city of _____, _____ County, where it offered for sale over-the-counter medicines, prescriptions, and sundries and solicited the entrance and patronage of the public.

3. Defendant kept the floor of said store waxed and polished, and on the date aforesaid certain cosmetics and soap products had fallen from a counter or otherwise had been allowed by defendant to be upon the floor of an aisle, 8 feet wide, in which customers were invited to walk, and said products were allowed by defendant to remain on the floor thereof for a period of 2½ hours prior to the accident hereinafter described.

4. On the aforesaid date plaintiff at the invitation of defendant entered said store and walked along the aisle to view the merchandise therein, and by reason of and in direct consequence of the negligence and carelessness of defendant in allowing said products to be and remain on the floor of the aisle aforesaid, plaintiff while proceeding in a reasonably safe and prudent manner stepped upon some of said products and was thereby caused to slip and fall violently to the floor.

5. Plaintiff suffered bodily injury and resulting pain and suffering, disability, disfigurement, mental anguish, loss of capacity for the enjoyment of life, expense of hospitalization, medical and nursing care and treatment, loss of earnings, loss of ability to earn money, and aggravation of a previously existing condition. The losses are either permanent or continuing and plaintiff will suffer the losses in the future.

31   6. Said injuries were not in any way due to contributory
32 negligence on the part of plaintiff.

33   WHEREFORE, Plaintiff demands judgment against defendant.

PROBLEM 2

Assume you have received the following memorandum from a paralegal in your office. Draft a complaint on behalf of Jack Richie.

MEMORANDUM

TO: Attorney

FROM: Paralegal

RE: Fall-Down Negligence Case of Jack Richie

While you were out, a new client stopped by. His name is Jack Richie, and he wants to sue the _____ law school. Here is his story.

He was on the way to a 3 o'clock interview yesterday for a job on the law school staff. He drove around the campus for a while. Unable to find a spot in the law school parking lot, he parked on the side of the road, under a tree in front of the law building.

After the appointment was over at 4, he hurried back to his car, as he had another job interview at 4:30. But his car wouldn't start when he turned the key in the ignition. So he went into the law building again to use a phone to call a mechanic.

When he came into the front office area, the secretary was using the telephone. But straight ahead was another office with no one there and a phone sitting on the desk. As he rushed in to grab the phone, he tripped on a typewriter cord that stretched across the floor. As he fell forward, he tried to grab the side of the desk to cushion his fall, but he ended up bumping his elbow badly as well as twisting his ankle. (He mentioned that he had sprained the ankle two months ago playing volleyball.)

Hearing the noise, a professor came into the office where Richie was on the floor. The professor gave Richie a ride to the emergency room. Richie told her he could get someone to pick him up. Meanwhile, while Richie was at the hospital, learning that he had a badly sprained ankle, his illegally parked car was towed.

Now Richie wants to sue. He will send you the receipt for the car towing bill, which was about $55. His hospital bills are so far about $275 to date, though he is supposed to continue to see the doctor, who threatens to put a cast on his ankle once the swelling subsides.

PROBLEM 3

Assume you have received the following memorandum from a paralegal in your office. Draft a complaint on behalf of Catherine Riddle.

MEMORANDUM

TO: Attorney

FROM: Paralegal

RE: Fall-down Negligence Case of Catherine Riddle

While you were out, I spoke with a student at the _____ law school, Catherine Riddle. She hurt herself on the stairs outside _____ Hall, a temporary law school annex. Apparently it had been drizzling when Cathy dropped off a book she had borrowed from a professor who has an office there.

Cathy said the stairs outside _____ Hall are made of unfinished wood. When I asked her for more details, she said they are about nine inches apart and about three feet wide. They have a railing, which is also made of wood. All but two of the stairs have rubber treads on them. Cathy slipped on the 10th or 11th step down, which didn't have a tread. (She counted the stairs—there are 18 altogether.) She said she was in a hurry when she went down the stairs, but she didn't think she was really rushing, and she was wearing her running shoes anyway. She said there were a lot of wet leaves on the stairs.

As she fell, she bounced down the remaining stairs, into a puddle at the bottom. She says she twisted her ankle, and now she wears a walking cast. This all happened a week ago today. She also mentioned there was part of a broken orange soda bottle at the bottom of the stairs, which cut her hand a little bit as she fell.

Cathy lives at _____ here in town. She wants you to sue the law school immediately as she needs the money to pay her doctor's bills. She has missed some classes already, due to her fall, and she is also behind in some of her assignments, so she wants to have this over as soon as possible.

PROBLEM 4

Draft an answer on behalf of the law school to the complaints you or another student drafted on behalf of Jack Richie and Catherine Riddle. Supply any reasonable allegations that you need to constitute affirmative defenses.

PROBLEM 5

Draft a complaint under your state's consumer protection statutes on behalf of a consumer who has a contract from a local health studio representing that the contract is for a lifetime membership. Include additional allegations that constitute an unfair or deceptive practice according to your state's statutes.

PROBLEM 6

Draft a complaint under your state's "lemon law" statutes on behalf of a consumer whose automobile brakes continue to fail after five attempts by the seller's service department to fix them. Include additional allegations that constitute failure to conform to other common express warranties.

PROBLEM 7

Draft a complaint under your state's "dram shop" statutes or alcoholic beverage control ("ABC") statutes on behalf of a pedestrian who has been injured by a minor driving a car after drinking six bottles of beer in the previous hour at a nearby bar.

Chapter 3

STYLE IN LEGAL DOCUMENTS

In E.B. White's famous essay on style in the little book that is generally referred to as "Strunk and White," he writes of style "in the sense of what is distinguished and distinguishing. ＊ ＊ ＊ When we speak of Fitzgerald's style," White writes, "we don't mean his command of the relative pronoun, we mean the sound his words make on paper. Every writer, by the way he uses the languge, reveals something of his spirit, his habits, his capacities, his bias. ＊ ＊ ＊ No writer long remains incognito." [1]

Like White's comments, most comments about style are subjective. Someone has a bold style; someone else has a turgid style. Style is flashy or tangled or refreshing. It is long-winded and pompous, or it is breezy or matter-of-fact. To characterize a novel in such terms is one thing. It is quite another thing to determine standards for appropriate style in drafting a contract or a statute. This is especially dangerous ground if White is right about writers not being able to remain incognito. White's words should challenge the legal drafter, for in legal documents the personality, beliefs, and style of the drafter as an individual must be removed as completely as possible.

Usually discussion of style in legal documents focuses on the primary value of consistency. To some extent it does not matter what conventions one adopts as long as they are observed consistently. If there is anything that characterizes the style of a well drafted legal document, it is that the drafter always says the same thing the same way and always says different things differently. Improving one's style requires more than attending consistently to any one of the matters discussed in this chapter. They all merit attention throughout any legal document.[2]

1. W. Strunk, Jr. and E. White, The Elements of Style 66–67 (3d ed. 1979).

2. For further discussion of style in particular contexts, see I. Alterman, Plain and Accurate Style in Court Papers (1987); C. Felsenfeld and A. Siegel, Writing Contracts in Plain English, ch. 6 (1981); W. Statsky, Legislative Analysis and Drafting, ch. 14 (2d ed. 1984).

CAVERS, THE SIMPLIFICATION OF GOVERNMENT REGULATIONS
8 Fed.B.J. 339, 345 (1947).

*   *   * It is only the cumulative effect of a large number of minor changes which can bring about a major improvement. In this respect, the analogy to streamlining is close. In the process of streamlining a locomotive, probably the removal of no single protuberance or angle would produce a perceptible difference in the operation of the train. The removal of fifty does.

I. MATTERS OF STYLE

A. TERMINOLOGY

Many people learn in English composition classes that repetition is a weakness and that variety in word choice is a strength. Certain misguided fiction writers take this advice to heart and try to tag every line of dialogue differently. The first speaker may be allowed merely to have "said" something, but the next one "replied," and then the first "answered," and after that somebody "whispered," "sighed," "breathed," or even "smiled" words in response. Sports reporters are particularly prone to this habit of using a different verb in every sentence. If one team "beat" another, the next team "defeated," "trounced," or "tromped" its opponent.

This constant variation can be irritating and distracting in any context. In legal drafting, it is totally unacceptable because the shifts make a reader wonder whether there is some hidden difference in meaning or reference. The drafter who is writing about condominiums and at one point refers to "units" dares not refer to "dwellings" later on. If one is writing about "rules," they should not later become "regulations."

Here is a section of a franchise tax board guideline that expresses definitions so variously that a reader might well question whether changes in wording throughout the guideline signify changes in meaning or not.

A. The following definitions shall apply to the construction of this guideline:

1. A "film" *means* the physical embodiment of a play, story or other literary or artistic work except that it *does not include* programs such as news and sports produced for telecast.

2. The word "film" *includes* a tape.

3. Each episode of a series of films produced for television exhibition *shall constitute* a separate film notwithstanding that the series relates to the same principal subject and is produced during a single television season.

4. "In release" *means* the date on which amortization of a film begins, and *is referred to* in the motion picture industry *as* the "accounting release date." For films owned by a television network, "in release" *means* the date on which the film is first telecast.

5. "Rerelease" *means* the release of any film for general theatrical and foreign distribution, syndication, or television network exhibition at any time after its initial distribution (release period) has terminated.

6. A "film" *is deemed to be* tangible personal property.

7. "Rent" *includes* license fees for the exhibition or telecast of films.

8. "Rate card" values *are* those published by Standard Rate and Data Service, Inc. [emphasis added throughout].

Just as it is important to use the same term consistently to refer to the same thing, it is also important not to give the same term more than one meaning or referent in the same document. For example, in a provision about "the United States" as a country, or as a geographical place, it would be inappropriate to say something like this: "The United States grants its citizens specified immunities." Such a statement refers to the United States government, not to the country itself.

B. PARALLEL CONSTRUCTIONS

Parallel ideas belong in parallel constructions whenever possible. The similarity in form helps a reader recognize the relationship in meaning. For example, the first sentence below uses parallel construction; the second does not.

Seller will pay for inspection, repairs, and painting.

Seller will pay for repairs, the bill for painting, and getting an exterminator to inspect for termites.

Again below, the first sentence uses parallel construction; the second does not.

The applicant shall obtain an application form from Room 250, fill it out, have his or her signature notarized, and file the completed form with the clerk in Room 254.

The applicant shall obtain an application form from Room 250 and fill it out, remembering that the signature must be notarized, and all completed applications must be filed with the clerk in Room 254.

The recommended parallel construction uses form to reinforce substance. In the first example, the series of nouns ("inspection," "repairs," and "painting") makes it easy to see at a glance that seller will pay for three things. In the second example, the series of verbs ("obtain," "fill out," "have notarized," and "file") makes it likewise easy to see that the application process has four steps. In fact, when there are several items in a parallel series, often it is helpful to use form even more bluntly to reinforce substance by numbering or lettering the items.

This principle of putting parallel ideas in parallel constructions functions most strictly in statute drafting, where it is sometimes called "normalizing." [3]

C. BREVITY

"Wordiness is a natural enemy of clarity * * *." [4] This is not to say that the shorter sentence is always the clearer one. If it takes more words to make a complicated concept clear, then clarity justifies the added length. However, lawyers are more often inclined to be too wordy than too brief.

1. *Needless Elaboration*

One of the most common forms of wordiness peculiar to legal documents is elaboration of details with no particular legal significance. Lawyers sometimes feel a pointless need to use language that is all-inclusive. Thus they fill consumer documents with a welter of details that many consumers cannot understand. Once one has been alerted to the problem, it is not difficult to change this habit. To demonstrate, here is the discussion by Carl Felsenfeld and Alan Siegel of how Citibank's consumer forms were streamlined.

C. FELSENFELD AND A. SIEGEL, WRITING CONTRACTS IN PLAIN ENGLISH
118–19, 121–23 (1981).*

The unsimplified model forms contain many examples of unnecessary elaboration. For instance, the old loan note refers to amounts that are unpaid "for a period in excess of 10 days." The new note uses the shorter but equally informative "more than 10 days."

Consider also the old note's description of debts that are covered by the collateral security. The security first applies to the loan that is covered by the note. The note calls this "the indebtedness of the undersigned hereunder." In the new note, it is called "this * * * debt."

The same security also covers the borrower's other debts to the bank. The old note calls them

all other indebtedness or liabilities of the undersigned to the bank, whether joint, several, absolute, contingent, secured, unsecured, matured or unmatured, under any present or future note or contract or agreement with the bank.

The new note just refers to "any other debt."

---

3. See Allen and Engholm, Normalized Legal Drafting and the Query Method, 29 J. Legal Educ. 380 (1978).

4. Siegel, To Lift the Curse of Legalese—Simplify, Simplify, 14 Across the Board 64, 70 (No. 6, June 1977).

* Copyright © 1981 by West Publishing Company. Reprinted by permission of the publisher.

The old note starts listing default events with these words:

In the event of default in the payment of this or any other Obligation or the performance or observance of any term or covenant contained herein or in any note or other contract or agreement * * *

A less verbose substitute (the concept not being carried into the new note) might be this: "If I break any promise to you * * *."

Both the old and new notes list various remedies that the bank will have if the borrower defaults. In general, these exist as a matter of law. There is therefore no requirement that they be catalogued in an agreement. While special consequences of a default, or special remedies—particularly "specific performance" of an obligation [73]—can be important in special cases, this consumer loan note involves none of them. The old note is being verbose when it describes the bank's legal rights upon the borrower's default by saying:

* * * the Bank shall have the right to exercise all the rights and remedies available to a secured party upon default under the Uniform Commercial Code (the "Code") in effect in New York at the time, and such other rights and remedies as may otherwise be provided by law.

The bank enjoys those enforcement rights whether or not they are mentioned in the note.[74] So the only apparent reason for this language is to inform the borrower. But what does the consumer borrower know of rights and remedies under the Code and other laws? The words are meaningless to the very audience to whom they are addressed. The new note eliminates this unjustifiable elaboration by saying:

You will also have other legal rights, for instance, the right to repossess, sell and apply security to the payments under this note and any other debts I may then owe you.

In the old note, the bank has the right upon default "to declare all or any part of the Obligations to be immediately due and payable, whereupon such Obligations shall become and be immediately due and payable." That language vibrates with importance. But it lacks legal significance. If the bank can declare the debts due, of course they *become* due; otherwise the declaration should not be there in the first place. The new note cuts through the pomposity and says: "You can then demand immediate payment of the balance * * *".

Here is another passage from the bank loan note where familiar, concrete words were used to supplant windy jargon:

73. See *Williston on Contracts*, Third Ed., Sec. 1423 B. fn. 4.

74. The ability to resort to collateral under the Code and also sue on the debt are permitted by Section 9–504 of the Code. Section 9–501 makes it clear that a secured party enjoys those rights even if they are not enumerated in the contract.

Old

Acceptance by the Bank of payments in arrears shall not constitute a waiver of or otherwise affect any acceleration of payment hereunder or other right or remedy exercisable hereunder.

New

You can accept late payments or partial payments, even though marked "payment in full", without losing any of your rights under this note.

Obviously, the traditional legal skills must be used to ensure that meaningful protection is not lost in the cause of simplification. Much elaboration may be meaningless. On the other hand, some words with the appearance of dross may be significant. Research must often precede the correct choice. The cooperative apartment sale contract is designed to bind both the seller and the buyer, one to sell and the other to buy. To accomplish this, the earlier text explicitly covered both sides of the transaction: "Seller agrees to sell and transfer and Purchaser agrees to buy the * * *". Is this cumbersome construction essential to the desired result? If it merely reads "Seller agrees to sell the * * *", is the buyer contractually bound to buy? * * *

* * *

* * * A reformation of the sentence can explicitly bind seller and buyer. Some creativity in writing achieves both clarity of language and legal specificity. While one continues to question the specific inclusion of both seller and buyer as a legal necessity, the solution eliminates any doubt that might result from a "Seller will sell the * * *" approach.

The old cooperative apartment sale contract, derived as it is from musty real estate forms, buries simple thoughts beneath needless elaboration. Paragraph 6, for example, begins:

> This sale is subject to the approval of the directors or shareholders of the Corporation as provided in the Lease or the corporate by-laws.

This sentence serves a much smaller purpose than the number of words would indicate. Who is to approve the sale—the directors or the shareholders? Is the underlying requirement in the lease or the by-laws? The buyer cannot tell. More important, even if these questions were answered they would not help the buyer understand or complete the transaction. If the granting of approval is a routine formality, it requires less elaboration than this; if it's more than routine, it requires more detail. Strictly speaking, this is a matter of choosing content, not just language. But it shows how a drafter who sought to be thorough has only been elaborate. In contrast, the new version says that: "* * * the Corporation must also give its approval."

Paragraph 16 of the old cooperative sale agreement illustrates another kind of elaboration:

> All representations, understandings and agreements had between the parties with respect to the subject matter of this agreement are

merged in this agreement which alone fully and completely expresses their agreement.

Compare this with the new version, which cuts through the elaboration. In the paragraph titled "Complete Agreement," it says: "Both parties agree that this contract sets forth all of their understandings." We discuss "word strings" below, but it is worth noting here that a traditional word string, "representations, understandings and agreements," has been replaced by a single word—"understandings"—which carries the intended meaning.

Here are more illustrations of needlessly elaborate language, and their plain English counterparts, from the old and new insurance policies.

BEFORE

This Policy shall not apply with respect to coverage

*   *   *

(e) to personal injury or property damage with respect to which an Insured under this Policy is also an Insured under a nuclear energy liability policy issued by Nuclear Energy Liability Insurance Association, Mutual Atomic Energy Liability Underwriters or Nuclear Insurance Association of Canada, or would be an Insured under any such Policy but for its termination upon exhaustion of its limit of liability.

AFTER

3. We won't cover any liability connected with a nuclear energy incident that's covered by one of the specialized nuclear energy insurance groups. Or would've been covered if the insurance liability limit hadn't been used up.

BEFORE

In the event that any provision of this policy is unenforceable by the Insured under the laws of any State or other jurisdiction wherein it is claimed that the Insured is liable for any injury covered hereby, because of non-compliance with any statute thereof, then this policy shall be enforceable by the Insured with the same effect as if it complied with such statute.

AFTER

If any of the terms of this policy should conflict with state or local law, you can enforce them as if they'd been changed to conform.

As these examples show, attempts to make a sentence all-inclusive only make it harder to understand. This form of verbosity creates another problem as well, by destroying the connective links between sentences. The result appears to be a list of separate, independent sentences, rather than a natural discourse in which each sentence builds on the one before and flows into the one that follows. Where the sentences in a text are not strongly linked, the whole text becomes difficult to follow:

BEFORE

Cancellation

This Policy may be cancelled by the Named Insured by surrender thereof to the Company or any of its authorized agents, or by mailing to the Company written notice stating when thereafter such cancellation shall be effective. This Policy may be cancelled by the Company by mailing to the Named Insured at the address shown in this Policy written notice stating when, not less than thirty (30) days thereafter, such cancellation shall be effective. The mailing of notice as aforesaid shall be sufficient notice and the effective date of cancellation stated in the notice shall become the end of the policy period. Delivery of such written notice either by the Named Insured or by the Company shall be equivalent to mailing. If the Named Insured cancels, earned premium shall be computed in accordance with the customary short rate table and procedure. If the Company cancels, earned premium shall be computed pro rata. Premium adjustment may be made at the time cancellation is effected or as soon as practicable thereafter. The check of the Company or its representative, mailed or delivered, shall be sufficient tender of any refund due the Named Insured. If this contract insures more than one Named Insured, cancellation may be effected by the first of such Named Insured for the account of all the Named Insureds: notice of cancellation by the Company to such first Named Insured shall be deemed notice to all Insureds and payment of any unearned premium to such first Named Insured shall be for the account of all interests therein.

AFTER

Can This Policy Be Cancelled?

Yes it can. Both by you and by us.

If you want to cancel the policy, hand or send your cancellation notice to us or our authorized agent. Or mail us a written notice with the date when you want the policy cancelled. We'll send you a check for the unearned premium, figured by the short rate table—that is, pro rata minus a service charge.

If we decide to cancel the policy, we'll mail or deliver to you a cancellation notice effective after at least 30 days. As soon as we can, we'll send you a check for the unearned premium, figured pro rata.

2. *Strings of Synonyms*

The other most common form of wordiness in legal documents is the string of synonyms such as "authorize and empower" or "rest, residue, and remainder." The old habit of using synonyms may have had sensible beginnings when legal documents in England had to be understood by people who spoke Anglo-Saxon and others who spoke French or Latin. Also, scriveners, who were paid by the word, may have added words on their own initiative. However, the habit has hung on long after any sensible purpose has disappeared. Today, it is usually enough to pick one term, probably the more familiar, and then use it consistently. Here are Felsenfeld and Siegel on the subject of strings of synonyms in the Citibank forms.

C. FELSENFELD AND A. SIEGEL, WRITING CONTRACTS IN PLAIN ENGLISH

124–26 (1981).*

Consider some of the word strings in the old bank promissory note and their treatment in the new version. Note that writing in a simpler manner often involves a new approach to the subject matter and not merely the elimination of words or the substitution of more familiar words. Sentences can be restructured entirely to read better. Generalizations can be made specific. Ideas scattered about the agreement can be brought together. Unnecessary substantive provisions can be dropped altogether.

For example, the old note, in providing for a late charge on instalments in default, uses the essentially unnecessary string to describe them:

due and remaining unpaid.

The revised version refers to the:

overdue instalment.

As another example, the old note holds the defaulting borrower obligated to pay the lender's:

costs and expenses.

The newer note reflects a combined legal, business, and language decision. Instead of generalizing and creating an open-ended world of "costs and expenses" to be paid for by the consumer, the new note establishes realistic events in advance. It refers specifically to:

attorney's fees ＊ ＊ ＊ and court costs.

Many other word strings appear in the old bank promissory note. The new one handles them in a variety of ways. For some, the unnecessary verbosity was eliminated:

Old	New
• indebtedness or liabilities (of the undersigned to the bank)	• debt (to you)
• shall have made and is hereby granted (a security interest)	• give (you what is known as a security interest)
• in and to	• in
• then and in any such event (describing the consequences of a default)	• you can then

Old

- due and payable

- rights and remedies

New

- immediate payment of the balance

- legal rights

For other word strings in the old note, the substantive content was eliminated, or the provisions were rewritten in an entirely new way. The old word strings in this category include:

- any and all

- performance or observance

- term or covenant

- contract or agreement

- evidencing or relating to

- nature or description

- fact or notice

Here are some additional word strings and their alternatives as they appear in the old and new versions of the cooperative apartment sale agreement:

Old

- sell and transfer (Par. 1)
- represents, warrants and covenants (Par. 4)
- right and power (Par. 4(a))
- full force and effect (Par. 4(e))
- representations, understandings and agreements (Par. 16)
- changed, discharged or terminated (Par. 17)
- cease and terminate (Par. 18)

New

- this sale
- assures

- has the right
- in effect
- understandings

- to change this contract, or to cancel it completely
- be considered cancelled

Other strings in the old agreement that were not specifically replaced in the new are:

- right, title and interest (Par. 2)

- in and to (Par. 2)

- terms, covenants and conditions (Par. 7)

- rules and regulations (Par. 7)

- cancel and terminate (Par. 13)

- fair and reasonable (Par. 15)

- obligation and liability (Par. 18)

The words in each string obviously do not have the same meaning. In many cases, such as *evidencing or relating to* and *in and to,* the differences are substantial. The drafter's job is to decide whether the several meanings are needed, in context, to accomplish the purpose of the contract.

D. TENSE

1. Present Tense

It is conventional to draft policy statements, conditions, and recitals as well as descriptions in a consistent present tense sequence. This is because documents "speak constantly." In other words, they speak not as of the time when they are drafted but whenever they are used. Thus it is appropriate to say:

> Unless one party gives the other party written notice of intent to terminate this agreement 30 days before the end of the term, this agreement renews itself from month to month.

> If any provision in this agreement is held invalid, the remaining provisions continue in effect.

Many drafters violate this convention. They draft policy statements in the future tense by mistake, saying:

> Unless one party shall give notice, this agreement shall renew itself.

> If any provision shall be held invalid, the remaining provisions shall continue in effect.

Sometimes, in a mistaken zeal for precision, they make things even worse, this way:

> Unless one party shall have been given notice, * * *.

> If any provision shall have been held invalid, * * *.

One of the most common misuses of the future tense is for definitions, as in: " 'Doing business' shall mean," or " 'private swimming pool' shall include." Instead, "doing business" means whatever it means and "private swimming pool" includes whatever it includes constantly from the moment the document comes into existence or takes effect.

2. Past and Present Perfect Tenses

Occasionally, it is acceptable to use the past tense or the present perfect tense to state conditions. For example:

> If a person other than the landlord repaired the damage [past tense], the landlord is not responsible for the quality of the work.

> If the premises have been condemned [present perfect tense], this agreement terminates.

However, since documents "speak constantly," these conditions could just as well be expressed in present tense.

3. Future Tense

The future tense is appropriate to express duties with respect to future conduct that are either imposed by some form of legislation or accepted by agreement. "Shall" expresses orders. "May" expresses discretionary authority. "Will" expresses agreement. Thus:

> "The landlord shall provide locks and keys," orders the statute.

> "The landlord may enter and repossess the premises upon termination of this agreement," asserts the landlord in the lease.

> "The tenant will keep the premises in good repair," says the properly drafted lease, reflecting that a contract recites agreements rather than giving orders.

However, many consumer contracts, drafted by the more powerful party, read more like statutes than contracts. They recite what the seller, lender, or landlord *will* do, but they order what the buyer, borrower, or tenant *shall* do. As consumer law imposes more requirements on contracts to be drafted in Plain English, there is more pressure on drafters to produce contracts that read like agreements instead of rule books.

Some of the mistakes drafters make in using "shall" and "will" may result from a gradual change over time in standard American usage. Formerly, "shall" was used in the first person and "will" in the second and third persons to express the simple future. For example:

I shall redraft the contract tomorrow.

You and she will be happy to see the finished product.

"Will" was formerly used in the first person and "shall" in the second and third persons to express determination or commands. For example:

I will stop smoking, no matter what.

You and he shall do what I say.

Today we no longer distinguish between the first person and the second and third persons in the future tense. People commonly use "will" for both the simple future declaration and also commands. "Shall" is usually reserved for special emphasis or for questions. For example:

I will redraft it tomorrow.

You and she will be happy to see it.

I will (shall) stop smoking, no matter what.

You and he will do what I say.

Shall I prepare a copy for you?

We would not say, "Will I prepare a copy?" But we would say, "Will you come by for it?" "Shall I" conveys the meaning of "Do you want me to" while "will" conveys a request for information.

There are no rules here to learn. This is merely a description of the common usage that is natural to speakers of English. On the other hand, it may explain some misuse of "shall" because people who are not sure what is correct tend to "overcorrect." They assume "shall" sounds more formal, authoritative, or somehow proper; they end up using it mistakenly as a result.

E. DISTINCTIONS AMONG "MAY," "SHALL," "MUST," AND OTHER TERMS OF AUTHORITY

A major source of confusion for drafters is the set of conventions for using "may," "shall," and other terms of authority.

R. DICKERSON, THE FUNDAMENTALS OF LEGAL DRAFTING

214 (2d ed. 1986).*

(1) To create a right, say "is entitled to."

(2) To create discretionary authority, say "may."

(3) To create a duty, say "shall."

(4) To create a mere condition precedent, say "must" (e.g., "To be eligible to occupy the office of mayor, a person must . . .")

(5) To negate a right, say "is not entitled to."

(6) To negate discretionary authority, say "may not."

(7) To negate a duty or a mere condition precedent, say "is not required to."

(8) To create a duty not to act (i.e., a prohibition), say "shall not."

Lawyers and legislators often make mistakes attempting to follow these conventions. One commentator reports that the across-the-board editorial check of legislative bills that produces the most substantive corrections is the check for correct use of "shall," "may," "must," and "should." [5]

One of the most common errors is known as the "false imperative." It is a false imperative to say that "it *shall be* a felony to commit murder." Such phrasing is inaccurate, assuming that the law is presently in effect; rather, it *is* a felony to commit murder. The confusion is between stating what the law is and directing people to do (or not do) things. To a large extent, laws and other legal statements are not directions. They are descriptions of the world as it is, or statements of policy. Thus it is appropriate to phrase them in the indicative mood. For example:

The rent *is* due on the first day of each month.

Accepting late rent *does not waive* the landlord's right to demand timely payment in the future.

The imperative mood is appropriate to give commands or directions. Technically, the imperative is always used in the second person. For example:

(You) *Be* careful.

(You) *Revise* several times for good drafting.

But statutes and most other regulatory documents are written in a style too formal for the second person. In them, commands and

* Copyright © 1986 by F. Reed Dickerson; published by Little, Brown & Company. Reprinted by permission of the author.

5. J. Davies, Legislative Law and Process in a Nutshell 183 (2d ed. 1986).

directions about future conduct are expressed in third person, and "shall" becomes the appropriate verb form. For example:

Dog owners shall put ID tags on their dogs.

Clinic applicants shall file application papers by June 1.

These are proper or "true" uses of the imperative. A "false imperative" phrases something as a command about future conduct when it should be an indicative statement about the present state of the law or policy. Sometimes false imperatives produce an unintended comic effect. For example:

Each child shall undergo vaccination by age six. (How is a five year old supposed to comply with this order?)

Each school week shall consist of 25 hours. (In other words, "You school weeks, get busy and make sure you consist of 25 hours.")

Another common mistake is to use "must" as though it were synonymous with the imperative "shall." For example:

The landlord must provide clean, safe common areas.

The tenant must provide the landlord reasonable access.

Technically, "must" should be reserved for conditions precedent. For example:

To be eligible for consideration, the applicant must submit a notarized application.

F. ACTIVE AND PASSIVE VOICE

Some legal documents appear to express false imperatives even though they actually do not. This is because they rely heavily on passive verbs. For example:

The notice shall be filed within 30 days.

The filing of the notice shall be regarded as prima facie evidence of compliance with this section.

Such sentences are grammatically acceptable. Most people would agree that they do not direct the notice or the filing to do anything.[6] Moreover, there is no particular reason to recast them so that the person filing the notice manages to get into the sentences as their subject.

This point is worth noting because many books about writing exhort writers to use active verbs instead of passive ones. Generally that is good advice. It is probably preferable to say, "The insured shall give notice to the insurer within 90 days," instead of saying, "The insured shall be given notice." The trouble with the passive verb in "The insured shall be given notice"—and in many sentences with passive verbs—is that the person doing the action does not get mentioned at all or else is relegated to the lesser status of an object. For

---

6. But see Kirk, Legal Drafting: Some Elements of Technique, 4 Tex.Tech L.Rev. 297, 311–12 (1973).

example: "The insurer shall be given notice *by the insured*." Also, active verbs take fewer words than passive verbs; therefore, writing with as many active verbs as possible produces more energetic, fast-paced prose than writing that moves slowly under the weight of the wordier passives.

Often, however, passive verbs are useful to keep provisions from being too specific. If there is some reason not to spell out who is responsible for filing notice, for example, then the passive verb serves well in the statement, "The notice shall be filed within 30 days." In other words, policy statements often properly focus on abstract concepts rather than people doing things. Passive verbs then are not automatically inferior to active verbs.

G. SINGULAR AND PLURAL

It is conventional to use the singular even when the sense is plural. For example, if a lease says, "The tenant is responsible for minor repairs," it is conventionally understood that the singular "tenant" applies to all the tenants if more than one are parties to the lease. Using a consistent singular is helpful to avoid some ambiguities that the plural can produce. For example, if a rule says, "Applicants shall file their forms before January 1," it is not clear whether one applicant has more than one form to file. If the number of forms per applicant is not at issue, it may be preferable to say, "Forms are due before January 1," or "December 31 is the deadline for filing forms." On the other hand, using the plural in reference to people is one convenient way to avoid the problems involved in using gender-specific pronouns.

H. NUMBERS

The drafter needs a consistent approach to presenting numbers: in figures ("4"), in words ("four"), or in the combination of figures and words ("four (4)"). Some people regard the combination as a useful safeguard against being harmed by a typographical error in figures, since such errors are easy to overlook in proofreading. If there is a conflict between the words and the figures, it is usually understood that the words prevail.[7]

The most common approach to numbers does not address the problem of potential typographical errors. According to this approach one uses words for the numbers one through nine and figures for the number 10 and higher numbers (as in this sentence). However, when 2 or more numbers appear in the same sentence, 1 of which is 10 or higher, figures are commonly used for all of the numbers (as in this sentence). Which approach one chooses does not matter very much; what matters is using it consistently. It is, incidentally, conventional in any approach to use words for any number that begins a sentence.

---

7. For the tongue-in-cheek view of one who believes that such careful people are actually taking the whole business (or themselves) too seriously, see Vanneman, Jr., Blame It All On O.P.E.C.? 65 ABA J. 1266 (1979).

It is also conventional to use figures for dates (January 4), time (4 p.m.), measurements (6 miles), amounts of money ($17—not $17.00), and percentages (3 percent—not 3%).

I. PUNCTUATION

In American prose generally, there has been a trend toward using less punctuation, which mainly means fewer commas. The saying goes, "When in doubt, leave it out." This trend has particular significance in the context of legal drafting. Every now and then somebody's artless drafting leaves a provision ambiguous or misleading because of a missing or misplaced comma. Law suits have been prosecuted over punctuation.[8]

An old practice was that when legislative bodies passed legislation, they passed what was read to them, that is, what they heard. After the vote, a clerk wrote down the legislation and put punctuation marks into it. These were thought not to be part of the law, and the law was to be construed without reference to punctuation.

That practice is, of course, not effective today,[9] but out of it comes a good idea for drafters. Lawyers do not want what they draft to end up in court because they depended on a comma or the absence of a comma to govern how a provision should be read. In other words, a sensible goal is to arrange the words so carefully that if a typist or printer inadvertently leaves out or puts in or moves a comma, the sense of what was intended will be so clear that no one will easily deny it. In short, it is wise to use as little punctuation as possible and to rely on it as little as possible to indicate meaning.

On the other hand, in spite of the general trend toward less punctuation, it is a good idea to put a comma before the last item in a series—even though many people do not do so. This sentence illustrates the point:

> The functions of statutes are to create rights, impose duties, prohibit and confer privileges.

Without a comma after "prohibit," it is possible to construe the sentence as saying that the functions are to: (1) create rights, (2) impose duties, and (3) prohibit and confer privileges. However, the drafter may intend to refer to four functions: (1) create rights, (2) impose duties, (3) prohibit, and (4) confer privileges. A comma after "prohibit" would eliminate the ambiguity.

Some people choose to put a comma before the last item in a series only when there is potential ambiguity, but such an approach requires stopping to assess every series one writes and making a deliberate choice each time whether to punctuate. It is far easier—and safer—to

8. See, for example, Lewis v. Carnaggio, 257 S.C. 54, 183 S.E.2d 899 (1971).

9. See, for example, Labbe v. Nissen Corp., 404 A.2d 564, 567 (Me.1979) ("Although punctuation is to be subordinated to the text, it is plainly a proper guide in the interpretation of statutes.").

make a habit of putting in the comma before the last item in *every* series.

J. NOMINALIZATIONS

In his book, *Style: Ten Lessons in Clarity and Grace,* Professor Joseph M. Williams devotes considerable attention to what he calls "nominalizations": nouns that have been derived from verbs or adjectives.[10] Nominalizations often end in "tion" or "ment," such as "rejection" and "violation" or "adjustment" and "alignment." Using nominalizations is not in itself a stylistic blunder. However, many sentences full of nominalizations produce a heavy, turgid style.

Professor Williams uses the following sentences to illustrate the problem:

> The claimant's *testimony* was that there was no medical *treatment* from July 27 until his *consultation* with a doctor on December 12.

> The claimant *testified* that he was not medically *treated* from July 27 until he *consulted* a doctor on December 12.

The first sentence is heavy with nouns. No human being is doing anything in it. In the second sentence, the claimant comes to life, doing things and having things done to him.

Here is another set of Professor Williams' examples:

> Your *compliance* with this provision is mandatory and *failure* to provide S with *proof* that such *insurance* is in effect constitutes *violation* of the Contract.

> You *must comply* with this provision. If you *do not prove* to S that you *are insured,* you *will violate* the Contract.

Sentences with human beings in action make documents easier to follow, just as they make any writing more interesting to read than sentences full of nominalizations.[11]

K. "AND/OR"

The hybrid conjunction and disjunction has caused legal trouble for years. Critics have railed against it, and judges have construed it against lawyers who were foolish enough to persist in using it.[12] In case after case, the comments about "and/or" reflect a degree of anger that matters of style rarely produce. Here is a typical condemnation.

EMPLOYERS' MUTUAL LIABILITY INS. CO. v. TOLLEFSEN
219 Wis. 434, 437, 263 N.W. 376, 377 (1935).

It is manifest that we are confronted with the task of first construing "and/or", that befuddling, nameless thing, that Janus-faced verbal

---

10. See especially 11–20 (2d ed. 1985).

11. The Dispositive Edge: Inventing Responsibility, (July 19, 1986) (presentation at conference of The Legal Writing Institute).

12. See numerous citations in McCarty, That Hybrid "and/or," 39 Mich.St.B.J. 9 (No. 5, May 1960).

monstrosity, neither word nor phrase, the child of a brain of someone too lazy or too dull to express his precise meaning, or too dull to know what he did mean, now commonly used by lawyers in drafting legal documents, through carelessness or ignorance or as a cunning device to conceal rather than express meaning with view to furthering the interests of their clients.

"In view of all this uncertainty and hostility the only safe rule to follow is not to use the expression in any legal writing, document or proceeding, under any circumstances." [13]

Among the contemporary scholars of legal drafting, Professor Mellinkoff is especially helpful in going beyond invective to show how "and/or" sometimes results in contradiction and other times in redundancy. He explains both what the trouble is and what to do about it.

DAVID MELLINKOFF, LEGAL WRITING: SENSE AND NONSENSE

55–56 (West Publishing Co., 1982). By permission.

The high failure rate of legal papers that depend on *and/or* for anything of importance should have long since eliminated it from the legal vocabulary. Yet it persists, and is widely used in legal and ordinary writings. For the writer in a hurry, for the writer content to let others solve the problems created by the writer, *and/or* is such a short, quick, and easy way out. It has a special currency in academia, where the lure of the scientific *(interface, parameter)* gulls some into confusing the compact form of *and/or* with the precision of a lopsided fraction.

One book on usage says its popularity even in "respectable places" means that it "is therefore acceptable current English." Most of the English usage people condemn it as ugly, unnecessary, and confusing. They usually end up blaming it on the law, saying (in charitable ignorance), "Maybe it's all right for them, but let them keep it."

This reverse smugness should give lawyers pause. Instances of non-legal *and/or* do not encourage imitation. They demonstrate its mindlessness ("Rape: The Hidden Crime.' [sic] Also shown is how other women can prevent *and/or* survive rape."), and its complicated silliness. (We look forward to seeing *and/or* hearing from you.)

Despite the relative simplicity of *A or B or both* (when such specification is necessary), legal writings continue to spew contradictions joined by an habitual *and/or*.

☐ For example:

    *   *   * the order was not made *and/or* was kept in abeyance.

    [Make it *or.*]

    *   *   * might be discharged *and/or* paroled at any time.

    [Make it *or.*]

13. *Id.* at 17.

*   *   * it was uniformly specified *and/or* implied.

[Make it *or*.]

Like a tic, *and/or* intrudes without effort, even when the writer has already covered all the possibilities.

☐ For example:

*   *   * the application of one or more of doctrines of A, B, C, *and/or* D.

[Make it *and*.]

If the lawyers did invent *and/or,* they owe it to the common language to atone, by now eliminating *and/or* from the legal vocabulary, and hope that the common language will follow. It is still confusing readers and costing litigants money. Anything *and/or* can do, ordinary English can do better.

L. GENDER

Gender-neutrality has received detailed coverage in much of the recent writing by experts on legal drafting.[14] They recognize the difficulties of avoiding gender-specific pronouns altogether, but they also take seriously the attempt to remove sexual bias and the appearance of such bias from legal documents. Most of them understand that even though it may be technically "correct" to use the word "man" to refer to women as well as men, it is also true that when someone uses "man" as a generic term for both sexes, the reader or listener is likely to visualize or think of a man.[15]

Moreover, legal classifications that use gender-specific words such as "he" and "man" always refer to men but may or may not refer to women. For example:

A person is eligible for this benefit if he is married and over the age of 18.

Such ambiguous classifications, especially in statutes, have produced enough legal problems to warrant finding a more effective solution than boilerplate gender-construction provisions[16] to the effect that "words importing the masculine gender include the feminine as well."[17]

---

14. See R. Dickerson, The Fundamentals of Legal Drafting 221–39 (2d ed. 1986); C. Felsenfeld and A. Siegel, above note 2, at 139–41; D. Mellinkoff, Legal Writing: Sense and Nonsense 47–51 (1982); R. Wydick, Plain English for Lawyers 65–67 (2d ed. 1985); Bagin, Are All Men Equal: The "Generic" Dilemma, Simply Stated 1 (No. 62, Jan. 1986) (Document Design Center newsletter); Romm, Avoiding Sexist Language, Quaint and Otherwise, 71 ABA J. 126 (May 1985).

15. For a detailed study of the ramifications of this process, see C. Miller and K. Swift, Words and Women (1976). For discussion in a legal context, see Collins, Language, History, and the Legal Process: A Profile of the "Reasonable Man," 8 Rut.–Cam.L.J. 311 (1977). For a study of how assumptions about the sexes affect thinking as well as writing, see Hofstadter, Metamagical Themas, 247 Scientific American 18 (Nov. 1982).

16. See Comment, Sexism in the Statutes: Identifying and Solving the Problem of Ambiguous Gender Bias in Legal Writing, 32 Buffalo L.Rev. 559, citations throughout (1983).

17. 1 U.S.C. § 1.

It is essential to find gender-neutral language that does not succumb to incorrect grammar, awkwardness, or simple nonsense. Professor Richard Wydick's practical advice is particularly attentive to these concerns.

R. WYDICK, PLAIN ENGLISH FOR LAWYERS
65–67 (2d ed. 1985) (footnotes omitted).*

Avoid Sexist Language

The very first section of the United States Code says that: "words importing the masculine gender include the feminine as well." Women are tired of that, and legal writers can no longer get away with it.

Whatever your personal beliefs about the role of women in society, you should avoid sexist language for the same reason that you avoid other language quirks—if you use sexist language, you will distract a part of your audience. And you will distract another part of your audience if you resort to clumsy or artificial constructions when trying to avoid sexist language.

Avoiding sexism gracefully is no easy task. Here are four suggestions that may help:

First, don't use expressions that imply value judgments based on sex. (For example, *a manly effort,* or *a member of the gentle sex.*)

Second, use sex-neutral terms where you can do so without artificiality. (For example, use *workers* instead of *workmen* and *reasonable person* instead of *reasonable man.* But don't concoct artificial terms like *waitpersons* to refer to servers in a restaurant.)

Third, use parallel construction when you are referring to both sexes. (For example, *husbands and wives,* not *men and their wives,* or *President and Mrs. Kennedy,* not *President Kennedy and Jackie.*)

Fourth, don't use sex-based pronouns when the referent may be of the opposite sex. For instance, don't use *he* every time you refer to judges. And don't use *she* either. The latter is just as distracting as the former. You can resort to the clumsy phrase *he or she* in moderation, but you can often avoid the need by using one of the following devices:

Omit the pronoun: For example, instead of *"the average citizen enjoys his time on the jury,"* you can say *"the average citizen enjoys jury duty."*

Use the second person instead of the third person: For example, instead of *"each juror must think for herself,"* you can say *"as a juror, you must think for yourself."*

Use the plural instead of the singular: For example, instead of "*each juror believes that he has done something worthwhile,*" you can say "*all jurors believe that they have done something worthwhile.*"

Repeat the noun instead of using a pronoun: For example, instead of "*a juror's vote should reflect her own opinion,*" you can say "*a juror's vote should reflect that juror's own opinion.*"

Alternate between masculine and feminine pronouns: For example, if you use *she* to refer to judges in one paragraph, use *he* to refer to lawyers in the next paragraph. Be aware that this device may look artificial, and that if you are careless you may perform a sex change on somebody in the middle of paragraph.

Use the passive voice: for the reasons explained in Chapter Four, use this device only in desperation.

The formerly favored view of "man" and masculine pronouns as generic terms for both sexes persists among some commentators,[18] some of whom employ sarcasm or joking tones to express their position.

FRIENDLY, LANGUAGE AND THE WOPERSONS' MOVEMENT
Washington Post, May 2, 1978, at A19.

Mankind means *humankind; womankind* has a place in the language only when a limitation is intended. *Mankind* is the inclusive word, and everyone knows it; not even the nuttiest word-fixer has suggested its replacement by *personkind.* Nor is anyone offended, much less misled, by Darwin's title "The Descent Of Man" or by thousands of similar constructions.[19]

Sarcasm and name-calling may not warrant serious attention. However, reluctance to innovate in drafting is not merely a joking matter.

D. HIRSCH, DRAFTING FEDERAL LAW
31 (1980) (Dept. of Health & Human Services publication).

If you can avoid using "he" to refer to people in general without contorting your sentences, that is all to the good. Do not forget, though, that as a draftsman your overriding objective is to express an idea as clearly and simply as you can, not to pursue a social ideology, no matter how lofty.

* * * Throughout this book I have referred to the "draftsman". I would be pleased to refer instead to the "drafter", except that a drafter is a horse. In a few years from now all new dictionaries may well include "draftsman" among the meanings of "drafter". Then I will use "drafter" instead of "draftsman". * * * [I]nnovation in devising new meanings for words is a flaw, not an asset, in a draftsman. The analogy is to the "creative" clerk who finds hitherto

---

18. For example, W. Strunk, Jr. and E. White, above note 1, at 60–61.

19. See also Younger, The English Language Is Sex–Neutral, 72 ABA J. 89 (June 1, 1986).

unthought of locations in which to file documents. Certainty of meaning largely depends upon the draftsman's unbendingly conservative use of language.

A year after that was written, *Webster's New Collegiate Dictionary* listed "drafter" as the noun form of the verb "draft," one of the meanings of which is "to practice draftsmanship." [20] The language does change. The drafter's function may not be to innovate, but neither is it to lag behind.

II. PROBLEMS

PROBLEM 1

Identify the stylistic blunders in the sentences below. Consider whether a sentence might be blunder-free in one kind of document but not in another.

1. This part shall be known as the "Residential Landlord and Tenant Act."

2. When it is claimed that the rental agreement or any provision thereof may be unconscionable, the parties shall be afforded a reasonable opportunity to present evidence with respect to the argument.

3. If either party institutes an action in a court of competent jurisdiction to adjudicate his right to the security deposit, the prevailing person is entitled to receive his court costs plus a reasonable fee for his attorney.

4. The court shall advance the cause on the calendar.

5. The landlord shall not abuse the right of access and/or use it to harass the tenant.

6. The term shall commence on _____, 19__, and shall continue from month to month.

7. Tenant will keep the premises in good order and condition. Landlord will otherwise maintain the property.

8. If Tenant abandons and/or vacates the premises, Landlord may at his option consider this agreement breached, terminate it and regain possession in the manner prescribed by law.

9. Notice upon Tenants shall be served as provided by law. If Tenant needs to notify Landlord of anything, this can be done by serving notice on the Manager of the demised premises at _____, who shall be authorized to accept service on behalf of Landlord.

10. Items furnished for the apartment must stay in that apartment.

PROBLEM 2

Assume that you are a member of a law school committee on academic policies. Someone has submitted the following first draft of a

20. At 341–42 (1981).

proposed policy. Mark it up to show what stylistic changes you recommend while remaining true to the apparently intended meaning. Also note any other revisions you think would help clarify meaning. Evaluate the policy statement according to everything you know so far about the principles of good drafting. What would you need to ask the proponent of the policy before you could sensibly redraft the policy statement?

ADVANCED WRITING AND RESEARCH REQUIREMENT

1 a. A student must receive a certificate of completion in Advanced
2   Writing and Research to graduate from _____ School of Law.
3   Any student wishing to fulfill the advanced writing and research
4   requirement must register with the Associate Dean of Students
5   within six weeks after the beginning of the semester.

6   A student can earn a certificate of completion in one of the
7   following manners:

8   (1) Writing a paper to the standards specified in section d below in
9   a large class or a seminar; or in an independent studies
10   program as specified in section c below;

11   (2) Completing an article of publishable quality for the Law Re-
12   view that is so certified by a member or members of the faculty
13   designated by the Dean;

14   (3) Such other programs as designated by the Dean.

15 b. Any student in a class designated as a seminar (to which a limit of
16   18 students will be imposed) has a right to fulfill the writing
17   requirement with that professor. Any professor teaching any other
18   upper division class that has 25 or less students must allow at least
19   six students in that class to fulfill the writing requirement, and any
20   professor in an advanced course of 51 or more must permit up to
21   two students.

22   If there are more requests from students in the class, faculty
23   members will choose students to work with, based upon the degree
24   to which proposed projects fall within the professors' expertise.

25   Part-time faculty may supervise papers only with the permission of
26   the Associate Dean. Permission usually will not be granted to
27   supervise more than two students per semester.

28 c. Independent Studies

29   Each professor will be required to supervise up to 3 new indepen-
30   dent study students a semester regardless of the number of papers
31   being supervised in other courses. He shall not be allowed to
32   supervise more than 3 without the written permission of the
33   Associate Dean.

34 d. Qualifications

35   To fulfill the Advanced Writing and Research requirement a paper
36   must be certified as on a level of good professional work for an

37 attorney. Work which is merely passing by academic standards
38 will not necessarily complete this requirement, even though the
39 paper fulfills the requirement for the course. The paper must
40 contain original work and not merely be a rehash of existing
41 sources.

42 Faculty members supervising writing requirements under any of
43 the methods stated above are expected to work intensively with the
44 students. This includes help in shaping the topic selected and/or
45 establishing schedules which will allow the student sufficient time
46 for rewriting and editing. Professors are expected to verify, with
47 independent research, if necessary, the accuracy and completeness
48 of the student's research. The supervising faculty member is
49 expected to give ample instruction to aid the student in completing
50 the project and to guarantee that he has developed sufficient
51 research and writing skills to be able to do such work in a
52 professional manner after graduation.

53 e. Notwithstanding the foregoing, completion of a year's work as a
54 tutor in the first year writing and research program, or the
55 academic assistance program, or a research assistantship for a full-
56 time faculty member which assistantship requires substantial expe-
57 rience will satisfy this writing requirement.

Chapter 4

THE PLAIN ENGLISH MOVEMENT

I. BACKGROUND

A. LEGALESE: THE TROUBLESOME LEGAL LANGUAGE

The Plain English Movement, sometimes called the Plain Language Movement, grew out of widespread public disenchantment with lawyers' pompous and often unintelligible language. Even lawyers have acknowledged the problem.

R. WYDICK, PLAIN ENGLISH FOR LAWYERS
3 (2d ed. 1985).

We lawyers cannot write plain English. We use eight words to say what could be said in two. We use arcane phrases to express commonplace ideas. Seeking to be precise, we become redundant. Seeking to be cautious, we become verbose. Our sentences twist on, phrase within clause within clause, glazing the eyes and numbing the minds of our readers.

The disparaging name for this kind of legal language is "legalese." Many critics have criticized it in general terms, but Professor Robert Benson has described it in great detail.

BENSON, THE END OF LEGALESE: THE GAME IS OVER
13 N.Y.U.Rev.L. & Soc.Change 519, 523–27 (1984–85)
(footnotes omitted).*

1. Characteristics of the Language

   a. Vocabulary

- Long words.

- Rare Old and Middle English words.

Examples: *aforesaid, witnesseth.*

---

* Copyright © 1985 by Robert W. Benson. Reprinted by permission of the author.

- Latin phrases.

Examples: *nolo contendere, assumpsit.*

- Common words with uncommon meanings.

Examples: *prayer, consideration.*

- Law French.

Examples: *estoppel, voir dire.*

- Terms of art.

Examples: *eminent domain, master and servant.*

- Argot.

Examples: *at issue, toll the statute.*

- Formalistic formulas.

Examples: *being first duly sworn, deposes and says; know all men by these present.*

- Frequent vague expressions.

Examples: *clearly erroneous, reasonable care.*

- Doublets.

Examples: *rights and remedies, free and clear.*

- Unusual prepositional phrases.

Examples: *as to, in the event of.*

- Use of *said* and *such* as articles.

Examples: *said agreement is signed, such payment as beneficiary requests.*

b. *Syntactic Features*

- Extremely long, complex sentences with many embedded clauses.
- Word lists.

Example: *all manner of action and actions, cause and causes of action, suits, debts, dues, sums of money, accounts, reckoning, bonds, bills, specialities, covenants, contracts, controversies, agreements, promises, variances, trespasses, damages, judgments, extents, executions, claims and demands.*

- Nominalizations, that is, nouns constructed from verbs, usually by adding an "ing," "tion," or "al" ending.

Example: *after consideration of the facts*, instead of *the court considered the facts.*

- Passives.

Example: *this agreement is signed by the buyer*, or *this agreement is signed* (a truncated passive), instead of the active form *buyer signs this agreement.*

- Negatives, sometimes double or triple negatives, using such words as *no, not, never, un-* (as a prefix), *unless, except, provided that, however.*

- Misplaced phrases. These are mostly prepositional phrases stuck into the middle of clauses in a way that, outside of the law, is meant only for laughs, as in "Throw Mama from the train a kiss," or "The man chased the cat with a broom in his underwear."

Examples: *a proposal to effect with the Company an assurance,* and *if in these instructions any rule, direction or idea is repeated.*

c. Organization

The linguists, in their own jargon, refer to this category as "discourse structure," by which they mean "how the individual sentences are organized relative to each other and . . . the coherence among sentences. . . ."

- Illogical ordering of ideas.

Lawyers frequently inform the reader of conditions, exceptions, and distracting details such as the date, or someone's address, or the source of authority, instead of announcing the big news and then filling in the supporting details, or using chronological, hierarchical, or some other logical order.

- Absence of pronouns.

This occurs not only between sentences, but within them, "with the result that this type of prose strikingly resembles that found in school primers. Jill said, 'Help Ben, Bill. Stop the ducks. Help Ben stop the ducks.' "

An example from a deed of trust:

Trustor agrees: . . . *[t]o provide, maintain and deliver to Beneficiary fire insurance satisfactory to and with loss payable to Beneficiary. The amount collected under any fire or other insurance policy may be applied by Beneficiary upon any indebtedness secured hereby and is such order as Beneficiary may determine, or at option of Beneficiary the entire amount so collected or any part thereof may be released to Trustor.*

David Crystal and Derek Davy, British linguists, were especially puzzled by this peculiarity of legalese: "But it is not simply that referential pronouns are avoided only where their use could raise genuine confusion; they seem to be eschewed as a species."

- Too many ideas in each sentence.

"[E]ach sentence is made to count for too much. In other kinds of prose, the writer often expresses an idea one way and then restates it in somewhat different form, giving the reader more time to digest it." Statutory language is particularly susceptible to this. For example:

Whoever, other than a special Government employee who serves for less than sixty days in a given calendar year, having been so employed as specified in subsection (d) of this section, within one year after such employment has ceased, knowingly acts as agent or attorney for, or otherwise represents, anyone other than the United States in any formal or informal appearance before, or, with the intent to influence, makes any oral or written communication on behalf of anyone other than the United States. . . .

d. Style

- Appearance of extreme precision. The result is often confusion and intimidation, instead of precision.

Example: *all manner of action I ever had, now have or . . . hereafter can, shall or may have . . . from the beginning of the world to the day of the date of these presents. . . .*"

- Impersonality.

The third person (he, she, it, buyer, seller, bank, etc.) is used consistently when the first (I, we) or second person (you) would be more natural.

- Declarative sentences which pronounce rights and duties.

Here, of course, form follows function, for it is a function of the law to declare rights and duties. A steady diet of the declarative form, however, can be oppressive and cause the reader to tune out.

- Conditional sentences.

These typically list numerous contingencies that must be satisfied in order to trigger some legal result. Here again, form follows function because the law must often draw many fine, conditional lines to indicate when it applies and when it does not. Ordinary English prose, however, handles contingencies in forms that are simpler than the long conditional sentence which is characteristic of legal prose.

- Pompous tone.

This is one of Mellinkoff's conclusions about legal language. Danet takes him to task for this and other findings that Danet considers "highly subjective judgments." This criticism is odd because, though not as easily identified as long sentences or passive verbs, tone certainly exists in written language and can be felt by the reader like a wet mackerel in the face, a velvet glove, or any number of sensations in between. If these are subjective judgments, an empirical study could at least discover the sensations perceived by most readers in the intended audiences. I would be surprised if such a study arrived at conclusions different from those drawn by Mellinkoff.

- Dull tone.

This is another of Mellinkoff's conclusions, and Danet criticizes this as a "subjective judgment." Like pomposity, dullness of tone is felt by readers, could be measured in an empirical study, and its existence in legal writing cannot plausibly be denied.

- Poetic devices.

Danet "unexpectedly discovered" in a bank loan form many prosodic, or word-music, features that are normally associated with poetry, such as alliteration, assonance, rhythm, rhyme, meter, and phonemic contrast. This is no surprise. These poetic features are easily observed in many legal documents. They probably stem from the law's ancient oral tradition, the archaic vocabulary still in use, and the original link between law and magic. For the same reasons, the parallel between legal language and Biblical language is striking.

- Odd graphic design.

Punctuation, capitalization, sectioning, headings, indentation, typeface, type size, and other graphic devices are frequently used in bizarre ways that do not tie into the meaning or importance of what is being said. Typically, these visual devices will either be completely absent, as in pages of long, solid blocks of grey prose with little punctuation, or will be so abundant that their purpose seems merely to paint the page with rococo decoration. When Crystal and Davy examined an insurance policy that was in the decorative style, they were determined to discover the graphics' logical link with meaning. They made heavy weather of it, like schoolboys struggling with a passage by the poet Browning, and their effort is recommended to all in need of comic relief. Lawyers seem not to know what people in the advertising and communication fields know: that the visual appearance of the graphics sends messages along with the text. The shortest and sweetest proof of this that I have seen is the sign along the highways in San Antonio, Texas reading "Littering is unLAWFUL."

B. THE BEGINNINGS OF THE PLAIN ENGLISH MOVEMENT

Some people credit President Jimmy Carter with founding the Plain English Movement in his famous executive order directing federal agencies to improve regulations:

EXEC. ORDER NO. 12,044
43 Fed.Reg. 12,661 (1978).

Regulations shall be as simple and clear as possible. * * * The head of each agency, or the designated official with statutory responsibility, shall approve significant regulations before they are published for public comment in the FEDERAL REGISTER. At a minimum, this official should determine that * * * the regulation is written in plain English and is understandable to those who must comply with it.

The main focus of the early Plain English Movement, however, was on consumer contracts, not on government documents. Consumers were routinely encountering form contracts for everything from buying a washing machine on credit to renting an apartment, and the contracts were often all but impossible to understand. The leading federal legislation included the Truth in Lending Act of 1968 and the Magnuson–Moss Warranty Act of 1975. By the end of the 1970's the first Plain English legislation began to make its way through several state legislatures. The purpose of the laws was: "to enable the average consumer, who makes a reasonable effort under the circumstances, to read and understand the terms of so-called form contracts and the like without having to obtain the assistance of a professional." [1]

---

1. Unenacted Maine bill quoted in D. Mellinkoff, Legal Writing: Sense and Nonsense 211 (1982).

II. THE PLAIN ENGLISH LAWS

The first broad state Plain English legislation was New York's Sullivan Law, named for its sponsor, Assemblyman Peter M. Sullivan. The law was signed by Governor Carey in 1977 and met with so much controversy that it was amended even before it became effective in 1978. See Table 1 for state Plain English legislation citations and Table 2 for federal citations. Since 1978 a number of states have enacted legislation covering various kinds of consumer contracts. Those with notably broad coverage are New York, Connecticut, Hawaii, New Jersey, and Minnesota. In general, Plain English laws regulate both the language and the format of consumer contracts. In general, the laws are of three types: (1) those that prescribe subjective standards of audience understanding, (2) those that prescribe objective tests of the documents themselves, and (3) those that prescribe subjective standards with objective guidelines.

Table 1

State Plain English Legislation

1. Plain English Statutes Applicable to Consumer Contracts Generally:

   Connecticut Gen.Stat.Ann. §§ 42–151 to –158 (1987).

   Hawaii Rev.Stat. § 487A–1 (1981).

   10 Maine Rev.Stat.Ann. §§ 1121 to –26 (1985).

   Minn.Stat.Ann. §§ 325G.29 to –.36 (1986).

   New Jersey Stat.Ann. 56:12–1 to –13 (1986).

   New York McKinney's Gen.Oblig.Law § 5–702 (1987).

   West Virginia Code, 46A–6–109 (1985).

2. Plain English Statutes Applicable to Insurance Contracts:

   Arizona Rev.Stat. § 20–1110.01 (1985).

   Arkansas Stats. §§ 66–3251 to –3258 (1980).

   Connecticut Gen.Stat.Ann. §§ 38–68s to –68x (1986).

   West's Fla.Stat.Ann. § 626–9641(f) (1985).

   Hawaii Sess. Laws 89 (1981).

   West's Ann.Ind.Code 27–1–26–1 to –12 (1986).

   24A Maine Rev.Stat.Ann. §§ 2438 to 2445 (1985).

   Maryland Code 1979, Art. 48A, § 490D.

   Mass.Gen.Laws Ann. c. 175, § 2B (1986).

   Minn.Stat.Ann. §§ 72C.01 to –.13 (1986).

   Mont.Code Ann. 33–15–321 to –329 (1985).

   Neb.Rev.Stat. §§ 44–3401 to –3408 (1984).

Nev.Rev.Stat. 687B.122 to –.128 (1981).

New Jersey Stat.Ann. 17B:17–17 to –25 (1985).

New Mexico Stat.Ann. 1986, §§ 59A–19–1 to –7.

New York McKinney's Ins. Law § 3102 (1985).

N.C.Gen.Stat. §§ 58–364 to –372 (1982).

North Dakota Century Code 26–1–36–13 to –16 (1985).

Ohio Rev.Code §§ 3902.01 to –.08 (1985).

36 Okla.Stat. 1985 § 36–3611.

Oregon Rev.Stat. 743.350 to –.370 (1985).

South Carolina Code 1985, §§ 38–3–61 to –64.

South Dakota Codified Laws 58–11A–1 to –9 (1986).

Tennessee Code Ann. §§ 56–7–1601 to –1609 (1984).

Virginia Code 1981, § 38.1–354.1 (1981).

West Virginia Code, 33–29–1 to –9 (1986).

Wisconsin Stat.Ann. 631.22 (1985).

Table 2

Federal Plain English Legislation

Act or Regulation	Citation	Date Effective
Truth in Lending Act of 1968	15 USC 1601–1666	1965
Regulation Z	12 CFR 226.1–226.1002	1969
Truth in Lending Simplification and Reform Act of 1980	(amended above)	1982
Fair Credit Reporting Act of 1970	15 USC 1681–1681t	1971
FTC Door to Door Sales Rule	16 CFR 429.1	1972
Real Estate Settlement Procedures Act of 1974	12 USC 2601–2617	1974
Employment Retirement Income Security Act of 1974	29 USC 1001–1381	1975
Magnuson–Moss Warranty—Federal Trade Commission Improvement Act	15 USC 2301–2312	1975
Fair Credit Billing Act	15 USC 1666–1666h	1975
Equal Credit Opportunity Act	15 USC 1691–1691f	1975
FTC Holder in Due Course Rule	16 CFR 433.1–433.3	1975
Truth in Leasing Act of 1976	15 USC 1667–1667e	1977
Electronic Fund Transfer Act	15 USC 1693–1693r	1980

A. LAWS WITH SUBJECTIVE STANDARDS

New York's law is an example of a law with subjective standards for the contracts it monitors. It says simply that they must be: "(1)

[w]ritten in a clear and coherent manner using words with common and every day meanings; (2) [a]ppropriately divided and captioned by [their] various sections." These standards are not only subjective; they are expressed in language that is vague, presumably on purpose. Here is the text of New York's law in full.

NEW YORK McKINNEY'S GEN.OBLIG.LAW
§ 5–702 (1987).

§ 5–702. Requirements for use of plain language in consumer transactions

a. Every written agreement entered into after November first, nineteen hundred seventy-eight, for the lease of space to be occupied for residential purposes, or to which a consumer is a party and the money, property or service which is the subject of the transaction is primarily for personal, family or household purposes must be:

1. Written in a clear and coherent manner using words with common and every day meanings;

2. Appropriately divided and captioned by its various sections.

Any creditor, seller or lessor who fails to comply with this subdivision shall be liable to a consumer who is a party to a written agreement governed by this subdivision in an amount equal to any actual damages sustained plus a penalty of fifty dollars. The total class action penalty against any such creditor, seller or lessor shall not exceed ten thousand dollars in any class action or series of class actions arising out of the use by a creditor, seller or lessor of an agreement which fails to comply with this subdivision. No action under this subdivision may be brought after both parties to the agreement have fully performed their obligation under such agreement, nor shall any creditor, seller or lessor who attempts in good faith to comply with this subdivision be liable for such penalties. This subdivision shall not apply to agreements involving amounts in excess of fifty thousand dollars nor prohibit the use of words or phrases or forms of agreement required by state or federal law, rule or regulation or by a governmental instrumentality.

b. A violation of the provisions of subdivision a of this section shall not render any such agreement void or voidable nor shall it constitute:

1. A defense to any action or proceeding to enforce such agreement; or

2. A defense to any action or proceeding for breach of such agreement.

c. In addition to the above, whenever the attorney general finds that there has been a violation of this section, he may proceed as provided in subdivision twelve of section sixty-three of the executive law.

B. LAWS WITH OBJECTIVE TESTS

At the other extreme are laws that present not only general standards but also detailed tests by which to determine whether a given document meets the standards. For objective tests, the lawmakers sometimes turn to the findings of people who have studied readability and produced tests of readability that work by figuring the average number of syllables per word and words per sentence. The best known is the Flesch Test, invented by Rudolf Flesch. Here is how it works.

R. FLESCH, HOW TO WRITE PLAIN ENGLISH
24 (1979).

Multiply the average sentence length by 1.015. Multiply the average word length by 84.6. Add the two numbers. Subtract this sum from 206.835. The balance is your readability score.

The scale shows scores from 0 to 100. Zero means practically unreadable and 100 means extremely easy. The minimum score for Plain English is 60, or about 20 words per sentence and 1½ syllables per word. Conversational English for consumers should score at least 80, or about 15 words per sentence and 1⅓ syllables per word.

The other commonly used test is the Gunning Fog Index. Its scoring system requires adding the average number of words per sentence and the percentage of words in the sample with three or more syllables. The resulting figure is then multiplied by 0.4. The result of that multiplication is the Fog Index (disregarding any figure to the right of the decimal). The Fog Index is supposed to correspond to the number of years of schooling someone needs to understand the tested piece of writing. Proponents of this test recommend that consumer documents have a Fog Index no higher than 10, the Fog Index of *Time*.[2]

Here is Connecticut's law, one that incorporates detailed objective tests.

CONNECTICUT GEN.STAT.ANN.
§§ 42–151 to –158 (1987).

§ 42–151. Definitions

The following definitions shall apply in this chapter:

(a) **Consumer.** A "consumer" is an individual who borrows, leases, buys or obtains money, property or services under a written agreement.

(b) **Consumer contract.** A written agreement is a "consumer contract," if:

(1) A consumer enters into the agreement primarily for personal, family or household purposes; and

---

2. Legal Services Corporation, Community Education Materials, Granby, Colorado Conference (1978).

(2) The agreement is one in which the consumer: (A) Borrows up to twenty-five thousand dollars or receives up to twenty-five thousand dollars in credit from a person who lends money or extends credit in the ordinary course of business; or (B) agrees to pay up to twenty-five thousand dollars to buy or lease personal property or services from a person who is acting in the ordinary course of business; or (C) leases any residential dwelling.

§ 42–152.　Standard of plain language

(a) **Standard.**　Every consumer contract entered into after June 30, 1980, shall be written in plain language.　A consumer contract is written in plain language if it meets either the plain language tests of subsection (b) or the alternate objective tests of subsection (c).　A consumer contract need not meet the tests of both subsections.

(b) **Plain language tests.**　A consumer contract is written in plain language if it substantially complies with all of the following tests:

(1) It uses short sentences and paragraphs; and

(2) It uses everyday words; and

(3) It uses personal pronouns, the actual or shortened names of the parties to the contract, or both, when referring to those parties; and

(4) It uses simple and active verb forms; and

(5) It uses type of readable size; and

(6) It uses ink which contrasts with the paper; and

(7) It heads sections and other subdivisions with captions which are in boldface type or which otherwise stand out significantly from the text; and

(8) It uses layout and spacing which separate the paragraphs and sections of the contract from each other and from the borders of the paper; and

(9) It is written and organized in a clear and coherent manner.

(c) **Alternate objective tests.**　A consumer contract is also written in plain language if it fully meets all of the following tests, using the procedures described in section 42–158:

(1) The average number of words per sentence is less than twenty-two; and

(2) No sentence in the contract exceeds fifty words; and

(3) The average number of words per paragraph is less than seventy-five; and

(4) No paragraph in the contract exceeds one hundred fifty words; and

(5) The average number of syllables per word is less than 1.55; and

(6) It uses personal pronouns, the actual or shortened names of the parties to the contract, or both, when referring to those parties; and

(7) It uses no type face of less than eight points in size; and

(8) It allows at least three sixteenths of an inch of blank space between each paragraph and section; and

(9) It allows at least one-half of an inch of blank space at all borders of each page; and

(10) If the contract is printed, each section is captioned in boldface type at least ten points in size. If the contract is typewritten, each section is captioned and the captions are underlined; and

(11) It uses an average length of line of no more than sixty-five characters.

§ 42–153. Coverage

(a) **Contracts covered.** This chapter shall apply to all consumer contracts made, entered into or signed by the consumer in this state after June 30, 1980.

(b) **Exclusions.** Mortgages, deeds of real estate, insurance policies and documents relating to securities transactions are not consumer contracts.

§ 42–154. Liability

Any creditor, seller or lessor which fails to comply with section 42–152 shall be liable to a consumer who is a party to the consumer contract for statutory damages of one hundred dollars plus, at the discretion of the court, an attorney's fee not to exceed one hundred dollars.

§ 42–155. Limitations on liability

(a) **Contracts with more than one party.** In any individual transaction, if there is more than one consumer who is a party to a single consumer contract, only one award of statutory damages may be made for that transaction.

(b) **Good faith.** No statutory damages or attorney's fee shall be awarded under this chapter for a violation of subsection (b) of section 42–152 if the creditor, seller or lessor has attempted in good faith to comply with that subsection.

(c) **Class actions.** No class action may be brought under this chapter.

(d) **Contracts prepared by the consumer.** No consumer may bring an action under this chapter on a contract which the consumer prepared.

(e) **Consumer represented by attorney at signing of contract.** No consumer may bring an action under this chapter on a contract, if:

(1) The consumer was represented at the signing of the contract by an attorney; and

(2) This fact is shown by the attorney's signed and dated statement on the contract.

(f) **Limitations on actions.** No consumer may bring an action under this chapter after the contract has been fully performed. No consumer may bring an action under this chapter more than six years after the date on which the contract was last signed.

§ 42–156. Exempt language

(a) **Required and authorized language.** The use of specific language expressly required or authorized by court decision, statute, regulation or governmental agency shall not be a violation of this chapter.

(b) **Legal descriptions of real property.** The use of a legal description of real property shall not be a violation of this chapter.

§ 42–157. Rights of parties

(a) **Enforceability.** A consumer contract shall remain enforceable, even though it violates this chapter.

(b) **Other consumer rights.** Nothing in this chapter shall preclude a consumer from making any claim or raising any defense which would have been available to the consumer if this chapter were not in effect.

(c) **Waiver.** A consumer may not waive the rights provided by this chapter, and any such waiver shall be void.

§ 42–158. Test procedures

Use the following procedures to determine compliance with subsection (c) of section 42–152:

(a) **Words.** To count the number of words in the contract, proceed as follows:

(1) Count every word used in the text of the contract.

(2) Do not count words or numerals used in headings, captions, signature lines, graphs or charts.

(3) Do not count single words or phrases used to identify the information required in a fill-in section of a contract, such as "Name" or "Address."

(4) Count as one word a contraction, hyphenated word, numeral, symbol, or abbreviation.

(5) Do not count words which are exempt under section 42–156.

(b) **Sentences.** A sequence of words is a "sentence," if:

(1) It expresses a complete thought; and

(2) It contains a subject and a verb, including the implied subject "you"; and

(3) It ends with a period. If it is an item in a list, it may end with a semicolon. If it is an introduction to a list, it may end with a colon.

(c) **Syllables.** A "syllable" is a unit of spoken language consisting of one or more letters of a word, as the word is divided by any dictionary. To count the number of syllables, proceed as follows:

(1) If there is more than one acceptable pronunciation for a word, use the one having fewer syllables.

(2) Count abbreviations, numerals, and symbols as one-syllable words.

(d) **Paragraphs.** A sequence of words is a "paragraph," if:

(1) It consists of one or more sentences; and

(2) It starts on a new line; and

(3) It is separated by at least three sixteenths of an inch of blank space from the text immediately preceding and following it.

(e) **Lists.** A sequence of words is a "list," if:

(1) Each item in the sequence is introduced by a numeral or letter; and

(2) Each item in the sequence starts on a new line.

(f) **Length of line.** (1) A printed text line does not exceed sixty-five characters if the distance between the inside left and inside right margins does not exceed the width of two and one-half alphabets of the typeface being used.

(2) A text line typed at ten characters per inch does not exceed sixty-five characters if the length of the line does not exceed six and one-half inches.

(3) A text line typed at twelve characters per inch does not exceed sixty-five characters if the length of the line does not exceed five and one-half inches.

(g) **Average number of words per sentence.** Count the total number of words and sentences in the contract, as described in this section. Then divide the number of words by the number of sentences. The result is the average number of words per sentence.

(h) **Average number of words per paragraph.** Count the total number of words and paragraphs in the contract, as described in this section. Then divide the number of words by the number of paragraphs. The result is the average number of words per paragraph.

(i) **Average number of syllables per word.** Count the total number of syllables and words in the contract, as described in this section. Then divide the number of syllables by the number of words. The result is the average number of syllables per word.

(j) **Special procedures for list formats.** To count sentences and paragraphs if a list format is used, proceed as follows:

(1) Examine the introduction to the list and each item in the list to see if it is a sentence or a paragraph.

(2) Do not count as part of any sentence the words "and," "or," "if," "if and only if," or "then," if they are used to link the items of the list to each other or to the introduction.

(3) If each item in the list is a sentence, count each as a sentence. If any item is not a sentence, count the entire list as part of the sentence and paragraph containing the introduction. Do not count an

item in a list as either a sentence or a paragraph if the subject or verb appears in the introduction.

(4) If each item in the list is a sentence but the introduction is not, count the introduction as part of the sentence containing the first item in the list.

(5) If each item in the list is a sentence and, in addition, each item is separated by at least three sixteenths of an inch of blank space from the sentences immediately preceding and following it, count each item as a paragraph.

C. LAWS WITH GUIDELINES

A third approach to Plain English legislation compromises between the subjective and the objective. Laws taking this approach present the subjective general standards and then present the objective detailed tests but only as guidelines. This approach rejects the rigidity of laws like Connecticut's. It also rejects the vagueness of laws like New York's. Here is New Jersey's law, which takes this approach.

NEW JERSEY STAT.ANN.
56:12–1 to –13 (1986).

56:12–1. Definitions

As used in this act:

"Consumer contract" means a written agreement in which an individual:

a. Leases or licenses real or personal property;

b. Obtains credit;

c. Obtains insurance coverage, except insurance coverage contained in policies subject to the "Life and Health Insurance Policy Language Simplification Act" (P.L.1979, c. 167, C. 17B:17–17 et seq.);

d. Borrows money;

e. Purchases real or personal property;

f. Contracts for services including professional services,

for cash or on credit and the money, property or services are obtained for personal, family or household purposes. "Consumer contract" includes writings required to complete the consumer transaction. "Consumer contract" does not include a written agreement involving a transaction in securities with a broker-dealer registered with the Securities and Exchange Commission, or a transaction in commodities with a futures commission merchant registered with the Commodities Futures Trading Commission.

56:12–2. Contracts to be written in simple, clear, understandable and easily readable way

A consumer contract entered into on or after the effective date of this amendatory and supplementary act shall be written in a simple, clear, understandable and easily readable way. In determining whether a consumer contract has been written in a simple, clear, understandable and easily readable way as a whole, a court, the Attorney General or the Commissioner of Insurance, in regard to contracts of insurance provided for in subsection c. of section 1 of this act (C. 56:12–1c.), shall take into consideration the guidelines set forth in section 10 of this act. Use of technical terms or words of art shall not in and of itself be a violation of this act.

56:12–3. Failure to comply; liability

A creditor, seller, insurer or lessor who fails to comply with section 2 of this act shall be liable to a consumer who is a party to the consumer contract for actual damages sustained, if the violation caused the consumer to be substantially confused about the rights, obligations or remedies of the contract, plus punitive damages in an amount up to $50.00. The creditor, seller, insurer or lessor shall also be liable for the consumer's reasonable attorney's fees and costs, not to exceed $2,500.00.

56:12–4. Class actions; limitation on punitive damages

Class actions may be brought under the provisions of this act, but the amount of punitive damages shall be limited to $10,000.00 against any one seller, lessor, insurer or creditor and the amount of attorney's fees may not exceed $10,000.00.

56:12–4.1. Reform or limit of provision of consumer contract by court; findings

In addition to the remedies provided in this act, a court reviewing a consumer contract may reform or limit a provision so as to avoid an unfair result if it finds that:

a.   a material provision of the contract violates this act;

b.   the violation caused the consumer to be substantially confused about any of the rights, obligations or remedies of the contract; and

c.   the violation has caused or is likely to cause financial detriment to the consumer.

If the court reforms or limits a provision of a consumer contract, the court shall also make orders necessary to avoid unjust enrichment. Bringing a claim for relief pursuant to this section does not entitle a consumer to withhold performance of an otherwise valid contractual obligation. No relief shall be granted pursuant to this section unless the claim is brought before the obligations of the contract have been fully performed.

56:12–5. Nonliability conditions

There shall be no liability under sections 3 and 4 if: a. both parties to the contract have performed their obligations under the contract, b. the creditor, seller, insurer or lessor attempts in good faith to comply with this act in preparing the consumer contract, c. the contract is in conformity with a rule, regulation, or the opinion or interpretation of the Attorney General or the Commissioner of Insurance, in regard to contracts of insurance provided for in subsection c. of section 1 of this act (C. 56:12–1c.), or d. the consumer supplied the contract or the portion of the contract to which the consumer objects.

56:12–6. Use of specific language

The use of specific language in a consumer contract required, permitted or approved by a law, regulation, rule or published interpretation of a State or Federal agency shall not violate this act.

56:12–7. Other claims not precluded

This act shall not preclude a debtor, buyer, insured or lessee from making any claims which would have been available to him if this act were not in effect.

56:12–8. Opinions on compliance of consumer contracts; review by attorney general; certification; fee

a. A creditor, seller, insurer, lessor or any person in the business of preparing and selling forms of consumer contracts may request an opinion from the Attorney General, or the Commissioner of Insurance, in regard to contracts of insurance provided for in subsection c. of section 1 of this act (C. 56:12–1c.), as to whether a consumer contract complies with this act.

The Attorney General or the Commissioner of Insurance, as the case may be, shall furnish the opinion within a reasonable period of time.

b. After reviewing the contract the Attorney General or the Commissioner of Insurance, as the case may be, shall: (1) certify that the contract complies with this act; (2) decline to certify that the contract complies with this act and note his objections to the contractual language; (3) decline to review the contract and refer the party submitting the contract to other previously certified contracts of the same type; (4) decline to review the contract because the contract's compliance with this act is the subject of pending litigation, or (5) decline to review the contract because the contract is not subject to this act.

c. Actions of the Attorney General or the Commissioner of Insurance, as the case may be, pursuant to this section are not appealable.

d. Any consumer contract certified pursuant to this section is deemed to comply with this act. Certification of a consumer contract pursuant to this section is not otherwise an approval of the contract's legality or legal effect.

e. Failure to submit a contract to the Attorney General or the Commissioner of Insurance, as the case may be, for review pursuant to this section does not show a lack of good faith nor does it raise a presumption that the contract violates this act. If pursuant to this section the Attorney General or the Commissioner of Insurance, as the case may be, refers a party to a previously certified contract, that the party chooses not to use the contract does not show a lack of good faith nor does it raise a presumption that a contract used by that party violated this act.

f. The Attorney General or the Commissioner of Insurance, as the case may be, may charge a fee, not to exceed $50.00, for the costs of reviewing a consumer contract pursuant to this section.

56:12–8.2. Power of commissioner of insurance to review and certify insurance contracts; effect on prior certification by Attorney General

The transfer to the Commissioner of Insurance of the power and duty to review and certify contracts of insurance provided for in subsection c. of section 1 of P.L.1980, c. 125 (C. 56:12–1c.) shall not affect any certification made by the Attorney General prior to the effective date of this act.

56:12–9. Application to dollar limitation on consumer contracts; nonapplication to real estate or insurance contracts

This act shall not apply to consumer contracts involving amounts of more than $50,000.00, but no dollar limitation shall apply to consumer contracts involving real estate or insurance.

56:12–10. Guidelines

a. To insure that a consumer contract shall be simple, clear, understandable and easily readable, the following are examples of guidelines that a court, the Attorney General or the Commissioner of Insurance, in regard to contracts of insurance provided for in subsection c. of section 1 of this act (C. 56:12–1c.), may consider in determining whether a consumer contract as a whole complies with this act:

(1) Cross references that are confusing;

(2) Sentences that are of greater length than necessary;

(3) Sentences that contain double negatives and exceptions to exceptions;

(4) Sentences and sections that are in a confusing or illogical order;

(5) The use of words with obsolete meanings or words that differ in their legal meaning from their common ordinary meaning;

(6) Frequent use of Old English and Middle English words and Latin and French phrases.

b. The following are examples of guidelines that a court, the Attorney General or the Commissioner of Insurance, in regard to contracts of insurance provided for in subsection c. of section 1 of this act (C. 56:12–1c.), may consider in determining whether the consumer contract as a whole complies with this act:

(1) Sections shall be logically divided and captioned;

(2) A table of contents or alphabetical index shall be used for all contracts with more than 3,000 words;

(3) Conditions and exceptions to the main promise of the agreement shall be given equal prominence with the main promise, and shall be in at least 10 point type.

56:12–11. Waiver of rights under act; effect of violation of act

No consumer contract shall contain a waiver of any rights under this act. A violation of this act will not render any consumer contract void or voidable, or serve as a defense in an action to enforce the consumer contract for breach thereof.

56:12–12. Injunction; attorney's fees and costs

The Office of the Attorney General, the Division of Consumer Affairs, the Department of the Public Advocate, the Commissioner of Insurance, in regard to contracts of insurance provided for in subsection c. of section 1 of this act (C. 56:12–1c.), or any interested person may seek injunctive relief. The court may authorize reasonable attorney's fees, not to exceed $2,500.00, and court costs in such a proceeding.

56:12–13. Severability

If any provision of this act, or its application to any person or circumstances, is held invalid, the remainder of the act and its application to other persons or circumstances shall not be affected.

D. MATTERS AFFECTING READABILITY

Regardless of whether they are objective tests or suggested guidelines, here are the typical directions for making documents more readable:

1. Avoid legalese; use words with common meanings instead.

2. Avoid wordiness. Especially avoid long sentences with complex structures and passive verbs.

3. Consider personalizing your writing, such as by saying, "I agree to pay you," instead of saying, "The mortgagor agrees to pay the mortgagee."

4. Divide material into paragraphs and other larger divisions, each with a heading. Use extra white space as well as tabulation to set off divisions.

5. Use indexes, tables of contents, and cross references to make individual provisions easy to find.

6. Choose type faces that aid readability. Boldface and italics are helpful devices for emphasis as long as they are used consistently and not overused. Blocks of solid capital letters are especially hard to read.

7. Choose serif type, which is easier to read than sans serif.

8. Use sufficient margins and contrast of ink to paper color to aid readability.

III. CRITIQUES OF PLAIN ENGLISH LAWS

A. CRITIQUE BY INTERESTED PARTIES

When the first states began to pass Plain English laws, lawyers were critical, as were the corporations that were suddenly required to redraft all of their form contracts. Corporations complained that there was no way to ensure that a redrafted contract would be in compliance with the laws before the corporation put it into use. Some of the legislation itself was not written in particularly plain language, prompting landlords, sellers, and lenders to complain that they should not have to do what legislators could not. Some also expressed the fear that converting to Plain English would make documents longer and thus actually discourage consumers from reading them—as well as increasing the cost of recording.[3]

Lawyers worried about the legal consequences of changing language if the changes had to include eliminating legal terms of art. Some worried that changing language to comply with a Plain English statute might result in violating some other statute. They anticipated a mountain of litigation, although it did not materialize.[4] These criticisms were, of course, from interested parties.

B. CRITIQUE BY LINGUISTS

Linguists were disinterested critics, but not at all uninterested. They insisted that all this effort to simplify could still leave contracts that were full of nonsense. For example, the story is told of the bank employee who spent a great deal of time trying to redraft the provision for figuring prepayment credit that is commonly known as the "rule of 78." She kept trying out drafts on people in the bank, and not one of the drafts was understandable. Finally she drew the conclusion that her drafting was not the problem; the problem was that the rule was too complicated to explain. The ultimate conclusion may be easier for the linguist than the lawyer: if the rule is too complicated to explain, it is a bad rule and ought to be scrapped.[5]

1. Readability Formulas

Linguist Veda Charrow criticizes readability formulas for not actually measuring comprehensibility.[6] In particular, she disapproves of Flesch's assumption that shorter words and sentences are more readable. She demonstrates her point with the following sentences:

3. Browne, Development of the FNMA/ FHLMC Plain Language Mortgage Documents—Some Useful Techniques, 14 Real Prop.Prob. & Tr.J. 696, 702–04 (1979).

4. See Block, Plain Language Laws: Promise v Performance, 62 Mich.B.J. 950, 950–51 (1983).

5. See Ross, On Legalities and Linguistics: Plain Language Legislation, 30 Buffalo L.Rev. 317, 341–51 (1981).

6. Let the Rewriter Beware 2–4 (1979) (Document Design Center pamphlet).

The happening of the accident creates a presumption of defendant's negligence. (10 words)

The very fact that the accident happened allows us to presume that the defendant was negligent. (16 words) [7]

Although the Flesch Test would rate the first sentence more readable by virtue of its fewer words, it is probably less readable because it relies heavily on abstract nominalizations rather than strong verbs.

Charrow also makes her point by comparing 2 sentences with the same number of words, 19:

This morning I got up and brushed my teeth and got dressed and ate breakfast and went to work.

The boy who the girl who hit the man in the white car kissed lives next door to me.

As she explains, the Flesch Test would find the first sentence less readable because it has more two-syllable words, yet the second sentence would probably cause more trouble for readers because it has more complex grammatical structure with subordinate clauses buried one inside another. [8]

Charrow is also critical of some of the other mechanical revisions Flesch and some other Plain English proponents recommend. She maintains that research shows that passive verbs make comprehension no more difficult than active verbs. [9] Moreover, she criticizes the Plain English phenomenon known as "whiz deletion," [10] which refers to removing relative pronouns and thus turning subordinate clauses into phrases. Removing the bracketed words in the following sentences would be "whiz" (for "wh— is") deletion:

The tenant, [who is] planning to arrive at noon, called ahead.

This rule, [which is] explained in detail on page 2, takes effect immediately.

According to Charrow the deletion makes sentences harder, not easier, to process.

Cutting words to simplify may make the writing sound like "disorganized baby talk." But it can also produce more serious trouble if it takes away examples, explanations, and contextual material that aid clarity. [11]

Language specialist Gertrude Block shares Charrow's concerns that attention to arbitrary formulas and statutory rules can end up making clarity and coherence suffer. Block tested a history textbook that Flesch had revised. She found that in the Flesch revision some facts

---

7. *Id.* at 5.

8. *Id.* at 4.

9. V. Charrow, What Is "Plain English," Anyway? 4 (1979) (Document Design Center pamphlet).

10. *Id.* at 5.

11. *Id.* at 7.

disappeared, others were modified, and still others appeared for the first time. In short, while Flesch might have made the text more interesting and easier to read, what he produced was neither as exact nor as complete as legal documents need to be.[12]

2. Personalization

The other characteristic of Plain English that has engendered considerable criticism is "personalization," which means using the personal pronouns "I" and "you" instead of referring to the parties to a contract by legal status, such as "mortgagor" and "mortgagee" or "lessor" and "lessee." Block questions whether personalization actually aids understandability,[13] and Charrow, who calls it "personal folksiness," worries that the arbitrary assignment of pronouns to parties may end up causing confusion about their identity. Professor Ross demonstrates with a prepayment clause the silly results that personalization can produce. Here is the clause:

> If I pay this loan off in full, ahead of schedule, I will not have to pay the full finance charge. I will pay a finance charge on the amount I have borrowed only for the number of days I have had the loan—from the day I received the loan until the day I pay off the loan.[14]

Here is what Professor Ross has to say about it:

ROSS, ON LEGALITIES AND LINGUISTICS: PLAIN LANGUAGE LEGISLATION
30 Buffalo L.Rev. 317, 348 (1981).*

* * * The consumer is referred to as "I" as if he were telling the Bank about rebates. Presumably it is the Bank that understands how rebates are computed. * * * The resulting tone is self-serving, like an advertisement in which a smiling consumer tells the bank how grateful he is that he will "not have to pay the full finance charge." This pretense that the consumer is writing to the bank may even be deceptive, implying a comprehension on the consumer's part that he does not in fact possess.

C. CRITIQUE BY REFORMERS OF CONSUMER LAW

A different sort of criticism of Plain English statutes has come from those who sought to reform consumer law. They focus on the limited value of Plain English laws no matter how they are written or enforced. The sense of the criticism is that the laws should not be regarded as panaceas. They do not offer substantial protection against adhesion contracts insofar as a form may be simplified without offering any meaningful alternatives to a consumer who does not have bargain-

---

12. Block, above note 4, at 954–55.

13. *Id.* at 954.

14. Ross, above note 5, at 347, quoting National Bank of Washington form, quoted in Washington Post, Aug. 24, 1977, § D, at 1, col. 2.

* Copyright © 1981 by Buffalo Law Review. Reprinted by permission of the Publisher.

ing power. Moreover, according to one critic, one major impediment to understanding contracts is that they overload consumers with information that consumers do not need at the point of entering an agreement.[15] If this is true, then the way to make contracts more readable is not merely to simplify and explain concepts but to excise nonessentials altogether.[16]

D. PUTTING THE CRITIQUES IN PERSPECTIVE

The main criticism, agreed upon by most all the critics, is that readability, while valuable, should never be allowed to take priority over clarity and accuracy. Thus formulas like the Flesch Test and Fog Index have lost favor. Likewise, there has been general agreement that terms of art with legal consequences should not be eliminated, although sometimes extra effort should go into defining such terms.

Most of the critics have taken care to distinguish between the unworkable extremes advocated by some Plain English proponents and the sensible reforms advocated by the movement generally. However, one critic who indicts the entire movement concludes that "much of the thinking behind the Plain English movement is naive, both about the complexities of language and about the extent to which linguistic reform can change sociolegal realities." [17]

Some criticize with an even sharper tongue, for example, "The Underground Grammarian."

R. MITCHELL, LESS THAN WORDS CAN SAY
153–54 (1979).

There is, of course, an alternative to the plain English fad * * *. We could simply decide to educate all Americans to such a degree that they could read and understand even the OSHA definition of an exit * * *. Just think what happens in the mind of the person who knows the difference between restrictive and nonrestrictive clauses. Anyone who understands that distinction is on the brink of seeing the difference between simple fact and elaborative detail and may well begin to make judgments about the logic of such relationships * * *. From that, it's not a long way to detecting non sequiturs and unstated premises and even false analogies.

Doubtless there will always be those who suspect that Plain English advocates ultimately intend to produce legal documents readable by first graders. This suspicion lends itself to such spoofs as this "Plain English Will."

15. Davis, Protecting Consumers from Overdisclosure and Gobbledygook: An Empirical Look at the Simplification of Consumer–Credit Contracts, 63 Va.L.Rev. 841, 855 (1977).

16. *Id.*

17. Danet, Language in the Legal Process, 14 Law & Soc. 445, 490 (1980).

THE PLAIN ENGLISH WILL

I am John Doe. This is my will. See my signature on this will. See my witnesses' signatures.

I revoke all my other wills and codicils.

See Sam Brown. I want him to be my personal representative. Please court, make him my personal representative. Sam is honest, I hope, and fair, I hope.

Sam won't serve? See Bob Baker. Bob will be personal representative.

See Mary Doe, my wife. Mary likes my personal effects. I give them to her. Also my bubble gum cards. My comic books. My baseball glove. My bat. My dog, Spot. If Mary kills me, naughty Mary. Do not give her my dog Spot. Nor my comic books.

See Tom. See Dick. See Harry. All Does' folks. Also, issue of me and Mary, I hope. Tom is 2. Dick is 3. Harry is 4. Mary is fertile.

See the residue of my estate. Give the residue to Mary. If she dies first, give it to Does' folks. Equally and outright.

See my personal representative. He is wise. He is strong. He has powers: to sell, to lease, with notice, without notice. Also to invest.

I'm not crazy. I know what I'm doing.

See my signature on _____ at _____, _____.

See my witnesses' signatures. We sign, watching each other. I say: "This is my will." They say, "Yes." Now see their signatures.[18]

IV. PLAIN ENGLISH WILLS: SOME SUGGESTIONS FROM PRACTITIONERS

A. A PLAIN ENGLISH WILL FORM

A Plain English will need not be a joke, however. In fact, Lawrence X. Cusack, a New York estate practitioner and author, has published a suggested form.[19] He drafted it after acknowledging that wills generally are "a warehouse of clutter," including unnecessary synonyms, recitals, and particularity.[20] He admits that many clients expect legalese in a will and might question the legal sufficiency of Plain English. However, he also says that six other lawyers who studied his Plain English will agreed with him that it is legally sufficient and does not suffer from any ambiguities.[21] He is careful to point out that modifications or additions may be necessary in particular

---

18. Anonymous (contributed by Professor David T. Smith).

19. The Plain English Will Revisited, July 1980 Tr. & Est. 42, 43.

20. Cusack, The Blue-Pencilled Will, August 1979 Tr. & Est. 33, 33.

21. *Id.* at 33–34.

cases, and, on the form itself, he expressly warns against non-lawyers using it without advice of counsel.[22] He also acknowledges that certain terms of art such as *per stirpes* are worth keeping, but with a brief explanation provided.[23] His premise is that a will needs to speak clearly both to the client and for the client to the probate judge.

B. REDUCING LEGALESE

Thomas S. Word, Jr., a Virginia practitioner, provides several examples of reducing traditional legalese in wills to Plain English, such as this redraft:

Original Will:

I, John Quincy Doe, now residing in the city of Richmond, State of Virginia, being of sound mind and memory, do hereby make, publish and declare this to be my last will and testament, hereby revoking, annulling and canceling any and all wills and codicils heretofore made by me.

Revised Will:

I, John Quincy Doe, of Richmond, Virginia, make this will, and revoke all earlier wills and codicils.[24]

Commentary accompanies each redraft. For example, Word comments on the above reduction from 49 words to 17.

WORD, A BRIEF FOR PLAIN ENGLISH
WILLS AND TRUSTS
14 U. of Rich.L.Rev. 471, 472 (1980).*

The distinction between "will" and "testament" left us long ago. "Publish and declare" should come at the end, in the attestation clause, if at all. Do annul and cancel add anything to revoke? * * * Would anyone think we were revoking someone else's will? ("And codicils" could be omitted, but I left it as a bow to tradition and because for some strange reason clients savor the word. In fact, the whole revocation clause is surplus—a complete will revokes all prior ones by operation of law.) (citations omitted)

In addition to showing how to reduce wordy and redundant clauses, Word shows how to excise legalese, unfamiliar words, and passive verbs.[25] These, of course, are the usual matters taken up by proponents of Plain English.

22. Cusack, above note 19, at 42–43.

23. *Id.* at 44.

24. Word, A Brief for Plain English Wills and Trusts, 14 U.Rich.L.Rev. 471, 472 (1980).

25. *Id.* at 475–78.

C. ORGANIZING A PLAIN ENGLISH WILL

Also, Word adds suggestions for organizing a Plain English will. In particular, he advocates removing technical material from the dispositive provisions and putting it in separate sections near the end. For example, he suggests moving to the end marital deduction formulas, facility of payment clauses, spendthrift clauses, and specific tax-related directions. This way, the client can read what the client needs to understand without having it cluttered by what the lawyer and the judge need to know. In the same vein, Word recommends incorporating by reference sections of the state statutes as a way of avoiding long recitations of such matters as the powers of the executor and the trustee. (He acknowledges the risk of having a client or beneficiary claim to be misled if incorporation by reference is overused.) [26]

D. THE DANGER IN NOT USING PLAIN ENGLISH

The lawyer who worries about taking the suggestions of Cusack and Word, and who is tempted instead to continue to rely on legalese, might consider the following case. A millionaire's trust contained a "no contest" clause that became an issue when the judge had to decide whether the clause should force the deceased millionaire's friend to forfeit her share of his estate. Here is the clause:

IN RE WEINGART, NO. P663511
(L.A.Super.Ct. March 21, 1983).

[The beneficiaries shall not] directly or indirectly aid, counsel, commence or prosecute any demands, claims, negotiations, suits, actions or proceedings in any court of law, or other arenas, having as an object: * * * the obtaining for anyone of (i) anything of value from this Trust or my estate, (ii) any of the assets of this Trust or my estate, or (iii) any assets in which I had an interest immediately prior to my death, grounded on, arising out of, or related to any claimed or actual agreement, representation or understanding not expressly set forth in a written and executed agreement that I would (or would not cause another to) deliver to anyone anything of value (directly or indirectly, in trust, by will, or otherwise) as a gift, or for services or any other thing of value (including by way of example but not limitation any employment or assistance) received by me or another. The word "another" includes any one or more (or combination thereof) people, partnerships, corporations, trusts, estates or other entities.

The judge "wrestled with the clause for at least a year" and eventually gave up and held it to be of no effect, so that the millionaire's friend took her share.[27]

---

26. *Id.* at 478–80.

27. See Benson, Plain English Comes to Court, 13 Litigation No. 1, 21, 22–23 (1986).

V. EXPANDING PLAIN ENGLISH REFORMS

In spite of both the serious criticisms and the jokes and parodies, the Plain English Movement has expanded. In fact, one explanation for the decline in introduction of new legislation is that there has been such widespread voluntary reform.[28] This may be because Plain English in large measure means writing well, and that means writing to be understood, which is not an especially controversial idea after all. Thus informal legislation or self-policing by industries, organizations, and individuals has become widespread. Moreover, plenty of help is now available for those who want to reform. Here are just some of the signs of the breadth of the movement's success.

A. REFORM AT CITIBANK: THE FIRST WAVE

Carl Felsenfeld began his advocacy of Plain English as a Vice President of Citibank. It was his voluntary conversion of the Citibank forms into Plain English in 1975 that inspired the first state Plain English legislation, New York's Sullivan Law. Felsenfeld went on to co-author with Alan Siegel *Writing Contracts in Plain English* (1981), an excellent contract drafting guide. Felsenfeld and Siegel both teach at Fordham University School of Law.

B. WRITING SPECIALISTS IN FIRMS AND LAW SCHOOLS

Some law firms have hired writing specialists as part- or full-time in-house editors and consultants to teach the lawyers to get rid of legalese and write in Plain English. This innovation began at the Wall Street law firm of Shearman and Sterling in 1978. The in-house writing specialist has long been recognized as a valuable part of legal education at several schools including the University of Florida. A nationally known scholar of legal writing, Gertrude Block, has served in that capacity at Florida since 1974.

C. INSURANCE INDUSTRY REFORMS

Many states that did not enact broad Plain English legislation did enact narrower provisions covering insurance policies. In response, the insurance industry decided to police itself. The National Association of Insurance Commissioners (NAIC) adopted model acts, one covering life and health policies, and the other covering property and casualty policies. A number of states have adopted the models as their legislation in the insurance fields or have promulgated regulations that reflect the NAIC models' readability standards. These standards require that insurance policies: (1) achieve a minimum score of 40 on the Flesch Test; (2) be printed in 10–point size type or larger; and (3)

---

28. Felsenfeld, The Future of Plain English, 62 Mich.B.J. 942, 943 (1983) (article introducing symposium on Plain English, including articles that survey its pro-gress in consumer and insurance contracts, lawsuit papers, judicial opinions, legislative drafting, and legal education).

include a table of contents or index if the policy is longer than 3 pages or more than 3,000 words.[29]

D. PRACTISING LAW INSTITUTE SEMINARS

The Practising Law Institute sponsored seminars on Plain English in 1979 and 1981, each with a course manual entitled *Drafting Documents in Plain Language.*

E. WYDICK'S PLAIN ENGLISH "BIBLE"

In 1979, Richard Wydick, a law professor at The University of California at Davis, expanded his famous article on Plain English [30] into a book by the same title, *Plain English for Lawyers* (2d ed.1985), which has become a "bible" for law schools and law offices.

F. MINNESOTA STATUTORY REFORM

In Minnesota, the Office of the Revisor of the Statutes began in 1981 the gradual process of revising that state's statutes into Plain English, using techniques recommended in the Document Design Center's *Guidelines for Document Designers.*[31] Here is an example of the transformation of one section, designed to clarify but not change the meaning.

458.02 Freight and Passenger Transportation Terminals
(1927 Version)

Any city in this state now or hereafter having a population of not less than 4,000 and not more than 50,000, shall have the power to acquire and hold in fee simple, by purchase or condemnation, land for the establishment of docks, quays, levees, wharves, landing places, railroad and other land transportation loading and unloading places, land or water freight and passenger stations, terminals and terminal buildings for any and all kinds of carriers and necessary equipment and appurtenances on any navigable stream within the limits of such city and may set aside such portions of the land when acquired, as the public needs may require, for use for public travel and shall devote the remainder thereof to the uses herein provided, or if required by the United States government.

---

29. As early as 1979, 25 states had taken some action to achieve readable insurance policies. R. Pressman, Legislative and Regulatory Progress on the Readability of Insurance Policies 14 (1979) (Document Design Center pamphlet, crediting the strong unifying influence of NAIC for the remarkable speed and breadth of Plain English reform in the insurance industry).

30. Plain English for Lawyers, 66 Cal.L. Rev. 727 (1978).

31. See Corbett, Revising Minnesota's Laws into Plain English, No. 70 Simply Stated 1, 1, 3 (December 1986/January 1987) (Document Design Center newsletter).

458.02 Power to Get Land for Transportation Facilities; Use (1985 Version)

Subdivision 1. **May get, hold.** A city with a population from 4,000 to 50,000 may acquire land on a navigable stream in the city by purchase or condemnation, and may hold it.

Subdivision 2. **Use.** The city may set aside when acquired, as much of the land as the public needs require for public travel. The remainder must be used as required by the federal government or for docks, quays, levees, wharves, landing places, railroad and other land transportation loading and unloading places, land and water freight and passenger stations, terminals and terminal buildings for carriers, and necessary equipment and appurtenances.

G. NLRB MANUAL

In 1983, the National Labor Relations Board adopted a *Style Manual* that "encourages the use of concise, plain English and provides rules and examples for improving legal writing, without legalese." [32]

H. MEDICARE REFORM

In 1984, a federal judge in New York ordered the government to rewrite Medicare benefit form letters in Plain English to meet due process standards. [33]

I. LAWYERS' BILLS

Lawyers have begun to understand that their clients are consumers and that communicating with them in Plain English benefits the lawyers as well as the clients. The Economics of Law Practice Section of the American Bar Association published an article to show how to draft bills in Plain English so that clients will quickly pay them. [34] For example, the article recommends that to project effort and concern for the client on the part of both the lawyer and other staff members, bills should use many action verbs such as "deposed," "researched," "briefed," "drafted," and "demanded." Bills should not use nouns ("phone call," "brief") or abbreviations that clients might not understand. [35]

J. UTILITY BILL REFORM IN NEW YORK

In October 1985, the New York Public Service Commission issued rules requiring residential gas and electric bills to be in Plain English. The rules required: (1) giving charges in terms of both amount of use and unit price, (2) using graphs to show the customer's energy use,

32. NLRB, Style Manual Preface ii (1983).

33. David v. Heckler, 591 F.Supp. 1033, 1035 (E.D.N.Y.1984).

34. Morgan, How To Draft Bills Clients Rush To Pay, July/August 1985 Legal Economics 22.

35. *Id.* at 22.

average use by residential customers, and average temperature for the billing period, (3) defining technical terms, and (4) using readable type.[36]

K. MODEL JURY INSTRUCTIONS

Under the auspices of the Federal Judicial Center in Washington, D.C., federal judges have drafted sets of model criminal jury instructions in Plain English.[37] Also, a committee of the Judicial Council of the Ninth Circuit drafted both criminal and civil instructions in Plain English that have been endorsed by the Council for use in the Ninth Circuit.[38] In 1987 Iowa's Uniform Civil Jury Instructions were redrafted in Plain English, with a redraft of the criminal instructions to follow.[39]

L. MODEL PLAIN LANGUAGE LEGISLATION

Professor Felsenfeld spearheaded a movement to convince the National Conference of Commissioners on Uniform State Laws to draft a Uniform Plain Language Act. Professor Felsenfeld found support for such legislation at a May 1986 conference of the Council of Better Business Bureaus. It turns out that consumers are not the only ones who see the value of Plain English legislation. Companies that engage in interstate commerce recognize that uniform legislation would make it easier for them to comply with the requirements in various states. Here is one proposal for model legislation.

NOTE, A MODEL PLAIN LANGUAGE LAW

33 Stanford L.Rev. 255, 296–300 (1981).*

A MODEL PLAIN LANGUAGE LAW

1. TITLE

This law can be cited as the Plain Language Act.

2. PURPOSES

(a) **Liberal Construction, Purposes:** This law is to be liberally construed to further its purposes, which are:

(1) to ensure that consumer contracts are written in simple format and plain language.

36. See N.Y. Utilities To Issue Clear Bills, No. 13 Simply Stated In Business 1 (January 1986) (Document Design Center publication).

37. See Federal Judicial Center Committee to Study Criminal Jury Instructions, Pattern Criminal Jury Instructions (1982).

38. Committee on Model Jury Instructions, Ninth Circuit, Manual of Model Jury Instructions for the Ninth Circuit (1985 ed.).

39. Letter to Iowa State Bar Association members from Donald C. Wilson, Chairman, Uniform Court Instructions Committee, Iowa State Bar Association (July 20, 1987).

* Copyright by the Board of Trustees of the Leland Stanford Junior University. Reprinted by permission of the publisher.

(2) to protect consumers against unfair or deceptive form contracts.

(b) **Severability:** The provisions of this law are severable. If one provision or application is held invalid, other provisions and applications shall remain law.

3. COVERAGE

(a) **Types of Contracts Covered:** A contract is covered by this law if it meets these three conditions:

(1) The contract is between a natural person and a person or organization acting in the ordinary course of business.

(2) The subject matter of the contract is commonly used for personal, family, or household purposes. This includes but is not limited to appropriate contracts for:

(A) sale or lease of real or personal property.

(B) services.

(C) mortgages.

(D) credit.

(E) insurance.

(F) common personal, family, or household investments, such as stocks, bonds, and mutual funds.

(3) The contract is signed after July 1, 1982. If a contract signed before that date includes an option to renew the contract, the renewal is not covered.

Drafting Note: This law is intended to cover all types of consumer contracts.

(b) **Related Documents:** Documents related to a covered contract which are intended to affect rights and duties under the contract are also covered.

Drafting Note: For example, a baggage receipt that limits liability and a certificate of completion for a home improvement are covered.

(c) **Form Sellers:** A form seller is a person or organization which in the ordinary course of business drafts and sells preprinted forms. Form sellers must comply with this law. If a covered contract violates this law and is based on a form sold by a form seller, the form seller is liable.

Drafting Note: Small businesses often buy preprinted contract forms from form sellers. While the small business has some control over whether its contracts are readable—it can shop for a readable form—most of the control over readability lies with the form seller. To ensure that form sellers simplify forms, this law can be enforced directly against them.

(d) **Language Required by Law:** This law does not apply to format or language required by state or federal law or regulation.

Drafting Note: This law does not affect format or language required by state law. Section 3(f) requires state agencies to simplify format or language required by *regulation*. Format or language required by federal law or regulation is beyond the reach of a state statute.

(e) **Bargained Language:** This law does not apply to language negotiated and specially chosen to suit both parties to a particular deal.

Drafting Note: This law does not cover language which was custom-made for a particular deal. This exception covers language altered to suit an individual consumer. It also covers contracts covering a group of consumers. For example, a group insurance policy may be largely based on the insurer's standard form, but also include language specially chosen to suit the group representative. The specially chosen language is not covered.

(f) **State Agencies:** State agencies that require or recommend format or language of covered contracts must promptly revise their regulations so that the format or language complies with this law. State agencies that approve the format or language of covered contracts must disapprove forms that do not comply with this law. This subsection can be enforced as provided in subsections 5(c) and (d).

4. STANDARD OF COMPLIANCE

Simple Format and Plain Language: A covered contract must be written in simple format and plain language. A contract is written in simple format if it is legible and easy to follow. A contract is written in plain language if it is concise and an average person can understand it. Simple format and plain language include but are not limited to the attributes listed below.

Drafting Note: This section uses both general standards and specific rules and standards to define simple format and plain language. The general standard gives the law the flexibility to adapt to new knowledge about how to communicate effectively. Specific rules and standards make the law easier to comply with and easier to enforce.

(a) **Simple Format:** A covered contract must:

(1) use 10–point or larger type, with at least 1 point of leading between lines.

Drafting Note: The rules on type size, spacing between lines, and index or table of contents (section 4(a)(6)) are consistent with most existing plain language laws. This helps ensure that businesses will not have to use a different form in each state.

(2) use paper and ink of sufficient quality and contrast to be easily legible.

(3) not use excessively long lines.

(4) be appropriately divided into sections and paragraphs. Each section must have an appropriate and conspicuous heading.

(5) put sections, paragraphs, and sentences in sensible order. Related ideas should be close together and in meaningful sequence.

(6) if longer than 3,000 words, have an index of principal sections or table of contents.

(7) if longer than 3,000 words, contain a conspicuous summary placed near the beginning of the contract.

Drafting Note: A summary section is important for long contracts because they can produce "information overload"; the reader is swamped by detail and misses the important parts. Readable summaries are presently required for insurance policies in a number of states, and for pension plans nationwide.

(b) **Plain Language:** A covered contract must:

(1) be concise, to the extent consistent with the goal of providing consumers with a clear explanation of the terms of the contract.

(2) use short and simple sentences.

(3) use words which an average person is likely to understand in context. Other words can be used only if there is no good alternative, and must be defined.

Drafting Note: There may be occasional need to use words which few people will understand, even in context. For example, a health insurance policy may need to use medical terms. This law allows use of such words as long as they are defined.

(4) keep double negatives, exceptions to exceptions, cross-references, and reference to definitions to the minimum needed for clarity. Definitions cannot contradict ordinary meaning.

(5) if written in English, score at least 50 on the Flesch readability test.

Drafting Note: The Flesch test is a reasonably good predictor of how easy a piece of writing is to read. When combined with other standards, it helps to ensure that contracts are written in plain language. Because it is precise, it makes both enforcement of and compliance with a plain language law easier.

A number of other states use the Flesch test to measure readability. These states require a minimum Flesch score of 40, 45, or 50. A score of 50 corresponds roughly to 12th–grade reading level.

(c) **Flesch Test Defined:**

(1) **Basic Formula:**

Let W = average number of words per sentence.

Let S = average number of syllables per word.

Then $R = 206.835 - [((1.015)W) + ((84.6)S)]$ is the Flesch readability score.

(2) **Parts of Contract Covered:** Only the running text is counted. Headings, tables, section numbers, and other parts

of the contract not written in complete sentences are not counted. Except for purposes of agency compliance with section 3(f), sentences required by law or regulation are not counted. Sentences which contain individual words or phrases required by law or regulation are counted.

(3) **Sentence Defined:** For the Flesch test, a sentence is any full unit of speech ending with a period, colon, semicolon, dash, question mark, or exclamation point.

(4) **Word Defined:** For the Flesch test, a contraction, hyphenated word, abbreviation, or single group of numbers, letters, and symbols is one word.

(5) **Syllable Defined:** For a word with more than one accepted pronunciation, use the pronunciation with the fewest syllables. For the Flesch test, an abbreviation or single group of numbers, letters, and symbols is one syllable.

(d) **Unenforceable Clauses:** No covered contract can contain a clause which purports to waive rights which statute, case law, or regulation say cannot be waived.

Drafting Note: Contracts sometimes include unenforceable clauses that deceive consumers about their legal rights. This section prohibits use of such clauses. It does *not* change the law governing which contract terms can be enforced.

5. REMEDIES

(a) **Actual Damages:** A natural person who is a party to a covered contract may recover actual damages from any person or organization who violates this law.

(b) **Penalties:** A natural person who is a party to a covered contract, and any law enforcement official (including but not limited to the attorney general, a district attorney, a city attorney, or a city prosecutor) may recover a penalty from any person or organization who violates this law.

The penalty in each action shall be at least $1,000, but not more than $1,000,000. If the penalty exceeds $1,000, 90% of the excess shall go to the state. The total penalty in any action or series of actions arising out of the same failure to comply by the same defendant shall not exceed $1,000,000 in one year. In fixing the penalty, the court shall consider all relevant factors, including but not limited to:

(1) How close to compliance was the defendant?

(2) How important is the transaction type to consumers?

(3) For how long has the defendant violated this law?

(4) How many consumers were affected by the violation?

(5) Was the violation intentional?

(6) What are the financial resources of the defendant?

(c) **Injunctions:** Any person or organization, whether or not a party to a covered contract, and any law enforcement official may bring an action to enjoin use of a contract that violates this law, or violation of subsection 3(f) of this law by a state agency.

> **Drafting Note:** This section encourages enforcement by allowing anyone to stop violations by obtaining an injunction. This provision is similar to Cal.Bus. & Prof.Code § 17204, which allows any private party to enjoin acts of unfair competition.

(d) **Attorney Fees:** Reasonable attorney fees, costs, and expenses shall be awarded for a successful action to enforce this law.

(e) **Class Actions:** Class actions may be brought for actual damages, but not for a penalty.

(f) **Good Faith Defense:** A defendant who proves a good faith effort to comply with this law has a complete defense to an action for damages or a penalty. Good faith includes continuing effort to review and revise forms to comply with this law.

> **Drafting Note:** This section protects a drafter who makes a conscientious but unsuccessful effort to comply with this law.

(g) **Effect of Noncompliance:** A covered contract can be enforced even if it does not comply with this law. But this law does not bar or limit any claims or defenses already provided by law. A defendant in a suit to enforce a covered contract has the right to counterclaim for violation of this law.

(h) **Statute of Limitations:** No action to enforce this law can be brought more than one year after both parties have completed their duties under the covered contract.

(i) **Non-waiver, Cumulative Remedies:** Rights under this law cannot be reduced or waived by contract. Remedies and penalties under this law are cumulative to each other and to all other remedies and penalties granted by law.

M. STATEMENT OF CLIENT'S RIGHTS IN FLORIDA

In June 1986, the Florida Supreme Court approved the Florida Bar's petition to amend the Florida Bar Rules of Professional Conduct, Rule 4–1.5(D),[40] regarding contingent fee arrangements. The rule now requires a *Statement of Client's Rights,* written in Plain English, to be read and signed by every client engaging an attorney on a contingent fee basis. Here is the required text of the Statement.[41]

STATEMENT OF CLIENT'S RIGHTS, RULES REGULATING THE FLORIDA BAR
494 So.2d 977, 1030–32 (1986).

Before you, the prospective client, arrange a contingent fee agreement with a lawyer, you should understand this statement of your rights as a client. This statement is not a part of the actual contract

---

40. The Florida Bar re Rules Regulating the Florida Bar, 494 So.2d 977, 1028–34 (1986).

41. Gertrude Block drafted the Statement.

between you and your lawyer, but, as a prospective client, you should be aware of these rights:

1.   There is no legal requirement that a lawyer charge a client a set fee or a percentage of money recovered in a case. You, the client, have the right to talk with your lawyer about the proposed fee and to bargain about the rate or percentage as in any other contract. If you do not reach an agreement with one lawyer you may talk with other lawyers.

2.   Any contingent fee contract must be in writing and you have three (3) business days to reconsider the contract. You may cancel the contract without any reason if you notify your lawyer in writing within three (3) business days of signing the contract. If you withdraw from the contract within the first three (3) business days, you do not owe the lawyer a fee although you may be responsible for the lawyer's actual costs during that time. If your lawyer begins to represent you, your lawyer may not withdraw from the case without giving you notice, delivering necessary papers to you, and allowing you time to employ another lawyer. Often, your lawyer must obtain court approval before withdrawing from a case. If you discharge your lawyer without good cause after the three-day period, you may have to pay a fee for work the lawyer has done.

3.   Before hiring a lawyer, you, the client, have the right to know about the lawyer's education, training, and experience. If you ask, the lawyer should tell you specifically about his or her actual experience dealing with cases similar to yours. If you ask, the lawyer should provide information about special training or knowledge and give you this information in writing if you request it.

4.   Before signing a contingent fee contract with you, a lawyer must advise you whether he or she intends to handle your case alone or whether other lawyers will be helping with the case. If your lawyer intends to refer the case to other lawyers he or she should tell you what kind of fee sharing arrangement will be made with the other lawyers. If lawyers from different law firms will represent you, at least one lawyer from each law firm must sign the contingent fee contract.

5.   If your lawyer intends to refer your case to another lawyer or counsel with other lawyers, your lawyer should tell you about that at the beginning. If your lawyer takes the case and later decides to refer it to another lawyer or to associate with other lawyers, you should sign a new contract which includes the new lawyers. You, the client, also have the right to consult with each lawyer working on your case and each lawyer is legally responsible to represent your interests and is legally responsible for the acts of the other lawyers involved in the case.

6.   You, the client, have the right to know in advance how you will need to pay the expenses and the legal fees at the end of the case. If you pay a deposit in advance for costs, you may ask reasonable questions about how the money will be or has been spent and how

much of it remains unspent. Your lawyer should give a reasonable estimate about future necessary costs. If your lawyer agrees to lend or advance you money to prepare or research the case, you have the right to know periodically how much money your lawyer has spent on your behalf. You also have the right to decide, after consulting with your lawyer, how much money is to be spent to prepare a case. If you pay the expenses, you have the right to decide how much to spend. Your lawyer should also inform you whether the fee will be based on the gross amount recovered or on the amount recovered minus the costs.

7. You, the client, have the right to be told by your lawyer about possible adverse consequences if you lose the case. Those adverse consequences might include money which you might have to pay to your lawyer for costs and liability you might have for attorney's fees to the other side.

8. You, the client, have the right to receive and approve a closing statement at the end of the case before you pay any money. The statement must list all of the financial details of the entire case, including the amount recovered, all expenses, and a precise statement of your lawyer's fee. Until you approve the closing statement you need not pay any money to anyone, including your lawyer. You also have the right to have every lawyer or law firm working on your case sign this closing statement.

9. You, the client, have the right to ask your lawyer at reasonable intervals how the case is progressing and to have these questions answered to the best of your lawyer's ability.

10. You, the client, have the right to make the final decision regarding settlement of a case. Your lawyer must notify you of all offers of settlement before and after the trial. Offers during the trial must be immediately communicated and you should consult with your lawyer regarding whether to accept a settlement. However, you must make the final decision to accept or reject a settlement.

11. If at any time, you, the client, believe that your lawyer has charged an excessive or illegal fee, you, the client, have the right to report the matter to The Florida Bar, the agency that oversees the practice and behavior of all lawyers in Florida. For information on how to reach The Florida Bar, call 904–222–5286, or contact the local bar association. Any disagreement between you and your lawyer about a fee can be taken to court and you may wish to hire another lawyer to help you resolve this disagreement. Usually fee disputes must be handled in a separate lawsuit.

_____   _____

Client Signature   Attorney Signature

_____   _____

Date   Date

N. LEGAL DRAFTING COURSES

Law schools have begun to develop much more comprehensive writing programs for students than were common even a few years ago. Legal Research and Writing courses are focusing more on Plain English. Legal Drafting courses received considerable attention at a 1986 conference sponsored by the Legal Writing Institute and the University of Puget Sound, entitled "Legal Writing: The Next Step." Professor Reed Dickerson led a seminar and workshop at Indiana University in 1987 on "Teaching Legal Drafting." Law schools have developed far more interest in Legal Drafting courses than they indicated in the American Bar Foundation's Lammers Report in 1977.[42]

VI. MAIN LESSONS OF THE PLAIN ENGLISH MOVEMENT

The Plain English Movement, whatever the excesses of some of its proponents, continues to have the effect of improving a lot of legal drafting that badly needed improving. The main lessons the movement has taught are collected in a National Institute of Education desk reference manual.[43] It explains and illustrates 25 principles that most affect clarity and ease of comprehension. These principles have been tested in research, and the manual also discusses the research supporting each. See Figure 1 for the 25 principles as listed in the manual's Table of Contents.

Figure 1

Document Design Guidelines *

Section A: Principles for Organizing Text
    A–1.   Put sentences and paragraphs in a logical sequence.
    A–2.   Give an overview of the main ideas of the text.
    A–3.   Use informative headings.
    A–4.   Make a table of contents for long documents.

Section B: Principles for Writing Sentences
    B–1.   Use the active voice.
    B–2.   Use personal pronouns.
    B–3.   Avoid nouns created from verbs; use action verbs.
    B–4.   Avoid whiz-deletions.
    B–5.   Write short sentences.
    B–6.   Do not insert excess information into a sentence.
    B–7.   List conditions separately.
    B–8.   Keep equivalent items parallel.
    B–9.   Avoid unnecessary and difficult words.

---

42. B. Lammers, Legislative Process and Drafting in U.S. Law Schools 10–12 (1977) (American Bar Foundation monograph).

43. B. Felker, F. Pickering, V. Charrow, V. Holland, and J. Redish, Guidelines for Document Designers (1981).

* Reprinted with permission from Guidelines for Document Designers, Document Design Center, American Institutes for Research.

B–10.   Unstring noun strings.

B–11.   Avoid multiple negatives.

Section C: Typographic Principles

C–1.   Use highlighting techniques, but don't overuse them.

C–2.   Use 8 to 10 point type for text.

C–3.   Avoid lines of type that are too long or too short.

C–4.   Use white space in margins and between sections.

C–5.   Use ragged right margins.

C–6.   Avoid using all caps.

Section D: Graphic Principles

D–1.   Use illustrations to supplement text.

D–2.   Use tables to supplement text.

D–3.   Use bar charts to supplement text.

D–4.   Use line graphs to supplement text.

When the document in question is a legal document, some additional principles apply:

A.   Keep substance as the main priority.   Next comes clarity, and then readability.   Fortunately, one of the common side-effects of converting complex material into Plain English is that the drafter ends up re-thinking the content as well as the form.   Restructuring produces reconceptualizing.   Ultimately the substance improves.

B.   Beware of needless synonyms.   In this connection, beware of all attempts to restate anything in different words.   It is an invitation to contradiction and contextual ambiguity.

C.   Scrap legalese, especially the needless "herein," "hereinabove," and "hereinafter" and the malignant "said."   The lawyer afflicted with legalese writes such nonsense as "my said wife" in a will, raising a question about how many wives the testator has.

VII.   THE CONVERSION OF A DOCUMENT: THE FHMA/FHLMC UNIFORM NOTE BEFORE AND AFTER PLAIN ENGLISH

As a review of the principles of Plain English with respect to both format and language, compare the two documents below.

Note 1 is a Federal National Mortgage Association (FHMA, sometimes called Fannie Mae)/Federal Home Loan Mortgage Corporation (FHLMC, sometimes called Freddie Mac) Uniform Note adapted for use in New York in 1975, before Plain English.   The original form was in type so small that it was nearly impossible to read.

Note 2 is the FHMA/FHLMC Uniform Multistate Fixed Rate Note dated 1983.

The results of this conversion were so successful that the new FNMA/FHLMC documents have been used as models by many other lenders.[44]

---

44.   See Browne, above note 3, at 698–
704.

NOTE 1

US $_____   _____ New York
                            City

                                      _____, 19__

FOR VALUE RECEIVED, the undersigned ("Borrower") promise(s) to pay _____, or order, the principal sum of _____ Dollars, with interest on the unpaid principal balance from the date of this Note, until paid, at the rate of _____ percent per annum. Principal and interest shall be payable at _____, or such other place as the Note holder may designate, in consecutive monthly installments of _____ Dollars (US $_____), on the _____ day of each month beginning _____, 19__. Such monthly installments shall continue until the entire indebtedness evidenced by this Note is fully paid, except that any remaining indebtedness, if not sooner paid, shall be due and payable on _____.

If any monthly installment under this Note is not paid when due and remains unpaid after a date specified by a notice to Borrower, the entire principal amount outstanding and accrued interest thereon shall at once become due and payable at the option of the Note holder. The date specified shall not be less than thirty days from the date such notice is mailed. The Note holder may exercise this option to accelerate during any default by Borrower regardless of any prior forbearance. If suit is brought to collect this Note, the Note holder shall be entitled to collect all reasonable costs and expenses of suit, including, but not limited to, reasonable attorney's fees.

Borrower shall pay to the Note holder a late charge of _____ percent of any monthly installment not received by the Note holder within _____ days after the installment is due.

Borrower may prepay the principal amount outstanding in whole or in part. The Note holder may require that any partial prepayments (i) be made on the date monthly installments are due and (ii) be in the amount of that part of one or more monthly installments which would be applicable to principal. Any partial prepayment shall be applied against the principal amount outstanding and shall not postpone the due date of any subsequent monthly installments or change the amount of such installments, unless the Note holder shall otherwise agree in writing. If, within twelve months from the date of this Note, Borrower make(s) any prepayments with money lent to Borrower by a lender other than the Note holder, Borrower shall pay the Note holder _____ percent of the amount by which the sum of prepayments made in such twelve month period exceeds twenty percent of the original principal amount of this Note.

Presentment, notice of dishonor, and protest are hereby waived by all makers, sureties, guarantors and endorsers, and shall be binding upon them and their successors and assigns.

Any notice to Borrower provided for in this Note shall be given by mailing such notice by certified mail addressed to Borrower at the Property Address stated below, or to such other address as Borrower may designate by notice to the Note holder. Any notice to the Note holder shall be given by mailing such notice by certified mail, return receipt requested, to the Note holder at the address stated in the first paragraph of this Note, or at such other address as may have been designated by notice to Borrower.

The indebtedness evidenced by this Note is secured by a Mortgage, dated _____, and reference is made to the Mortgage for rights as to acceleration of the indebtedness evidenced by this Note.

_____   _____

_____   _____

Property Address   (Execute Original Only)

NOTE 2

_____, 19__, _____ , _____
                  (City)   (State)

[Property Address]

1. BORROWER'S PROMISE TO PAY

In return for a loan that I have received, I promise to pay U.S. $_____ (this amount is called "principal"), to the order of the Lender. The Lender is _____. I understand that the Lender may transfer this Note. The Lender or anyone who takes this Note by transfer and who is entitled to receive payments under this Note is called the "Note Holder."

2. INTEREST

Interest will be charged on unpaid principal until the full amount of principal has been paid. I will pay interest at a yearly rate of _____%.

The interest rate required by this Section 2 is the rate I will pay both before and after any default described in Section 6(B) of this Note.

3. PAYMENTS

(A) Time and Place of Payments

I will pay principal and interest by making payments every month.

I will make my monthly payments on the _____ day of each month beginning on _____, 19__. I will make these payments every month until I have paid all of the principal and interest and any other charges described below that I may owe under this Note. My monthly payments will be applied to interest before principal. If, on _____, _____, I still owe amounts under this Note, I will pay those amounts in full on that date, which is called the "maturity date."

I will make my monthly payments at _____ or at a different place if required by the Note Holder.

(B) Amount of Monthly Payments

My monthly payment will be in the amount of U.S. $_____

4. BORROWER'S RIGHT TO PREPAY

I have the right to make payments of principal at any time before they are due. A payment of principal only is known as a "prepayment." When I make a prepayment, I will tell the Note Holder in writing that I am doing so.

I may make a full prepayment or partial prepayments without paying any prepayment charge. The Note Holder will use all of my prepayments to reduce the amount of principal that I owe under this Note. If I make a partial prepayment, there will be no changes in the due date or in the amount of my monthly payment unless the Note Holder agrees in writing to those changes.

5. LOAN CHARGES

If a law, which applies to this loan and which sets maximum loan charges, is finally interpreted so that the interest or other loan charges collected or to be collected in connection with this loan exceed the permitted limits, then: (i) any such loan charge shall be reduced by the amount necessary to reduce the charge to the permitted limit; and (ii) any sums already collected from me which exceeded permitted limits will be refunded to me. The Note Holder may choose to make this refund by reducing the principal I owe under this Note or by making a direct payment to me. If a refund reduces principal, the reduction will be treated as a partial prepayment.

6. BORROWER'S FAILURE TO PAY AS REQUIRED

(A) Late Charge for Overdue Payments

If the Note Holder has not received the full amount of any monthly payment by the end of _____ calendar days after the date it is due, I will pay a late charge to the Note Holder. The amount of the charge will be _____% of my overdue payment of principal and interest. I will pay this late charge promptly but only once on each late payment.

(B) Default

If I do not pay the full amount of each monthly payment on the date it is due, I will be in default.

(C) Notice of Default

If I am in default, the Note Holder may send me a written notice telling me that if I do not pay the overdue amount by a certain date, the Note Holder may require me to pay immediately the full amount of principal which has not been paid and all the interest that I owe on that amount. That date must be at least 30 days after the date on which the notice is delivered or mailed to me.

(D) No Waiver By Note Holder

Even if, at a time when I am in default, the Note Holder does not require me to pay immediately in full as described above, the Note Holder will still have the right to do so if I am in default at a later time.

(E) Payment of Note Holder's Costs and Expenses

If the Note Holder has required me to pay immediately in full as described above, the Note Holder will have the right to be paid back by me for all of its costs and expenses in enforcing this Note to the extent not prohibited by applicable law. Those expenses include, for example, reasonable attorneys' fees.

7. GIVING OF NOTICES

Unless applicable law requires a different method, any notice that must be given to me under this Note will be given by delivering it or by mailing it by first class mail to me at the Property Address above or at a different address if I give the Note Holder a notice of my different address.

Any notice that must be given to the Note Holder under this Note will be given by mailing it by first class mail to the Note Holder at the address stated in Section 3(A) above or at a different address if I am given a notice of that different address.

8. OBLIGATIONS OF PERSONS UNDER THIS NOTE

If more than one person signs this Note, each person is fully and personally obligated to keep all of the promises made in this Note, including the promise to pay the full amount owed. Any person who is a guarantor, surety or endorser of this Note is also obligated to do these things. Any person who takes over these obligations, including the obligations of a guarantor, surety or endorser of this Note, is also obligated to keep all of the promises made in this Note. The Note Holder may enforce its rights under this Note against each person individually or against all of us together. This means that any one of us may be required to pay all of the amounts owed under this Note.

9. WAIVERS

I and any other person who has obligations under this Note waive the rights of presentment and notice of dishonor. "Presentment" means the right to require the Note Holder to demand payment of amounts due. "Notice of dishonor" means the right to require the Note Holder to give notice to other persons that amounts due have not been paid.

10. UNIFORM SECURED NOTE

This Note is a uniform instrument with limited variations in some jurisdictions. In addition to the protections given to the Note Holder under this Note, a Mortgage, Deed of Trust or Security Deed (the "Security Instrument"), dated the same date as this Note, protects the

Note Holder from possible losses which might result if I do not keep the promises which I make in this Note. That Security Instrument describes how and under what conditions I may be required to make immediate payment in full of all amounts I owe under this Note. Some of those conditions are described as follows:

Transfer of the Property or a Beneficial Interest in Borrower. If all or any part of the Property or any interest in it is sold or transferred (or if a beneficial interest in Borrower is sold or transferred and Borrower is not a natural person) without Lender's prior written consent, Lender may, at its option, require immediate payment in full of all sums secured by this Security Instrument. However, this option shall not be exercised by Lender if exercise is prohibited by federal law as of the date of this Security Instrument.

If Lender exercises this option, Lender shall give Borrower notice of acceleration. The notice shall provide a period of not less than 30 days from the date the notice is delivered or mailed within which Borrower must pay all sums secured by this Security Instrument. If Borrower fails to pay these sums prior to the expiration of this period, Lender may invoke any remedies permitted by this Security Instrument without further notice or demand on Borrower.

WITNESS THE HAND(S) AND SEAL(S) OF THE UNDERSIGNED.

_____ (Seal)
Borrower

_____ (Seal)
Borrower

_____ (Seal)
Borrower

_____ (Seal)
Borrower

[*Sign Original Only*]

VIII. THE GOAL OF DRAFTING IN PLAIN ENGLISH

In his *Persuasive Writing* column in the ABA Journal, Irving Younger has this to say about legalese such as "hereinafter" and "said": "These are show-off words. Anyone who uses them wants the world to see that it's a lawyer talking, for only lawyers use these words. There's no need to remind the world that you're a lawyer ∗ ∗ ∗."[45]

45. Younger, Symptoms of Bad Writing, 72 ABA J. 113 (May 1, 1986).

When the drafter reaches the stage of choosing actual wording, there is particular temptation to adopt the wording of old

The ultimate goal of drafting documents in Plain English is to produce understanding and thus to prevent disputes. The Plain English approach is not new. Here is what LeRoy Marceau had to say in 1965. Although he writes expressly about union contracts, his checklist spells out the characteristics of well drafted documents in general.

L. MARCEAU, DRAFTING A UNION CONTRACT
xxvii–xxviii (1965).*

* * * The ideal union contract, while difficult to create, is not difficult to envision. It would have the following characteristics:

1.   When a reader wants to learn what the rule is, on any subject the contract covers, an index or table of contents will quickly refer him to the page the rule is on.

2.   When he turns to the page, he will find a prominent caption showing the place on the page where the rule appears.

3.   Everything that the contract has to say about the subject will be said (or at least referred to) at that place. The reader may be referred to other sections for details, but the rule set forth will be reasonably complete.

4.   The language setting forth the rule will be subject to only one possible interpretation.

5.   It will be so clear-cut that one can easily tell whether it applies to the existing facts. "6 a.m.," for example, is preferable to "dawn."

6.   The rule set forth will accurately state what the parties have agreed on.

7.   The rule will be stated simply enough to be understood by the people who can be expected to use the contract.

8.   The rule will be short enough that those people can grasp it readily, and possibly remember it.

9.   The rule will be adaptable to changing conditions. That is, despite the normal changes that can be expected to occur, the rule will continue to meet the desires of the parties; and will require amendment only when a particularly far-reaching change occurs.

10.   When the rule must be amended, it will be possible to amend it without changing many other parts of the contract.

Notice that the foregoing are characteristics of a *complete* contract rather than of any single isolated provision. Good drafting implies a complete job. There is no way to make one section of a contract

forms for boilerplate clauses. The beginning of documents is a common location for boilerplate. Because getting started on any new piece of writing is often the hardest part, many documents still begin with traditional legalese from old forms. For analysis of how much opening boilerplate hangs on out of tradition rather than out of legal necessity, and for demonstrations of how to convert to simpler beginnings with just as valid legal effect, see Kirk, Legal Drafting: How Should a Document Begin? 3 Tex.Tech L.Rev. 233, 233–38, 247–63 (1972).

adequate if the other sections are to remain nebulous. For a contract is an integrated whole; it is not a mere collection of unrelated provisions. Since each provision will be interpreted in the light of the whole, one cannot hope to draft the provision unless there is a foundation and framework of the contract for him to fit it into. Many a provision which might be a masterpiece if standing alone has become a monstrosity when injected into a contract with which it does not mesh. It follows that one who starts with a nebulous contract cannot hope to transform it into an orderly contract by a series of amendments. To create a masterpiece one must start with a fresh canvas.

IX. PROBLEMS

PROBLEM 1

Below are several Truth in Lending statements drafted by creditors to comply with federal and state law. How readable is each one? Do they go so far in the interest of readable format that they sacrifice accuracy or completeness of substance? What Plain English features do you find in these statements that are worth using in legal drafting generally? Which features, if any, would you avoid other than in consumer documents?

STATEMENT 1

IN CASE OF ERRORS OR INQUIRIES ABOUT YOUR BILL

The Federal Truth in Lending Act requires prompt correction of billing mistakes.
1. If you want to preserve your rights under the Act, here's what to do if you think your bill is wrong or if you need more information about an item on your bill:
    a. Do not write on the bill. On a separate sheet of paper, write (you may telephone your inquiry but *doing so will not preserve your rights under this law*) the following:
        i. Your name and account number.
        ii. A description of the error and an explanation (to the extent you can explain) why you believe it is an error. If you only need more information, explain the item you are not sure about and, if you wish, ask for evidence of the charge, such as a copy of the charge slip. Do not send in your copy of a sales slip or other document unless you have a duplicate copy for your records.
        iii. The dollar amount of the suspected error.
        iv. Any other information (such as your address) which you think will help the Bank to identify you or the reason for your complaint or inquiry.
    b. Send your billing error notice to the address on your bill which is listed after the words "Send inquiries to:".
    Mail it as soon as you can, but in any case, early enough to reach the Bank within 60 days after the bill was mailed to you. If you have authorized your bank to automatically pay from your checking or savings account any credit card bills from that bank, you can stop or reverse payment on any amount you think is wrong by mailing your notice so the Bank receives it within 16 days after the bill was sent to you. However,

you do not have to meet this 16–day deadline to get the Bank to investigate your billing error claim.

2.   The Bank must acknowledge all letters pointing out possible errors within 30 days of receipt, unless the Bank is able to correct your bill during that 30 days. Within 90 days after receiving your letter, the Bank must either correct the error or explain why the Bank believes the bill was correct.   Once the Bank has explained the bill, the Bank has no further obligation to you even though you still believe that there is an error, except as provided in paragraph 5 below.

3.   After the Bank has been notified, neither the Bank nor an attorney nor a collection agency may send you collection letters or take other collection action with respect to the amount in dispute; but periodic statements may be sent to you, and the disputed amount can be applied against your credit limit.   You cannot be threatened with damage to your credit rating or sued for the amount in question, nor can the disputed amount be reported to a credit bureau or to other creditors as delinquent until the Bank has answered your inquiry.   *However, you remain obligated to pay the parts of your bill not in dispute.*

4.   If it is determined that the Bank has made a mistake on your bill, you will not have to pay any finance charges on any disputed amount.   If it turns out that the Bank has not made an error, you may have to pay finance charges on the amount in dispute, and you will have to make up any missed minimum or required payments on the disputed amount.   Unless you have agreed that your bill was correct, the Bank must send you a written notification of what you owe;   and if it is determined that the Bank did make a mistake in billing the disputed amount, you must be given the time to pay which you normally are given to pay undisputed amounts before any more finance charges or late payment charges on the disputed amount can be charged to you.

5.   If the Bank's explanation does not satisfy you and you notify the Bank *in writing* within *10* days after you receive its explanation that you still refuse to pay the disputed amount, the Bank may report you to credit bureaus and other creditors and may pursue regular collection procedures.   But the Bank must also report that you think you do not owe the money, and the Bank must let you know to whom such reports were made.   Once the matter has been settled between you and the Bank, the Bank must notify those to whom the Bank reported you as delinquent of the subsequent resolution.

6.   If the Bank does not follow these rules, the Bank is not allowed to collect the first $50 of the disputed amount and finance charges, even if the bill turns out to be correct.

7.   If you have a problem with property or services purchased with a credit card, you may have the right not to pay the remaining amount due on them, if you first try in good faith to return them or give the merchant a chance to correct the problem. There are two limitations on this right:

    a.   You must have bought them in your home state or if not within your home state within 100 miles of your current mailing address; and

    b.   The purchase price must have been more than $50.

However, these limitations do not apply if the merchant is owned or operated by the Bank, or if the Bank mailed you the advertisement for the property or services.

STATEMENT 2

In Case of Errors or Inquiries About Your Bill

The Federal Truth in Lending Act requires prompt correction of billing mistakes. The Act's provisions, which are summarized below with respect to its billing error resolution procedures, will control in the event of conflict with your Agreement.

1. If you want to preserve your rights under the Act, here's what to do if you think your bill is wrong or if you need more information about an item on your bill:

   a. Do not write on the bill. On a separate sheet of paper write (you may telephone your inquiry but **doing so will not preserve your rights under this law,**) the following:

      i. Your name and account number.

      ii. A description of the error and an explanation (to the extent you can explain) why you believe it is an error.

      If you only need more information, explain the item you are not sure about and, if you wish, ask for evidence of the charge such as a copy of the charge slip or Charge Card check. Do not send in your copy of a sales slip or other document unless you have a duplicate copy for your records.

      iii. The dollar amount of the suspected error.

      iv. Any other information (such as your address) which you think will help the Bank with which you have your agreement, (hereinafter called "Bank") to identify you or the reason for your complaint or inquiry.

   b. Send your billing error notice to the address on your bill which is listed after the words: "Send Inquiries To:".

      Mail it as soon as you can, but in any case, early enough to reach the Bank within 60 days after the bill was mailed to you. If you have authorized your Bank to automatically pay from your checking or savings account any credit card bills from that Bank, you can stop or reverse payment on any amount you think is wrong by mailing your notice so the Bank receives it within 16 days after the bill was sent to you. However, you do not have to meet this 16–day deadline to get the Bank to investigate your billing error claim.

2. The Bank must acknowledge all letters pointing out possible errors within 30 days of receipt, unless the Bank is able to correct your bill during that 30 days. Within 90 days after receiving your letter, the Bank must either correct the error or explain why the Bank believes the bill was correct. Once the Bank has explained the bill, the Bank has no further obligation to you even though you still believe that there is an error, except as provided in paragraph 5 below.

3. After the Bank has been notified, neither the Bank nor an attorney nor a collection agency may send you collection letters or take other collection action with respect to the amount in dispute; but periodic statements may be sent to you, and the disputed amount can be applied against your credit limit. You cannot be threatened with damage to your credit rating or sued for the amount in question, nor can the disputed amount be reported to a credit bureau or to other creditors as delinquent until the Bank has answered your inquiry. **However, you remain obligated to pay the parts of your bill not in dispute.**

4. If it is determined that the Bank has made a mistake on your bill, you will not have to pay any finance charges on any disputed amount. If it turns out that the Bank has not made an error, you may have to pay finance charges on the amount in dispute, and you will have to make up any missed minimum or required payments on the disputed amount. Unless you have agreed that your bill was correct, the Bank must send you a written notification of what you owe; and if it is determined that the Bank did make a mistake in billing the disputed amount, you must be given the time to pay which you normally are given to pay undisputed amounts before any more finance charges or late payment charges on the disputed amount can be charged to you.

5. If the Bank's explanation does not satisfy you and you notify the Bank **in writing** within 10 days after you receive its explanation that you still refuse to pay the disputed amount, the Bank may report you to credit bureaus and other creditors and may pursue regular collection procedures. But the Bank must also report that you think you do not owe the money, and the Bank must let you know to whom such reports were made. Once the matter has been settled between you and the Bank, the Bank must notify those to whom the Bank reported you as delinquent of the subsequent resolution.

6. If the Bank does not follow these rules, the Bank is not allowed to collect the first $50 of the disputed amount and finance charges, even if the bill turns out to be correct.

7. If you have a problem with property or services purchased with a credit card, you may have the right not to pay the remaining amount due on them, if you first try in good faith to return them or give the merchant a chance to correct the problem. There are two limitations on this right:

    a. You must have bought them in your home state or if not within your home state within 100 miles of your current mailing address; and

    b. The purchase price must have been more than $50.

However, these limitations do not apply if the merchant is owned or operated by the Bank, or if the Bank mailed you the advertisement for the property or services.

STATEMENT 3

YOUR BILLING RIGHTS

KEEP THIS NOTICE FOR FUTURE USE

This notice contains important information about your rights and our responsibilities under the Fair Credit Billing Act.

Notify Us in Case of Errors or Questions About Your Bill:

If you think your bill is wrong, or if you need more information about a transaction on your bill, write us on a separate sheet at the address listed on the front of your bill. Write to us as soon as possible. We must hear from you no later than 60 days after we sent you the first bill on which the error or problem appeared. You can telephone us, but doing so will not preserve your rights.

In your letter, give us the following information:

*   Your name and account number.
*   The dollar amount of the suspected error.
*   Describe the error and explain, if you can, why you believe there is an error.
    (A) Do not send in your copy of a sales or credit slip unless you have a duplicate copy for your records.
    (B) However, if additional information is needed, describe the item in question. The Bank may impose a charge of up to $5 for each copy of a sales slip, requested by you for your records, to help defray cost to the Bank for providing the copy(s).

If you have authorized us to pay your credit card bill automatically from your savings or checking account, you can stop the payment on any amount you think is wrong. To stop the payment your letter must reach us three business days before the automatic payment is scheduled to occur.

Your Rights and Our Responsibilities After We Receive Your Written Notice:

We must acknowledge your letter within 30 days, unless we have corrected the error by then. Within 90 days, we must either correct the error or explain why we believe the bill was correct.

After we receive your letter, we cannot try to collect any amount you question, or report you as delinquent. We can continue to bill you for the amount you question, including finance charges, and we can apply any unpaid amount against your credit limit. You do not have to pay any questioned amount while we are investigating, but you are still obligated to pay the parts of your bill that are not in question.

If we find that we made a mistake on your bill, you will not have to pay any finance charges related to any questioned amount. If we didn't make a mistake, you may have to pay finance charges, and you will have to make up any missed payments on the questioned amount. In either case, we will send you a statement of the amount you owe and the date that it is due.

If you fail to pay the amount that we think you owe, we may report you as delinquent. However, if our explanation does not satisfy you and you write to us within ten days telling us that you still refuse to pay, we must tell anyone we report you to that you have a question about your bill. And, we must tell you the name of anyone we reported you to. We must tell anyone we report you to that the matter has been settled between us when it finally is.

If we don't follow these rules, we can't collect the first $50 of the questioned amount, even if your bill was correct.

Special Rule for Credit Card Purchases:

If you have a problem with the quality of property or services that you purchased with a credit card, and you have tried in good faith to correct the problem with the merchant, you may have the right not to pay the remaining amount due on the property or services. There are two limitations on this right:

    (a) You must have made the purchase in your home state or, if not within your home state, within 100 miles of your current mailing address; and

    (b) The purchase price must have been more than $50.

These limitations do not apply if we own or operate the merchant, or if we mailed you the advertisement for the property or services.

STATEMENT 4

In Case of Errors or Inquiries About Your Bill

The Federal Truth in Lending Act, the _____ Truth-in-Lending Act and the _____ Uniform Consumer Credit Code requires prompt correction of billing mistakes.

1.   If you want to preserve your rights under the Act, here's what to do if you think your bill is wrong or if you need more information about an item on your bill:

    a.   Do not write on the bill. On a separate sheet of paper write (you may telephone your inquiry but <u>doing so will not preserve your rights under this law)</u> the following:

        i. Your name and account number.

        ii. A description of the error and an explanation (to the extent you can explain) why you believe it is an error.

            If you only need more information, explain the item you are not sure about and, if you wish, ask for evidence of the charge such as a copy of the charge slip. Do not send in your copy of a sales slip or other document unless you have a duplicate copy for your records.

        iii. The dollar amount of the suspected error.

        iv. Any other information (such as your address) which you think will help the creditor to identify you or the reason for your complaint or inquiry.

    b.   Send your billing error notice to:

        Mail it as soon as you can, but in any case, early enough to reach the creditor within 60 days after the bill was mailed to you. If you have authorized your bank to automatically pay from your checking or savings account any credit card bills from that bank, you can stop or reverse payment on any amount you think is wrong by mailing your notice so the creditor receives it within 16 days after the bill was sent to you. However, you do not have to meet this 16–day deadline to get the creditor to investigate your billing error claim.

2. The creditor must acknowledge all letters pointing out possible errors within 30 days of receipt, unless the creditor is able to correct your bill during that 30 days. Within 90 days after receiving your letter, the creditor must either correct the error or explain why the creditor believes the bill was correct. Once the creditor has explained the bill, the creditor has no further obligation to you even though you still believe that there is an error, except as provided in paragraph 5 below.

3. After the creditor has been notified, neither the creditor nor an attorney nor a collection agency may send you collection letters or take other collection action with respect to the amount in dispute; but periodic statements may be sent to you, and the disputed amount can be applied against your credit limit. You cannot be threatened with damage to your credit rating or sued for the amount in question, nor can the disputed amount be reported to a credit bureau or to other creditors as delinquent until the creditor has answered your inquiry. However, you remain obligated to pay the parts of your bill not in dispute.

NOTICE: **See reverse side for important information regarding your rights to dispute billing errors.**

STATEMENT 5

In case of errors or inquiries about your bill.

The Federal Truth in Lending Act and the _____ Uniform Consumer Credit Code require prompt correction of billing mistakes.

1. If you want to preserve your rights under the Act, here's what to do if you think your bill is wrong or if you need more information about an item on your bill:

a. Do not write on the bill. On a separate sheet of paper write (you may telephone your inquiry but **doing so will not preserve your rights under this law**) the following:

  i. Your name and account number.

  ii. A description of the error and an explanation (to the extent you can explain) why you believe it is in error.

  If you only need more information, explain the item you are not sure about and, if you wish, ask for evidence of the charge such as a copy of the charge slip. Do not send in your copy of a sales slip or other document unless you have a duplicate copy for your records.

  iii. The dollar amount of the suspected error.

  iv. Any other information (such as your address) which you think will help identify you or the reason for your complaint or inquiry.

b. Send your billing error notice to: _____

  Mail it as soon as you can, but in any case, early enough to reach _____ within 60 days after the bill was mailed to you.

2. _____ must acknowledge all letters pointing out possible errors within 30 days of receipt, unless we are able to correct your bill during that 30 days. Within 90 days after receiving your letter _____ must either correct the error or explain why we believe the bill was correct. Once we have explained the bill, there is no further obligation to you even though you still believe that there is an error, except as provided in paragraph 5 below.

3. After _____ has been notified, neither we nor an attorney nor a collection agency may send you collection letters or take other collection action with respect to the amount in dispute. Periodic statements may be sent to you. You cannot be threatened with damage to your credit rating or sued for the amount in question, nor can the disputed amount be reported to a credit bureau or to other creditors as

delinquent until we have answered your inquiry. **However, you remain obligated to pay the parts of your bill not in dispute.**

4. If it is determined that _____ has made a mistake on your bill, you will not have to pay any finance charges on any disputed amount. If it turns out that we have not made an error, you may have to pay finance charges on the amount in dispute, and you will have to make up any required payments on the disputed amount. Unless you have agreed that your bill was correct, we must send you a written notification of what you owe; and if it is determined that we did make a mistake in billing the disputed amount, you must be given the time to pay which you normally are given to pay undisputed amounts before any more late payment finance charges on the disputed amount can be charged to you.

5. If _____ explanation does not satisfy you and you notify us **in writing** within 10 days after you receive the explanation that you still refuse to pay the disputed amount, _____ may report you to credit bureaus and other creditors and may pursue regular collection procedures. But we must also report that you think you do not owe the money, and we must let you know to whom such reports were made. Once the matter has been settled between you and _____, we must notify those to whom we reported you as a delinquent of the subsequent resolution.

6. If _____ does not follow these rules, we are not allowed to collect the first $50 of the disputed amount and finance charges, even if the bill turns out to be correct.

7. If you have a problem with property or services purchased with a credit card, you may have the right not to pay the remaining amount due on them, if you first try in good faith to return them or give the seller a chance to correct the problem. There are two limitations on this right:

    a. You must have bought them in your home state or if not within your home state within 100 miles of your current mailing address; and

    b. The purchase price must have been more than $50.

        However, these limitations do not apply if the seller is owned or operated by _____, or if _____ mailed you the advertisement for the property or services.

PROBLEM 2

Redraft the following apartment lease in Plain English.

Apartment Lease

1 THIS LEASE, made this _____ day of _____ A.D., 19__, by and
2 between _____, owner and proprietor of the _____ or _____ his
3 duly authorized agent, both of _____, hereinafter called the Lessor,
4 and _____ of _____ hereinafter called the Lessee _____.

5 WITNESSETH, That in consideration of the sum of _____ Dollars
6 paid by the Lessee _____, which said sum is hereby acknowledged to
7 have been received as paid payment of rents accruing under this Lease,
8 and in the further consideration of the covenants, agreements and
9 conditions herein contained, on the part of the Lessee _____ to be
10 kept, done and performed, the said Lessor does hereby lease to the
11 Lessee _____ Apartment No. _____ on the _____ floor in the
12 _____, situated _____, with the full understanding that _____
13 family consists of _____ adults and _____ child _____ and no
14 more.

15 TO HAVE AND TO HOLD THE SAME for the full term of _____
16 from the _____ day of _____ A.D., 19__, to the _____ day of

17 _____, 19__, the said Lessee _____ yielding and paying to the Lessor
18 therefor the total rent of _____ Dollars.

19   And the said Lessee _____ covenant _____ with the Lessor to
20 pay said rent in advance in _____ payments, the first payment of
21 _____ Dollars on the _____ day of _____ A.D., 19__, which said
22 sum has been paid and acknowledged herein, and the remaining pay-
23 ments as follows, namely:

24 _____

25 _____

26 _____

27 _____

28 _____.

29   AND THE SAID LESSEE _____ further covenant _____ and
30 agree _____ not to use nor permit to be used the premises leased for
31 any illegal, immoral or improper purposes; not to make nor permit any
32 disturbance, noise or annoyance whatsoever detrimental to the prem-
33 ises or to the comfort and peace of any of the inhabitants of said
34 building or its neighbors, and particularly, said Lessee _____ agree
35 _____ that under no circumstances will _____ allow or
36 permit their child or children to play in the halls, lobby, porches or
37 staircases of said building or in any other way to annoy the tenants of
38 other Apartments, and the Lessor does hereby receive the right to
39 terminate this lease at any time this condition is permitted to exist;
40 not to assign this lease nor sub-let any part of the premises here leased,
41 except with the written consent of the owner and only at a price which
42 shall be an amount not less than the proportional rate for the full term;
43 not to use said premises for any other purpose than as a private
44 dwelling for the members of _____ family; to pay the cost of repairing
45 all damage to the apartment occasioned by the Lessee _____ or any of
46 _____ family; and especially the cost of removing foreign substances
47 from toilets and sinks.

48   AND THE LESSEE _____ hereby covenant _____ and agree
49 _____ that if default is made in the payment of rent as above set forth
50 or any part thereof, or if said Lessee _____ or _____ family shall
51 violate any of the covenants, agreements and conditions of this lease,
52 then the Lessee _____ shall become a tenant at sufferance, hereby
53 waiving all right of notice to vacate said premises, and the Lessor shall
54 be entitled to reenter and retake possession immediately of the demised
55 premises, and the entire rent for the rental period next ensuing shall at
56 once be due and payable and may forthwith be collected by distress or
57 otherwise as provided by law; and will at the end of _____ term
58 without demand quietly and peaceably deliver up the possession of said
59 premises in as good condition as they now are (ordinary wear and the
60 decay and damage by fire or the elements only excepted).

61   SAID LESSEE _____ hereby acknowledges receipt of the articles
62 enumerated on the reverse side of this lease and by agreement made a
63 part hereof and further covenants and agrees to assume full responsi-

64 bility for said articles and to make good any damage or deficiency
65 therein at the expiration of this lease; to return all linens clean and
66 pay for cleaning of same upon termination of lease.

67 And the Lessor, upon performance of the said covenants, agree-
68 ments and conditions by said Lessee _____ hereby covenants that the
69 said Lessee _____ shall have the quiet and peaceable enjoyment of
70 said premises, herein reserving the right to inspect said premises so
71 often as shall be deemed necessary and to show the apartment at
72 reasonable hours to prospective tenants during the thirty days next
73 prior to the expiration of this lease.

74 Witness our hands and seals this _____ day of _____ A.D., 19__.
75 Signed and sealed in the presence of:

76 _____ _____ (Seal)
77   Lessor.

78 _____ _____ (Seal)
79   Agent for Lessor.

80 _____ _____ (Seal)
81   Lessee.

82 _____ _____ (Seal)
83   Lessee.

PROBLEM 3

Below are three different release forms. Read them first to get an idea of the contents. Then draft a release form in Plain English, using these forms as models only to the extent that their language and format measure up to Plain English standards.

RELEASE

1   _____ 19__
2 In consideration of _____ dollars to _____ paid by _____ the
3 receipt whereof is hereby acknowledged _____ hereby remise, release
4 and forever discharge the said _____
5 from all debts, demands, actions, causes of action, suits, dues, sum and
6 sums of money, accounts reckonings, bonds, specialties, covenants,
7 contracts, controversies, agreements, promises, doings, omissions, vari-
8 ances, damages, extents, executions and liabilities and any and all
9 other claims of every kind, nature and description whatsoever, both in
10 LAW and EQUITY, which against the said _____
11 or _____ heirs, executors, administrators, successors or assigns
12 _____ now have or ever had from the beginning of the world to this
13 date and more especially on account of _____
14 _____
15 _____
16 _____

17 _____
18 _____

19 Executed as a sealed instrument this day and year above written.

20 Signed in presence of   _____

21 _____   _____

RELEASE AND SETTLEMENT OF CLAIM

1   **For the sole consideration of** _____ Dollars, to me/us in hand
2 paid, the receipt of which is hereby acknowledged, I/we _____, Releas-
3 or(s), being over 21 years of age, do hereby release, and forever dis-
4 charge _____,
5 Releasee(s) and all other persons, firms or corporations from any and
6 all claims, demands, rights, actions or causes of action on account of or
7 in any way growing out of any and all personal injuries (and conse-
8 quences thereof, including death, and specifically including, also, any
9 injuries which may exist, but which at this time are unknown and
10 unanticipated and which may develop at some time in the future, and
11 all unforeseen developments arising from known injuries) and any and
12 all property damage resulting or to result from an accident that
13 occurred on or about the _____ day of _____ 19__, and do hereby for
14 myself/ourselves, my/our heirs, executors, administrators, successors,
15 assigns and next of kin covenant to indemnify and save harmless the
16 said above-named Releasee(s) and said persons, firms or corporations
17 above-referred to, from all claims, demands, costs, loss of services,
18 expenses, and compensation on account of or in any way growing out of
19 said accident or its results both to person and property.

20   **It is expressly understood and agreed that** the acceptance of the
21 said above amount is in full accord and satisfaction of a disputed claim,
22 and that the payment of the said above amount is not an admission of
23 liability.

24   **In Witness Whereof,** I/we have hereunto set my/our hand and
25 seal this _____ day of _____ 19__.

26   SIGNATURE: _____(L.S.)

27   _____(L.S.)

28   CERTIFICATE OF WITNESSES

29   **We certify that this release** was signed in our presence by the
30 above who acknowledged that he/they understood it fully.

31 Witness _____   Witness _____

32 Address _____   Address _____

RELEASE OF ALL CLAIMS

1   FOR AND IN CONSIDERATION OF the payment to me/us of the
2 sum of Dollars ($_____), and other good and valuable consideration,
3 I/we, being of lawful age, have released and discharged, and by these
4 presents do for myself/ourselves, my/our heirs, executors, administra-
5 tors and assigns, release, acquit and forever discharge _____
6 and any and all other persons, firms and corporations of and from any
7 and all actions, causes of action, claims or demands for damages, costs,
8 loss of use, loss of services, expenses, compensation, consequential
9 damage or any other thing whatsoever on account of, or in any way
10 growing out of, any and all known and unknown personal injuries and
11 death and property damage resulting or to result from an occurrence or
12 accident that happened on or about the _____ day of _____, 19__, at
13 or near_____.

14   I/we hereby acknowledge and assume all risk, chance or hazard
15 that the said injuries or damage may be or become permanent, progres-
16 sive, greater, or more extensive than is now known, anticipated or
17 expected. No promise or inducement which is not herein expressed has
18 been made to me/us, and in executing this release I/we do not rely
19 upon any statement or representation made by any person, firm or
20 corporation, hereby released, or any agent, physician, doctor or any
21 other person representing them or any of them, concerning the nature,
22 extent or duration of said damages or losses or the legal liability
23 therefor.

24   I/we understand that this settlement is the compromise of a
25 doubtful and disputed claim, and that the payment is not to be con-
26 strued as an admission of liability on the part of the persons, firms and
27 corporations hereby released by whom liability is expressly denied.

28   This release contains the ENTIRE AGREEMENT between the
29 parties hereto, and the terms of this release are contractual and not a
30 mere recital.

31   I/we further state that I/we have carefully read the foregoing
32 release and know the contents thereof, and I/we sign the same as my/
33 our own free act.

34   WITNESS _____ hand and seal this _____ day of _____, 19__.
35 **WITNESSES**

36   **CAUTION! READ BEFORE SIGNING**

37 _____
38 ADDRESS_____   }   _____
39 _____
40 ADDRESS_____   _____

Chapter 5

CONCEPTS AND CONSTRUCTS: THE DRAFTING PROCESS

Drafting is a process, but it is misleading to spell out its steps in any particular order, for that might suggest that the steps are, or should be, the same for everybody every time. That is not the case, and yet it is possible to make some suggestions based on the experience of successful practitioners. Also, it is important to recognize that drafting is itself part of a larger planning process that lawyers undertake for their clients. The steps do not occur separately, one at a time, but are inextricably linked.[1]

I. SOME CONTINUING CONCERNS

Some matters that the drafter must regard as continuing concerns are beyond the scope of this book.

A. LEGAL CONTEXT

The external legal context in which the contract or other document is to function should figure into all parts of the planning. It goes without saying that the drafter needs to research all applicable law thoroughly.

B. CIRCUMSTANTIAL CONTEXT

The drafter should become as fully informed as possible about the circumstantial context in which the document is to operate, such as the customs of any businesses involved. In this regard, it may be necessary to consult experts on technical matters outside the drafter's realm of expertise.

---

1. See Macneil, A Primer of Contract Planning, 48 S.Cal.L.Rev. 627, 643 (1975). This chapter reflects much of Macneil's discussion at 643–51. Although Macneil focuses expressly on contracts, the process also applies to other planning documents. See also R. Dick, Legal Drafting 29–40 (2d ed. 1985); R. Dickerson, The Fundamentals of Legal Drafting 51–69 (2d ed. 1986).

C. NEGOTIATING CONTEXT

Even one who is a novice at negotiation needs to keep in mind that it is not done exclusively before the drafting starts. Moreover, it helps to keep in mind that one of the effects of the continuing nature of negotiation is that all plans are to some extent subject to change.

II. GETTING THE FACTS

The lawyer engaged in planning needs to gather facts about the parties' goals and also about the means by which they expect to attain those goals. This is not merely a matter of gathering information. As the lawyer begins to ask questions, that process can give new shape to the facts. Pursuing details about means, for instance, can produce new perceptions about goals. At this stage the lawyer might uncover potential conflicts of interest among multiple parties. The lawyer also might discover that the client has not planned carefully enough. Advising the client about such matters requires tact because the client may think the lawyer too cautious about remote possibilities and what the client regards as minor risks.

A. GENERATING QUESTIONS TO ASK THE CLIENT

When preparing to draft a document for an individual client, the drafter should regard that client as one of the most important resources. "Researching the client" should not be left to casual conversation. It is a good idea to have questions written down to make sure nothing is left out. Many lawyers develop checklists for frequently drafted documents such as wills, corporate by-laws, or marital separation agreements. The more work one does in a given field, the more refined the checklist or intake questionnaire becomes.

Questions can be generated from a number of sources, such as:

1. Research into the law on the subject.

2. Conversations with experts on any technical matters involved.

3. Explication of any document already in use by the client and now to be redrafted.

4. Study of similar documents or forms used by others.

5. Study of checklists or questionnaires used by others. To demonstrate how long and comprehensive checklists can be, here is a sample checklist for drafting a partnership agreement.

R. DICK, LEGAL DRAFTING

40–46 (2d ed. 1985).*

CHECK–LIST FOR PARTNERSHIP AGREEMENT

1. *Name*

(1) What is the proposed name of the partnership?

(2) Is this name likely to be confused with any other well-known names in this type of business?

2. *Partners*

(1) What are the names and addresses of all partners?

(2) Are all partners over the age of majority?

3. *Business Aspects*

(1) What type of business is proposed?

(2) Will the partnership require leased premises or ownership of buildings and what will be needed for inventory, furniture, fixtures and equipment?

(3) Do one or more of the partners already have a suitable lease or own a suitable building? If not, how much cash outlay is required for periodic payments under a lease or for a purchase? If a purchase is in the offing, will there be mortgage financing? Will the building be acquired as partnership property? Can the partnership realistically meet mortgage payments, utility costs, salaries and other expenses?

(4) Have the proposed partners discussed appropriate banking arrangements and fixed on a suitable line of credit for this type of business?

(5) If expansion of business is contemplated, where will the capital come from for expansion?

(6) What are the financial backgrounds and resources of the partners?

(7) Is the partnership to take over an existing business? If so, are properties of that business to be transferred into the partnership? Are any insurance policies, manufacturing licenses or royalty agreements to be assigned to the partnership? Will the new partnership assume all debts and liabilities of an existing business? Will the fiscal year and auditors for the existing business be the same for the new partnership? Will the existing business be formally dissolved?

(8) Will the partnership business be one with a high element of risk? If so, would a corporation be preferable?

4. *Principal place of business*

(1) Where will the partnership locate?

(2) Will there be branch offices in the same province or in other provinces?

5. *Life of partnership*

(1) When will the partnership begin?

(2) How long is the partnership expected to last? If indefinitely, then what are the contingencies for dissolution?

6. *Capital contributions, percentage division of profits and percentage interests*

(1) What is each partner expected to contribute in money or property? Is there a time limit when contributions are to be made? If contributions are periodic what is the interest rate to be charged, if any, on the unpaid balance?

(2) Is any property being loaned by a partner (such as a library, vehicles or tools)?

(3) What is the value of any property contributions made by a partner?

(4) Is part of the profits to be left in the partnership business as extra capital?

(5) What is the percentage division of the initial money and property contributions?

(6) If the partnership is an existing one, what percentage interest has each partner in the new partnership after adding new partners? In other words, what percentage of capital, goodwill, work in progress, receivables and furniture and fixtures will each partner own in the new partnership?

(7) Does goodwill have any value at all in this type of partnership? If so, should a formula be inserted in the agreement for calculation of goodwill on the admission of new partners?

(8) Does the percentage division of profits correspond to the percentage ownership interest in the partnership? Will this division of profits change periodically depending on the performance of each partner? How will the performance of each partner be measured? If the percentage division of profits changes, will there be a corresponding adjustment in the percentage ownership interest?

(9) Will new or young partners be permitted to acquire a percentage ownership interest or will they be confined to a percentage division of profits?

(10) Will there be ownership and non-ownership units or common, profit-sharing units and preferred-ownership units for the partnership? For any common profit-sharing units will goodwill be fixed or frozen?

(11) If there is to be a periodic change of the percentage division of profits, will this be done by secret ballot under the control of an

auditor with each partner evaluating only the performance of the other partners according to an agreed method?

(12) Are profits divisible quarterly? Will monthly statements be prepared by the auditors to watch closely the performance of the business?

(13) Will the partners have entertainment or promotional expense accounts or will these be personal?

7. *Management*

(1) Are the partners to have equal authority in management?

(2) Will there be two groups of partners—ownership and non-ownership partners, senior and junior partners, active and silent partners or partners owning common units and others owning common and preferred units?

8. *Attention to partnership matters*

(1) Are all partners to attend to partnership matters full time?

(2) Are there any activities that are prohibited?

(3) What will happen if one partner is asked to serve on a government board, committee or commission for a temporary period?

9. *Accounting matters*

(1) Will the partnership accounting be on an accrual basis?

(2) May any partner inspect the books at any time?

(3) Will there be a reserve for bad debts?

(4) Will the partners have drawing accounts?

(5) Are the partners to share any loss according to their percentage-ownership interests?

10. *Expulsion, mental incompetency, withdrawal, death, disability or bankruptcy of a partner*

(1) What are the grounds and method for expulsion of a partner?

(2) How long must a partner be disabled to fall within the disability provisions?

(3) What notice of withdrawal is required and how is it to be given?

(4) Should there be a restraint-against-trade clause if a partner withdraws, such as not engaging in medical practice for five years within five miles of a medical clinic?

(5) Is there to be a clause enabling the continuation of the business by the remaining partners after expulsion, mental incompetency, withdrawal, death, disability or bankruptcy?

(6) How is the value of the interest of the withdrawing partner to be determined? What is the time period for payment? Will an expelled partner have any right to be compensated for goodwill?

(7) Will there be a separate buy-sell agreement to compel the estate of a deceased partner to sell his interest and the surviving partners to buy that interest?

(8) Will the buy-sell agreement be funded by life insurance? If so, will term insurance, convertible term or whole life insurance be used?

(9) What proportion of each policy on the life of any one partner will the other partners own?

(10) Is any partner uninsurable or rated as a high risk because of a lung condition, etc.?

(11) Will there be a trustee under the buy-sell agreement?

(12) Should the surviving partners be entitled to an assignment to them of any policy or policies held by the deceased on their lives upon payment of the cash surrender values to the estate of the deceased?

(13) If a partner is found by court order to be mentally incompetent or incapable of managing business affairs, is that partner considered to have withdrawn from the partnership and offered that partner's interest for sale at a valuation to be determined under the partnership agreement?

(14) Will there be a compulsory retirement clause at 65 or will the partner at 65 be bought out over a period of 5 years until age 70 and still be active in the business?

(15) Will the partners collectively wish to direct the investment of cash reserves built up under the insurance policies that fund the buy-sell agreement where interest rates are higher than insurance lending rates?

11. *Dissolution*

(1) Under what conditions is the partnership dissolved?

(2) Do only senior partners act as liquidators? How are "senior partners" defined for this purpose?

––––––

Sophisticated computer software is now available to improve client questionnaires that serve as the basis for complex documents. The process works this way. The law firm first creates a master form on the computer that contains all of the various provisions that have appeared in all of the individual documents of some particular type, say, acquisition agreements or multi-party loan agreements, drafted in the past by senior members of the firm. From the master form a questionnaire is formed. The questions appear on the screen. When the answers are typed on the keyboard, the answers trigger which follow-up questions to ask and which irrelevant questions to skip. The computer program also checks for consistency among answers; it adjusts tenses, plurals, and other grammatical matters; and it allows for editing in response to both law and fact changes. The ultimate effect of such a program is that every lawyer in a firm can draft even complex documents that benefit from the best thinking of all the members of the firm.[2]

B. GENERAL AREAS OF FOCUS FOR ANY CHECKLIST

Any checklist of questions should be tailored to the particular kind of document envisioned, and as much as possible to the factual setting for the particular client's document.[3] Here are some general areas that particular questions should develop.

1. Questions About Client's Purposes

a. What is the client's present situation in relation to the document?

b. Does the client expect the document to change the situation or to solidify it? What does the client expect the document to accomplish?

c. How does the client expect to use the document? Is it to cover one situation with one other party, or is it to be used as a form over time and thus to apply to many parties and many variations in situation?

d. Has the client negotiated with anyone regarding this document? Are negotiations still in progress? Have negotiations resulted in any oral agreements or anything else that needs to be incorporated into the document?

e. Has the client had previous transactions similar to the one to which this document will relate? What were those previous transactions like?

f. Does the client know other parties to be involved? What does the client know about them? How does the client feel about them?

2. Trouble–Shooting Questions

a. What potential problems should the document resolve so as to keep the law from stepping in to resolve them?

b. What are any potential threats to a smooth-sailing transaction?

c. Does the client want a "tight" document that covers everything and leaves nothing to risk or a "loose" document that assumes some risks in the interest of doing good business? It is important to consider the client's style and understand that sometimes legal decisions are made in a context that also contains business decisions.

3. Questions to Assess the Client

These are not questions to ask the client but questions to ask oneself about the client.

2. Harrington, Help in Drafting Complex Documents, Nat'l L.J., Nov. 11, 1985, at 14.

3. To get an idea of what good checklists encompass in a variety of legal contexts, see B. Becker, B. Savin, D. Becker, and D. Gibberman, Legal Checklists (Callaghan) (1975 and cumulative supplements) (looseleaf service).

a. How much does the client understand about the transaction at hand and about its legal ramifications? Is the client sophisticated or naive?

b. Is the client perceptive? Can the client's statements be trusted as accurate, honest, consistent?

c. Is the client so totally focused on one aspect of the transaction that others are being neglected? Does the client need help to think about neglected matters? It is important to remember that the lawyer is the trouble shooter, but the client is the policy maker. Finding out what the client wants to accomplish is often a matter of finding out about underlying policies that may or may not be expressed directly in the document. Nonetheless, short of drafting an unconscionable or otherwise illegal document, the lawyer must never lose sight of the goal: achieving what the client—not the lawyer—wants.

III. LAYING THE CONCEPTUAL FOUNDATION

Only rarely must the drafter operate in a vacuum with no models at all, but commonly the available models are poorly drafted or not entirely relevant. These may provide some building blocks, but the drafter often has no one single document to use as a foundation.

The prospect of having to draft "from scratch" is more frightening than redrafting someone else's document or relying on someone else's form; however, it may also produce a better document, especially if the content as well as the form of the model is insufficient. Models can foster the temptation to accept something that looks all right under cursory inspection even though careful analysis would reveal serious flaws in it. In contrast, when the drafter is compelled to build a document from the foundation up, the result may be more carefully planned and thoroughly tested.

A. FORMING CONCEPTS

The first step in the construction process is a thinking rather than a writing step—although many people do their best thinking on paper. Much of what goes on when people think is to form concepts, which is a process of producing general ideas about specific facts. If people did not conceptualize, or generalize, the world would be a muddle in which every single thing the senses encountered would be regarded as different from every other thing. Thus, the tendency to generalize is a way of achieving some order out of chaos.

When preparing to draft a planning or legislating document, there is a special need first to form clear concepts and find appropriate levels of generality in which to express them. It is worth it to stop and think at the conceptual level about what the document is going to accomplish. Clients often provide a welter of particulars and either no concept at all or poorly conceived concepts. Furthermore, the lawyer may increase the store of essential, but chaotically disorganized, facts by looking at the client's business records, assessing the business risks involved, and attending to the client's particular requests.

Even if beginning with someone else's document as a model, one may discover that its language reflects either muddled conceptualization or insufficient generalization. In the search for appropriate concepts and generalities, the purpose is not to find some ultimate and perfect truth. It would be difficult to write a single word if such standards governed. Instead all that matters is a level of generality that is useful as a kind of shorthand to keep from having to write down every single thing that might happen in the future.

DICKERSON, TOWARD A LEGAL DIALECTIC
61 Ind.L.J. 315, 318 (1986).*

For the lawyer-planner, "truth" means a clear-eyed understanding of what results are needed and what elements in the process of concept selection and formation and the use of language are best adapted to reaching those results.

B. SOLVING CONCEPTUAL PROBLEMS

Here are two examples of how the process works.

1. The Trouble With "Extortion by Theft"

First, consider the following statutory provision:

SECTION 4. Extortion by Theft of Agricultural Products

It shall be unlawful for any person to obstruct, retard, prevent, delay or otherwise interfere with the production, transportation, shipment, delivery, purchase, sale, barter or marketing of any perishable agricultural or dairy product, or to cause the transportation, shipment, delivery, purchase, sale, barter or marketing of any perishable agricultural or dairy product to be obstructed, retarded, prevented, delayed or otherwise interfered with, by coercing, threatening, intimidating, or attempting to coerce, threaten or intimidate any person who owns, grows, produces, buys, sells, barters or markets any such product, or who is engaged in the transportation, delivery, shipment or marketing of any such product, for the purpose of inducing, extorting or compelling such person to join any organization, or to contribute money, services or any other thing of value to such organization or to any person or persons whomsoever, or to contribute money or other thing of value to any person or persons on the condition, express or implied, that the production, transportation, shipment, delivery, marketing, purchase, sale or barter of such product will not be obstructed, retarded, prevented, delayed or otherwise interfered with. Any person who shall violate any of the provisions of this act shall be deemed guilty of a felony and upon conviction thereof shall be fined in any sum not

---

exceeding one thousand dollars ($1,000) and imprisoned for a period of not less than one (1) nor more than five (5) years.

Readers who try to wade through this provision at a reasonable speed usually find themselves sinking in the mire. The provision has served as the raw material for a redrafting problem in some Legal Drafting classes. The students discovered that part of the trouble comes from unnecessary repetition, and part of it comes from including too many synonyms. What happened when the students set about paring the provision down was that they began to argue about which terms to keep. If they kept "interfere with," did they need any of the preceding terms: "obstruct, retard, prevent, delay"? Or was "interfere" too broad a term? Were the other terms necessary to put limits on the sense of "interfere"? In the alternative, should one of the more narrow terms be used alone instead of "interfere"? Similar arguments ensued about the other lists.

Also, the students were troubled by the title: "Extortion by Theft of Agricultural Products." Someone noticed that "extorting" was buried in one of the lists in the middle of the provision, and "theft" never came up at all. This led to rethinking about what the statute was designed to prohibit. The final drafts that the different students produced were not alike in most respects, but the word "theft" had disappeared from everybody's version. Perhaps the statute was intended to prohibit theft by extortion, but certainly not extortion by theft. Most of the students decided that extortion was the central concept. They kept some general term about extortion in the title, and they took "extorting" out of the list buried in the middle. They had discovered that if a concept is the whole, it cannot also be one of the parts.

2. The Trouble With "Inability to Act"

Consider a trust document that provides for what to do if the trustee is "unable to act by reason of death, disability, or absence from the country." [4] Assuming these are the possibilities the client/settlor has thought of, the lawyer looks at the list and realizes that resignation, another real possibility, is missing. But the solution may not be simply to add it. Why take on the responsibility for thinking of every possibility and including them all? Besides, another look at the original language reveals something else wrong. Resignation is not an inability to act; it is a refusal. Thus comes the discovery that the original concept—inability to act—was not adequate. The document ends up referring to what to do if the trustee "does not serve for any reason." In short, testing ideas about particulars leads to refining concepts, which in turn leads to changing general language.

---

4. See J. Johnson, A Draftsman's Handbook for Wills and Trust Agreements 13 (1961).

C. CONCEPTS AS "TYPE FACTS"

What has happened here is that the lawyer has found the lowest common denominator among the particulars. That is the concept that is best adapted to reach the needed result. In other words, the lawyer has arrived at what Professor Irvin Rutter calls a "type fact," a generalization about the behavior of a kind of thing, as opposed to a "unique fact," a statement about a particular thing that happened.[5] The statements that lawyers produce as planners rely heavily on type facts, just as the statements they produce as litigators rely heavily on unique facts. In short, for the planner, type facts turn into concepts.[6]

D. THE LEGAL CONSEQUENCES OF CONCEPTUAL CHANGES

Just as changing insights can lead to changing the general terms that name concepts, changing the terms can have far-reaching legal consequences. Consider what happened at the University of California at Berkeley when the University announced a plan to reclassify all its various graduate student teaching positions under the single general title: "graduate student instructor."

Before the reclassification in July 1985, there had been three classifications: "teaching assistant," "teaching associate," and "acting instructor." The acting instructors had received higher pay than those in the other classifications. Their status had also enabled them to teach beyond the four years to which other graduate students were limited. The additional teaching years were critical to students working on a Ph.D. These benefits disappeared with the reclassification. However, it appeared to the graduate students that the main purpose for the reclassification was to defeat their attempt to unionize. The University wanted to regard them as teacher trainees rather than employees and thus ineligible to bargain.[7]

In short, concepts—and the terms that name them—can be used as tools to achieve a particular legal result; they can also spark a legal battle.

---

5. Designing and Teaching the First–Degree Law Curriculum, 37 U.Cin.L.Rev. 9, 85 (1968).

6. See Dickerson, Toward a Legal Dialectic, 61 Ind.L.J. 315, 326–27 (1986).

7. For an account of the Berkeley students' charges of unfair labor practices filed with the California Public Employ-

ment Relations Board, see Berkeley Graduate Students Protest Job Reclassification, Chron. of Higher Educ., Oct. 2, 1985, at 27, 30. For a report of the Administrative Law Judge's ruling in the graduate students' favor, see Cal. Graduate Students Eligible for Bargaining, Chron. of Higher Educ., Mar. 4, 1987, at 2.

IV. ORGANIZING THE DOCUMENT: THE DRAFTER AS ARCHITECT AND CONSTRUCTION ENGINEER

A document long enough or complicated enough to need separate parts should be planned with attention to three organizational matters: division, classification, and sequence.

A. DIVISION

1. *Tests for Division Schemes*

The first stage of organizing a body of material is to divide the whole into parts. If the drafter has already produced abstract concepts to bring order to the collection of chaotic facts involved, that general language may convert easily into headings for parts. The drafter, of course, has the power not only to label the parts but also to decide how many there should be. If the division of material to go into the document is technically sound, it should meet the following tests:

  a. The parts (and their headings) should be mutually exclusive.

  b. Added together, they should equal the whole.

  c. There should be one consistently applied principle to govern the division, such as chronology, size, rank, or degree of importance.

To illustrate the tests, here is a division that fails all three tests: dividing a whole called "human beings" into parts called "men," "women," and "American." First, the parts do not exclude each other insofar as Americans include both men and women. Second, the parts do not equal the whole insofar as children as such are not included. Third, the division begins as if governed by sex but then shifts as if governed by nationality.

In some contexts it is important to divide material and label the parts strictly according to these tests. Such strictness does not always work sensibly, however, when dividing a document such as a contract into sections. In particular, it often is not fruitful to spend time thinking of some principle of division that can be consistently applied to produce a set of headings for parts of a contract. To do so would be to force conceptualization at such an abstract level that it would not help readers. It is important, however, to give thought to how many parts are practical for the document in question.

2. *Headings*

It is especially important to give thought to informative headings for the sections. Courts have been known to refuse to enforce provisions in sections of documents with headings that did not clearly inform readers of their content. For example, consider this disclaimer of warranty provision from a contract for the sale of an automobile:

9. *Factory Warranty:* Any warranty on any new vehicle or used vehicle still subject to a manufacturer's warranty is that made by the manufacturer only. The seller hereby disclaims all warranties, either express or implied, including any implied warranty of merchantability or fitness for a particular purpose.

The heading here was found to be misleading, and thus the provision was ineffective as a seller's attempt to disclaim warranties.[8]

Some states have statutes expressly prohibiting misleading headings in insurance contract forms. The Washington state insurance commissioner may disapprove of a form with a misleading heading;[9] in Arkansas[10] and Oklahoma,[11] the commissioner is required to disapprove of such a form.

One way to avoid uninformative headings is to avoid abstract nouns altogether and have headings that are phrases about actions or decisions instead. For example, an insurance policy might give up headings like "Coverage" and "Exclusions" and instead have headings like "What Damaged Property We Insure."

Every heading, whether it heads a major division or a subdivision, should be numbered or lettered. Otherwise there is no easy way to refer to it or find it in the document, unless the entire document is line-numbered. Even then it is an aid to readers to number or letter every division and subdivision.

B. CLASSIFICATION

Classification involves deciding which material goes in each division or subdivision. The decisions should depend on where readers may be expected to look for various provisions. The main principle of classification is to put closely related provisions together. What this means in practice is that exceptions should go together with the general rules to which they relate, and definitions should go in the context where the defined terms are used.

If there are many exceptions or many definitions, it may be more practical to have separate sections for them to avoid excessive repetition and to make amendment easy. This is a "modular" theory of drafting, more appropriate perhaps for statutes than for contracts. It favors what is convenient for the drafter, rather than the reader, especially if the document is intended as a form to be used for many parties over a long period of time. It also values economy of statement over clarity. However, the result is sometimes a document so heavy with cross-references that it is likely either to confuse or to misinform. If clarity and easy use as a reference document are the primary values, then repetition seems less a flaw and more an aid to understanding.

---

8. Blankenship v. Northtown Ford, Inc., 95 Ill.App.3d 303, 306–07, 50 Ill.Dec. 850, 420 N.E.2d 167, 170–71 (1981).

9. West's Rev.Code Wash.Ann. 48.44.020.

10. Arkansas Stats. § 66–3210.

11. 36 Okla.Stat. § 3611.

It may seem logical to expect that final decisions about division are made first and then classification happens as a separate following stage. However, in practice, drafters sometimes discover while in the midst of classifying that they need to rethink divisions. If one part becomes overloaded, it may be worth it to subdivide so that information is not buried. If a part ends up with almost nothing in it, perhaps it should be consolidated with another part. However, all parts need not be of similar length.

C. SEQUENCE

1. Making Parts Easy To Find

The sequence in which parts occur in the document should also be governed by what makes information easy to find. Often the easiest order for drafter and reader alike is chronological order. It may help to think about what circumstances or events are likely to cause a party to want to look something up in the contract. This approach to sequence is consistent with headings that focus on actions rather than abstractions. Sometimes this approach works best with headings that are questions. For example, an insurance policy might have sections headed: "What causes of loss are covered?" and "How do I make a claim?" Often the document is used for reference, and not necessarily read straight through from beginning to end.

Here are some other principles that can govern the sequence of parts of contracts:

a. General provisions before special ones such as exceptions.

b. More important provisions before less important ones.

c. Often used provisions about ordinary events before less often used ones about extraordinary events. In a lease, for example, provisions about maintenance duties and rent payments should precede provisions about destruction of the premises and abandonment by the tenant.

d. "Housekeeping" provisions last. Housekeeping provisions cover such matters as amendments, governing law, and severability of any provisions found to be unenforceable.

Severability clauses are of dubious value. The absence of such a clause in a statute does not prevent a court from excising invalid provisions to preserve the constitutionality of a statute. Likewise a severability clause does not prevent a court from striking down a whole act if preserving part of it would produce unreasonable, unconstitutional, or absurd results.[12] Courts have also refused to excise an unenforceable clause from a paragraph in a contract and instead stricken the entire paragraph in spite of a severability clause.[13] Moreover, a sever-

---

12. Small v. Sun Oil Co., 222 So.2d 196, 199 (Fla.1969).

13. Richard P. Rita Personnel Services Intern., Inc. v. Kot, 229 Ga. 314, 317, 191 S.E.2d 79, 82 (1972).

ability clause has not saved an entire agreement when a court found it tainted.[14]

2. Document Design: Some General Conclusions

The principles governing sequence overlap. It would be impossible to put them all to work at once without contradiction. They are, therefore, merely general principles for consideration. Moreover, as one drafts and redrafts, changes are likely to occur in all three stages of the organizational process: division, classification, and sequence. The plans need not be finally settled before drafting the text of individual provisions. On the contrary, the design of a complex document is often in flux until the polishing stages of the final draft.

Professor Dickerson regularly refers to the design of legal documents as "architecture" insofar as the legal architect "must participate in exploring the objectives, sketch the structural framework, fill in the broad surfaces, work out the significant details, and add the aesthetic touches." [15] The concept of document design as architecture applies most precisely to the design of statutes and codes; however, one can appropriately describe all good legal document design as architectural in its attention to detail and consistency.

V. GETTING IT ALL ON PAPER: THE WRITING STAGES

If the lawyer has imposed some organization on the process of questioning the client, such as by using a good checklist, the fact-gathering part of the drafting process can also begin to shape the document. In any event, the client's goals should govern the organization. To achieve efficiently a clear, concise document, the following writing stages are generally regarded as essential.

A. OUTLINE

Many people groan at the thought of making an outline. Fresh in the memory comes the image of the fifth or sixth grade English teacher, or maybe the graduate student who taught Freshman English in college. Somehow there were always too many rules about making outlines. The idea was to outline the term paper *before* composing it, but many an outline—required to be turned in with the paper—was actually produced *after* the paper was written.

1. Outlining as Explication

Even the outline written after the fact is itself a valuable mechanism, although it functions very differently from the outline written before the document. Outlining a document or part of a document that

---

14. Schuylkill County Tax Claim Bureau v. Tremont Township, 522 A.2d 102 (Pa.Cmwlth.1987).

15. R. Dickerson, Legislative Drafting 12 (1954).

already exists is a form of explication of the text. It can reveal problems of ambiguity, lack of clarity, or missing material. It can also lead to new ideas about how to reorganize material. If the document under construction is to be a reconstruction of an existing document, a detailed outline can serve as a valuable diagnostic tool to see just how much revision is in order.

2. *Outlining as a Planning Tool*

If the document is a new one, the outline serves as a planning tool. At the outset it may be no more than a list of topics (single words or phrases) to indicate the scope of the subject matter to be covered. These topics, if they are broad enough, may easily convert later into division headings in the document. Some people find the broad topic outline sufficient, especially if the document is fairly short and simple.

If the content is complex or includes a great many separate provisions, it helps first to produce a planning outline that consists of broad topics plus words or phrases to list the matters to be covered under each topic. If the items in the lists naturally separate into groups, then subdivision headings may also emerge from the outline.

3. *Outlining as a Technique for Dividing and Subdividing*

The material also may cause some parts of the outline to be subdivided into more levels than other parts. The possibilities are infinite, but here are some examples to illustrate the idea.

```
I.                        I.                        I.
    A.                        II.                       A.
    B.                            A.                    B.
    C.                            B.                II.
        1.                        C.                    A.
        2.                        D.                III.
II.                               E.                    A.
    A.                        III.                       B.
        1.                        A.                         1.
        2.                        B.                    C.
        3.                        C.
    B.
```

The outline on the left and the one in the middle above are equally reasonable. The variations in amount or depth of detail do not signal any particular trouble. One might be suspicious of Division "I" in the middle outline, however, because it has no subdivisions while Division "II" has several. That may signal that "I" is nothing more than an "Introduction" and contains no substance. But that is only a suspicion.

The outline on the right does have some problems by traditional outline standards that are worth attention. Division "II" has a subdivision "A" but no "B," and Division "III.B" has a subdivision "1" but no "2." Traditional standards insist that every "A" must have a "B," and every "1" must have a "2." This standard is not a piece of rigidity for its own sake. It comes from the idea that an outline is a mechanism for dividing a whole into parts. In other words, if "II.A" has no "B" to follow it, "II" must not be complicated enough to warrant subdivision. Division "II.A" should be part of "II." Likewise, "III.B.1" should be part of "III.B." If an outline is functioning as a form of explication, an "A" without a "B" or a "1" without a "2" may signal something missing in the material or a concept not fully enough developed.

4. Advantages of Outlining in Detail

The major advantages of producing a detailed planning outline for a new document rather than only a broad topic outline are that the detailed outline:

a. Helps ensure that material is not inadvertently left out.

b. Makes it easier to see any need to change the sequence of coverage before paragraphs are written and transitions are built in.

c. Makes it easier to keep on writing at the actual writing stage rather than having to stop often to think about what comes next.

Just as early outlining is valuable, so can early writing be valuable—before all the research and thinking are done. During the outlining or writing, as Professor Dickerson puts it, the draft can begin to "talk back," producing new ideas about the substance and altering the conceptual construct.[16]

B. FIRST DRAFT

The more preliminary work the drafter has done, the easier it should be to write the first draft. Even so, the drafter should take courage in the knowledge that writing is difficult for most people. Most of those who say otherwise either don't know what they are talking about or don't mean it. "There's nothing to writing. All you do is sit down at a typewriter and open a vein."[17] It is worth it to make the process as painless as possible. Here are a few ideas that have worked for some people.

1. Starting in the Easiest Spot

There is no good reason why a draft should have to be written beginning to end. If a section that will end up further on in the document is easier or more interesting to write, it makes sense to start with it. Whatever has the capacity to get the drafter past staring at the blank paper makes sense. In fact, many introductory sections are wordy and slow-moving because they are written while the drafter is still trying painfully to get under way.

16. Dickerson, Legal Drafting: Writing as Thinking, or, Talk-back from your Draft and How To Exploit It, 29 J.Legal Educ. 373, 376–79 (1978).

17. R. Smith, quoted in No. 73 Simply Stated 3 (April 1987) (Document Design Center newsletter).

2. Stopping In the Middle of Something Good

Once a drafter gets going, there is an unfortunate tendency to keep going until the drafting bogs down in some difficulty. Then, of course, it is equally difficult to come back to it. It can be a smart trick on oneself to leave the desk when the drafting is speeding along. Then coming back to it is easier and so is getting under way. This often means stopping in the middle of a section rather than after its conclusion so that there is not yet another beginning to face cold.

3. A Word About Audience

While writing the first draft, it is a good idea to keep in mind that the primary audience, usually non-lawyers, are the people who need to understand what the document obligates them to do. On the other hand, lawyers and judges are always a potential secondary audience.

C. REVISIONS

It is usually safe to say that the more times a document is revised, the better it becomes. This means that it is worth it to go through it "one more time" as long as the time is available and not too expensive in terms of other pressing work. The client is to be pitied whose lawyer turns something out once—even in longhand or on the dictaphone— hands it over to a secretary for typing, and never sees it again until it appears with a cover letter ready for signature. That lawyer, to say nothing of the client, is missing the opportunity for all the valuable talk-back that successive drafts can yield. Worse yet, that lawyer risks serious errors escaping uncaught.

D. CONSISTENCY CHECKS

A series of checks is necessary to ensure that anything repeated in the course of the document receives consistent treatment throughout. Reading the document straight through, even slowly and carefully, is not a satisfactory way to accomplish this. There are too many things to look for to keep them all in mind at once. Not only do mechanical matters such as format, punctuation and spelling need to be consistent, but terms need to be used consistently with their definitions, and all provisions that relate to the same topic dare not contradict each other. These rigorous consistency checks through the entire document, one matter at a time, particularly distinguish drafting legal documents from all other forms of writing.

E. REVIEW BY OTHERS

Before regarding a drafting job as finished, the drafter should receive the benefit of review by others if possible. One is always too close to one's own work to see it with the clear eye of others. Colleagues can give one kind of useful review by virtue of their legal acumen. However, if a consumer document is under review, a layperson as reviewer can often tell better whether the document speaks clearly. Likewise, if a business document is under review, the best reviewer might be one who is knowledgeable about the given kind of business.

To benefit most from review, the drafter should not merely sit back and passively receive the reviewer's comments. The drafter should ask questions or at least have questions in mind. One may be able to learn more from the reviewer by asking the reviewer to answer the following questions:

1. Is anything missing?
2. Is the document too long or too short?
3. Is it too complicated or too simple for its primary audience?
4. Are there any serious interruptions?
5. Are there too many or too few subdivisions?
6. Is the whole presentation easy or hard to read? [18]

VI. PROBLEMS

SET A

Below is a form contract for the purchase and sale of real estate. Study it with particular attention to paragraphs 2, 12, and 16. What is paragraph 16 about: warranties? rights? duties? What gaps do you find in its coverage? Do paragraphs 12 and 16 overlap? Think about what paragraph 16 authorizes or requires and when, with respect to both execution of the contract and closing. Also think about its location in the sequence of provisions in the contract along with paragraph 2, which provides the blank space for addenda before execution.

---

18. See R. Dick, above note 1, at 39–40.

REALTOR®

GAINESVILLE BOARD OF REALTORS®, INC.
DEPOSIT RECEIPT AND
PURCHASE AND SALE AGREEMENT
CONVENTIONAL FINANCING*

Date _____ 19_____

Receipt is hereby acknowledged by _____, hereinafter called REALTOR, of the sum of

_____ (_____) (by check)

from _____, hereinafter called BUYER, as a deposit

and as a part of the purchase price on account of an offer to purchase the property of _____

_____, hereinafter called SELLER, said property being in _____ County, Florida, and described as follows:

_____

Also known as: _____
Together with the following personal property:

The SELLER hereby agrees to sell said property to the BUYER and the BUYER hereby agrees to purchase said property from the SELLER upon the following terms and conditions:

1. PURCHASE AND SALES PRICE $ _____
    Payable as follows:

    (a) Deposit paid herewith .... $ _____
    (b) Additional Deposit .... _____
    (c) Cash at Closing (U.S. cash, certified or cashiers check) .... _____
    (d) Balance payable .... _____
    (e) _____ _____

    TOTAL PURCHASE AND SALES PRICE $ _____

2. TERMS AND CONDITIONS:

* Copyright © 1987 by Gainesville [Fla.] Board of Realtors. Reprinted by permission.

3. ABSTRACT-TITLE INSURANCE POLICY. (Check one) The SELLER shall furnish either ☐ an abstract from earliest records to date, showing his title to be marketable or insurable, or ☐ SELLER shall furnish an ALTA Owner's Title Insurance Binder and Policy insuring marketable title from a recognized Title Insurance Company doing business in this area, and Abstract or Title Insurance Binder to be delivered to the BUYER, or his Attorney or Agent, whose name is _____ within _____ days from _____.

4. EXAMINATION OF TITLE: The BUYER or his Attorney shall have _____ days within which to examine said Abstract of Title or Title Binder and to signify his willingness to accept the same, whereupon the transaction shall be concluded on _____ or such earlier date as may be mutually agreeable.

If the title is unmarketable, the SELLER shall have _____ days or a reasonable period of time within which to cure the designated defects in the title that render same unmarketable or uninsurable in the opinion of the BUYER or his said Agent, and the SELLER hereby agrees to use reasonable diligence in curing said defects, and upon the defects being cured and notice of that fact being given to the BUYER or his said Agent, this transaction shall be closed within _____ days of delivery of said notice. At the option of the BUYER, upon SELLER's failure or inability to correct the marketability of the title within the time limit or a reasonable period of time, the SELLER shall deliver the title in its existing condition, otherwise the earnest money deposit shall be returned to the BUYER upon demand therefor, and all rights and liabilities on the part of the BUYER arising hereunder shall terminate. Provided, however, that in the event of disagreement between the SELLER and the BUYER or his said Agent, as to the marketability of the title, the SELLER may offer a binder for an ALTA Form A or equivalent policy issued by a recognized title insurance company doing business in this area, agreeing to insure said title against all exceptions other than those mentioned in this agreement and the standard printed exceptions, which binder shall be conclusive that said title is marketable, said Binder and policies pursuant thereto shall be paid for by the BUYER.

5. KIND OF CONVEYANCE: Conveyance of title shall be by full WARRANTY DEED to _____ free and clear of all encumbrances and liens of whatsoever nature, except taxes for the current year, and except as herein otherwise provided. The SELLER shall also deliver to the BUYER a lien and possession affidavit at closing.

6. RESTRICTIONS, EASEMENTS, LIMITATIONS: The BUYER shall take title subject to: zoning, restrictions, prohibitions and other requirements imposed by governmental authority; restrictions and matters appearing on the plat or otherwise common to the subdivision; public utility easements of record; taxes for year of closing and subsequent years, assumed mortgages and purchase money mortgages, if any; other: _____ provided, however, that there exists at closing no violation of the foregoing and that the marketability of title, and they do not prevent the use of the Property for _____ purpose(s).

7. EXPENSES: BUYER shall pay for the following expenses: (a) Title examination and title opinion; (b) Recording of deed; (c) All expenses relative to all Notes and Mortgages or Contract for Deed, and transfer of existing mortgages; (d) Survey, if any; (e) BUYER's Attorney's fee.
SELLER shall pay for: (a) Real Estate Compensation; (b) Abstract or Title Insurance; (c) Preparation of Instruments of Conveyance; (d) Documentary Stamps on Deed; (e) Termite Inspection Fee; (f) SELLER's Attorney's Fee.

8. PRORATIONS: All taxes for the current year, rentals, insurance premiums, association assessments and interest on existing mortgages (if any) shall be prorated as of the date of closing with BUYER paying for the day of closing. If part of the purchase price is to be evidenced by the assumption of a mortgage requiring deposit of funds in escrow for payment of taxes, insurance or other charges, the BUYER agrees to reimburse the SELLER for escrowed funds assigned to BUYER at closing, with all mortgage payments to be current at the time of closing.

9. SURVEY: If the BUYER desires a survey of the property, he may have the property surveyed at his expense prior to the closing date. If the survey shows any encroachments on the land herein described, or that the improvements located on the land herein described encroach on other lands, or any shortages, written notice to that effect along with a copy of the survey shall be given to the SELLER and the same shall be treated as defects in title to be eliminated by SELLER.

This form is for the exclusive use of members in good standing of the Gainesville Board of REALTORS® unless its use by another person is authorized in writing by the Board of Directors.

REVISED 5/87, © 1984 Gainesville Board of REALTORS®, Inc. All Rights Reserved

10. PURCHASE MONEY MORTGAGES TO SELLER: The purchase money note and mortgage, if any, shall provide for a 30 day grace period in the event of default if it is a first mortgage and a 15 day grace period if a second mortgage; shall provide for right of prepayment in whole or in part without penalty; and shall not provide for acceleration or interest adjustment in event of resale of the property; and shall be otherwise in form and content in accordance with covenants established by the Eighth Judicial Circuit Bar Association. Said mortgage shall require all prior liens and encumbrances to be kept in good standing and shall forbid modifications of or future advances under prior mortgage(s).

11. VARIANCE IN AMOUNT OF FINANCING TO BE ASSUMED: Any variance in amount of financing to be assumed from the amount stated herein shall be added to or deducted from: purchase money financing if such is contemplated by this Agreement, otherwise, said variance shall be added to or deducted from the cash at closing, provided that if such procedure results in an increase in cash due at closing in excess of $500.00 or _____, said variance shall be added to or deducted from the cash at closing, provided that if such procedure results in an increase in cash due at closing in excess of $500.00 or _____ BUYER shall not be obligated to perform unless Seller reduces the purchase price by the amount of the excess over the herein specified sum.

12. TERMITES, OR OTHER INFESTATION: SELLER shall furnish to BUYER or his attorney or his agent at least 5 days prior to closing a certificate of a locally licensed entomologist dated within thirty days prior to closing, showing any improvements on the premises, exclusive of fences and _____ to be apparently free from active infestation (other than infestation by wood destroying fungi) or visible damage (including that caused by wood destroying fungi) by termites or other wood destroying organisms as required to be disclosed by Florida law. In the event active infestation or visible damage is found to be present, the SELLER shall bear the costs of remedying such active infestation and damage. Should the cost of such treatment and repair exceed $ _____, the SELLER may elect to terminate this agreement and all rights and liabilities of all parties shall be at an end and the deposit shall be returned to BUYER, unless the BUYER elects to proceed with the transaction, having the above amount deducted from the purchase price. "Damage" as used in this paragraph shall mean only damage that affects the structural integrity of the structure and its components.

13. PAVING, SEWER AND SIMILAR LIENS, ASSESSMENTS AND FRONT FOOTAGE CHARGES: SELLER shall be responsible for payment of all charges relating to paving, sidewalk and other assessments whether in place or under construction as of the date of this Contract. Public utility fees, assessments, or front footage charges shall be paid as follows:
Check one (1):
( ) SELLER shall pay (or has paid) all costs of utilities including sewer and water frontage charges, sewer and water capital facilities charges and water meter charges.
( ) SELLER shall pay (or has paid) sewer and water front footage charges only.
( ) The subject property is presently not served with central water or sewer or SELLER shall not pay any cost of utilities

14. DESTRUCTION OF PREMISES: If any improvements located on the above described premises at the time of the execution of this binder are damaged by fire or other casualty prior to closing, and can be restored to substantially the same condition within a period of thirty (30) days after such destruction occurs, SELLER shall so restore the improvements, and the closing date shall be extended accordingly. If such restoration cannot be completed within said period of time, this Contract, at the option of the BUYER, shall terminate and the deposit shall be returned to BUYER. All risk of loss prior to closing shall be borne by SELLER

15. FAILURE OF PERFORMANCE: If BUYER fails to perform this Contract within the time specified (including payment of all deposits hereunder), the deposit(s) paid by BUYER may be retained by or for the account of SELLER as agreed upon liquidated damages, consideration for the execution of this Contract and in full settlement of any claims; whereupon BUYER and SELLER shall be relieved of all obligations under this Contract; or SELLER, at SELLER's option, may proceed in equity to enforce SELLER's rights under this Contract. If, for any reason other than failure of SELLER to make SELLER's title marketable after diligent effort, SELLER fails, neglects or refuses to perform this Contract, the BUYER may seek specific performance or elect to receive the return of Buyer's deposit(s) without thereby waiving any action for damages resulting from Seller's breach.

16. INSPECTION, REPAIR AND MAINTENANCE: Unless otherwise stated in this Agreement, SELLER warrants that: (a) the roof, (excluding the facia and soffit) does not have any visible evidence of leaks or structural damage. In the event repairs or replacements are required, SELLER shall pay up to $ _____ for such repairs or replacements by an appropriately licensed person. However, if the cost for such repairs or replacements exceeds $ _____ BUYER or SELLER may elect to pay such excess, failing which either party may cancel this Contract; (b) SELLER further warrants that the septic tank, pool, all major appliances, heating, cooling, electrical, plumbing systems and machinery are in good working condition. In the event repairs or replacements are required, SELLER shall pay up to $ _____ for such repairs or replacements by an appropriately licensed person. However, if the cost for such repairs or replacements exceeds $ _____, BUYER or SELLER may elect to pay such excess, failing which either party may cancel this Contract. BUYER may, at BUYER's expense, have inspections made of the roof and said items by an appropriately licensed person dealing in the construction, repair and maintenance thereof and shall report in writing to SELLER such deficiencies within said period, BUYER shall be deemed to have waived SELLER's warranties as to deficiencies not reported in writing to SELLER such deficiencies within said period, BUYER shall be deemed to have waived SELLER's warranties as to deficiencies not reported is first. Unless BUYER reports such deficiencies within said period, BUYER shall be deemed to have waived SELLER's warranties as to deficiencies not reported. In the event SELLER is unable to correct the failures prior to closing, the sums may be paid into escrow at closing to cover the cost of repairs or replacements. SELLER agrees to provide availability of utilities for inspection upon a reasonable notice. Notwithstanding the provisions hereof, between the date of this Contract and the closing, SELLER shall maintain the real and personal property in the condition herein warranted, reasonable wear and tear excepted, and shall maintain the lawn and shrubbery, in substantially the same condition as exists upon the date of execution of this Contract. BUYER's designee shall be permitted reasonable access for inspection prior to closing in order to confirm the compliance with the maintenance requirements.

17. POSSESSION: BUYER shall be given possession of said property _____

18. ATTORNEY'S FEES AND COSTS: If any litigation arises under this agreement between BUYER and SELLER, the prevailing party shall be entitled to recover from the non-prevailing party all reasonable costs incurred in the trial court and on appeal by the prevailing party including a reasonable attorney's fee.

19. OTHER AGREEMENTS: This Contract constitutes the entire agreement between the parties, and any changes, amendments, or modifications hereof shall be void unless the same are reduced to writing and signed by the parties hereto.

20. TIME FOR ACCEPTANCE: If this Contract is not executed by all parties hereto on or before _____, 19 _____, the aforesaid deposit shall be, at the option of the BUYER, returned to him, and the Contract shall be null and void. The date of the Contract for purposes of performance shall be regarded as the date of execution by the last party to the Contract.

21. Disbursement of closing proceeds shall be made as soon after closing as final title certification and examination have been made, but which shall be no later than five (5) business days after closing. The binder deposits referred to herein shall be held in accordance with applicable statutes.

22. Typewritten or handwritten provisions inserted in this form shall control all printed provisions in conflict therewith.

23. THIS IS A LEGALLY BINDING CONTRACT AND SHALL NOT BE RECORDED UNLESS OTHERWISE AGREED TO BETWEEN THE PARTIES. IF NOT FULLY UNDERSTOOD, SEEK COMPETENT LEGAL ADVICE. DO NOT SIGN UNTIL ALL BLANKS ARE COMPLETED. YOUR REALTOR RECOMMENDS THAT YOU OBTAIN TITLE INSURANCE OR A TITLE OPINION FROM YOUR ATTORNEY.

By: _____   By: _____

      REALTOR

Dated this _____ day of _____, 19 _____

WITNESSES:

      BUYER:

_____

I, or we, agree to purchase the above described property on the terms and conditions stated in the foregoing instrument.

_____

I, or we, agree to sell the above mentioned property to the BUYER, or his nominee, on the terms and conditions stated in the above instrument, and by the signatures

attached on the _____ day of _____, 19 _____ signify our acceptance and

approval of the proposed sale.

WITNESSES:

      SELLER:

_____

_____

SELLER agrees to pay the licensed real estate Broker (REALTOR®) named below, at time of closing, from the disbursements of the proceeds of sale, compensation in the amount of _____ for his services in effecting the sale by finding a BUYER ready, willing and able to purchase pursuant to the foregoing Contract. In the event BUYER fails to perform and the deposit(s) is retained, 50% thereof, but not exceeding the REALTOR's fee above computed, shall be paid to the REALTOR, as full consideration for REALTOR's services including costs expended by REALTOR, and the balance shall be paid to SELLER. If the transaction shall not be closed because of refusal or failure of SELLER to perform, the SELLER shall pay said fee in full to REALTOR on demand. In any litigation concerning the brokerage fee, the prevailing party shall be entitled to recover reasonable attorney fees and costs.

By: _____

(Name & Address of Selling REALTOR)

_____ (Seller)

_____ (Name of Listing REALTOR)

_____ (Seller)

PROBLEM 1

You represent buyers who want to make an offer on a house with some suspicious looking cracks in the basement wall. Your clients have a friend who is a retired construction engineer and who is willing to inspect the house at no cost to the buyers. He is not now licensed as an engineer or inspector. If their friend finds some serious problem, they want the contract to be void; they will not be content with the seller's either making repairs before closing or leaving some amount in escrow after closing to pay for repairs made by the buyers.

Using the form contract as the offer to purchase, draft an addendum as paragraph 2 to accommodate the buyers' wishes, or otherwise amend the form to accomplish the same result.

PROBLEM 2

You represent sellers who have received an offer to purchase their home. Under paragraph 2, the buyers have typed: "Sellers to repair and/or replace porch roof." In paragraph 16, the buyers have typed "$3000" in each of the blanks.

Your clients anticipate a problem with these buyers over the porch roof, and they would like to prevent it if possible. They acknowledge that the roof leaks. The buyers saw the stains on the ceiling when they came to look at the house. The sellers are willing to make reasonable repairs, but they don't think they should have to replace the whole roof, which is what it appears the buyers want.

Draft a counter-offer on behalf of the sellers. They want protection, but they also want to keep these buyers. It's a buyers' market in your area, and your clients are eager to move to an apartment since they have both recently retired.

PROBLEM 3

As counsel to the Board of Realtors, redraft paragraph 16 so that it prevents as many conflicts between buyers and sellers as possible. Make any accompanying revisions in other paragraphs needed to carry out your reconceptualization of the parties' rights and responsibilities regarding inspection and repairs.

SET B

Your client has brought you a form lease that she has been using in another state in her property rental business. She has just moved to your area and anticipates continuing in the same business. She would like you to go over the lease and recommend improvements. In particular, she wants a "comprehensive provision on security deposits."

First, look over the materials below: (1) the lease, (2) a section of a state landlord-tenant statute on security deposits, and (3) sample security deposit provisions from miscellaneous leases. A series of problems follows these materials. (If your state has landlord-tenant statutes, you might refer to them as the applicable law. Otherwise assume the security deposit section given here governs. Also, assume the sample security deposit provisions are from assorted leases drafted by others that you happen to have in your files. Do not accept any of them uncritically as a model.)

RENTAL AGREEMENT—LEASE

1 Made and entered into this _____ day of _____ 19__ between
2 _____, agent for Landlord, and _____, Tenant, whereby the Land-
3 lord agrees to rent to said Tenant the property located and known as
4 _____ in the City of _____, _____, County of _____, State of
5 _____ on the following terms and conditions: Rental Rate _____ per
6 month, to begin on the _____ day of _____ 19__ on a lease basis,
7 term of lease to be _____ months with option to renew on date of
8 termination. Tenant to give Landlord notice of intention not later
9 than 15 days prior to termination date of lease. Landlord reserves the
10 right to adjust the rent at the termination of the original lease and/or
11 upon receipt of notification of Tenant's intention to extend lease.

TENANT AGREES AS FOLLOWS:

13 1. PAYMENT OF RENT—To pay on the due date the monthly rent,
14   in advance, to Agent at _____.

15 2. UTILITIES, RENT, GLASS, DOORS—To pay all utility bills when
16   due, to keep sewerage pipes at said premises clear of obstructions
17   and to replace all broken or missing glass, damaged doors or other
18   parts during Tenant's occupancy.

19 3. REPAIRS AND MAINTENANCE—To accept the premises in its
20   present condition; to maintain the premises in good condition and
21   repair, natural wear and tear excepted; to make no alteration to
22   said property without the written consent of the Landlord.

23 4. LIABILITY AND INJURY—To relieve and indemnify Landlord
24   and/or Agent from any liability for:

25   A. Inability for any reason beyond the control of Landlord and/or
26   Agent to deliver possession of this property to said Tenant on
27   the effective rental date above written.

28   B. Damage or injury from any cause whatsoever which may be
29   sustained by Tenant, Tenant's property or any other person for
30   any cause whatsoever.

31 5. DAMAGE TO PROPERTY—To pay all costs for damage caused by
32   Tenant's negligence or lack of care.

33 6. INSPECTION OF PREMISES—To permit the Landlord or his
34   Agent to enter the premises at any reasonable time upon four (4)
35   hours written notice prior thereto, to show the property to prospec-
36   tive purchasers or Tenants, to inspect the premises; also to display
37   on the premises for sale signs and/or rental signs, after due notice
38   of the termination of the tenancy has been given by either party
39   hereto.

7. LAWN AND SHRUBBERY—To take proper care of the lawn and shrubbery, including mowing, trimming and weeding. Tenant shall not remove any shrubbery without written consent of the Landlord.

8. SUBLETTING ASSIGNING—Tenant shall not sublet the whole or any part of the premises, nor assign this agreement, or any interest therein. A violation of this covenant shall constitute a breach of this agreement. Tenant shall forfeit the term, and the Landlord shall have the right to evict Tenant.

9. USE OF OCCUPANCY—Tenant is not to put the premises to any use which is illegal or to any use other than that for which it is rented, to-wit-, for the use and occupancy as a dwelling by Tenant, and his family, consisting of _____ adults and _____ children. No pets other than _____.

10. TELEVISION AERIALS—Tenant shall not be at liberty to erect any television aerial upon the premises hereby rented (leased) without first securing permission from the Landlord.

11. AGENCY—Agent may act for Landlord in all matters relating hereto.

12. EXPENSE OF ENFORCEMENT—If rent is not received within three (3) days after due, a late charge of $5.00 shall be added. If rent and late charge not paid within fifteen (15) days after rent due, entire rental for remainder of rental period shall be due and payable and Landlord shall have such remedies as are provided by law in such cases. If tenant defaults in payment of rent or in compliance with other provisions of this Agreement and it is necessary to place same in hands of an attorney, Tenant agrees to pay a reasonable attorney's fee and all Court costs.

SPECIAL STIPULATIONS

SECURITY DEPOSIT $_____, refundable within _____ days after vacating and subject to premises being clean and intact. Any violation of above terms will result in forfeiture of any part of said deposit.

_____

_____

Signed, sealed and delivered in presence of

_____   _____ (Seal)

_____   _____ (Seal)

FOR AGENCY

_____ By _____ (Seal)

LANDLORD–TENANT STATUTE

83.49 Deposit money or advance rent; duty of landlord and tenant.—

(1) Whenever money is deposited or advanced by a tenant on a rental agreement as security for performance of the rental agreement or as advance rent for other than the next immediate rental period, the landlord or his agent shall either:

(a) Hold the total amount of such money in a separate non-interest-bearing account in a _____ banking institution for the benefit of the tenant or tenants. The landlord shall not commingle such moneys with any other funds of the landlord or hypothecate, pledge, or in any other way make use of such moneys until such moneys are actually due the landlord;

(b) Hold the total amount of such money in a separate interest-bearing account in a _____ banking institution for the benefit of the tenant or tenants, in which case the tenant shall receive and collect interest in an amount of at least 75 percent of the annualized average interest rate payable on such account or interest at the rate of 5 percent per year, simple interest, whichever the landlord elects. The landlord shall not commingle such moneys with any other funds of the landlord or hypothecate, pledge, or in any other way make use of such moneys until such moneys are actually due the landlord; or

(c) Post a surety bond, executed by the landlord as principal and a surety company authorized and licensed to do business in the state as surety, with the clerk of the circuit court in the county in which the dwelling unit is located in the total amount of the security deposits and advance rent he holds on behalf of the tenants or $50,000, whichever is less. The bond shall be conditioned upon the faithful compliance of the landlord with the provisions of this section and shall run to the Governor for the benefit of any tenant injured by the landlord's violation of the provisions of this section. In addition to posting the surety bond, the landlord shall pay to the tenant interest at the rate of 5 percent per year, simple interest.

(2) The landlord shall, within 30 days of receipt of advance rent or a security deposit, notify the tenant in writing of the manner in which the landlord is holding the advance rent or security deposit and the rate of interest, if any, which the tenant is to receive and the time of interest payments to the tenant. Such written notice shall:

(a) Be given in person or by mail to the tenant.

(b) State the name and address of the depository where the advance rent or security deposit is being held, whether the advance rent or security deposit is being held in a separate account for the benefit of the tenant or is commingled with other funds of the landlord, and, if commingled, whether such funds are deposited in an interest-bearing account in a _____ banking institution.

(c) Include a copy of the provisions of subsection (3).

Subsequent to providing such notice, if the landlord changes the manner or location in which he is holding the advance rent or security deposit, he shall notify the tenant within 30 days of the change according to the provisions herein set forth. This subsection does not apply to any landlord who rents fewer than five individual dwelling units. Failure to provide this notice shall not be a defense to the payment of rent when due.

(3)(a) Upon the vacating of the premises for termination of the lease, the landlord shall have 15 days to return the security deposit together with interest if otherwise required, or in which to give the tenant written notice by certified mail to the tenant's last known mailing address of his intention to impose a claim on the deposit and the reason for imposing the claim. The notice shall contain a statement in substantially the following form:

This is a notice of my intention to impose a claim for damages in the amount of _____ upon your security deposit, due to _____. It is sent to you as required by s. 83.49(3), _____ Statutes. You are hereby notified that you must object in writing to this deduction from your security deposit within 15 days from the time you receive this notice or I will be authorized to deduct my claim from your security deposit. Your objection must be sent to   (landlord's address) .

If the landlord fails to give the required notice within the 15-day period, he forfeits his right to impose a claim upon the security deposit.

(b) Unless the tenant objects to the imposition of the landlord's claim or the amount thereof within 15 days after receipt of the landlord's notice of intention to impose a claim, the landlord may then deduct the amount of his claim and shall remit the balance of the deposit to the tenant within 30 days after the date of the notice of intention to impose a claim for damages.

(c) If either party institutes an action in a court of competent jurisdiction to adjudicate his right to the security deposit, the prevailing party is entitled to receive his court costs plus a reasonable fee for his attorney. The court shall advance the cause on the calendar.

(4) The provisions of this section do not apply to transient rentals by hotels or motels as defined in chapter 509; nor do they apply in those instances in which the amount of rent or deposit, or both, is regulated by law or by rules or regulations of a public body, including public housing authorities and federally administered or regulated housing programs including s. 202, s. 221(d)(3) and (4), s. 236, or s. 8 of the National Housing Act, as amended, other than for rent stabilization. With the exception of subsections (3), (5), and (6), this section is not applicable to housing authorities or public housing agencies created pursuant to chapter 421 or other statutes.

(5) Except when otherwise provided by the terms of a written lease, any tenant who vacates or abandons the premises prior to the expira-

tion of the term specified in the written lease, or any tenant who vacates or abandons premises which are the subject of a tenancy from week to week, month to month, quarter to quarter, or year to year, shall give at least 7 days' notice by certified mail to the landlord prior to vacating or abandoning the premises, which notice shall include the address where the tenant may be reached. Failure to give such notice shall relieve the landlord of the notice requirement of paragraph (3)(a).

(6) For the purposes of this part, a renewal of an existing rental agreement shall be considered a new rental agreement, and any security deposit carried forward shall be considered a new security deposit.

(7) Upon the sale or transfer of title of the rental property from one owner to another, or upon a change in the designated rental agent, any and all security deposits or advance rents being held for the benefit of the tenants shall be transferred to the new owner or agent, together with any earned interest and with an accurate accounting showing the amounts to be credited to each tenant account. Upon the transfer of such funds and records as stated herein, and upon transmittal of a written receipt therefor, the transferor shall be free from the obligation imposed in subsection (1) to hold such moneys on behalf of the tenant. However, nothing herein shall excuse the landlord or agent for a violation of the provisions of this section while in possession of such deposits.

(8) Any person licensed under the provisions of s. 509.241, unless excluded by the provisions of this part, who fails to comply with the provisions of this part shall be subject to a fine or to the suspension or revocation of his license by the Division of Hotels and Restaurants of the Department of Business Regulation in the manner provided in s. 509.261.

(9) In those cases in which interest is required to be paid to the tenant, the landlord shall pay directly to the tenant, or credit against the current month's rent, the interest due to the tenant at least once annually. However, no interest shall be due a tenant who wrongfully terminates his tenancy prior to the end of the rental term.

SECURITY DEPOSIT PROVISIONS FROM MISCELLANEOUS LEASES

Lease A

5. The above referenced security deposit is a deposit by tenant with the landlord as security for the faithful performance by the tenant of all the terms of this agreement. The deposit shall be held in a manner allowed by law and shall be returned to the tenant on the full and faithful performance by him of all the provisions of the lease. The security deposit and advance rent shall be forfeited as liquidated damages, without prior notice to tenant, if the tenant fails to take possession or otherwise leaves or abandons the rented premises prior to the expiration of the term of this lease, and if landlord elects to

terminate the lease as opposed to continuing the lease in force and re-renting it for tenant's benefit as provided in paragraph (8) herein. If the security deposit is applied at the end of the stated term of this lease or for any other defaults of tenants then the security deposit shall be applied to actual damages and the balance returned or notice given to tenant pursuant to the _____ Statutes. If the lease is terminated for failure to pay rent then the security deposit shall be deemed liquidated damages for costs and expenses of renting the apartment but landlord shall also be entitled to any unpaid rent and any actual damages for physical harm done to the leased premises or any other costs incurred by landlord.

Lease B

4. $_____ as security has been deposited. Landlord may use therefrom such amounts as are reasonably necessary to remedy Tenant's defaults in the payment of rent, to repair damages caused by Tenant, and to clean the premises if necessary upon termination of tenancy. If used toward rent or damages during the term of tenancy, Tenant agrees to reinstate said total security deposit upon five days written notice delivered to Tenant in person or by mailing. Security deposit or balance thereof, if any, shall be mailed to Tenant at last known address within 14 days of surrender of premises.

Lease C

SECURITY Tenant is notified that the security deposit paid is
DEPOSIT held by the Landlord in a non-interest bearing escrow
3. account at _____.

If Tenant fails to take occupancy of the unit as agreed the Security Deposit is forfeited. Landlord may apply a portion or all of the Security Deposit to the cost of cleaning or repairs occasioned by Tenant's occupancy or use of the apartment, reasonable wear and tear excepted. Tenant will be notified of any claim against the Security Deposit within 15 days after the unit is surrendered to the Landlord's possession and after the termination date of the lease. If the Tenant vacates prior to the termination date of the lease, and gives Landlord written notice by certified mail seven (7) days in advance of intention to vacate, notification of claim will be made within 15 days after reletting of the apartment.

If the lease is fulfilled and there are no claims against the Security Deposit, refund will be made to the Tenant within 15 days of the termination of the lease.

If the Security Deposit does not cover all costs of the breach of the lease, Landlord may pursue all legal remedies to collect all costs or damages, including court costs and attorney's fees.

Tenant shall not use Security Deposit as last month's rent.

Lease D

7. To pay a security deposit of $_____ to secure Resident's pledge of full compliance with the terms of this agreement. NOTE: *This may not be used to pay rent under any circumstances!!* Any damages not previously reported as required in Paragraph 5 above will be repaired at Resident(s)' expense with funds other than Security Deposit.

Lease E

3) SECURITY DEPOSIT: Lessee agrees to pay Lessor the sum of _____ Dollars ($_____) as a security deposit held in escrow and as a guarantee against damage or loss and cleaning if necessary, to the rental unit, above normal wear and tear. This deposit is refundable less charges, if any, no later than fifteen (15) days after termination of this rental agreement. Lessee acknowledges that the leased premises were clean to his/her satisfaction prior to his/her occupancy.

Lease F

3. **DEPOSIT MONEY:** Lessee agrees to pay Lessor the sum of _____ ($_____) Dollars as deposit money to be held in escrow as required by law to guarantee against any damage, loss, or necessary cleaning to the unit where such damage, loss or cleaning exceeds normal wear and tear. The deposit money also may be used to pay for any damages suffered as the result of Lessee's breach of this Agreement. The deposit money is refundable, less any charges, no later than fifteen (15) days after the termination of this Rental Agreement unless otherwise provided by law. The Lessor shall have no obligation to return same to Lessee if Lessee defaults in performance of its promises herein contained. Lessee acknowledges that the leased premises were cleaned to his satisfaction prior to his occupancy. Landlord may retain Security Deposit or prepaid rent as a cancellation charge or as liquidated damages if Tenant fails to take occupancy of the premises as agreed or violates any of the terms of this lease. Security Deposit shall never be construed or intended to be applied as rent.

Lease G

On execution of this lease, Lessee deposits with Lessor the additional sum of One Hundred Fifty and no/100 Dollars ($150.00), receipt of which is hereby acknowledged by Lessor, as security for the full and faithful performance by Lessee of this lease, and the sum of Four Hundred Fifty and no/100 Dollars ($450.00) as the rent for the first and last months of the lease term. Upon vacating the premises for termination of the lease, Lessor shall return such deposit to Lessee in the manner provided by statute.

Lease H

2A. No part of your security deposit will be held in an interest bearing account. Landlord is holding your security deposit in a separate non-interest bearing account for the benefit of the tenants. This means that your security deposit is held in said account and cannot be: (1) commingled with other funds of the Landlord; (2) hypothecated, pledged, or in any other way used by the Landlord until such money is actually due the Landlord.

2B. Landlord is holding your security deposit in an interest bearing account at _____ located at _____. FIVE PER CENT (5%) interest will be paid to the benefit of the tenant since the security deposit money is held in an interest bearing account. Tenant will receive his accumulated interest upon vacating the premises. If a claim is imposed against tenant's security deposit money for damages, cleaning, nonpayment of rent, etc., interest will only be paid on that portion of the security deposit returned to tenant.

3. Your security deposit money will be returned to you within fifteen (15) days after termination of the lease agreement less any charges for damages above normal wear and tear. You are also hereby informed of your right to recover the deposit money under Section _____, _____ Statutes, as follows:

> "The Landlord has 15 days after the tenant vacates the premises for termination of rental agreement to impose a claim against the tenant's security deposit. If the Landlord fails to give the tenant notice of such claim within 15 days the Landlord waives his rights to retain the deposit and must return it to the tenant pursuant to Section _____, _____ Statutes."

I acknowledge that the Landlord has made the above disclosures to me this _____ day of _____, 19__, and I have read, understand and agree to be bound by each of them.

Lease I

(1) Tenants hereby agree to pay the following sums of money to Landlord in consideration of this lease:

$_____ for rent for period _____

$_____ rent held in escrow for last month _____

$_____ security deposit subject to terms stated in Section (2).

$_____ total of which $_____ has been paid on the signing of this agreement with

$_____ due on or before _____

(2) In the event Tenant fails to take occupancy of the premises or violates any of the terms of this lease the money deposited as security for the performance of the rental agreement shall be forfeited by the Tenant and retained by Landlord. At the termination of the rental period, in the event the Tenant is not in default in the performance of this agreement, Landlord shall give notice to tenant pursuant to Sec-

tion _____ Statutes, 19__, of his intent to deduct from said security deposit the cost of cleaning, unpaid rent, or repairs due to Tenant's use of the unit and furnishings, reasonable wear and tear expected, and pursuant to said statute, refund to Tenant any un-used portion. In the event Tenant breaches any covenant of this agreement, said money deposited as security for the performance of this agreement may be retained by Landlord and applied to damages due Landlord for such default without affecting Landlord's right to pursue all legal remedies to collect all costs or damages, including court costs and reasonable attorney fees sustained as a result of Tenant's breach of the terms and conditions of this lease. The monies deposited by Tenant as advanced rent or as security for the performance of this agreement shall be maintained by Agent in a special non-interest bearing account for the benefit of Tenants pursuant to section _____ Statutes. Bank _____

Lease J

2. SECURITY DEPOSITS: TENANT agrees to pay LANDLORD as a security deposit the sum of $_____ as security for the prompt payment of the rentals and other sums due or which may become due hereunder and the performance of all agreements herein of TENANT. Such deposit is to be refunded to TENANT upon his removal from the premises at the expiration or termination of this Rental Agreement, or any renewal thereof, after there has been deducted any and all rentals and other service charges due LANDLORD under the terms hereof, then remaining unpaid. In the event of a bona fide sale, subject to this Rental Agreement, LANDLORD shall have the right to transfer such security deposit to the purchaser for the benefit of TENANT, and LANDLORD shall be considered and will be thereby released by TENANT from all liability for the return of such security deposit, and TENANT agrees in such event to look solely to the new LANDLORD/ purchaser for the return of the deposit and for the performance of the obligations hereunder by LANDLORD. In event the sums due hereunder by TENANT to LANDLORD exceed the security deposit for repairs aforesaid or under any provisions hereof, then TENANT agrees to pay any additional sums due over and above said security deposit to LANDLORD within thirty (30) days after notification of such sums due LANDLORD. Your security deposit and or advanced rent are being held in a non-interest bearing account in the _____ Bank of _____, _____.

Separate Document attached to Lease J

Date _____

Received From _____ $_____ Dollars [ ] Cash [ ] Check [ ] M.O. as Security Deposit for the property: _____ City of _____ Zip _____ Balance of $_____ Due on or before _____

Management agrees that, subject to the conditions listed below, this security deposit will be returned in full.

Undersigned agrees that this security deposit may not be applied as rent, and that the full monthly rent will be paid on or before the first day of every month including the last month of occupancy.

_____

BY Property Manager

_____

Resident

_____

Resident

RELEASE OF THE SECURITY DEPOSIT IS SUBJECT TO THE FOLLOWING PROVISIONS:

1. Full term of lease has expired.
2. _____ days notice was given prior to leaving residence.
3. No damage to property beyond fair wear and tear.
4. Entire residence, including range, exhaust fan, refrigerator, bathroom, closets and cabinets are clean. Refrigerator to be defrosted.
5. No stickers or scratches or holes on walls. Eight small nail holes permitted.
7. No unpaid late charges or delinquent rents.
8. All keys are returned.
9. All debris and rubbish and discards placed in proper rubbish containers.
10. Forwarding address left with management.
11. When applicable—yard cut and cleaned.

The costs of labor and materials for cleaning and repairs, and delinquent payments will be deducted from Security Deposit if the above 11 provisions are not complied with. The Security Deposit will be refunded by a check, mailed to the forwarding address, made payable to all persons signing the Lease.

PROBLEM 1

Draft a set of questions to ask your client before working further on the lease.

PROBLEM 2

Outline the lease as it is. Keep the numbered headings just as they are; under each heading, make a phrase outline of the content of the section. Based on your outline, what structural and conceptual flaws do you discover in the lease?

PROBLEM 3

Outline a proposed redraft of the lease. Along with major headings, include subheadings where appropriate and a phrase outline of the content you propose to include.

PROBLEM 4

After evaluating the security deposit provisions you have from other leases, draft a security deposit provision consistent with the applicable statute. Make sure you have a clear concept of what a security deposit is. What is its purpose? How can the landlord use the money and under what circumstances? Does the provision actually operate as a liquidated damages clause? If not, how does it differ from such a clause?

PROBLEM 5

Redraft the entire lease.

SET C

As legal advisor to your county's commissioners, you have been asked to review two ordinances from other counties that are now proposed for adoption in yours.

PROBLEM 1

Below is Ordinance No. 82–19, commonly known by its proponents as "the swimming pool ordinance." Draft questions to ask its proponents.

PROBLEM 2

Outline the ordinance as it is. Be prepared to discuss how you evaluate its conceptualization and organization.

PROBLEM 3

Outline your proposed redraft of the ordinance. Be prepared to justify any substantive policy changes you propose.

PROBLEM 4

Redraft the ordinance to improve its conceptual and organizational structure. Take care that you make no substantive policy changes without authorization.

ORDINANCE NO. 82–19

1   AN ORDINANCE PROVIDING FOR THE CONSTRUCTION AND
2   MAINTENANCE OF FENCES AND SAFETY BARRIERS FOR
3   SWIMMING POOLS, PROVIDING FOR PERMITS, PROVIDING
4   FOR TYPES OF SAFETY BARRIERS AND FENCES PERMIT-
5   TED, PROVIDING AN EFFECTIVE DATE.

6 BE IT ORDAINED BY THE BOARD OF COUNTY COMMISSIONERS
7 OF _____ COUNTY, _____:

8   SECTION 1: <u>Intent.</u> It is recognized that swimming pools which
9 are not surrounded by fences or safety barriers pose a threat to the
10 safety of the citizens of _____ County, _____, especially young

children. The purpose of this ordinance is to provide a minimum standard of protection against the hazards of unprotected and easily accessible swimming pools.

SECTION 2: Definitions. As used in this ordinance the following terms shall have the following meanings:

Swimming Pool—Any constructed or prefabricated pool used for swimming or bathing over 24″ in depth measured between the floor of the pool and the maximum water level.

Swimming Pool (Private)—Shall be defined to include all constructed or assembled pools which are used as a swimming pool in connection with a residence whether single or multi-family and are available for use only to the family of the owner or owners and their private guests or invitees.

Swimming Pool (Public)—Shall be defined to include any constructed or prefabricated pool other than a private pool.

SECTION 3: Permits. Before any work is commenced, permits shall be secured for all swimming pools and for the safety barriers. Plans shall contain all details necessary to show compliance with the terms and conditions of this ordinance. No swimming pool permit shall be issued unless simultaneously therewith a permit is secured for the erection of the required safety barrier. If the premises are already enclosed, as hereinafter provided, a permit for the safety barrier shall not be required if, upon inspection of the premises, the existing barrier and gates are proven to be satisfactory.

SECTION 4: Required for final inspection of pool. No swimming pool final inspection and approval shall be given by the Building and Zoning Codes Department, unless there has been erected a safety barrier as hereinafter provided. No pool shall be filled with water unless a final inspection has been made and approved, except for testing purposes as may be approved by the Building and Zoning Codes Department.

SECTION 5: Types permitted. The safety barriers shall take the form of a screened-in patio, a wooden fence, a wire fence, a rock wall, a concrete block wall or other materials so as to enable the owner to blend the same with the style of architecture planned or in existence on the property.

SECTION 6: Height. The minimum height of the safety barrier shall not be less than four feet.

SECTION 7: Location of barrier. The safety barrier shall be erected either around the swimming pool or around the premises on which the swimming pool is erected. In either event, it shall enclose the area entirely, prohibiting unrestrained admittance to the enclosed area.

SECTION 8: Gates. Gates shall be of the spring lock type, or equivalent, so that they shall automatically be in a closed and fastened position at all times.

SECTION 9: <u>Wooden fences.</u> In the wooden type fence, the boards, pickets, louvers, or other such members, shall be spaced, constructed, and erected so as to make the fence not easily climbable or penetrable.

SECTION 10: <u>Walls.</u> Walls whether of the rock or block type shall be erected to make them not easily climbable.

SECTION 11: <u>Wire fences.</u> Wire fences shall be the two inch chain link or diamond weave nonclimbable type, or of an approved equal, with top rail. They shall be of a heavy, galvanized material.

SECTION 12: <u>Refusal of permit.</u> It shall be within the discretion of the director of the Building and Zoning Department to refuse approval of any barrier which, in his opinion, does not furnish the safety requirement of this section i.e., that is high enough and so constructed to keep children of pre-school age from getting over or through it.

SECTION 13: <u>Maintenance.</u> It shall be the responsibility of the owner or occupant of the premises upon which a swimming pool is hereafter erected to maintain and keep in proper and safe condition the safety barrier required and erected in accordance with this ordinance.

SECTION 14: <u>Exemptions.</u> The provisions of this ordinance shall not apply to above ground swimming pools, access to which is gained by a ladder or other portable device or movable device such as a swing up ladder which can be easily removed from the pool or otherwise secured to accomplish the minimum level of protection afforded by this ordinance.

SECTION 15: <u>Applicability.</u> The provisions of this ordinance shall apply to all new private swimming pools, the construction of which commences after the effective date.

SECTION 16: <u>Variances.</u> Variances from the provisions of this ordinance may be applied for and received from the _____ County Zoning Board of Adjustment where it is demonstrated that unique circumstances dictate that the provisions of this ordinance would serve no useful purpose and further that the purposes of this ordinance would not be frustrated by the granting of such variance.

SECTION 17: <u>Warning.</u> The degree of protection afforded by this ordinance is considered reasonable for regulatory purposes. The provisions of this ordinance shall not be construed by any person to replace that degree of care which is required to properly supervise and control either their own premises or their own children who may wander upon the premises of another where a swimming pool is located. The degree of protection afforded by this ordinance is declared to be minimal and it is specifically recognized that any safety barrier may be surmounted under the proper circumstances.

SECTION 18: <u>Severability.</u> It is declared to be the legislative intent that if any section, subsection, sentence, clause or provision of this ordinance is held invalid, the remainder of the ordinance shall not be affected.

103   SECTION 19: <u>Effective date.</u> This ordinance shall take effect upon
104 receipt of the official acknowledgement from the Office of the Secretary
105 of the State of _____ that this ordinance has been filed with said
106 office.

PROBLEM 5

Below is Ordinance 84–10, known as "the false alarm ordinance." Draft questions to ask its proponents.

PROBLEM 6

Outline the ordinance as it is. Be prepared to discuss how you evaluate its conceptualization and organization.

PROBLEM 7

Outline your proposed redraft of the ordinance. Be prepared to justify any substantive policy changes you propose.

PROBLEM 8

Redraft the ordinance to improve its conceptual and organizational structure. Take care that you make no substantive policy changes without authorization.

_____ COUNTY FALSE ALARM ORDINANCE 84–10

1   WHEREAS, there are presently in use within the unincorporated
2 area of _____ County certain hardware and other radio and electroni-
3 cally controlled alarm systems which are privately owned and operated;
4 and,

5   WHEREAS, these privately owned burglary and robbery alarm
6 systems are causing substantial misuse of the manpower and resources
7 of the Office of the Sheriff by causing the dispatch of patrol units to the
8 scene of numerous false alarms thus removing the units from patrol
9 and causing them to be out of service when a true need or emergency
10 situation could exist; and,

11   WHEREAS, telephone alarm devices regulated or programmed to
12 make connection with the Sheriff's Office could seize and hold Sheriff's
13 office telephone lines to the exclusion of other calls; and

14   WHEREAS, the current high incidence of false alarms and the
15 misuse of telephone alarm devices is deemed to constitute a threat to
16 the people of the County and is obstructive of efficient protection;

17   NOW, THEREFORE, BE IT ORDAINED, BY THE BOARD OF
18 COUNTY COMMISSIONERS OF _____ COUNTY, _____;

19   Section 1. <u>Definitions.</u>

20   a) "Alarm system" shall mean any mechanical, electrical or ra-
21 dio-controlled device which is designed to be used for the detection of
22 any unauthorized entry into a building, structure or facility, or both,
23 and which emits a sound or transmits a signal or message when

activated. Alarm Systems include, but are not limited to, direct dial telephone devices, audible alarms and proprietor alarms. Excluded from the definition of alarm systems are devices which are designed or used to register alarms that are audible, visible, or perceptible in or from any motor vehicle or auxiliary device installed by telephone companies to protect telephone systems from damage or disruption of service.

b) "False alarm" shall mean the activation of any alarm signal by an alarm system which is responded to by the Sheriff's Office, and which is not caused or precipitated by an actual or attempted burglary or other attempted unlawful act or activity, or other emergency reasonably requiring the services of the Sheriff's Office. An alarm will be deemed to be valid only when substantial physical evidence exists which would clearly indicate a criminal act was the sole reason for activation of the alarm. Examples include, but are not limited to: freshly broken windows, doors, or locks; obvious indications of forced illegal entry; missing property, etc. Alarm systems which activate from simply shaking of doors or rattling of windows are not properly installed or maintained and are deemed to be emitting a "false alarm".

c) "Person" shall mean any natural person, firm, partnership, association, corporation, company or organization of any kind.

d) "Sheriff" shall mean the Sheriff of _____ County, or his designated representative.

e) "Automatic dialing device" shall mean an alarm system which automatically sends over regular telephone lines, by direct connection, or otherwise, a pre-recorded voice message or coded signal indicating the existence of the emergency situation that the alarm system is designated to detect, but shall not include such telephone lines exclusively dedicated to an alarm system which are permanently active and terminate within the communication center of the Sheriff's Office.

f) "Residential premises" shall mean any structure or combination of structures which serve as dwelling units including single family as well as multi-family units.

g) "Commercial premises" shall mean any structure or area which is not defined herein as residential premises.

h) "Fee" shall mean an assessment of costs imposed pursuant to this ordinance to defray the expense of responding to a false alarm.

Section 2. Notification and Registration. Every person who shall own, operate, or lease any alarm system as defined herein within the unincorporated area of _____ County, whether existing or to be installed in the future, shall, within thirty (30) days of the effective date of this ordinance for existing alarm systems or prior to installation of alarm systems installed after the effective date of this ordinance, notify the Sheriff, on forms to be provided by the Sheriff's Office of the following information:

1. The type, make, model of the alarm system.

2. Whether installed in a residential or commercial premise, and the location of the alarm system, including the street address or specific directions to where the alarm system is located.

3. The name, address, business and/or home telephone number of the owner or lessee of the alarm system. In the event that the owner or lessee of the alarm system is a business entity, partnership, or corporation, the business shall indicate the name, street address, and telephone number of the agent designated by the business to be responsible for contacting.

4. The names, addresses and telephone numbers of not less than two (2) persons to be notified to respond in the event of an alarm activation. The responder persons so listed must be available at all times and be authorized to enter the premises and deactivate the alarm system. It shall be the responsibility of the owner, operator, or lessee of the alarm system to keep the listing current.

5. Such other information as the Sheriff shall deem necessary or appropriate.

Section 3. Response to False Alarm; Required Reports; Corrective Action; Penalties and Disconnection.

a) For the purpose of this ordinance, responsibility for a false alarm shall be borne by the owner, operator, or lessee of the alarm system.

b) A response to a false alarm shall result when any Deputy Sheriff is dispatched to or responds to the activation of any alarm system.

c) The following shall be required by each person who owns, operates or controls any premise, commercial or residential, for each incident of a response to a false alarm by the Sheriff's Office.

1. For a response to a premise at which no other false alarm has occurred from the effective date of this ordinance or within the preceding six (6) month period, whichever shall be less, a written report, on forms prescribed by the Sheriff's Office shall be filed with the Sheriff's Office within ten (10) days after notice to do so, setting forth the cause of such false alarm, the corrective action taken, whether the alarm has been inspected by an authorized serviceman, and such other information as the Sheriff may reasonably require to determine the cause of such false alarm and corrective action necessary. No fee shall be charged for the first response.

2. For a second or third response to false alarms to any premise, commercial or residential, within six (6) months after the first response, no fee shall be assessed, but a written report shall be required as for a first response.

114 3. For a fourth false alarm response to any premise, commercial
115 or residential, within six (6) months after such third response of a false
116 alarm and for each succeeding response within six (6) months of the
117 preceding response, a fee of TWENTY–FIVE DOLLARS ($25.00) shall
118 be charged; a written report and inspection shall be required/and if
119 such fourth false alarm or any such succeeding false alarm is a result of
120 failure to take necessary corrective action, the Sheriff may order the
121 disconnection of such alarm system. For failure to pay the required
122 fee, the Sheriff may order the disconnection of any alarm system. It
123 shall be a violation of this ordinance not to disconnect, or to reconnect
124 such alarm system until such corrective action is taken and the fee is
125 paid, provided that no disconnection shall be ordered on any premise
126 required by law to have an alarm system in operation. Any order for
127 disconnection shall be rescinded by the Sheriff upon presentation of
128 demonstrative evidence of corrective action and inspection, as may be
129 required by the Sheriff, and a finding that adequate corrective action
130 has been taken and the required fee has been paid.

131 Section 4. Requirement to Respond to Premise when Alarm is
132 Activated. The owner, operator, or lessee or a listed responder of an
133 alarm system is required to respond by reporting to the premises or
134 facility within thirty (30) minutes from the time of the notification by
135 Sheriff of the activation of any alarm system, whether false or not.
136 Failure to respond shall be deemed a violation of this ordinance by the
137 owner, operator or lessee of the alarm system.

138 Section 5. Deactivation of Audible Alarms Within Thirty Minutes.
139 It shall be a violation of this ordinance to maintain an alarm system or
140 audible alarm which does not deactivate within thirty (30) minutes of
141 its activation.

142 Section 6. Automatic Dialing Devices. It shall be a violation of
143 this ordinance for any person to install, maintain, own, possess or
144 operate any automatic dialing device alarm system regulated or
145 programmed to make connection with any telephone number installed
146 in the Sheriff's Office, except to such telephone number(s) which may
147 be determined and designated by the Sheriff.

148 Section 7. Requirement of Auxiliary Power Supply. It shall be a
149 violation of this ordinance for any person to install, maintain, own,
150 possess or operate any alarm system which does not have an auxiliary
151 power supply which activates in the event of a power failure or
152 electrical outage.

153 Section 8. Right to a Hearing. Upon written request of the
154 person assessed a fee or ordered to disconnect an alarm, a hearing may
155 be held before the Sheriff or his designee to review such assessment or
156 disconnect order. Such request must be made within fifteen (15) days
157 after the date of the notice of assessment or disconnect order. At the
158 hearing, such evidence as is deemed necessary may be presented.

159   Section 9. <u>General Penalty.</u> Anyone convicted of a violation of, or
160 failure to comply with, any of the provisions of this ordinance shall be
161 punished as provided by law.

162   Section 10. <u>Severability.</u> If any section, subsection, sentence,
163 clause, provision or part of this ordinance shall be held invalid for any
164 reason, the remainder of this ordinance shall not be affected thereby,
165 but shall remain in full force and effect.

166   Section 11. <u>Effective Date.</u> October 12, 1984.

Chapter 6

CHOOSING LANGUAGE: VAGUENESS, GENERALITY, AND AMBIGUITY

I. FLEXIBILITY THROUGH VAGUENESS AND GENERALITY

It is a widely held but mistaken notion that the goal of legal writing, particularly legal drafting, is absolute precision. Not only is such a goal impossible to reach; in legal drafting, it is undesirable. Instead the goal is, or should be, "a precisely appropriate degree of imprecision." [1]

This is not double-talk. This goal recognizes that legal documents are plans for a future full of circumstances that neither the drafter nor the client can presently know about. Thus documents need to be flexible. The most useful language to accomplish flexibility is often vague rather than precise, general rather than particular.[2] When the drafter uses language to make a document flexible, the user receives the delegated authority to interpret later when the circumstantial context can be brought to bear on the interpretation.[3]

A. VAGUENESS DISTINGUISHED FROM AMBIGUITY

Professor Dickerson has defined vagueness as "the degree to which, independent of equivocation, language is uncertain in its respective application to a number of particulars." [4] This definition's reference to

---

1. C. Curtis, It's Your Law 76 (1954).

2. See Kirk, Legal Drafting: Some Elements of Technique, 4 Tex.Tech L.Rev. 297, 300 (1973).

3. Curtis, A Better Theory of Legal Interpretation, 3 Vand.L.Rev. 407, 419–25 (1950).

4. R. Dickerson, The Fundamentals of Legal Drafting 39 (2d ed. 1986); see Farns-

worth, Some Considerations in the Drafting of Agreements: Problems in Interpretation and Gap Filling, 23 Record of N.Y. C.B.A. 105, 106 (1968) (vagueness as result of words that do not refer to "a neatly bounded class but a distribution about a central norm").

equivocation distinguishes between vagueness and ambiguity. It is a useful distinction because vagueness is often both purposeful and valuable while ambiguity is usually inadvertent and dangerous.

Some commentators use the terms "ambiguity" and "vagueness" as though they were synonymous. However, when they treat "purposive" ambiguity as a deliberate device to delegate the authority to interpret, the commentators appear to be talking about vagueness but calling it ambiguity.[5] For example, here is historian Henry Steele Commager writing about the framers of the United States Constitution.

COMMAGER, MEESE IGNORES HISTORY IN DEBATE WITH COURT
N.Y. Times, Nov. 20, 1985, at A31, col. 3.*

* * * Quite deliberately, they fell back on *ambiguous* words and phrases: "Republican form of government," "unreasonable searches and seizures," "cruel and unusual punishment," "provide for the general welfare" and many others, confident that future generations would have the good sense to define this language in terms "adequate to the exigencies" of politics and government.

Indeed, Nathaniel Gohrman of Massachusetts candidly said of the finished document that "the *vagueness* of the terms constitutes the propriety of them." And as a consequence of the delegates' foresight, the "rigid" American Constitution proved as flexible as the "unwritten" British one [emphasis added].

The distinction between ambiguity and vagueness is worth preserving. Ambiguity equivocates; if a word is ambiguous, there are usually only two or three possibilities as to what it means. If a word is vague, there are many more possibilities. Vagueness is a matter of degree.

The only words that are totally precise (the opposite of vague) are words that refer to only one thing or one person such as "the Mona Lisa," "William Shakespeare," or "the current Queen of England." Note that the reference to the current Queen is more precise than a reference to Queen Elizabeth would be. "England's Queen Elizabeth" could refer to Elizabeth I as well as Elizabeth II. That term is ambiguous. A reference to "Queen Elizabeth" is also vague. There may be unknown numbers of local festival queens and the like named Elizabeth as well as somebody's dog or cat. But there is only one "current Queen of England."

It is true, however, that context can eliminate vagueness just as it can ambiguity. A reference to Queen Elizabeth's meeting on a particular date with England's Prime Minister Margaret Thatcher would be neither vague nor ambiguous.

---

5. See Dickerson, above note 4, at 35, note 5; see, for example, Miller, Statutory Language and the Purposive Use of Ambiguity, 42 Va.L.Rev. 23, 23–24, notes 29, 30 and accompanying text (1956).

As this example illustrates, nearly all terms are vague to some degree. Even though precise reference is the exception rather than the rule, some words are more vague than others. Perhaps the most vague are references to colors, smells, sounds, and other things that we know by the senses. What does "red" mean? Or "loud" or "bitter" or "cold"? What does "high" mean? Or "near"? Even though we might have a difficult time explaining such concepts to make sure someone else perceives them in exactly the same way we do, we do not avoid using the terms at all. We largely rely on context to make meaning precise. For example, people do not have difficulty distinguishing between a "bitter divorce" and a "bitter lemon pie."

B. VAGUENESS ASSOCIATED WITH GENERALITY

Just as the distinction between vagueness and ambiguity is worth preserving, the association between vagueness and generality is worth acknowledging. "Vagueness is normally used in the philosophy of language in connection with general terms * * *." [6]

Strictly speaking, vagueness and generality are distinguishable. General terms refer to several, perhaps many, particulars, but the exact particulars referred to are capable of being identified. In other words, the intended scope of general terms is clear, while the intended scope of vague terms is not. A reference to "this state's statutes" is general but not vague, assuming the context provides the name of the state. A reference to "my heirs at law" is general but not vague, assuming the context indicates whose heirs, when they are to be determined, and according to what state's law.

Although it is possible to distinguish between vague and general terms, it is of dubious value to devote very much time and energy to doing so. It is not the label that matters. What matters is that the drafter be alert to the need for flexibility, or elasticity, in documents that describe future events and prescribe or proscribe future behavior. Here is Henry Steele Commager again on the delegates to the 1787 Constitutional Convention.

COMMAGER, MEESE IGNORES HISTORY IN DEBATE
WITH COURT
N.Y. Times, Nov. 20, 1985, at A31, col. 2–3.*

* * * Because the delegates were free from the arrogance of supposing they could anticipate the future, that is just what they did. They laid down broad general principles for grants of power, and restraints on power, assigning to the national Government powers of a general nature and leaving to the states those of a local nature—and this in language flexible enough to anticipate an ever-changing society, econo-

6. Christie, Vagueness and Legal Language, 48 Minn.L.Rev. 885, 886 (1964).

my and political crises. That is how Abraham Lincoln interpreted the Constitution during the greatest crisis of our history: The Constitution was flexible enough to enable him to do whatever was necessary to save the union.

If the distinction between vagueness and generality is to be preserved at all, it may help to remember the difference between type facts and unique facts. Unique facts get expressed in more particular terms. They report the past and are the language of pleadings and other litigation documents. Thus a complaint alleges that "the landlord failed to repair the front steps." In contrast, a lease, looking to the future, expresses type facts in general terms. It refers to "the landlord's duty to maintain the common areas." It may move still farther from precision and refer to "remedies for breach of duty."

It often does not matter at what point the language is no longer merely general but becomes vague as well.[7] "Language, at any rate in legal documents, does not fix meaning. It circumscribes meaning."[8]

C. TIGHTENING AND LOOSENING LANGUAGE

What matters is whether the term the drafter has chosen will stretch to cover the particular circumstance to which somebody later wants to apply it—or the circumstance somebody wants it not to reach. For example, Charles C. Curtis describes the process of drafting an agreement for an unsecured loan. The vice-president of a bank, the client, wants a provision about the borrower's duty to keep a certain amount of "working capital." But "working capital" might be too vague. The drafter chooses to say, "the excess of the total current assets over current liabilities, determined in strict accordance with sound accounting practice by * * * independent certified accountants * * *." The drafter chooses the modifiers with special care. "Independent certified" keeps "accountants" from stretching far enough to cover the borrower's own accountants or uncertified accountants. On the other hand, "sound" allows "accounting practice" to stretch far enough to cover current practices that are subject to customary discretion within the profession of accountancy.[9] This kind of elasticity should not be denigrated as an abdication of the drafter's power to legislate precisely. Instead the elasticity acknowledges that the fabric of business dealings and the fabric of the social structure require individuals to be able to decide what is reasonable under the current circumstances.

This same recognition of the value of imprecision is reflected in the concepts that serve as constitutional principles.

---

7. For discussion of the theory that lawyers deal in the general and the particular rather than the abstract and the concrete, see Curtis, above note 1, at 59–60.

8. *Id.* at 67.

9. *Id.* at 67–68.

MARTIN v. HUNTER'S LESSEE
14 U.S. (1 Wheat.) 304, 326 (1816).

The constitution unavoidably deals in general language. It did not suit the purposes of the people, in framing this great charter of our liberties, to provide for minute specifications of its powers, or to declare the means by which those powers should be carried into execution. It was foreseen that this would be a perilous and difficult, if not an impracticable, task.

Thus our legal literature is full of references to "due process," "equal protection," and a wealth of other such imprecise terms. They were intended to be so. Now and then someone urges something like the argument that "interstate commerce" does not include interstate telegraph companies because telegraph did not exist when the Framers chose that term, but such an argument does not usually get very far.[10] One of the clearest instances of choosing vague terms on purpose to allow for future variations in circumstance was in the U.S. Supreme Court's direction to integrate the schools "with all deliberate speed." [11] Legislators assume the same kind of general control over the future without committing anyone to specifics when they direct:

> The tenant shall not unreasonably withhold consent to the landlord to enter the dwelling unit from time to time * * *.

Likewise, contracting parties engage in the same sort of flexible social control when they agree in a lease:

> In case the premises should be damaged by fire, wind, rain, or other cause beyond the control of both landlord and tenant, then the premises will be repaired within a reasonable time at the expense of landlord.

II. THE DANGERS OF VAGUENESS AND GENERALITY

Vagueness and generality do sometimes cause trouble. Occasionally a statute is held void for vagueness. In the realm of both public and private documents, there is always the possibility of the reader in bad faith who insists that now means next year or here means three states to the west.

For instance, the story is told of the man who posted a sign on his barn saying, "Please do not ask permission to hunt." When he found hunters in his woods and asked them whether they had read his sign, they told him they had and assumed from it that he meant he wanted

---

10. For example, see Pensacola Tel. Co. v. Western Union Tel. Co., 96 U.S. (96 Otto) 1 (1877).

11. Brown v. Bd. of Educ. of Topeka, Kansas, 349 U.S. 294, 301, 75 S.Ct. 753, 757 (1955).

hunters to go ahead without bothering him. What this amounts to, of course, is "purposely pretending not to hear." [12]

But the danger of someone's saying "this" means "that" exists with respect to almost any term. For example, parties to a contract have argued about the word "chicken." Did it mean only a young chicken suitable for broiling or frying or any chicken meeting the contract's specification on weight and quality? [13] In another sales contract, one party argued that "minimum 50% protein" in horsemeat scraps could stretch to mean 49.5%.[14] An insured once argued that a fire insurance policy covering lumber stored in "sheds" covered lumber in the basement of a two-story warehouse.[15]

It probably would be impossible to anticipate and thus prevent such interpretations. Even if it were possible, it would require such wordy detailing of particulars that documents would become nearly impossible to wade through.

III. THE DANGERS OF OVERPARTICULARITY

Listing particulars or even several fairly general terms is a common device to try to give a clear idea of the meaning of vague terms. This has been likened to drawing several overlapping circles to bring attention to the overlapping area. It is a way of using vagueness to aid precise understanding.[16]

Thus the lease provision about damage to the premises does not refer merely to "cause beyond the control of both landlord and tenant" but also mentions "fire, wind, and rain" to give more of an idea of the kind of damage contemplated. Snow damage would probably be included. A baseball through a window thrown by the tenant's visiting grandchild might not be.

However, this device for clarifying vague terms can produce a great deal of trouble through the operation of the canon *expressio unius est exclusio alterius,* which means that to express one thing is to exclude similar alternatives not mentioned. The lesson the canon teaches is to avoid lists of particulars because they usually cannot be exhaustive. The danger is that some particular that is left out will be regarded as purposefully omitted.[17]

12. AP dispatch, reported in Christie, above note 6, at 887, note 3.

13. Frigaliment Importing Co. v. B.N.S. Int'l Sales Corp., 190 F.Supp. 116, 117 (S.D. N.Y.1960).

14. Hurst v. W.J. Lake & Co., 141 Or. 306, 309, 16 P.2d 627, 628 (1932).

15. Easton v. Washington County Ins. Co., 391 Pa. 28, 32–33, 137 A.2d 332, 335 (1957).

16. Christie, above note 6, at 895–96.

17. For analysis of how this canon has been called into service to help reverse a well established interpretation of federal immigration law, see INS v. Phinpathya, 464 U.S. 183, 104 S.Ct. 584 (1984); Pelta, INS v. Phinpathya: Literalist Statutory Interpretation in the Supreme Court, 23 San Diego L.Rev. 401 (1986).

Omitting a particular can cause trouble; so can applying the canon to determine it a purposeful omission. Consider the case of the physician who withdrew from his partnership in a clinic. The partnership agreement limited his right to practice for two years within a given area, and the remaining partners in the clinic sued to enforce the agreement. The trial court found for the clinic. The appellate court reversed the judgment, holding that the partnership agreement was void under a statute respecting contracts in restraint of trade. Here is the pertinent part of the statute.

> (1) Every contract by which anyone is restrained from exercising a lawful profession, trade or business of any kind, otherwise than is provided by subsections (2) and (3) hereof, is to that extent void.
>
> (2) One who sells the good will of a business, or any shareholder of a corporation selling or otherwise disposing of all of his shares in said corporation, may agree with the buyer, and one who is employed as an agent or employee may agree with his employer, to refrain from carrying on or engaging in a similar business and from soliciting old customers of such employer within a reasonably limited time and area, so long as the buyer or any person deriving title to the good will from him, and so long as such employer continues to carry on a like business therein. Said agreements may, in the discretion of a court of competent jurisdiction be enforced by injunction.
>
> (3) Partners may, upon or in anticipation of a dissolution of the partnership, agree that all or some of them will not carry on a similar business within a reasonably limited time and area.

The court figured out that since subsection (1) refers to "profession, trade or business," and subsection (2) refers only to "business," then subsection (2) must omit professions and trades on purpose. Accordingly, the court decided that the exception described in subsection (2) did not apply to the professional partnership. The applicable provision of the clinic's agreement was unacceptably in restraint of trade.[18]

The state supreme court quashed the decision, taking the position that the statute had been adopted from another state and thus should be construed as it had been in the courts of the other state, where the exception applied to professions and trades as well as businesses.[19] The supreme court relied heavily on the dissent to the appellate opinion, which has no kind words for the majority's use of the canon.

AKEY v. MURPHY

229 So.2d 276, 279–80 (Fla.App.1969) (Mann, J., dissenting).

In the search for meaning there are no shortcuts, and Latin is no substitute for thought. Of course expressio unius est exclusio alterius if the alterius is excluded from the unius by context or common sense. But in the statute we here interpret, *"business"* is first used following the words *"profession, trade or "* and followed by *"of any kind."* Thus

18. Akey v. Murphy, 229 So.2d 276, 279 (Fla.App.1969).

19. Akey v. Murphy, 238 So.2d 94, 95–96 (Fla.1970).

where "business" recurs in subsections (2) and (3) it is used in its generic sense which includes within ejusdem generis "profession" and "trade." At least the Attorney General, mirabile dictu, so thought in 1964 when he opined that physicians could indeed enter into such an agreement as is here involved. Op.Atty.Gen. 064–121. But neither *expressio* nor *ejusdem* determines the correct interpretation of a statute. These Latin labels are affixed *after* interpretation by us judges. When they are taken seriously, as *expressio unius* is here, as factors in the process of decision, the result often distorts legislative intent.

The first step in statutory construction is a reading of the entire statute:

"542.12 Contracts in restraint of trade invalid; exceptions.—

"(1) Every contract by which anyone is restrained from exercising a lawful profession, trade or business of any kind, otherwise than is provided by subsections (2) and (3) hereof, is to that extent void.

"(2) One who sells the good will of a business, or any shareholder of a corporation selling or otherwise disposing of all of his shares in said corporation, may agree with the buyer, and one who is employed as an agent or employee may agree with his employer, to refrain from carrying on or engaging in a similar business and from soliciting old customers of such employer within a reasonably limited time and area, so long as the buyer or any person deriving title to the good will from him, and so long as such employer continues to carry on a like business therein. Said agreements may, in the discretion of a court of competent jurisdiction be enforced by injunction.

"(3) Partners may, upon or in anticipation of a dissolution of the partnership, agree that all or some of them will not carry on a similar business within a reasonably limited time and area.

"(4) This section does not apply to any litigation which may be pending, or to any cause of action which may have accrued, prior to May 27, 1953."

I cannot read into that statute any intention on the part of our Legislature to enact a blanket prohibition against contracts not to compete and then to permit them between those engaged in *business* but not between those engaged in *professions* or *trades*.

* * *

In truth the time is overdue to rescue the law of statutory interpretation from Latin as the Second Vatican Council rescued the Mass. Max Radin wrote: "In all this what room is there for the standard 'canons of interpretations,' for *ejusdem generis, expressio unius,* and the entire coterie or band of phrases and tags and shibboleths which are so wearisomely familiar? I should be tempted to deny that they have ever resolved an honest doubt, if a general negative were provable. Certainly it is hard to find an instance in which they did more than invest with the appropriate symbolic uniform a conclusion that should have been quite as respectable in the ordinary civilian clothes of sober common sense." A Short Way With Statutes, 56 Harv.L.Rev. 388 (1942).

———

Even though the canons do not fare well in this dissent, it is also true that adopting another state's construction of an adopted statute is itself only another construction device, not inherently more, or less, sensible for its lack of a Latin name.

Ejusdem generis is another Latin-named canon that poses a threat to the drafter of lists. *Ejusdem generis* means "of the same kind." The canon provides a method for limiting the meaning of a general term at the end of a list of more particular ones. For example, if a statute allows a tax deduction for losses from "fire, storm, shipwreck, or other casualty," a deduction is probably not allowed for loss of a diamond ring by negligently dropping it into a lake. When figuring out how restrictive the general term is, the interpreter should keep in mind that the purpose of adding the general term was presumably to account for reasonable possibilities left out of the list of particulars because the drafter did not think of them.[20]

The canon poses a threat to the drafter because an interpreter may excessively narrow the meaning of a term in light of the preceding terms associated with it. For instance, the Williams Act[21] prohibits "any fraudulent, deceptive, or manipulative acts or practices, in connection with any tender offer." In 1985, the U.S. Supreme Court held that a withdrawal of one tender offer and substitution of another was not manipulative because "manipulative" meant deceptive or fraudulent.[22]

The dangerous error of overparticularity is especially common in wills[23] and trusts.[24] Consider, for example, the following all too typical directions to an executor. The particularity works as a constant invitation to think about what other particulars are not mentioned and why not.

> Section 1. I direct my Executor, as promptly as practicable after my death, to pay from and out of my residuary estate all my just debts, if any there be, my burial expenses, including the cost of a marker and the engraving of the marker at my grave, all costs and expenses of administering and settling my estate and all lawful taxes assessed by reason of my death against my taxable estate or any part thereof, including estate, inheritance, succession, transfer and any other taxes, by whatever name called, whether levied by the Federal Government or by any State Government or political subdivision of any State, and such taxes shall not be charged against or collected from any legatee or devisee of any share or part of my estate, other than my residuary

20. See W. Statsky, Legislative Analysis and Drafting 90–91 (2d ed. 1984).

21. 15 U.S.C. § 78n(e) (1982).

22. Schreiber v. Burlington Northern, Inc., 472 U.S. 1, 8, 105 S.Ct. 2458, 2462 (1985).

23. See E. Schlesinger, English as a Second Language for Lawyers, 12 Inst. on Est. Plan. para. 708 (1978).

24. See J. Johnson, A Draftsman's Handbook for Wills and Trust Agreements 10–13 (1961).

estate, or from the beneficiary or beneficiaries of any insurance policy or policies on my life and the proceeds of which are included as a part of my taxable estate, or from any person who receives or acquires at my death, in any manner whatsoever, any property or any interest in any property which is considered or treated as a part of my estate for the purpose of computing any one or more of the aforesaid taxes.[25]

For comparison, consider the following recitation of the powers of a personal representative. Without the redundancies of the above provision, it is easier to assess the value of the particulars included here.

I appoint my wife, _____, as PERSONAL REPRESENTATIVE of my estate and direct that she serve without bond. In addition to the powers conferred upon personal representatives by law, she shall have full power, in her discretion and without any court order or proceeding to lease, or to sell pursuant to option or otherwise at public or private sale and upon such terms as she shall deem best, any real or personal property belonging to my estate, without regard to the necessity of such sale for the purpose of paying debts, taxes or devises; or to retain any or all of such property not so required, without liability for any depreciation thereof; to make distribution in kind; to assign or transfer certificates of stock, bonds or other securities; to adjust, compromise and settle all matters of business and claims in favor of or against my estate; to continue any unincorporated business for the period of administration, or to incorporate any business in which I may be engaged at the time of my death and to continue that incorporated business throughout the period of administration; and to do any and all things necessary or proper to complete the administration of my estate, all as fully as I could do myself.

Instead of trying to predict every possible particular, the drafter should reduce general terms to the lowest common denominator. The drafter walks a tightrope between language so vague that it invites misunderstanding and language so particular that an interpreter in bad faith is able to slip out from under some provision by claiming not to be covered by its exact terms. Learning to be sure-footed on the tightrope between precision and imprecision becomes increasingly important as the scope of malpractice continues to widen. Attorneys who draft wills and contracts must be especially on guard against being found negligent for drafting errors,[26] especially errors arising out of some form of ambiguity.

IV. THE NATURE OF AMBIGUITY

Written material is ambiguous if on its face it has two or more distinct and mutually exclusive meanings. Usually an ambiguity is an

---

25. Quoted in Word, A Brief for Plain English Wills and Trusts, 14 U.Rich.L.Rev. 471, 473 (1980).

26. For discussion of cases in which vagueness or ambiguity has led to liability to clients and sometimes to third parties, see Comment, Attorney Malpractice in California: The Liability of a Lawyer Who Drafts an Imprecise Contract or Will, 24 U.C.L.A.L.Rev. 422 (1976).

equivocation, that is, an uncertainty between only two meanings. The writing literally says two things equally. For example:

Only persons who are doctors and lawyers qualify.

Must one be both a doctor and a lawyer to qualify, or is it enough to be one or the other? Also, what about a Ph.D.? Does one with a doctorate in literature qualify? Here is another example.

Persons who reside in New York and New Jersey have 90 days in which to file claims.

Does the 90–day rule apply to everyone who resides in New York and also to everyone who resides in New Jersey? Probably. Possibly, however, the rule applies only to a much smaller group—those who have at least two residences, one in New York and one in New Jersey. Thus the statement of the rule is equivocal.

Usually the word "equivocate" has derogatory connotations. A person who equivocates is thought to be evasive, Janus-faced or "two-faced," one who "speaks out of both sides of the mouth." On the other hand, in some contexts—poetry, in particular—ambiguity deserves praise. The language of metaphor is the language of ambiguity. Likewise in some legal writing, ambiguity is a valuable tool. The defense counsel, composing answers to interrogatories or a letter to plaintiff's counsel, may benefit from ambiguity as a means of keeping from making dangerous admissions while still being technically responsive to questions asked.

Professor Arthur Leff's definition of "ambiguity" in his unfinished law dictionary discusses both its virtues and vices.

A. LEFF, THE LEFF DICTIONARY OF LAW: A FRAGMENT
94 Yale L.J. 1855, 2007 (1985).*

ambiguity. A state of language in which the meaning to be conveyed is subject to uncertainty, in which the writing can plausibly mean one thing, or another, or still another or more. In legal writing, of course, it is always said that ambiguity is to be avoided, since people's rights and duties so often arise out of language and depend upon its meanings. But every natural language is to some extent ambiguous. Unlike languages of mathematical logic, which are designed for almost no purpose but to avoid ambiguity, ordinary languages have other jobs to do—to express nuance, to be pleasant to the mind and ear, subtly to reverberate word to word and context to context so as to express things not just accurately, but richly and fully. Thus, almost anything written in a real language *can* be seen to convey more than one precise meaning, and indeed the creation and use of ambiguity is one of the prime techniques of literature. In fact, intentional ambiguity is sometimes desired in law too, as when parties to a contract would

* Reprinted by permission of The Yale Law Journal Company and Fred B. Roth-man & Company from *The Yale Law Journal,* Vol. 94, pp. 1855, 2007.

rather not face a potential issue, preferring instead to deal with the issue ambiguously and leave the solution of the problem, should it arise, to determination by subsequent litigation.

Hence, while unambiguous writing is important to law, even when desired it is an aim never fully realizable. One does the best one can. While there are famous instances of apparently perfect clarity being insufficient (as when "one thousand" turned out to mean "1200" in the rabbit trade, and "white selvage" was shown to refer to "dark selvage"), it is usually possible to write most things with enough exactness to serve the legal purpose at hand, *i.e.,* to express only one plausible meaning in the particular context. Legal problems do arise, however, because one wants neither to bind people to things they did not mean, nor to allow every previous agreement and meaning to be opened up to the uncertainty of subsequent litigation. A contract should not *ordinarily* be at risk of a subsequent claim by a party that by "black" he meant "white." But what if he did—and the other party knew it?

The central problem is this: Once something is found "ambiguous" *at law,* it is up for grabs. There is, for instance, an "ambiguity exception" to the **parol evidence rule.** Testimony about unwritten understandings is allowed to clarify "ambiguities" in contract interpretation. There are even rules of thumb, *e.g.,* that ambiguous language should be interpreted "*contra proferentem,*" or "*contra stipulatorem,*" *i.e.,* against the profferer or writer thereof, or even "*contra venditorem,*" *i.e.,* against the seller in an ambiguous sales contract. And there is the practically important rule that all ambiguities in any insurance contract will be interpreted against the insurance company. The difficulty, then, is to take a language necessarily always somewhat ambiguous, and decide when it is ambiguous enough that one should allow subsequent argument about what it really was meant to mean in the face of a pretty clear "objective" meaning.

Ambiguity in legal drafting is almost never appropriate. When it happens, it is usually inadvertent, not purposeful. The owner and contractor who sign the building contract do not want to go to court after the house is built to have a judge or jury determine the price. When the contract is discovered to be ambiguous, it is so in spite of the intentions of the parties. Each of them knows precisely what the contract says. It is not at all vague. The trouble is that it says one definite thing to one person and another definite thing to the other.

One of the most important tasks of the lawyer as drafter is to be aware of the potential for ambiguity in documents and to edit carefully to remove inadvertent ambiguity. If an ambiguity is patent, that is, obvious on the face of the document, courts commonly construe it against the drafter. If the ambiguity is latent and is not discovered until trouble develops, the drafter will still suffer the results of confusion where there might have been clarity. Ambiguity comes in three forms: semantic, syntactic, and contextual.[27]

V. THE DANGERS OF AMBIGUITY

A. SEMANTIC AMBIGUITY

1. Double- and Multi-meaning Words

Semantic ambiguities occur because words often have more than one meaning. Most double-meaning words cause no confusion because the context of surrounding words clarifies the meaning. This is true of homonyms, which are words spelled and pronounced identically but different in meaning. For example: After a game of pool, they jumped in the pool. Another example: She serves on boards that are concerned about the price of shingles and boards. Notice that there are no homonyms in this sentence: He is bored with serving on the board. Here the difference in spelling clarifies meaning without any need to look to context.

In the sentence above about doctors and lawyers, the uncertainty whether "doctor" includes Ph.D. is a problem of semantic ambiguity. In fact, in that sentence, "doctor" has more than two possible meanings. What about veterinarians, dentists, osteopaths, and chiropractors? Do they qualify? Here the context is no help.

When one discovers potential semantic ambiguity in one's own drafting, it is wise to look first to the context. Can the ambiguity be prevented by choosing surrounding words carefully? If context is no help, then it is wise to add words, perhaps a synonym, to clarify which meaning is intended. For instance, "residence" may mean legal domicile; it may also mean usual place of abode. In a contest between economy and clarity, clarity should always win.

2. Some Special Cases

a. Dates

Careless phrasing of references to dates can produce inadvertent ambiguity. Here are the common ambiguous phrasings:

The option extends *from* May 5 *to* May 8. (Is it available on May 5? On May 8?)

The option extends *from* May 5 *until* May 8. (Is it available on May 5? On May 8?)

The option is open *between* May 5 and May 8. (Is it open on May 5? On May 8?)

The option must be exercised *by* May 8. (Including *on* May 8?)

---

27. For detailed discussion of the forms of ambiguity, with examples of the many possibilities, see R. Dick, Legal Drafting 61–73 (2d ed. 1985).

With the following phrasing instead, the ambiguities disappear.

The option is available *after* May 4 and *before* May 8.

The option must be exercised *before* May 8.

b. Ages

Careless phrasing of references to age can also produce inadvertent ambiguity.

Ambiguous phrasing:

This option is open to anyone between the ages of 21 and 30.

Clearer substitute:

This option is open to anyone 21 years old or older and under 31.

Ambiguous phrasing:

This option is open to anyone who is more than 21 years old.

Clearer substitutes, depending on intended meaning:

This option is open to anyone who has passed his or her 21st birthday.

This option is open to anyone who is 22 years old or older.

c. Number

Using the singular rather than the plural often avoids ambiguity. Consider this ambiguous sentence:

Persons with hardships shall file affidavits in support of applications for exemption.

Must one person have more than one hardship to be entitled to exemption? How many affidavits per person? Per hardship? This muddle disappears if the sentence says:

A person with a hardship shall support an application for exemption by affidavit.

Another solution is to take people out of the sentence altogether and make it a shorter generic version.

The way to prove hardship is by affidavit.

d. Provisos

The phrase "provided that" produces so much ambiguity that it is wise to avoid it as much as possible. For example:

These by-laws may be amended at any regular meeting at which a quorum is present, by a majority vote of the members present, *provided* that notice of the vote was given as *provided* in the by-laws, and further *provided* that amendments that affect requirements of these by-laws for votes other than majority votes must pass with votes of not less than the amount called for in the requirements to be affected by the proposed amendment.

The proviso about notice is a condition precedent. The sentence should say: "*if* notice was given."

The phrase "notice of the vote was given as provided in the by-laws" produces no ambiguity. This sentence uses "provided" to refer to a provision in a document. It is not a proviso.

The final use of "provided that" does not set forth another condition precedent for conducting the vote. This proviso introduces a new rule altogether. It would better be stated in a separate sentence with a transitional signal such as "however."

B. SYNTACTIC AMBIGUITY

Syntactic ambiguity is uncertainty of meaning resulting from the arrangement of words in a sentence rather than from multiple meanings of an individual word. Context is often no help at all in clarifying the meaning. In fact, it is the arrangement of words together in the immediate context that produces the ambiguity. Professor Layman Allen argues that lawyers tend to be experts in their manipulation of semantic uncertainty; however, he offers no such compliments regarding lawyers' skills at manipulating syntax.

L. ALLEN, TOWARDS A NORMALIZED LANGUAGE TO CLARIFY THE STRUCTURE OF LEGAL DISCOURSE, VOL. II, DEONTIC LOGIC, COMPUTATIONAL LINGUISTICS AND LEGAL INFORMATION SYSTEMS
349, 349 (1981).

The members of the legal profession, which holds itself out to the public as expert in the art of communicating, perform at about the level of rank amateurs in the expression of structure. We are innocently and inadvertently introducing structural uncertainties into our writings to a degree that is a professional disgrace—enough so, that it often ought to be sufficient grounds for a successful malpractice action.

1. *Conjunctions and Other Verbal Glue*

In the sentence, "Only persons who are doctors and lawyers qualify," it is syntactic ambiguity that makes it impossible to know whether one person must have two professions to qualify. The troublesome word is "and," a coordinating conjunction. Conjunctions and prepositions are often responsible for syntactic ambiguity because they are the glue in a sentence, the words that signify how the content words—the nouns and verbs—relate to each other.

It is possible, of course, to say that common sense resolves the ambiguity if context does not. Relatively few people are both medical doctors and lawyers. The number practicing both professions simultaneously is minuscule. Thus common sense dictates that the sentence means that those who qualify are both doctors and other people who are lawyers. Besides, if the sentence appeared in the context of some paragraph, that wider context would probably resolve the ambiguity.

However, "common sense" does not always solve such problems. It is particularly dangerous to rely upon in a world of legal interests and potential readers in bad faith.

a. The Ambiguous "Or"

For instance, consider the effects of the emphasized "or" in this U.S. Department of State form.

> I certify that I have read the names of the above listed organizations, and that I am not now, nor have I ever been, a member of, in association with, or affiliated with, *or* that I have not contributed to any of such organizations, except as indicated and explained below [emphasis added].

Professor Allen has used this sentence to show the value of tabulated form as a tool for revealing syntactic ambiguities:

L. ALLEN, LOGIC AND LAW
Law and Electronics 203 (1962).

I certify

1. that I have read the names of the above listed organizations, and

2. A) that I am not now, nor have I ever been, a member of, in association with, or affiliated with, or

   B) that I have not contributed to any such organizations,

3. except as indicated and explained below.

Is it possible that the draftsman really meant "or" between 2A and 2B; so that merely having failed to contribute to any such organization allows one to sign the oath with impunity?

Now consider the emphasized "or" in this statute.

> Any male person who, knowing a female person is a prostitute, lives or derives support or maintenance in whole or in part from the earnings or proceeds of her prostitution, or from money loaned or advanced to or charged against her by any keeper or manager or inmate of a house or other place where prostitution is practiced or allowed, or who solicits *or* receives compensation for soliciting for her, is guilty of pimping, a felony * * * [emphasis added].

A man charged under this statute argued that the final clause should be read to mean "who solicits compensation or receives compensation." Since there was no evidence that he either solicited compensation or received compensation, he argued he was innocent. The State of California, wanting to convict him for pimping, argued that the clause should be read to mean "who solicits for her or receives compensation for soliciting for her." In this case, the trial judge construed the ambiguous "or" in favor of the defendant.[28]

---

28. People v. Smith, 44 Cal.2d 77, 79–80, 279 P.2d 33, 34–35 (1955).

b. The Ambiguous "And"

Now consider the final "and" in this statute.

No person shall engage in or institute a local telephone call, conversation or conference of an anonymous nature and therein use obscene, profane, vulgar, lewd, lascivious or indecent language, suggestions or proposals of an obscene nature *and* threats of any kind whatsoever [emphasis added].

A man charged under this statute argued that there was nothing in the State's bill of particulars to substantiate that he had made any threats. The statute, he argued, outlawed obscene language *and* threats in an anonymous phone call. One without the other was not enough to violate the statute. His position was not only arguable; he prevailed, that is, until the Louisiana Supreme Court deduced that "and threats" was properly interpreted as "or threats." [29] Here is an analysis of the statute.

ALLEN AND ENGHOLM, NORMALIZED LEGAL DRAFTING AND THE QUERY METHOD

29 J. Legal Educ. 380, 384–87, 399 (1978).[*]

Hill was charged with unlawfully making an anonymous telephone call to a woman during which he used obscene, profane, vulgar, lewd, lascivious and indecent language and threats. In response to a motion for a bill of particulars, the state conceded that Hill made no specific threats other than those inherent in words to the effect that he desired sexual intercourse with the woman he called. Subsequently, the district court dismissed the prosecution, basing the dismissal on an interpretation of the statute that required both obscene language *and* threats as distinct elements of the crime.

The state appealed to the Louisiana Supreme Court, contending that the district court's dismissal was based upon an erroneous interpretation of the statute. As originally enacted, the statute read:

No person shall engage in or institute a local telephone call, conversation or conference of an anonymous nature and therein use obscene, profane, vulgar, lewd, lascivious or indecent language, suggestions or proposals.

and the phrase "of an obscene nature and threats of any kind whatsoever" was added later. The prosecution argued that the "and" in the added phrase should be read disjunctively in order to fulfill the intent of the legislature in enlarging the scope of the statute. The intended effect would have been achieved by drafting the statute to read "No person shall X or Y". Therefore, it argued, the court should construe the "and" as an "or".

This same position can be expressed differently—and more persuasively—to achieve the same result. Instead of the straining argument

---

29. State v. Hill, 245 La. 119, 125–26, 157 So.2d 462, 464 (1963).

[*] Copyright © 1978 by Journal of Legal Education. Reprinted by permission of the publisher.

to interpret the "and" as "or" to achieve the legislative intent, the more persuasive argument is to merely interpret "and" as a full-sentence connecting "and" rather than a sentence-part connecting "and".

Thus, where the statute formerly said, "No person shall X", it was amended to say, "No person shall X and Y". The intent of this language, it could have been argued, was to provide that "No person shall X, *and* no person shall Y", rather than as "No person shall (X *and* Y)". Represented diagramatically (using the actual language of the statute), the state's position, in effect, was (and could have actually been so argued):

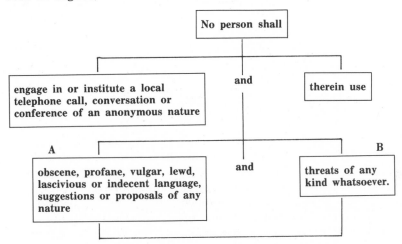

1. No person shall engage in or institute a local telephone call
   * * * and therein use **A,** and

2. No person shall engage in or institute a local telephone call
   * * * and therein use **B.**

Hill argued the opposite. He claimed that the legislature used the word "and" in order to restrict the scope of the statute. Where there was formerly a single element to the crime, now it was necessary to show that the defendant made threats in a telephone call in addition to using obscene, profane, etc., language. Since he had failed to make threats in the telephone call upon which his prosecution was based, the district court had properly dismissed the charge. Hill's position can also be represented by a diagram:

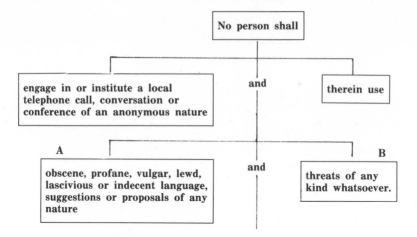

No person shall engage in or institute a local telephone call
* * * and therein use **A** and **B**.

Ultimately, the Louisiana Supreme Court resolved the case by
interpreting the disputed "and" as an "or".

* * *

It is notable that in reaching the conclusion it did, the court ignored
the common law maxim that criminal statutes are to be construed
strictly. It is fair to ask whether the ambiguity was deliberate. Does
deliberately incorporating this syntactic ambiguity (if it was done
deliberately) in this Louisiana criminal statute serve a useful policy
goal? Or is it simply another example of inadvertent ambiguity that is
easily overlooked when drafting statutory language?

* * *

The results of this normalizing process are two ways of normalizing the Louisiana statute that regulates anonymous telephone conversations (1) by converting its ambiguous within-sentence syntax into
unambiguous between-sentence syntax, and (2) by merely disambiguat-
ing the relevant aspects of its within-sentence syntax. From the
viewpoint of facilitating the more extensive use of computers in helping to process and analyze legal prose, the first alternative is preferable. It could be written as follows:

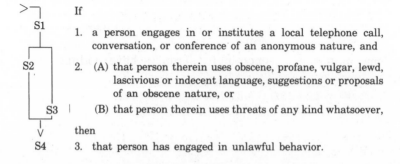

The second alternative could be written:

No person shall engage in or institute a local telephone call, conversation or conference of an anonymous nature and therein use any of the following:

1. obscene, profane, vulgar, lewd, lascivious or indecent language, suggestions or proposals of an obscene nature, or

2. threats of any kind whatsoever.

Neither of these alternatives deals with the other ambiguities (other than the one that arose in the Hill case) in this statute. They are probably inadvertent ones, also, that should be resolved.[30]

2. Modifiers

a. Squinting Modifiers

The expression "squinting modifier" is a somewhat awkward but nonetheless standard metaphor used to refer to a modifier that may modify what precedes it or what follows. For example:

The client with the foot broken *recently* filed an action.

One section on this page needing revision *surely* is not to be quoted.

Does the section surely need revision, or is it surely not to be quoted?

The client with the foot broken *recently* filed an action.

Was the foot broken recently, or did the client file recently?

b. Modifiers Preceding or Following Compounds

Modifiers preceding or following compounds may modify all compounded items or only the closest item. For example:

The report is required of educational institutions and corporations making charitable donations.

Must the corporations be educational, and must the educational institutions make charitable donations for the report to be required of them?

3. Pronoun Reference

The most common pronominal ambiguity occurs in a sentence with a plural pronoun and more than one plural noun as possible referent. For example:

The parties have reviewed the contractual terms, brought in their witnesses, and have several disagreements about them. Do the parties disagree about the witnesses, about both witnesses and terms, or possibly only about terms?

Some ambiguous pronominal references have nothing to do with plurals, however. For example:

The lawyer told her client that she was right.

Who was right? The lawyer? Or the client?

The accountant tried to keep his client from losing the tax advantages, which was not easy.

---

30. See also Dickerson, Obscene Telephone Calls: An Introduction to the Read-ing of Statutes, 22 Harv.J. on Legis. 173 (1985).

What was not easy? Losing the tax advantages? Or trying to keep his client from losing them?

4. *Punctuation*

a. *Commas*

Sometimes careless placement of a comma produces ambiguity. For example:

> Have you used another name in employment, or in making applications within the last five years?

The comma suggests that if you used another name in employment ten years ago, you should answer the question yes. In other words, the five-year limitation seems to refer only to making applications even though the "common sense" analysis suggests that probably the questioner cares only about uses of another name in the past five years either in employment or in applications.

Irregular punctuation in a provision of the Florida Constitution produced a syntactic ambiguity that sent a case to the Florida Supreme Court. Article V, Section 4(b)(1) reads:

> District courts of appeal shall have jurisdiction to hear appeals, *that may be taken as a matter of right,* from final judgments or orders of trial courts * * * not directly appealable to the supreme court or a circuit court * * * [emphasis added].

The State wanted to appeal an order granting a motion for judgment of acquittal in a criminal case; it relied on the commas setting off "that may be taken as a matter of right," arguing that the provision authorized appeal as a matter of right from every order. Here is the outcome of the State's argument.

STATE v. CREIGHTON

469 So.2d 735, 736–40, 741 (Fla.1985) (footnotes omitted).

* * *

The state brought an appeal from the trial court's judgment and the district court of appeal dismissed the appeal. The issue before us is whether the state is entitled to appellate review of the trial court's order granting judgment of acquittal.

Section 924.07, Florida Statutes (1981), authorizes appeals by the state in criminal cases as follows:

The state may appeal from:

(1) An order dismissing an indictment or information or any count thereof;

(2) An order granting a new trial;

(3) An order arresting judgment;

(4) A ruling on a question of law when the defendant is convicted and appeals from the judgment;

(5) The sentence, on the ground that it is illegal;

(6) A judgment discharging a prisoner on habeas corpus;

(7) An order adjudicating a defendant insane under the Florida Rules of Criminal Procedure; or

(8) All other pretrial orders, except that it may not take more than one appeal under this subsection in any case.

Such appeal shall embody all assignments of error in each pretrial order that the state seeks to have reviewed. The state shall pay all costs of such appeal except for the defendant's attorney's fee.

A trial court's order granting a motion for judgment of acquittal is not among the rulings set out in the statute and thereby identified as appealable by the state in criminal cases. In dismissing the state's appeal, the district court cited *Whidden v. State,* 159 Fla. 691, 32 So.2d 577 (1947), which held that the state's right of appeal in criminal cases is purely statutory. Thus the district court indicated that its dismissal of the appeal was based on the lack of statutory authority. The state argues, however, that it has a right to an appeal conferred not by statute, but by the Constitution of Florida.

The state relies on article V, section 4(b)(1), Florida Constitution, which provides in pertinent part that the district courts of appeal

> shall have jurisdiction to hear appeals, that may be taken as a matter of right, from final judgments or orders of trial courts . . . not directly appealable to the supreme court or a circuit court.

The state argues, in effect, that this provision confers upon any litigant the right to appeal a final judgment or order of a trial court. As authority for this proposition, the state relies on *State v. W.A.M.,* 412 So.2d 49 (Fla. 5th DCA), *review denied,* 419 So.2d 1201 (Fla.1982). In that decision, the district court of appeal held the state could appeal an order of speedy-trial discharge in a juvenile case, even though "no statute or rule authorize[d] it," on the ground that article V, section 4(b)(1), conferred a constitutional right of appeal. *Id.* at 50.

The district court in *W.A.M.* relied upon *Crownover v. Shannon,* 170 So.2d 299 (Fla.1964), where this Court held that the constitutional provision pertaining to the jurisdiction of the district courts of appeal did indeed confer a right to appeal final judgments of trial courts. The district court in *W.A.M.* acknowledged that *Crownover* was decided under a previous version of the constitution and that the difference in language is "substantial," but simply concluded: "we do not believe such changes were intended to eliminate the right of appeal from final-judgments." 412 So.2d at 50.

The argument of the state in support of its effort to overturn the decision of the district court in the instant case requires for its proper resolution some discussion of constitutional history. In 1956, article V of the Florida Constitution was substantially revised. Among the amendments was the provision creating the district courts of appeal.

Prior to the establishment of the district courts of appeal in 1957, the Supreme Court of Florida had

> appellate jurisdiction in all cases at law and in equity originating in Circuit Courts, and of appeals from the Circuit Courts in cases arising before the Judges of the County Courts in matters pertaining to their probate jurisdiction and in the management of the estates of infants, and in cases of conviction of felony in the criminal courts, and in all criminal cases originating in the circuit courts.

As can readily be seen, the Supreme Court was, under article V of the Constitution of 1885, prior to the 1956 revision, the single court of general appellate jurisdiction of major cases.

In *Whidden v. State,* 159 Fla. 691, 32 So.2d 577 (1947), this Court said, "The state's right to appeal is purely statutory, and is found in Sections 924.07 and 924.08, Fla.Stat.1941 * * *." *Id.* at 692, 32 So.2d at 578. Applying that principle, the Court held that an order of a county judge quashing an instrument charging a criminal offense could be appealed by the state to the circuit court. The Court's opinion shows that it was accepted as obvious that the existence of statutes defining the circumstances under which the state could appeal adverse rulings in criminal cases was to be controlling. Thus it is clear that before the 1956 amendment, the state's right of appeal was purely statutory. *State v. Frear,* 155 Fla. 479, 20 So.2d 481 (1945).

In 1956 article V was revised and the district courts of appeal were created. The appellate jurisdiction of those courts was defined in pertinent part as follows:

> (3) *Jurisdiction.* Appeals from trial courts in each appellate district, and from final orders or decrees of county judge's courts pertaining to probate matters or to estates and interests of minors and incompetents, may be taken to the court of appeal of such district, as a matter of right, from all final judgments or decrees except those from which appeals may be taken direct to the supreme court or to a circuit court.

> The supreme court shall provide for expeditious and inexpensive procedure in appeals to the district courts of appeal, and may provide for review by such courts of interlocutory orders or decrees in matters reviewable by the district courts of appeal.

> The district courts of appeal shall have such powers of direct review of administrative action as may be provided by law.

Art. V, § 5(3), Fla.Const. of 1885 (1956). The *Crownover v. Shannon* decision, relied upon by the district court in *W.A.M.* as discussed above, was an interpretation of the above-quoted language, specifically the indication that "appeals * * * may be taken * * * as a matter of right * * *." Although it had been opined that the definition of the new district courts' appellate jurisdiction was not intended to create any substantive rights not existing before, but only to re-allocate jurisdiction, see Opinion of the Attorney General 056–306 (October 16, 1956), this Court in *Crownover* said:

> The right to appeal from the final decisions of trial courts to the Supreme Court and to the District Courts of Appeal has become a part of the Constitution and is no longer dependent on statutory authority or subject to be impaired or abridged by statutory law, but of course subject to rules promulgated by the Supreme Court regulating the practice and procedure.

Crownover v. Shannon, 170 So.2d at 301. It should be noted that *Crownover* was a civil case.

Crownover stands for the legal proposition that the 1956 amendment defining the appellate jurisdiction of the district courts, by using language different from that used to define appellate jurisdiction in article V prior to the 1956 amendment, had created a constitutional right of appeal that did not exist under prior law. If indeed the 1956 change of language was intended to have such effect, then it would follow that a subsequent substantial change in the constitutional language was similarly intended to alter the effect of the jurisdictional provisions.

Where there is a significant change in the language of the constitution, it is to be presumed that the change was intentional and was intended to have a different effect from the prior language. *See, e.g., In re Advisory Opinion to the Governor,* 112 So.2d 843 (Fla.1959); *Swartz v. State,* 316 So.2d 618 (Fla. 1st DCA 1975). The 1956 language interpreted in *Crownover,* providing that "[a]ppeals * * * may be taken to the court of appeal * * * as a matter of right," art. V, § 5(3), Fla. Const. of 1885, was eliminated by the 1972 revision of article V. As has been stated previously the present language brought about by the 1972 revision provides that the district courts of appeal "shall have jurisdiction to hear appeals, that may be taken as a matter of right, from final judgments or orders of trial courts * * * not directly appealable to the supreme court or a circuit court." Art. V, § 4(b)(1), Fla.Const. The elimination of the language found dispositive in *Crownover* must be taken as having intended to negate the interpretation given by *Crownover* that the constitution had bestowed a right of appeal, thus returning to the longstanding rule stated in *State v. Whidden* that the state's right of appeal is controlled by statute.

Principles of English usage indicate that the present language was not intended to provide that all final orders and judgments are appealable as a matter of constitutional right. The word "that" is the restrictive, or defining pronoun. It introduces matter that defines, restricts, modifies, or qualifies the matter to which it refers. On the other hand, the word "which" is the nonrestrictive or nondefining pronoun and is used to introduce a separate, independent, or additional fact about the matter referred to. W. Strunk and E.B. White, *The Elements of Style* 53 (1972). So, the clause, "that may be taken as a matter of right," restricts the term "appeals" so as to apply the grant of jurisdiction only with regard to appeals that may be taken as a matter of right. Nothing is said about the circumstances under which a litigant has the right to take an appeal. The reader is in effect told to look elsewhere to determine whether there is such a right. In order to plainly say that all final judgments may indeed be appealed as a matter of right, the constitution would have to use the clause "*which* may be taken as a matter of right." In such a context, "which" does not define or restrict such appeals but independently describes them, adding information in a way that would have independent substantive effect. *See* M. Kammer and C. Mulligan, *Writing Handbook* 117–18, 138, 151–52 (1953). If the word "which" had been used instead of "that," one could logically interpret the language to confer upon a litigant the right to appeal a final judgment or order. *See also* H.W. Fowler, *Modern English Usage* 713 (1937). But we must look at the language actually used, and that language indicates that the question of when an aggrieved litigant is entitled to an appeal is a matter to be determined by sources of authority other than the constitution.

Moreover, during the period from 1957 through 1972, when the language underlying the *Crownover* decision (a civil case) was in effect, the courts of Florida continued to operate under the assumption that the state's right of appeal in criminal cases was governed by statute. *See, e.g., Carroll v. State,* 251 So.2d 866 (Fla.1971); *Jenkins v. Lyles,* 223 So.2d 740 (Fla.1969); *State v. Diamond,* 188 So.2d 788, 789 (Fla.1966); *State v. Harris,* 136 So.2d 633 (Fla.1962); *State v. Schroeder,* 112 So.2d 257 (Fla.1959); *State v. Shouse,* 177 So.2d 724 (Fla. 2d DCA 1965); *Balikes v. Speleos,* 173 So.2d 735 (Fla. 3d DCA 1965). Cases decided after the 1972 revision of article V still recognize the right of appeal as a matter of substantive law controllable by statute not only in criminal cases but in civil cases as well. *See, e.g., State ex rel. Sebers v. McNulty,* 326 So.2d 17 (Fla.1975); *Clement v. Aztec Sales, Inc.,* 297 So.2d 1 (Fla. 1974); *State v. Matera,* 378 So.2d 1283 (Fla. 3d DCA 1979); *State v. I.B.,* 366 So.2d 186 (Fla. 1st DCA 1979); *State v. Brown,* 330 So.2d 535 (Fla. 1st DCA 1976); *see generally* Fla.R.App.P. 9.140, Committee Note.

This understanding is in keeping with the common-law rule that a writ of error would lie for the defendant but not for the state. Thus it is now generally held that, unless expressly provided for by statute, in criminal cases the state is not entitled to appeal adverse judgments and orders. *See United States v. Sanges,* 144 U.S. 310, 12 S.Ct. 609, 36 L.Ed. 445 (1892). The general common-law rule applied not only to judgments rendered upon verdicts of acquittal but also to determinations of questions of law. *Id.*

> The weight of authority is overwhelming, not only in this country but in England, that the writ will not lie at the instance of the State, and it is evident from the character of the legislation on the subject in this State that it has never been contemplated that the State could further pursue parties who had obtained judgment in their favor in

prosecutions by indictment, whether by the judgment of the court or the verdict of a jury.

State v. Burns, 18 Fla. 185, 187 (1891). In view of this virtual prohibition of the common law, we can see sections 924.07 and 924.071 as strictly limited and carefully crafted exceptions designed to provide appellate review to the state in criminal cases where such is needed as a matter of policy and where it does not offend against constitutional principles. The existence of these statutes and the established understanding of their purpose are incompatible with the suggestion that article V, section 4 confers a right on any litigant to appeal any adverse final judgment or order.

In view of the above considerations—the fact that *Crownover* interpreted constitutional language that has been changed, that court decisions decided after the constitutional change make clear that appeals by the state are governed by statute, that *Crownover* itself was an aberration in interpretation of the pre–1973 language, that the present constitutional language merely allocates jurisdiction rather than conferring appeal rights, and that the common-law rule provides insight into the meaning and purpose of the criminal appeal statutes—we reaffirm the principle that the state's right of appeal in criminal cases depends on statutory authorization and is governed strictly by statute.

*   *   *

For the foregoing reasons, the decision of the district court of appeal, dismissing the state's appeal from a judgment of acquittal, is approved.

———

The combination of questionable punctuation—or lack of it—and an ambiguously placed modifier can produce no end of trouble. Consider the case of the trucking company ordered by the Interstate Commerce Commission (ICC) to stop shipping in certain parts of Connecticut, Pennsylvania and New Jersey. The ICC Certificate of Public Convenience and Necessity that caused the trouble authorized the company to ship:

> Between points in Connecticut, Pennsylvania, New Jersey, and New York *within 100 miles of Columbus Circle, New York, N.Y.,* on the one hand, and, on the other, points and places in Connecticut, Delaware, Maryland, Massachusetts, Pennsylvania, New Jersey, New York, and Rhode Island [emphasis added].

The company argued that "within 100 miles of Columbus Circle, New York, N.Y." modified only "New York," leaving the company free to ship anywhere in Connecticut, Pennsylvania, and New Jersey. The ICC argued that the 100–mile limitation applied to all 4 states. Here is how the federal district court in New Jersey resolved the problem.

T.I. McCORMACK TRUCKING CO. v. UNITED STATES

298 F.Supp. 39, 41–42 (1969).

*   *   *

Initially, it must be noted that, as a matter of grammatical construction, there can be no question but that the 100–mile provision in the Sub 70 Certificate applies only to New York. Whether the grammatical rule be designated as the "Doctrine of the Last Antecedent," or as a matter of simple common sense, the absence of a comma after the Certificate's first reference to "New York" indicates most clearly that this is the case. As a result, all that remains for consideration is the Commission's contention that the effect to be given to its own special expertise in construction of technical terms of art compels that this court defer to it in a case of simple grammatical construction such as is presented here.[2]

That contention was dealt with thoroughly in the first *McCormack* opinion, 251 F.Supp. at 534–536, where strong distinction was made between Commission construction of "commodity descriptions" and Commission construction of territorial descriptions. In the case of the former, it was pointed out, there is involved "an area wherein the Commission's great familiarity with customary trade usage and with industry-wide understanding of prior Commission interpretations is critical." As a result, it was concluded, wide latitude should be given to Commission interpretation of commodity descriptions. However, in the case of Commission construction of territorial descriptions, such as are involved in the McCormack matter, it was pointed out, with citation to the Commission's own statements in its original Order of March 26, 1962:

> "The disputed language in McCormack's certificate is non-technical in nature. *There is no apparent reason for example, why a similar territorial description in a statute or contract should be given any different meaning,* *   *   * no policy or presumption favoring a liberal or strict construction for the purpose of granting a larger or smaller quantum of operating authority. (Emphasis supplied). 89 M.C.C. at 10."

251 F.Supp. at 536. This court continues to believe that the conclusion reached in the original *McCormack* decision was a cogent one; as a result, no great deference will be paid to the Commission's rather unusual reading of the Sub 70 Certificate. The court holds that, as a matter of law, the Certificate permits plaintiff to deal in Connecticut, Pennsylvania, and New Jersey, without reference to the 100 mile

---

2. In framing the issue in such a manner, the court, of course, does not find it necessary to consider the merits of the Commission's attempted invocation of its "expertise." On this question, see the dissenting opinion of Commissioner Webb, 102 M.C.C. at 583.

limitation contained therein, which applies only to operations in New York State.

The Order of the Interstate Commerce Commission dated August 5, 1966 will be set aside and enjoined.

*   *   *

———————

The majority opinion gives the impression that the disputed provision is actually quite simple and not worthy of such controversy. However, that is the way it is with ambiguities. One person reads something one way; someone else reads it another. Each one has a theory about punctuation, grammar, "plain meaning," or legislative history as the only proper foundation on which to base a reading. Often neither acknowledges that the provision is ambiguous, in spite of the fact that if it were not, they probably would not be arguing about it in the first place.

In the trucking company's case, the majority consisted of only two people, members of a three-judge panel. The dissenting third judge wrote more than twice as much about the case and the presence or absence of a "dangerous comma." Here is part of the dissenting opinion.

T.I. McCORMACK TRUCKING CO. v. UNITED STATES

298 F.Supp. 39, 45–47 (1969) (McLaughlin, J., dissenting).

What we have before us is a 1948 certificate of public convenience and necessity issued by the Interstate Commerce Commission. The unquestioned intent of the Commission was to apply the hundred mile limitation to all points and places in the four states named in the document. Because of the involved irregular routes allowed, the certificate was obviously not easy to draft; to a layman that task could well have been nigh impossible. Even so, as we have seen, the Commission never contended that each of the words in the "within 100 hundred miles of Columbus Circle, N.Y. *   *   * " phrase were technical words of art but does say and has established that "Collectively the words have a definite and distinctive meaning in the context here considered." As such and having in mind that in this connection the uncontradicted intent of the Commission as to the content of the certificate was to include all four states of the certificate within the hundred mile limitation of Columbus Circle, it was not only "common sense" but high level specialized judgment to use the Commission rightly recognized expertise to make sure that the language chosen supported the Commission's purpose. That was only the beginning of the firm, unalterable designation of the routes allowed by the granting Authority. McCormack Company which had applied for and had received the said certificate knew exactly what the Commission had allowed in its territorial designation. McCormack formally verified that in writing and under those precise conditions accepted the certificate as drafted and without reservation. Not long after that, definitely at least by the time its new ownership took over, plaintiff was deliberately transporting interstate freight over routes beyond the scope of its certificate. Plaintiff has persisted in that course down to and including this moment. It never brought a proceeding before the Commission in an effort to vindicate its action. The only reason it appears here as plaintiff is because it is again in effect appealing from a Commission decision upholding the certificate as granted.

We have seen how McCormack in the beginning contended that the Commission by some mysterious informal wave of the hand allowed plaintiff the additional routings. In passing, that of itself is the strongest possible admission that the original, sharply limited certificate meant what the Commission had always maintained it did. Having made no progress with its enlargement allegation, McCormack came into this Court in its 1966 appeal with a new proposition. It produced a person described in the prior court opinion as a "linguist". He, from the absence of a comma after the first "New York" in the phrase involved, concluded that McCormack was given unrestricted rights in all four states. The "New Standard Dictionary of the English Language" (1944) states the prime meaning of linguist to be "an adept in languages; one who is acquainted with several languages". The second meaning of the word is given as "a student of the history or science of language; a philologist". This particular linguist has no Interstate Commerce Commission experience whatsoever. There is no suggestion that he has any understanding of irregular routings. The linguist's pronouncement is seconded by four attorneys also produced on behalf of the plaintiff. At oral argument the main reliance for the plaintiff for the comma disposition was stated as the truly scholarly H.W. Fowler in his book "Modern English Usage" (1965 Ed.) p. 588. However, there is no mention of Fowler in plaintiff's briefs. What Fowler deals with on p. 588 and also on pp. 587 and 589 is the murky comma world. The most Mr. Fowler and his revisionist suggest is the recasting of sentences instead of using the crude device of the intrusive comma. On p. 588, it is said "In ambiguous appositions. Insertion or removal of commas is seldom a sufficient remedy, and indeed it is usually impossible. The thing is to remember that arrangements in which apposition commas and enumeration commas are mixed up are dangerous and should be avoided."

Amazingly there is no mention either, oral or written by plaintiff of the great American authority in this field, Wilson Follett. The latter's definitive book "Modern American Usage" (1966) is of much the same view as Fowler. Follett lays the comma to an uneasy rest at p. 401, saying "The comma can cause trouble equally by its absence, by its presence, and by wrong placement." Neither Fowler nor Follett ever intimate that a comma quibble in circumstances as those before us should ever be given serious attention.

The certificate, intended to be granted by the Commission and so granted in 1948, down to and through the current litigation has never been attacked as unreasonable. And there is no claim that the Commission has ever varied from its 1948 view of its grant. Plaintiff, having agreed to and accepted the original territory, later desiring more, simply took it. Its unfounded statement that the Commission merely closed its eyes, went beyond its statutory grant, beyond its authority and extended the area allowance, just fell apart and is not here referred to by plaintiff. Instead came the incredible argument that despite the Commission's intention, the plaintiff's acquiescence and the fact that the Commission had always upheld its 1948 position completely, nevertheless, because of the absence of at best a most questionable comma, the certificate, which contained what the Commission intended to grant and did grant and what plaintiff intended to receive and did accept, is to be construed twenty years after it was allowed in a manner significantly different from what the Commission gave and what the plaintiff knowledgeably was given.

There has been nothing arbitrary, capricious or clearly erroneous in the Commission's actions throughout the twenty years of this certificate. There is no excuse in this case to allow the desperate use of a "dangerous comma" to reverse a decision of the Commission which was soundly within its discretion.

I would affirm the decision of the Commission.

b. Semi-colons

Although most ambiguous punctuation problems are comma problems, the semi-colon is also sometimes the culprit. Does it separate phrases or clauses that stand independently on their own, or is it merely a comma in disguise?

Consider the case of an Indiana couple who appealed their conviction for illegal sale of fireworks. Here is the statute they relied upon for their defense.

> Nothing in this act shall be construed to prohibit any resident wholesaler, dealer, or jobber to sell at wholesale such fireworks as are not herein prohibited; *or the sale of any kind of fireworks provided the same are to be shipped directly out of state;* or the use of fireworks by railroads or other transportation agencies for signal purposes or illumination, or the sale or use of blank cartridges for a show or theater, or for signal or ceremonial purposes in athletics or sports, or for use by military organizations [emphasis added].

The defendants had sold at retail some fireworks that were permitted by statute only to be sold wholesale. They argued that this was legally acceptable because they ascertained that the purchaser was from Illinois and he signed a statement that he was "going to immediately ship all Indiana illegal fireworks directly out of the state of Indiana * * *."

The court of appeals accepted the defendants' view of the matter and reversed the conviction. Here is what the Indiana Supreme Court had to say about it.

HILL v. STATE

488 N.E.2d 709, 710–11 (Ind.1986).

* * *

Counsel points out that this section is structured as a series, each ending with a semicolon, followed by the word "or" as an introduction to the next exception on the list. The common understanding of such a series of phrases is that each stands on its own as a separate exception. Under this reading, he argues, the Hills engaged in a "sale of any kind of fireworks provided the same are to be shipped directly out of state" and thus did not violate the law.

The State's position has been that Ind.Code § 22–11–14–4 was intended to exempt wholesale transactions for shipping out of state. Responding to this argument, defense counsel interrupted the prosecutor five times during final argument in the trial court to insist that the sale to Oakley was a retail sale. The prosecutor provided the trial judge with copies of minutes from the town planning commission indicating that the operator of New–Line Fireworks, which was on land zoned for wholesale operations, represented that fireworks were not stored on the premises and were delivered to customers "through the mail or by a truck." When a party cannot keep his own story straight, it requires additional concentration to treat his arguments seriously.

While it is true that the common meaning given the punctuation used in Ind.Code § 22–11–14–4 would suggest that an exemption exists for fireworks sold wholesale or retail for shipment out of state, we are not obligated to engage in a debate on the significance of semicolons and disjunctives when doing so renders the statute absurd or produces a result repugnant to the apparent intent of the legislature. *Spaulding v. Harvey* (1856), 7 Ind. 429.

The framework provided by the General Assembly seems plain enough. It manifests a desire to reduce the number of children and adults burned or injured by fireworks. The legislature has determined that certain fireworks are safe for retailing to the general public and that others are not. Dealers are allowed to sell all fireworks at wholesale and all fireworks may be shipped out of state. Appellants see in this scheme the proverbial loophole: the customer walks in the store, signs a statement that he intends to ship all illegal fireworks out of state, buys individual items, and drives away. Although Oakley was asked to show his drivers license to show that he was not an Indiana resident, if we accept the Hills' argument that they are exempted because the fireworks were to be "shipped directly out of state", the residence of the purchaser would be of little moment.

We conclude that reading the phrase "shipped directly out of state" as an exception to the rule that only certain listed fireworks can be sold at retail required that the term "shipped" be read to mean a method of delivery which does not result in the product being placed in general distribution within the state. It means that jobbers may sell crates of fireworks and ship them to Illinois; it does not mean that fireworks salesmen can have their customers sign a form and then hand them a paper bag of cherry bombs.

This loophole is closed. The judgment of the trial court is affirmed.

C. CONTEXTUAL AMBIGUITY

Contextual ambiguity results when two different parts of the same document say contradictory things. Occasionally contextual ambiguity occurs within one sentence. For example:

> State regulations are not preempted only when they conflict with federal law.

Common sense suggests that the drafter intends to say that the regulations are preempted only when they conflict or that the regulations are not preempted except when they conflict. However, the sentence combines two ways to make its point and so says the opposite of what the drafter presumably intends.

More often contextual ambiguity results from contradiction between two sentences rather than within one. For example, consider what it would be like to try to conduct a college inventory of equipment according to the following instructions:

> Items valued at more than $100 are included in the inventory. The standard items consist of desks, chairs, credenzas, tables, lamps, typewriters, personal computers, filing cabinets, dictating equipment, calculators, and other electrical equipment. Items omitted from the lists include: library chairs, wastebaskets, staplers and other desk accessories.

When the contradictory phrases are close together, the contradiction is at least easy to spot. Contextual ambiguity is often the most difficult type to discover, however, because the contradictory clauses or sentences may be far removed from each other. It is not until one party relies on one of them and another party relies on the other that the ambiguity is discovered.

The case below illustrates the typical process a court goes through to attempt to reconcile contradictory clauses. Here the customers of a truck rental company thought they had a lease with an option to purchase, giving them the right to return the trucks when the contract was terminated. The rental company read the "Truck Lease Service Agreement" to say that at termination, there was to be an absolute sale of the trucks to the customers. When the customers returned the trucks, the rental company sold them at a loss and sued for breach of contract to collect the difference. The court resolved the controversy by looking to a section of the contract that both the rental company and the customers overlooked.

TRANSPORT RENTAL SYSTEMS, INC.
v. HERTZ CORP.

129 So.2d 454, 455–56 (Fla.App.1961).

* * *

The contract in question is very complete and in great detail. It contains 29 provisions, all of which apply only to the leasing of trucking equipment, with the exception of the two sections hereinafter quoted.

The breach of the contract for which damages were claimed was alleged to have occurred under Section (18) and subsections (a) and (b) thereof which read as follows:

"(18) Either party shall have the right to cancel this agreement on any Anniversary of the date on which the last vehicle delivered to Customer hereunder shall have entered Customer's service under this agreement, by giving to the other party, at least thirty (30) days prior to such termination date, notice in writing of its intention so to terminate this agreement.

(a) In the event either party shall elect to cancel this agreement, then Customer agrees to purchase the vehicles then covered by this agreement and Lessor agrees to sell said vehicles to Customer, upon the basis set out in sub-section (b) hereof.

(b) In the event of cancellation of this agreement, the purchase by Customer of the vehicles covered hereby shall be for cash or upon terms suitable to Lessor and at the original value thereof, as specified in Schedule A and/or other Schedule A's attached hereto, less depreciation, computed upon the bases of the time which has elapsed from the date the vehicles shall have entered the service of Customer until the date Customer shall have exercised this option to purchase, and at the depreciation rate set forth in Schedule A and/or other Schedule A's attached hereto, provided, however, that the purchase price of such vehicles under this option shall not in any event be less than fifteen (15) per cent of the original value, as set out in Schedule A and/or other Schedule A's attached hereto."

the plaintiff claiming that same provided for an absolute sale of the vehicles to the defendants.

The vehicles were returned by the defendants to the plaintiff upon termination of the contract. The plaintiff then sold the vehicles at private sale. The damages for the breach were claimed to be a sum of money equal to the difference between the amount realized from the sale of the vehicles and the amount the plaintiff would have been entitled to receive for the vehicles under the terms of the contract. This amount was established to be the sum of $18,000. It is apparent that the jury allowed only one-half of this amount as plaintiff's damages for the breach, but this is not material in resolving the issue.

The main contention of the defendants was that the above-quoted provision of the contract was only an option to purchase, giving the defendants, lessees under the contract, the right to return the goods upon termination of the contract.

Defendants' motion to dismiss the complaint for its failure to state a cause of action was denied. Likewise, defendants' motion for a directed verdict upon the issue involved because of the plaintiff's failure to show a breach by the defendants of the contract was denied.

The arguments of counsel were centered primarily around an interpretation of the above referred to provision of the contract. Also, the briefs of the parties are confined almost entirely to a construction of this provision. Apparently, Section (16) of the contract, which reads as follows:

> "(16) Customer agrees that upon the expiration of the period for which any vehicles delivered under this agreement respectively shall have been leased or upon the cancellation or termination of this agreement, all of the vehicles delivered under this agreement to Customer will be returned to Lessor at the garage at which such delivery shall have been made (or such other garage in the same city as may have been designated by Lessor), in as good mechanical condition and running order as they were when received by Customer, ordinary wear and tear excepted."

was either disregarded or entirely overlooked. This provision can only be construed as implying a right to return the vehicle upon termination of the contract and sets forth the conditions upon which the return is to be made. This is a reasonable inference and no other inference or intention can possibly be applied to its terms. When this provision is considered along with Section (18) and its subsections and the other provisions of the contract, the contract must be considered as a lease agreement with an option, upon termination of the contract, in the lessees to either return the vehicles or buy the same upon the terms set forth in Section (18) and its subsections.

Section (16) would not have been inserted had it not been intended to serve some purpose in expressing the intention of the parties. An implication of law arising from one clause of a contract indicating that another is unnecessary does not justify that such other clause is superfluous. 7 Am.Jur., Contracts, 95. It is a cardinal rule in the construction of contracts that the intention of the parties thereto will be ascertained from a consideration of the whole agreement. 7 Fla. Jur., Contracts, Sec. 77. If a contract contains clauses which are apparently repugnant to each other, they must be given such an interpretation as will reconcile them if possible. 7 Fla.Jur., Contracts, Sec. 91. The real intention, as disclosed by a fair consideration of all parts of a contract, should control the meaning given to mere words or particular provisions when they have reference to the main purpose. 7 Fla.Jur., Contracts, Sec. 88, p. 155; 12 Am.Jur., Contracts, Sec. 252; 7 Fla.Jur., Contracts, Sec. 87. These general principles of construction are well-settled statements of the law in this state.

Upon applying these general principles of construction to the contract in question, it can only be concluded that the contract in question was a lease agreement with an option to the lessees, upon termination of the lease agreement, to either return the property or buy the same. The lessees chose to return the same to the lessor's assignee, the appellee herein. There was, therefore, no breach of the contract and the defendants, the appellants herein, were entitled to judgment as a matter of law upon this particular element of alleged damages.

* * *

Inadvertent contextual ambiguity can easily creep into a contract or legislative document with many related sections. That is why issue-by-issue checks for substantive consistency are essential. Computers can produce a high degree of mechanical consistency in such matters as spelling and capitalization and in some instances even parallel sentence construction. Symbolic logic is also available as a tool for consistency.[31] But ultimately the human being who drafts the document is responsible for its internal substantive consistency. When the drafter does not carry out this responsibility, the door is open for the court to step in, sometimes with surprising results.

VI. PROBLEMS

PROBLEM 1

You are legal advisor to your county commissioners. One of them has brought you the text of a proposed ordinance and asked you to evaluate its choice of language. Section 1 of the ordinance is below. Redraft it to reflect your evaluation, especially with respect to degree of generality and particularity and of vagueness and precision.

1 SECTION 1. It shall be unlawful for any person, firm or corpora-
2 tion to convey or transport garbage, offal or other rubbish upon any
3 public highway, road or street in that part of _____ County outside
4 the incorporated cities located therein, unless such garbage, offal or
5 other rubbish is conveyed or transported in a vehicle with a water-tight
6 metal body provided with a tight metal cover or covers and so con-
7 structed as to prevent any of the contents from leaking, spilling, falling
8 or blowing out of such vehicle, and such vehicle shall at all times,
9 except when being loaded or unloaded, be completely and securely
10 covered so as to prevent offensive odors escaping therefrom and so that
11 no part of the contents thereof shall be at any time exposed.

PROBLEM 2

You represent a building contractor who brought an action to enforce a mechanic's lien for the amount he claims to be due on a

---

31. See Allen, Symbolic Logic: A Razor-Edged Tool for Drafting and Interpreting Legal Documents, 66 Yale L.J. 833 (1957).

contract to build a home. Someone else represented him at the trial level, where the judgment was for the home owner, who argued successfully that the maximum amount due under the contract could not exceed $34,500.

Both your client and the home owner agree that the cost of construction was $35,380. In addition to $34,500, your client insists the owner owes $3,538, which is a 10 per cent fee provided for in their contract. In other words, your client claims $38,038.

Assume that you have agreed to represent the contractor in his appeal. Moreover your client wants to prevent a similar conflict arising in the future; therefore, he wants you to redraft his form contract to eliminate any ambiguity about price.

Here is the provision that caused the trouble. Study it to see how many different interpretations are reasonable. Then redraft it.

1   3. In consideration of the performance by the said contractor of
2 all of the covenants and conditions contained in this agreement and
3 contained in the plans and specifications the owners agree to pay to the
4 contractor an amount equal to the amount of all material furnished by
5 the contractor and the labor furnished by the contractor together with
6 payroll taxes and Insurance, also together with the sum total of the net
7 amount due the subcontractors performing work or furnishing work for
8 said construction. The Owners also agree to pay to the contractor, in
9 addition to the amount specified hereinabove, a fee equal to 10% of the
10 actual cost of the said residence, said fee to be paid after completion of
11 said residence and acceptance thereof by the Owners. It is specifically
12 agreed by and between the parties that notwithstanding the agreement
13 hereinabove by the owners shall not be required, under the terms of
14 this agreement, to pay to the contractor any amount in excess of the
15 sum of Thirty-Four Thousand, Five Hundred Dollars ($34,500.00) which
16 is the estimated cost of construction, plus the fee provided for herein.

PROBLEM 3

You represent a local moving company engaged exclusively in local moves of household goods. Your client has been using a bill of lading form that is common, with minor variations, among national moving companies. Your client operates in a heavily competitive market and does not want unnecessarily to scare off business. You have been asked to redraft the form.

Below are the first three paragraphs, which recite the terms of the carrier's liability. Evaluate their choice of language, and also evaluate conceptualization and organization. Then redraft.

TERMS AND CONDITIONS

1 1. PERILS ASSUMED—The carrier assumes obligation against all
2 risks of direct physical damage or loss to the property to be moved,

3 packed, stored, shipped, forwarded, or otherwise handled from any
4 external cause except as hereinafter excluded.

5 2. The carrier shall be liable only for its failure to use ordinary care
6 and then only on the basis of customer's declared valuation of the
7 goods. The burden of proving negligence or failure to use the care
8 required by law shall be upon the customer.

9 3. No liability shall be provided for loss or damage caused by or
10 resulting from: An act, omission, or order of shipper, including damage
11 or breakage resulting from improper packing by shipper; insects,
12 moths, vermin, ordinary wear and tear, or gradual deterioration; defect
13 or inherent vice of the article, including susceptibility to damage
14 because of atmospheric conditions such as temperature and humidity or
15 change therein; hostile or war-like action in time of peace or war
16 including action in hindering, combating, or defending against an
17 actual, impending or expected attack; any weapon of war employing
18 atomic fission or radioactive force whether in time of peace or war; or
19 insurrection, rebellion, revolution, civil war, usurped power, or action
20 taken by governmental authority in hindering, combating, or defending
21 against such occurrence, seizure, or destruction under quarantine or
22 customs regulations, confiscation by order of any government or public
23 authority, or risks of contraband, or illegal transportation or trade; any
24 strike, lockout, labor disturbance, riot, civil commotion, or any act of
25 any person or persons taking part in any such occurrence or distur-
26 bance; and acts of God.

PROBLEM 4

If your state has statutes authorizing "living wills" but not prescribing the language to be used in a living will, draft a form consistent
with your statutes for use by your firm's clients. If your state has no
such statutes, for the purpose of this problem assume the following
sections apply.

**765.02 Right to make declaration instructing physician con-
cerning life-prolonging procedures; policy statement.** The Legislature finds that every competent adult has the fundamental right to
control the decisions relating to his own medical care, including the
decision to have provided, withheld, or withdrawn the medical or
surgical means or procedures calculated to prolong his life. This right
is subject to certain interests of society, such as the protection of
human life and the preservation of ethical standards in the medical
profession. The Legislature further finds that the artificial prolonga-
tion of life for a person with a terminal condition may secure for him
only a precarious and burdensome existence, while providing nothing
medically necessary or beneficial to the patient. In order that the
rights and intentions of a person with such a condition may be
respected even after he is no longer able to participate actively in
decisions concerning himself, and to encourage communication among
such patient, his family, and his physician, the Legislature declares

that the laws of this state recognize the right of a competent adult to make an oral or written declaration instructing his physician to provide, withhold, or withdraw life-prolonging procedures, or to designate another to make the treatment decision for him, in the event that such person should be diagnosed as suffering from a terminal condition.

765.03 Definitions. As used in ss. 765.01–765.15, the term:

(1) "Attending physician" means the primary physician who has responsibility for the treatment and care of the patient.

(2) "Declaration" means:

(a) A witnessed document in writing, voluntarily executed by the declarant in accordance with the requirements of s. 765.04; or

(b) A witnessed oral statement made in accordance with the provisions of s. 765.04 by the declarant subsequent to the time he is diagnosed as suffering from a terminal condition.

(3) "Life-prolonging procedure" means any medical procedure, treatment, or intervention which:

(a) Utilizes mechanical or other artificial means to sustain, restore, or supplant a spontaneous vital function; and

(b) When applied to a patient in a terminal condition, serves only to prolong the process of dying.

The term "life-prolonging procedure" does not include the provision of sustenance or the administration of medication or performance of any medical procedure deemed necessary to provide comfort care or to alleviate pain.

(4) "Physician" means a person licensed to practice medicine in the state.

(5) "Qualified patient" means a patient who has made a declaration in accordance with ss. 765.01–765.15 and who has been diagnosed and certified in writing by the attending physician, and by one other physician who has examined the patient, to be afflicted with a terminal condition.

(6) "Terminal condition" means a condition caused by injury, disease, or illness from which, to a reasonable degree of medical certainty, there can be no recovery and which makes death imminent.

765.04 Procedure for making a declaration; notice to physician.

(1) Any competent adult may, at any time, make a written declaration directing the withholding or withdrawal of life-prolonging procedures in the event such person should have a terminal condition. A written declaration must be signed by the declarant in the presence of two subscribing witnesses, one of whom is neither a spouse nor a blood relative of the declarant. If the declarant is physically unable to sign the written declaration, his declaration may be given orally, in which event one of the witnesses must subscribe the declarant's signature in the declarant's presence and at the declarant's direction.

(2) It is the responsibility of the declarant to provide for notification to his attending physician that the declaration has been made. In the event the declarant is comatose, incompetent, or otherwise mentally or physically incapable, any other person may notify the physician of the existence of the declaration. An attending physician who is so notified shall promptly make the declaration or a copy of the declaration, if the declaration is written, a part of the declarant's medical records. If the declaration is oral, the physician shall likewise promptly make the fact of such declaration a part of the patient's medical record.

765.06 Revocation of declaration. A declaration may be revoked at any time by the declarant:

(1) By means of a signed, dated writing;

(2) By means of the physical cancellation or destruction of the declaration by the declarant or by another in the declarant's presence and at the declarant's direction; or

(3) By means of an oral expression of intent to revoke.

Any such revocation will be effective when it is communicated to the attending physician. No civil or criminal liability shall be imposed upon any person for a failure to act upon a revocation unless that person has actual knowledge of such revocation.

————

If you use the above statutes as the applicable law, assume you have received the following memorandum from a senior partner in your firm, directing your attention to a variety of matters.

MEMORANDUM

TO: Junior Partner

FROM: Senior Partner

RE: Living Will Form

When you draft a living will form for us, will you keep in mind the following:

1. Some of our clients are far more sophisticated than others—everybody from Ph.D.'s to people who never graduated from high school. They all need to understand what the declaration says; on the other hand, the form should not insult anyone's intelligence.

2. Please get into the form a place for the client to say who is to make treatment decisions if the client cannot communicate.

3. Section 765.04 restricts who can be witnesses. Our form should have language to make the restriction clear to the people getting ready to sign as witnesses. Also, I have read that some other states require that both witnesses not be related to the declarant by blood or marriage and also that they not be entitled to any of the declarant's estate either by will or by operation of law. Some have gone even further and

disallowed the attending physician, the physician's employees, employees of a health facility where the declarant is a patient, or anyone who has a claim against the declarant's estate. I can't make up my mind whether it would be a good idea to add some or all of these restrictions. Will you think about them and add any that you decide belong there. Then, after I see your draft, we can talk about this whole issue of whether we should urge our clients to restrict the witnesses more tightly than our statute does.

4. Section 765.03(5) purports to be a definition, but it actually turns out to express a rule about physicians certifying terminal conditions. Most of our clients probably won't be diagnosed and certified to be afflicted with a terminal condition at the time they sign their declarations; however, some may be. See if you can make the form flexible enough to provide for listing the name and address of any physicians who have certified that the declarant has a terminal condition.

5. I think it would be a good idea to mention in the declaration the right to revoke it and also the basic information about how to revoke. In other words, let's use the form itself as a means of making sure our clients know about their revocation rights. Some states make living wills automatically expire after a certain period of time, usually five years. Think about building in automatic expiration as an alternative to—or in addition to—reciting the revocation rights. Draft according to what you conclude would be the best way to handle the possibility of clients changing their minds.

6. I would like to protect our clients by adding a provision that a copy is going to the client's doctor with directions to make it part of the client's medical record. This way, if the client has a doctor who will not comply with the living will, the client will have a better chance of finding that out in time to decide whether to change doctors.

7. I read a horror story once about living wills being put in a hospital emergency room file because they were understood to be directions not to resuscitate declarants who suffered heart failure at the hospital resulting from injuries in car accidents and other such casualties. Please take special care to prevent our form from being misconstrued that way.

8. We seem to be stuck with the vague term "terminal condition" as defined by Section 765.03(6). See if you can figure out a way for our form to give the client more power and the doctor less to determine what "imminent" means in the statement that a terminal condition is one which makes death imminent.

9. Our clients might want to specify whether food and water are to be provided by gastric tube or intravenously or not at all. What do you think of adding language to give them the option?

P.S. Here are some forms I have come across. If you find anything useful, help yourself.

TO MY FAMILY, MY PHYSICIAN, MY LAWYER, MY CLERGY-
MAN—

TO ANY MEDICAL FACILITY IN WHOSE CARE I HAPPEN TO BE—

TO ANY INDIVIDUAL WHO MAY BECOME RESPONSIBLE FOR
MY HEALTH, WELFARE OR AFFAIRS

Death is as much a reality as birth, growth, maturity and old age—it is
the one certainty of life. If the time comes when I, _____ can no
longer take part in decisions for my own future, let this statement
stand as an expression of my wishes, while I am still of sound mind.

If the situation should arise in which there is no reasonable expectation
of my recovery from physical or mental disability, I request that I be
allowed to die and not be kept alive by artificial means or "heroic
measures". I do not fear death itself as much as the indignities of
deterioration, dependence and hopeless pain. I, therefore, ask that
medication be mercifully administered to me to alleviate suffering even
though this may hasten the moment of death.

This request is made after careful consideration. I hope you who care
for me will feel morally bound to follow its mandate. I recognize that
this appears to place a heavy responsibility upon you, but it is with the
intention of relieving you of such responsibility and of placing it upon
myself in accordance with my strong convictions, that this statement is
made.

Signed _____

Date _____

Witness _____

Witness _____

Copies of this request have been
given to _____

_____

_____

_____

———

DECLARATION

Declaration made this _____ day of _____, 19__. I, _____,
willfully and voluntarily make known my desire that my dying not be
artificially prolonged under the circumstances set forth below, and I do
hereby declare:

If at any time I should have a terminal condition and if my
attending physician has determined that there can be no recovery from

such condition and that my death is imminent, I direct that life-prolonging procedures be withheld or withdrawn when the application of such procedures would serve only to prolong artificially the process of dying, and that I be permitted to die naturally with only the administration of medication or the performance of any medical procedure deemed necessary to provide me with comfort care or to alleviate pain.

In the absence of my ability to give directions regarding the use of such life-prolonging procedures, it is my intention that this declaration be honored by my family and physician as the final expression of my legal right to refuse medical or surgical treatment and to accept the consequences for such refusal.

If I have been diagnosed as pregnant and that diagnosis is known to my physician, this declaration shall have no force or effect during the course of my pregnancy.

I understand the full import of this declaration, and I am emotionally and mentally competent to make this declaration.

(Signed) _____

The declarant is known to me, and I believe him or her to be of sound mind.

Witness _____

Witness _____

————

DECLARATION

I have the primary right to make my own decisions concerning treatment that might unduly prolong the dying process. By this declaration I express to my physician, family and friends my intent. If I should have a terminal condition it is my desire that my dying not be prolonged by administration of death-prolonging procedures. If my condition is terminal and I am unable to participate in decisions regarding my medical treatment, I direct my attending physician to withhold or withdraw medical procedures that merely prolong the dying process and are not necessary to my comfort or to alleviate pain. It is not my intent to authorize affirmative or deliberate acts or omissions to shorten my life rather only to permit the natural process of dying.

Signed this _____ day of _____

Signature _____

City, County and State of residence _____

————

DIRECTIVE TO PHYSICIANS

Directive made this _____ day of _____ (month, year).

I _____, being of sound mind, willfully, and voluntarily make known my desire that my life shall not be artificially prolonged under the circumstances set forth below, do hereby declare:

1. If at any time I should have an incurable injury, disease, or illness certified to be a terminal condition by two physicians, and where the application of life-sustaining procedures would serve only to artificially prolong the moment of my death and where my physician determines that my death is imminent whether or not life-sustaining procedures are utilized, I direct that such procedures be withheld or withdrawn, and that I be permitted to die naturally.

2. In the absence of my ability to give directions regarding the use of such life-sustaining procedures, it is my intention that this directive shall be honored by my family and physician(s) as the final expression of my legal right to refuse medical or surgical treatment and accept the consequences from such refusal.

3. If I have been diagnosed as pregnant and that diagnosis is known to my physician, this directive shall have no force or effect during the course of my pregnancy.

4. I have been diagnosed and notified at least 14 days ago as having a terminal condition by _____, M.D., whose address is _____, and whose telephone number is _____. I understand that if I have not filled in the physician's name and address, it shall be presumed that I did not have a terminal condition when I made out this directive.

5. This directive shall have no force or effect five years from the date filled in above.

6. I understand the full import of this directive and I am emotionally and mentally competent to make this directive.

Signed _____

City, County and State of Residence _____

The declarant has been personally known to me and I believe him or her to be of sound mind.

Witness _____

Witness _____

PROBLEM 5

Your client AM brings you a handwritten page and tells you, "My friend MG and I own a big piece of land together, which we have subdivided into 10 lots. Now we're ready to sell the land. Here is the contract we drew up. We trust each other, but we want a good legal contract. Get this into proper form for us, okay?"

After reading the handwritten contract, what do you need to ask AM before redrafting? Try to anticipate as fully as possible any problems you will have redrafting the contract so that you can do the job after only one conversation with AM. Here is what the handwritten page says over the signatures of the two friends.

1) 50%/50% of quick bulk sale that both parties agree to.

2) $\frac{2}{3}$ (MG) $\frac{1}{3}$ on profits up to $91,000. 50%—50% on anything over $91,000.

3) 150 K or better offer on bulk sale we will both agree to sell.

4) Money will be divided: According to above formulas.

Chapter 7

CLARITY THROUGH CONSTRUCTION

I. CANONS OF CONSTRUCTION

If the drafter does not take charge of making meaning clear, courts sometimes rely upon the canons, or rules, of construction to govern how to choose one of two or more contradictory meanings. However, these are not actually rules with the force of law. They are customs, and a given canon may or may not be followed in a given situation.[1]

Restrictive canons of construction were originally an English device to preserve the common law from legislative meddling, and that sense of them became an American idea as well in the maxim: "Statutes passed in derogation of the common law * * * should be construed strictly * * *."[2] However, the twentieth century has given us some changing views of the relationship between the common law and the canons of statutory construction. The New Deal era brought constrictions on the common law and more liberally construed remedial legislation.[3] The era of expansion of civil rights legislation brought new deference to administrative interpretations of legislation through regulations.[4] The 1980's brought back deference to the common law accompanied by a reluctance to interfere with contract and property rights and an inclination to construe regulatory statutes narrowly.[5] One study notes that nineteenth century restrictive canons were used more in the 1980's than during the New Deal era and that expansive

---

1. For a detailed discussion of how the canons function, see the examples in a specific context—the interpretation of collective bargaining agreements by labor-management arbitrators—in Elkouri and Elkouri, How Arbitration Works 342–65 (4th ed. 1985).

2. Ross v. Jones, 89 U.S. (22 Wall.) 576, 591 (1874).

3. See, for example, SEC v. C.M. Joiner Leasing Corp., 320 U.S. 344, 350–51, 64 S.Ct. 120, 124–25 (1943).

4. See, for example, Griggs v. Duke Power Co., 401 U.S. 424, 433–34, 91 S.Ct. 849, 854–55 (1971).

5. See, for example, Schreiber v. Burlington Northern, Inc., 472 U.S. 1, 8, 105 S.Ct. 2458, 2462 (1985).

canons were used far less in the 1980's.[6] In such an era, the plain meaning doctrine reigns. Broad remedial purposes get short shrift.

Perhaps the most important thing about the canons is the value of making a document so free from ambiguity that they need not be invoked. On the other hand, realistically, the need for interpretation arises fairly often. In the realm of contracts, this is so partly because the negotiation process sometimes makes removing all ambiguities more dangerous than keeping some of them.

SHULMAN, REASON, CONTRACT AND LAW IN LABOR RELATIONS

68 Harv.L.Rev. 999, 1004 (1955).*

No matter how much time is allowed for the negotiation, there is never time enough to think every issue through in all its possible applications, and never ingenuity enough to anticipate all that does later show up. Since the parties earnestly strive to complete an agreement, there is almost irresistible pressure to find a verbal formula which is acceptable, even though its meaning to the two sides may in fact differ. The urge to make sure of real, consensus or to clarify a felt ambiguity in the language tentatively accepted is at times repressed, lest the effort result in disagreement or in subsequent enforced consent to a clearer provision which is, however, less favorable to the party with the urge. With agreement reached as to known recurring situations, questions as to application to more difficult cases may be tiredly brushed aside on the theory that those cases will never—or hardly ever—arise.

KIRK, LEGAL DRAFTING: SOME ELEMENTS OF TECHNIQUE

4 Tex.Tech L.Rev. 297, 300 (1973).**

* * * [T]he generality, the vagueness, the flexibility, of the "language of the law" puts the lawyer on the horns of a dilemma. By assumption, the parties to the document are agreeing to specific solutions to specific problems that may possibly arise in the course of their transaction; but the "language of the law" that the lawyer has available inevitably depends upon the circumstances. Charles P. Curtis once suggested that drafting be done in these general, vague, flexible terms.[15] The parties could wait until the difficulty had aris-

---

6. Harris, The Politics of Statutory Construction, 1985 Brigham Young U.L.Rev. 745, 787.

* Copyright © 1955 by the Harvard Law Review Association.

** Copyright © 1973 by Texas Tech University Law Review. Reprinted by permission of the publisher.

15. Curtis says the author of a word or phrase delegates to the user of the docu-

ment the power to interpret it when necessary—and when the circumstances surrounding the need for interpretation are known. The most important criterion for interpretation is consistency with the rest of the law. Curtis, A Better Theory of Legal Interpretation, 3 Vand.L.Rev. 407, 419–25 (1950).

en—and the facts were known—and could then, in a retrospective decision true to common law method, determine what the term meant under the circumstances. But this means that the parties to the document have abandoned, to the generality of the language of the law, and to the retrospective method of the common law, the opportunity to agree in advance upon the rules that are to be used to settle the difficulties that arise in their transaction.

The maxims or principles of legal interpretation—for wills, for statutes, for contracts, and the like—are the means by which courts retrospectively give particular substance to the general, vague, flexible "language of the law." [16] These maxims and principles will always be necessary because it is impossible to predict all of the difficulties that can arise in a transaction or all of the circumstances under which these difficulties can occur. Nevertheless, in the transaction that is based on the consent of two parties, the assumption is that the parties have the opportunity to fix the rules that will be used to solve difficulties that occur during their transaction and that they have in fact done so.[17] * * *

Some states codify some of the canons in their constitution or in an opening code title to govern the entire code. Even more common are statutes directing a given construction of a particular chapter or even a particular section. The Commissioners on Uniform State Laws have drafted rules of construction for uniform statutes. It may be interesting to speculate whether codification of a canon gives it any greater weight than those that remain grounded only on case law, but ultimately it matters more what courts do than what they say about why they do it.[7] The most important thing to recognize about the canons is how slippery they are and how dangerous it is to rely on any of them.[8] Professor Llewellyn gives ample evidence of why this is so.[9]

---

16. This is the basis for the concept that language that is clear on its face not only need not be interpreted but cannot be interpreted by a court. As to statutes, see 2 J.G. Sutherland, Statutes and Statutory Construction § 4502 (3d ed. F. Horack 1943). As to contracts, see 3 A. Corbin, Contracts § 542 (1960); 4 S. Williston, Contracts § 609 (3d ed. W.H.E. Jaeger 1961).

17. The parole evidence rule is a codification of these assumptions; and the broadened recognition of "partial" integration extends the concept to all contractual transactions. Restatement (Second) of Contracts §§ 235(3), 236(2), 237(1) (Tent. Draft No. 5, 1970).

7. Memorandum from Professor Mary Ellen Caldwell to Barbara Child (Fall 1986)

(on file at U. of Fla. College of Law Legal Drafting Dept.).

8. There is no absolute certainty even in such trusted maxims as the rule that penal statutes are to be strictly construed. "The rule is still invoked, but so variously and unpredictably, and it is so often conflated with inconsistencies, that it is hard to discern widespread adherence to any general policy of statutory construction." Jeffries, Legality, Vagueness, and the Construction of Penal Statutes, 71 Va.L.Rev. 189, 219 (1985).

9. See also Posner, Legal Formalism, Legal Realism, and the Interpretation of Statutes and the Constitution, 37 Case W.Res.L.Rev. 179 (1986).

LLEWELLYN, REMARKS ON THE THEORY OF APPELLATE DECISION AND THE RULES OR CANONS ABOUT HOW STATUTES ARE TO BE CONSTRUED

3 Vand.L.Rev. 395, 401–06 (1950) (footnotes omitted).*

CANONS OF CONSTRUCTION

Statutory interpretation still speaks a diplomatic tongue. Here is some of the technical framework for maneuver.

THRUST	BUT	PARRY
1. A statute cannot go beyond its text.		1. To effect its purpose a statute may be implemented beyond its text.
2. Statutes in derogation of the common law will not be extended by construction.		2. Such acts will be liberally construed if their nature is remedial.
3. Statutes are to be read in the light of the common law and a statute affirming a common law rule is to be construed in accordance with the common law.		3. The common law gives way to a statute which is inconsistent with it and when a statute is designed as a revision of a whole body of law applicable to a given subject it supersedes the common law.
4. Where a foreign statute which has received construction has been adopted, previous construction is adopted too.		4. It may be rejected where there is conflict with the obvious meaning of the statute or where the foreign decisions are unsatisfactory in reasoning or where the foreign interpretation is not in harmony with the spirit or policy of the laws of the adopting state.
5. Where various states have already adopted the statute, the parent state is followed.		5. Where interpretations of other states are inharmonious, there is no such restraint.
6. Statutes *in pari materia* must be construed together.		6. A statute is not *in pari materia* if its scope and aim are distinct or where a legislative design to depart from the general purpose or policy of previous enactments may be apparent.

THRUST	BUT	PARRY

7. A statute imposing a new penalty or forfeiture, or a new liability or disability, or creating a new right of action will not be construed as having a retroactive effect.

7. Remedial statutes are to be liberally construed and if a retroactive interpretation will promote the ends of justice, they should receive such construction.

8. Where design has been distinctly stated no place is left for construction.

8. Courts have the power to inquire into real—as distinct from ostensible—purpose.

9. Definitions and rules of construction contained in an interpretation clause are part of the law and binding.

9. Definitions and rules of construction in a statute will not be extended beyond their necessary import nor allowed to defeat intention otherwise manifested.

10. A statutory provision requiring liberal construction does not mean disregard of unequivocal requirements of the statute.

10. Where a rule of construction is provided within the statute itself the rule should be applied.

11. Titles do not control meaning; preambles do not expand scope; section headings do not change language.

11. The title may be consulted as a guide when there is doubt or obscurity in the body; preambles may be consulted to determine rationale, and thus the true construction of terms; section headings may be looked upon as part of the statute itself.

12. If language is plain and unambiguous it must be given effect.

12. Not when literal interpretation would lead to absurd or mischievous consequences or thwart manifest purpose.

13. Words and phrases which have received judicial construction before enactment are to be understood according to that construction.

13. Not if the statute clearly requires them to have a different meaning.

14. After enactment, judicial decision upon interpretation of particular terms and phrases controls.

14. Practical construction by executive officers is strong evidence of true meaning.

15. Words are to be taken in their ordinary meaning unless they are technical terms or words of art.

15. Popular words may bear a technical meaning and technical words may have a popular signification and they should be so construed as to agree with evident intention or to make the statute operative.

THRUST BUT PARRY

16. Every word and clause must be given effect.

16. If inadvertently inserted or if repugnant to the rest of the statute, they may be rejected as surplusage.

17. The same language used repeatedly in the same connection is presumed to bear the same meaning throughout the statute.

17. This presumption will be disregarded where it is necessary to assign different meanings to make the statute consistent.

18. Words are to be interpreted according to the proper grammatical effect of their arrangement within the statute.

18. Rules of grammar will be disregarded where strict adherence would defeat purpose.

19. Exceptions not made cannot be read.

19. The letter is only the "bark." Whatever is within the reason of the law is within the law itself.

20. Expression of one thing excludes another.

20. The language may fairly comprehend many different cases where some only are expressly mentioned by way of example.

21. General terms are to receive a general construction.

21. They may be limited by specific terms with which they are associated or by the scope and purpose of the statute.

22. It is a general rule of construction that where general words follow an enumeration they are to be held as applying only to persons and things of the same general kind or class specifically mentioned (*ejusdem generis*).

22. General words must operate on something. Further, *ejusdem generis* is only an aid in getting the meaning and does not warrant confining the operations of a statute within narrower limits than were intended.

23. Qualifying or limiting words or clauses are to be referred to the next preceding antecedent.

23. Not when evidence sense and meaning require a different construction.

24. Punctuation will govern when a statute is open to two constructions.

24. Punctuation marks will not control the plain and evident meaning of language.

25. It must be assumed that language has been chosen with due regard to grammatical propriety and is not interchangeable on mere conjecture.

25. "And" and "or" may be read interchangeably whenever the change is necessary to give the statute sense and effect.

26. There is a distinction between words of permission and mandatory words.

26. Words imparting permission may be read as mandatory and words imparting command may be read as permissive when such construction is made necessary by evident intention or by the rights of the public.

Thrust	But	Parry
27. A proviso qualifies the provision immediately preceding.	27. It may clearly be intended to have a wider scope.	
28. When the enacting clause is general, a proviso is construed strictly.	28. Not when it is necessary to extend the proviso to persons or cases which come within its equity.	

II. TABULATED STRUCTURE

A. AVOIDING AMBIGUITY

Instead of counting on some canon of construction to resolve ambiguities, the drafter should take special care to avoid them. One of the most successful ways to avoid syntactic ambiguity in particular is to set material out on the page in a form that makes clear how its parts relate to each other. For example, consider this sentence:

Psychiatric service is covered only if it is furnished by a group practice organization, by a hospital, or by a community mental health center which furnishes comprehensive mental health services.

Is it only community mental health centers that must furnish comprehensive mental health services in order to provide covered psychiatric service? Or does that requirement also apply to group practice organizations and hospitals? The provision can be set out two different ways depending on which meaning is intended.

Meaning 1

Psychiatric service is covered only if it is furnished by

1. a group practice organization,
2. a hospital, or
3. a community mental health center which furnishes comprehensive mental health services.

Set out this way, the provision expressly requires that a community mental health center furnish comprehensive mental health services. It also expressly does not impose that requirement on group practice organizations and hospitals.

Meaning 2

Psychiatric service is covered only if it is furnished by

1. a group practice organization,
2. a hospital, or
3. a community mental health center

which furnishes comprehensive mental health services.

Set out this way, the provision expressly imposes the requirement on all three service providers.

B. EMPHASIZING ALTERNATIVE AND CUMULATIVE ITEMS

There is another advantage to presenting a sentence with its parallel parts set off from the rest of the sentence in a tabulated column. It provides visible emphasis of whether the parallel items are alternative or cumulative.

1. *Emphasis of Alternative Items*

If the company defaults in paying

      (a) taxes,

      (b) rents, or

      (c) other like charges,

the security under this mortgage becomes enforceable.

2. *Emphasis of Cumulative Items*

Any person guaranteeing a signature warrants that

      (a) the signature was genuine;

      (b) the signer was an appropriate person to endorse; and

      (c) the signer had legal capacity to sign.

C. TABULATED SENTENCE STRUCTURE FOR PARALLEL ITEMS

1. *Formalities*

When using tabulated structure for material that is an integral part of a sentence, certain formalities are important to observe. They are to ensure that the tabulated structure aids clarity rather than inadvertently destroying it.

a. The material constitutes a complete sentence in which every word is essential to the meaning.

b. The indented items are parallel in construction. In the term of Professors Allen and Engholm they are "normalized."

c. The indented items begin with lower case letters rather than capitals. This is to emphasize that they are within a sentence rather than self-contained entities.

d. At the end of each item except the last one, there is a comma or a semi-colon. When the items are short and when there is no punctuation within any single item, most drafters prefer commas to semi-colons.

e. After the next to the last item, it is essential to put either "and" or "or" to indicate whether the items are cumulative or alternative. Some drafters choose to put the "and" or "or" after every item except the last one when there are many, and especially if they take more than one page. This compensates for the reader's inability near the beginning to glance easily at the end of the list to discover whether the items are cumulative or alternative.

f. Each item follows smoothly from the introductory words that precede the tabulated material. Likewise, any concluding words follow smoothly from each item. Thus, if any introductory words and any concluding words are read with any one of the items alone, a coherent, grammatical sentence results. For example, consider again this sentence:

If the company defaults in paying

    (a) taxes,

    (b) rents, or

    (c) other like charges,

the security under this mortgage becomes enforceable.

One can extract from this sentence a coherent statement about rents alone by reading both introductory and concluding words together with the chosen item from the tabulated material, rents:

If the company defaults in paying * * * rents, * * * the security under this mortgage becomes enforceable.

The tabulated structure in this sentence thus passes the test.

2. Potential Coherence Problems

Here is one way that tabulated sentence structure can go wrong if the drafter does not carefully integrate the introductory and concluding material. Consider this sentence:

If the estate exceeds $30,000,

    (a) each child is entitled to a distributive share in the balance over $30,000; and

    (b) if the estate is $30,000 or less, no child is entitled to any distributive share.

Reading the introductory material with division (b) makes clear what has gone wrong. It makes no sense to say:

If the estate exceeds $30,000, if the estate is $30,000 or less, no child is entitled to any distributive share.

But that is precisely one of the two things the above sentence says. Here is how it should have been presented.

    (a) If the estate exceeds $30,000, each child is entitled to a distributive share in the balance over $30,000; and

    (b) if the estate is $30,000 or less, no child is entitled to any distributive share.

Here is another example of tabulated sentence structure that falls apart.

The various

    1. cities

    2. counties,

> 3.   states, and
>
> 4.   the nation

are all having economic difficulties.

If the sentence is read using only item 4, it says:

> The various the nation are all having economic difficulties.

Here is a corrected version.

> The various
>
> > 1.   cities,
> >
> > 2.   counties, and
> >
> > 3.   states, and

the nation are all having economic difficulties.

These sentences are so short and simple that they actually do not warrant tabulated structure in the first place. They are tabulated here only to show how tabulated sentence structure can go wrong. In a long and complicated sentence, such incoherence may be more difficult to spot. If a sentence with tabulated structure looks suspicious, the best way to test it is by reading the introductory material along with just the last item or another item near the end. The further away from the introductory material, the more likely an error is to occur.

D.   LISTS DISTINGUISHED FROM TABULATED SENTENCE STRUCTURE

Sometimes it is convenient to indent and number a list of items merely because it is a list. If the list is preceded by some introductory language, the results may look like tabulated sentence structure. However, list structure differs from tabulated sentence structure essentially in that the point of the sentence with a list in it is clear before the list begins, and the items in the list function almost as various possible ways to fill a blank. For example:

> This chapter applies to the purchase by any of the following agencies of all services for which payment is authorized:
>
> > 1.   The Department of the Army.
> >
> > 2.   The Department of the Navy.
> >
> > 3.   The Department of the Air Force.

Here are the characteristics of list structure.

1.   The sentence above could be written:

> This chapter applies to the purchase by _____ of all services for which payment is authorized.

Then any one of the listed agencies could be written into the blank, and later on if someone with the power to do so decided that the chapter also applied to the Coast Guard, it also could be written into the blank, whereupon it would become item 4.

2.   The listed items here are in parallel construction just as they are in tabulated sentence structure. If material is not in parallel form, it is not appropriate in the first place for either tabulated sentence structure or list structure, or else it needs to be reconstructed to make it appropriate.

3. The items in the list begin with capital letters. They are not functional parts of a sentence and embedded into it. Rather, they are self-contained items and as independent as items on a laundry list.

4. After each item there is a period, which further signifies the independence of each item. Sometimes lists are presented with no punctuation after the items; however, this may leave the introductory material as a sentence without an end, which is not advisable.

5. There is no "and" or "or" relating the last item in the list to those preceding it. This is because the items are neither alternative nor cumulative. Rather, the same thing (the introductory material) is being said independently about each item. Conceivably, it could be said about other items too, either now or later; therefore, what happens to be now the last item on the list should not be thought of as finally the last one, or as the end of the sentence. For all practical purposes, the "end of the sentence" is the end of the material preceding the list, and each item on the list is an equally available substitute for the language "any of the following agencies," which is essentially nothing more than a blank to be filled in.

E. CHOOSING BETWEEN TABULATED SENTENCE STRUCTURE AND LIST STRUCTURE

The two types of structure lend themselves to different kinds of material, so that the drafter should make a conscious choice to use one or the other.

1. Tabulated Sentence Structure

Tabulated sentence structure is appropriate only when dividing up an existing complete sentence to show the relationships among its parts. Such structure is particularly useful to set out cumulative requirements, as in "You must do this, this, this, *and* this to comply with the law", or lists of alternative prohibitions, as in "If you do this, this, this, *or* this, you will be subject to penalty."

2. List Structure

List structure is appropriate for giving examples. The language "for example" or "for instance" or some phrase including "the following" often signals list structure, which is appropriate when it is understood that the list is not exhaustive and may be augmented in the future.

F. CHECKLIST FOR USING TABULATED SENTENCE STRUCTURE AND LIST STRUCTURE

Tabulated sentence structure and list structure are valuable devices to aid understanding. Inadvertent errors in form can cancel out the value, however. When incorporating either of these structures, it is important to observe these principles:

1. Use either structure judiciously. Do not overtabulate uncomplicated, unambiguous material.

2. Make sure that tabulated items are in parallel constructions.

3. Decide whether the material lends itself to tabulated sentence structure or list structure, and then observe the formalities for the structure chosen.

4. In tabulated sentence structure, make sure to indicate whether the items are alternative or cumulative.

5. If you use tabulated sentence structure, make sure that the sentence makes sense when you read the introductory material followed by each item by itself. If there is any concluding material, that also must read smoothly with each item separately.

III. PROBLEMS

PROBLEM 1

Explain what produces the ambiguity in each of the following provisions. Then redraft each provision to make it unambiguous.

    a. My executor shall divide the remainder of my property equally between all of my nieces and my nephew.

If there are 11 nieces, does the nephew get $\frac{1}{2}$ or $\frac{1}{12}$?

    b. I hereby deed the property to Michael Howard, a single man, and Robert Mern and Anne, his wife.

Does Howard get $\frac{1}{2}$ or $\frac{1}{3}$ interest?

    c. Officers shall be elected on a vote of the members representing not less than $\frac{3}{4}$ of the capital stock of the membership.

Must a candidate receive $\frac{3}{4}$ of the vote to be elected, or do $\frac{3}{4}$ of the members constitute a quorum for voting purposes?

    d. No person shall have sexual intercourse with a child of the age of 14 years, or under.

If a person has sexual intercourse with a child whose fourteenth birthday was three months ago, is the act in violation of the statute?

PROBLEM 2

Explain what is wrong with the structure in the following sentences.

Sentence a

(1) The application shall contain:

    (a) The applicant's name and address.

    (b) Birthday.

    (c) Shall be filed with the Department of State.

Sentence b

(a) The landlord shall make reasonable provisions for:

1.   The extermination of rats, mice, roaches, ants, wood-destroying organisms, and bedbugs.   When vacation of the premises is required for such extermination, the landlord shall abate the rent.

2.   Locks and keys.

3.   The clean and safe condition of common areas.

Sentence c

(a) General Rule.   If

(1) any improvements located on the premises at the time of the execution of this binder are damaged by fire or other casualty prior to closing; and

(2) those improvements can be restored to substantially the same condition within a period of 30 days after such destruction occurs; and

(3) the Seller restores the improvements, then the closing date shall be extended accordingly, and

(4) the Buyer shall have no option to terminate this contract.

(5) All risk of loss prior to closing shall be borne by the Seller.

PROBLEM 3

Use tabulated sentence structure to present the following provision so that it is clear what different kinds of transactions are "consumer transactions"—and how many kinds there are.   Make clear what modifies what.   At the same time, take care not to over-tabulate.

1   (1) "Consumer transaction" means a sale, lease, assignment, award
2   by chance, or other disposition of an item of goods, a consumer service,
3   or an intangible to an individual for purposes that are primarily
4   personal, family, or household or that relate to a business opportunity
5   that requires both his expenditure of money or property and his
6   personal services on a continuing basis and in which he has not been
7   previously engaged, or a solicitation by a supplier with respect to any of
8   these dispositions.

PROBLEM 4

Below are three provisions that have figured in court disputes. Decide how you would construe them and why.   Then redraft them to remove any possible ambiguity and ensure that even a reader in bad faith could not plausibly support an interpretation other than yours. Remember that the goal of careful drafting is not merely to prevail in litigation; it is to prevent litigation.   Moreover, one cannot be sure that a court's construction of an ambiguous provision will be sensible, assuming "sensible" means according to the drafter's intention.

Case 1

The judge dismissed an indictment against the defendant for Class B theft. The State appealed, arguing that the governing statute authorizes dismissals only involving Class D and Class E crimes. Here is the statute.

1   When a person has been admitted to bail or is committed by a
2 judge, or is indicted, or held upon a complaint and warrant for an
3 assault or other Class D or E crime as defined by Title 17–A, section 4–
4 A, for which the party injured has a remedy by civil action, except
5 aggravated assaults, assaults upon or resistance of a law enforcement
6 officer as defined by Title 17–A in the execution of his duty, and
7 assaults of such officers, if the injured party appears before the judge or
8 court, and in writing acknowledges satisfaction for the injury, the court,
9 on payment of all costs, may stay further proceedings and discharge the
10 defendant. The judge may exonerate the bail and release the obligors,
11 supersede the commitment by his written order and exonerate the bail
12 of the witnesses.

Should the Class B theft dismissal stand?

Case 2

The defendant was found guilty of violating a zoning ordinance prohibiting lodging houses in a Class 1A District. She rented rooms on the second and third floors of her house in a Class 1A District to six roomers. She did not serve meals to anyone. Her roomers paid rent either weekly or monthly. There was no dispute that her house was occupied as a lodging house, but the defendant claimed that the ordinance permitted her to rent rooms to five or more roomers as long as she did not furnish table board to more than four. Here is the relevant part of the ordinance.

1   Subject to the off street parking regulations set forth in Sections
2 800 to 814, an accessory use customarily incident respectively to a Class
3 1A or Class 1B District use shall be permitted in such respective district
4 when such accessory use, building or structure is located upon the same
5 lot with the main use or building to which it is accessory provided that:

*   *   *

6   (4) Rooms only in the main building may be rented, and table
7 board furnished for pay to not more than four persons, for definite
8 periods of not less than one week, provided no window display sign, sign
9 board or other visual or sound device is used to advertise such use and
10 no culinary facilities in addition to those provided for one family are
11 used.

Should the defendant be able to keep her roomers as long as they take their meals elsewhere?

Case 3

Four town council members were defendants in a civil action to oust them from office for paying themselves a salary. In a separate civil action, a court had adjudged the salary void. They repaid the money, and there was no criminal prosecution. When the State sought to oust them from office, they argued there could be no ouster without prior criminal conviction. The State argued that ouster was a separate penalty authorized by statute and not dependent on conviction. Here is the statute.

1   No alderman or councilman of any town, organized hereunder,
2 shall, during the term for which he shall have been or shall be elected,
3 accept, take or receive to his own use, from the town of which he shall
4 be an alderman or councilman, any sum of money or other thing of
5 value, other than that which is, by this chapter provided to be paid to
6 such alderman or councilman, for his services as such alderman or
7 councilman; and every person who shall violate the provisions of this
8 section, shall be deemed guilty of a misdemeanor and upon conviction
9 thereof, in any court of competent jurisdiction, shall be fined not less
10 than one hundred dollars, nor more than three hundred dollars, such
11 fine to go to the school fund of the county in which such town shall be
12 located; and he shall also cease to be an alderman or councilman, as
13 the case may be, of such town.

Should the council members be allowed to stay in office?

Chapter 8

WORKING WITH DENSE
MATERIAL

I. EXPLICATION: THE TESTING PROCESS

If a drafting job involves redrafting all or part of an existing document, an initial sketch outline usually reveals fairly quickly which sections are so densely packed that they are not easily penetrable.

If a provision is suspect, either because it is exceptionally complex or because it is hard to read and may be fraught with ambiguities, then the drafter will probably benefit from a full-dress explication of the sort a literary scholar might perform on a poem. This entails close reading, line by line, for both semantic and syntactic analysis. In other words, it is important to attend both to what individual words mean and to how the words and phrases relate to each other. A technical knowledge of linguistics is not necessary to perform a careful explication.

Through explication, the drafter discovers far more than simply what the provision means. The drafter can criticize it intelligently and discover how best to redraft it so that it will better meet its users' needs. This analysis usually becomes a process of questioning the meaning of some sentences or the purposes of the whole document. The questions may be ones to ask the client, who is the policy-maker. They may lead to other forms of research. In any event, the important thing is to write them down right away. They will be useful later, and it usually turns out to be a mistake to rely on memory to dredge them up on cue. Several decoding techniques are available.

A. THE ROADMAP [1]

Initially it may be helpful to analyze a suspect provision in a loose, informal way by making a rough chart of it with circles and arrows and notes in the margin. This is akin to bookbriefing an opinion in a casebook. The drafter can grasp major concepts and find major gaps or

---

1. See Benson, Up a Statute with Gun and Camera: Isolating Linguistic and Logical Structures in the Analysis of Legislative Language, 8 Seton Hall Legis.J. 279, 287–91 (1984).

contextual ambiguities. If the hieroglyphics are easily decoded, this may be the only explication device needed.

A variation of this technique is to make a roadmap of the logical structure by going through the material and circling the words "if," "then," "and," "or," and "but." "However" and "except" can be regarded as variants of "but." "Also" and "in addition" can be regarded as variants of "and." Other variants may appear as well. It is also a good idea to circle "not" and its variants.

B.   THE SENTENCE DIAGRAM [2]

If the structure of an individual sentence is garbled or particularly dense, it is helpful to draw a rough sentence diagram. One need not be an expert at grammar and diagraming formalities. The only necessary grammatical skills are the ability to distinguish subjects, verbs, and objects, and the ability to attach modifiers to what they modify. Diagraming is especially good for weeding out syntactic ambiguities, particularly squinting modifiers.

C.   COMPLETE TABULATION

If the troublesome material is too long and complicated to yield to charting by the roadmap or the diagram, then one can test it by setting it out on paper with its parallel parts grouped and set apart by indentation. This process is essentially the same as using tabulated sentence structure to present material, with one major difference. Tabulated sentence structure as a presentation device indents only those particular parallel items that are fraught with potential ambiguity or that deserve special emphasis.

However, when the drafter uses this process as a testing tool, it involves indenting virtually if not literally every set of parallel items in the material under scrutiny. The process helps to reveal syntactic ambiguities and other problems in sentence structure. Sometimes the process can both reveal an ambiguity and provide the mechanism for resolving it.

1.   *Tabulated Sentence Structure: A Quick Review*

It may be helpful first to review how tabulated sentence structure works. Consider the following syntactically ambiguous provision:

> A tax credit is available for stocks, notes, and obligations issued by the U.S. government.

Is the credit available for all stocks and all notes no matter who issues them and only those obligations that are issued by the U.S. government, or must the stocks and notes as well as the obligations be issued by the U.S. government to be eligible for the credit?

The drafter might not initially notice the ambiguity. But if the provision is set out as follows, the ambiguity emerges.

---

2. See *id.* at 292–96.

A tax credit is available for

    (1) stocks,

    (2) notes, and

    (3) obligations issued by the U.S. government.

When the words appear on paper in this tabulated structure, the drafter is forced to consider the alternative possibility.

A tax credit is available for

    (1) stocks,

    (2) notes, and

    (3) obligations

issued by the U.S. government.

At that point, the only thing to do is to find out from the policy-maker which meaning is intended and then draft accordingly. What the drafter dare not do is decide which way it ought to be as if the drafter were the policy-maker.

But there is another point to be made here as well—about reading and writing rather than ethics. One could read and reread the tax credit provision and not discover the ambiguity in it. Even seasoned drafters often fail to discover ambiguity when they merely read a provision. That is why it is so important to engage in the physical act of setting the words down on paper and having to elect where to indent. When the hand hesitates, and the drafter is tempted to scratch something out and move it, that indicates the trouble in a provision the reader could have sworn was clear.

2. Complete Tabulation: An Example

To see how complete tabulation works as a tool to test dense material, consider this section of the service contract of a security alarm company called SOS.[3]

a. The Dense Material

CANCELLATION BY SOS

1   This agreement may be canceled, without previous notice, by SOS
2 if the Central Station, connecting wires or equipment within Client's
3 premises are destroyed by fire or other catastrophe, or so substantially
4 damaged that it is impracticable to continue service. It may likewise
5 be canceled by Client if Client's plant is so destroyed or damaged.
6 Advance payments made for service to be supplied after the date of
7 termination will be refunded to Client. This contract may be terminat-
8 ed by SOS at any time if it is unable to secure or retain the connections
9 or privileges necessary to send signals between Client's premises and
10 the Central Station or between the Central Station and the _____

3. Adapted from contract used as drafting problem material in R. Dickerson,
Materials on Legal Drafting 108–09 (1981).

11 Police Department. SOS is not liable for any damages or penalty as a
12 result of such a termination. Advance payments made for service to be
13 supplied after the date of termination will be refunded to Client.

b. The Dense Material Completely Tabulated

A. This agreement may be canceled, without previous notice, by SOS
if

  1. the Central Station,

  2. connecting wires or

  3. equipment within Client's premises

are

  1. destroyed by

      a. fire or

      b. other catastrophe, or

  2. so substantially damaged that it is impracticable to continue
      service.

B. It may likewise be canceled by Client if Client's plant is so

  1. destroyed or

  2. damaged.

Advance payments made for service to be supplied after the date of
termination will be refunded to Client.

C. This contract may be terminated by SOS at any time if it is unable
to

  1. secure or

  2. retain

the

  1. connections or

  2. privileges

necessary to send signals

  1. between Client's premises and the Central Station or

  2. between the Central Station and the _____ Police Department.

SOS is not liable for any

  1. damages or

  2. penalty

as a result of such a termination.

Advance payments made for service to be supplied after the date of
termination will be refunded to Client.

c. Questions Raised About the Dense Material

The process of setting the material out in this structure generates a
number of questions. Some are simple questions of fact, but others are
major conceptual questions that warrant discussion with SOS, the

drafter's client. Consider the following questions, and decide whether they are easily answerable. Which ones would warrant discussion with SOS before redrafting? What further questions does the explication raise?

1. Why does "A" say the agreement may be "canceled" and "C" say "terminated"? What is the difference?

2. Should "A" refer to "connecting wires within Client's premises" as well as "equipment within Client's premises"?

3. In "B," what does "likewise" mean? Does it mean without previous notice? If not, why should Client have to give notice under these circumstances but SOS not have to?

4. Why is "A" about premises and "B" about plant? Are they the same place?

5. In "B," what does "so" mean? Is this a reference to fire or other catastrophe?

6. Why does Client get no refund under "A" but only under "B" and "C"?

7. May SOS be liable for damages or penalty under "A"? Under "B"?

8. Why is a provision for cancellation by Client buried in the middle of a section headed "Cancellation by SOS"?

II. CONTINUING EXPLICATION IN LATER STAGES OF DRAFTING

The process of explication continues throughout the redrafting stages. After discovering what the initial explication yields, the drafter decides how to organize a redraft to meet the client's needs. Deciding about organization leads to deciding about related conceptual problems in the original draft. Also, issues about the form of a document lead to issues about its substance. Form and substance are inextricably related; explication refines that relationship.

Professor David Mellinkoff's central approach to improving bad legal writing is explication.

DAVID MELLINKOFF, LEGAL WRITING: SENSE AND NONSENSE

xiii (West Publishing Co., 1982). By permission.

* * * Whether it's your legal writing or someone else's, THE QUESTION is always in order: *"Does it have to be like this?"*

If you are writing, The Question will keep you from becoming another piece of office equipment, unconcerned with consequences or the possibilities of improvement.

If you are reading, vary the emphasis. First, softly: "Does it *have* to be like this?" Then louder: "Does it have to be like *this*?" Annoy the writer into explaining. Occasionally, the explanation will be convincing. More often, it won't satisfy you—or the writer. And you may end up with something closer to human understanding.

III. PRESENTING COMPLEX MATERIAL

Some of the techniques that work to test dense material turn out to be useful for presentation as well.

A. THE DECISION TREE

A rigorous version of the loose roadmap is a decision tree,[4] which reduces conditions and results to a series of yes or no questions and answers. An accurate and complete decision tree makes a provision very easy for a reader to follow, but it is not always easy to make. It involves three stages:

1. The material is divided up into as many discrete propositions as possible.

2. Each proposition is divided into an assertion and its negation, in order to make the list exhaustive and the items on it mutually exclusive.

3. The propositions are put into a logical sequence.[5] The propositions should move from general to specific subject matter so that the first question will produce an immediate result in as many cases as possible, and each successive question moves to a lower common denominator, producing a result for fewer cases.[6]

To illustrate, here is a provision in a homeowner's insurance policy followed by a decision tree explicating it (Figure 1).

BENSON, UP A STATUTE WITH GUN AND CAMERA: ISOLATING LINGUISTIC AND LOGICAL STRUCTURES IN THE ANALYSIS OF LEGISLATIVE LANGUAGE
8 Seton Hall Legis.J. 279, 297, 298 (1984).*

This policy insures against direct loss to the property covered by the following perils:

    1.   Fire or Lightning, excluding loss resulting from electrical injury or disturbance to electrical appliances, devices, fixtures or wiring caused by electrical currents artificially generated, unless fire ensues, and then only for the loss caused by such ensuing fire.

---

4. See Benson, above note 1, at 296–300.

5. Wason, The Drafting of Rules, 118 (Part 1) New L.J. 548, 549 (1968).

6. Benson, above note 1, at 298.

Figure 1

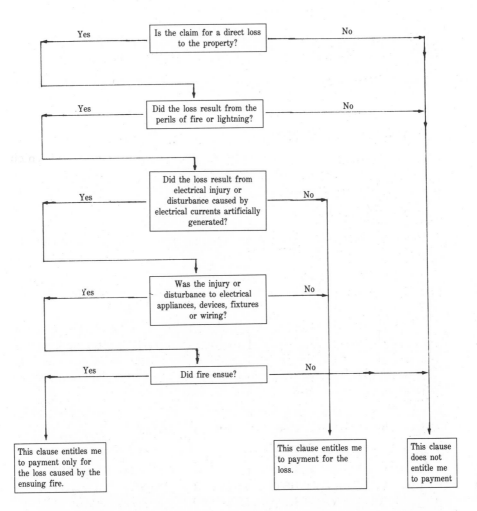

The decision tree is good for assessing over-all conceptual scheme. If there is something irrational or arbitrary in the provision or if there is a gap in its coverage, the decision tree is likely to reveal the problem.[7] The decision tree can also be adapted to produce and fill out standard forms through computer programs.[8]

B. THE GRAPH OF LOGICAL STRUCTURE

Logical graphs [9] are variations on decision trees. However, instead of focusing on yes and no questions, they focus on the logical relation-

7. Fitzgerald and Spratt, Rule Drafting—I, 119 (Part 2) New L.J. 991, 992 (1969).

8. For an example of how a tax statute gets transformed into a computer program for computing individuals' tax liability, see Fitzgerald and Spratt, Rule Drafting—III, 119 (Part 2) New L.J. 1052, 1052–54 (1969).

9. See Benson, above note 1, at 301–05.

ships expressed by "if" (conditions), "then" (results), "and" (cumulatives), "or" (alternatives), and "but" (exceptions). To illustrate, here is a provision about retirement pensions, followed by a decision tree presenting it (Figure 2) and then a graph of its logical structure (Figure 3).

WASON, THE DRAFTING OF RULES

118 (Part 1) New L.J. 548, 548 (1968).*

The earliest age at which a woman can draw a retirement pension is 60. On her own insurance she can get a pension when she reaches that age, if she has then retired from regular employment. Otherwise she has to wait until she retires or reaches age 65. At age 65 pensions can be paid irrespective of retirement. On her husband's insurance, however, she cannot get a pension, even though she is over 60, until he has reached age 65 and retired from regular employment, or until he is 70 if he does not retire before reaching that age.

Figure 2

```
┌─────────────────────────────────────────────────────────┐
│                                                           │
│                    MARRIED WOMAN'S                        │
│              (FLAT RATE) RETIREMENT PENSION               │
│                                                           │
│   1.  I am under 60 Yes        ..       .. NO PENSION     │
│                     No         ..       .. read Q.2       │
├─────────────────────────────────────────────────────────┤
│   2.  I am claiming (a)  on own                           │
│                          insurance    .. read Q.3         │
│                     (b)  on husband's                     │
│                          insurance    .. read Q.5         │
├─────────────────────────────────────────────────────────┤
│   3.  I am under 65 Yes        ..       .. read Q.4       │
│                     No         ..       .. PENSION        │
├─────────────────────────────────────────────────────────┤
│   4.  I am working  Yes        ..       .. NO PENSION     │
│                     No         ..       .. PENSION        │
├─────────────────────────────────────────────────────────┤
│   5.  my husband's  (a)  less than 65  .. NO PENSION      │
│       age is        (b)  between 65                       │
│                          and 69        .. read Q.6        │
│                     (c)  70 or more    .. PENSION         │
├─────────────────────────────────────────────────────────┤
│   6.  my husband    Yes        ..       .. PENSION        │
│       has retired   No         ..       .. NO PENSION     │
│                                                           │
└─────────────────────────────────────────────────────────┘
```

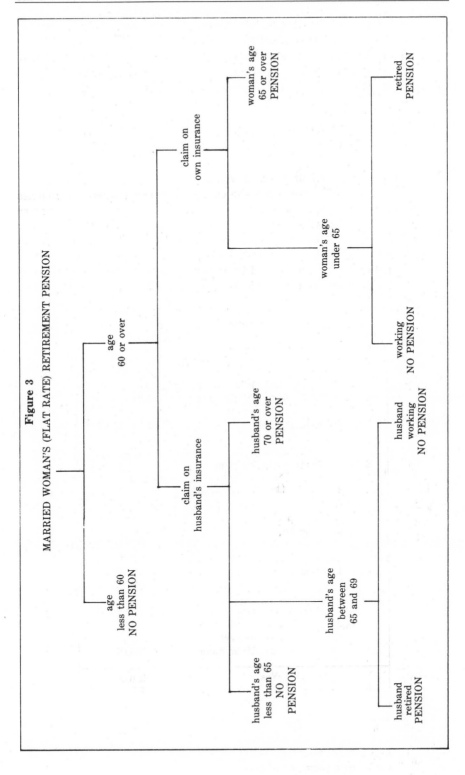

Figure 3

MARRIED WOMAN'S (FLAT RATE) RETIREMENT PENSION

Decision trees and graphs may be too schematic to serve as the sole method of presenting contractual and legislative provisions. It would be difficult, for instance, to quote part of a graph, and legal documents need to be easily quoted with precise reference given. On the other hand, in informal settings, users may benefit from the presentation of rules and regulations in tree or graph form.

One study compared a group of people who read a complex set of regulations in its original textual form and another group who read the regulations in the form of a decision tree. The group who used the decision tree solved problems according to the regulations in hypothetical cases faster and more accurately than the other group. They also made more favorable comments about the regulations.[10]

Decision trees and graphs are especially helpful for document users who want to find the answer to a particular problem. They can quickly rule out the details and alternatives that do not apply, and they need not try to keep in mind all the answers to earlier questions as they move down the tree or graph.[11]

C. NORMALIZATION

More helpful for revealing the whole of a complex conceptual scheme is the process that Professors Allen and Engholm call "normalization."[12] This is a sophisticated variation of tabulation. It goes a step further to present complex material in a format that not only reveals ambiguities but also resolves them and makes material much easier to read. The difference between normalization and complete tabulation for strict explication is that explication does not change the word choice or word order of the original material. It changes only the placement of the words on the page so that existing parallel constructions are set off in indented columns. Normalization takes some liberties with wording so that parallel ideas that were not originally expressed in parallel constructions are converted into parallel constructions in order to draw attention to the parallels.

Allen and Engholm focus on the relationships between parallel conditions and parallel results in contractual and legislative documents. Thus their normalized versions of complex provisions line up a parallel list of conditions headed by an introductory "If" and then line up a parallel list of results headed by a transitional "then." They might express the provision about the tax credit this way.

10. Wason, above note 5, at 549.

11. Fitzgerald and Spratt, above note 8, at 991.

12. For discussion of symbolic logic as a normalizing mechanism, see Allen and En-gholm, The Need for Clear Structure in "Plain Language" Legal Drafting, 13 J.L. Reform 455 (1980).

If

1. stocks,

2. notes, and

3. obligations

are issued by the U.S. government,

then

a tax credit is available for them.

A sentence set out with its parallel parts normalized looks somewhat like an outline in that they both have parallel parts indented and numbered or lettered. However, it is important to keep in mind the distinction between normalized text and an outline. A sentence in normalized form is still a *complete sentence*. An outline, on the other hand, is an *abbreviated version* or a skeleton of a whole rather than the whole itself broken into parts.

Allen and Engholm demonstrate how the process works.

ALLEN AND ENGHOLM, NORMALIZED LEGAL DRAFTING AND THE QUERY METHOD

29 J.Legal Educ. 380, 387–88, 400 (1978).*

Statutory or contractual language, although sometimes relatively free of syntactic ambiguity, is frequently unnecessarily complicated. If the purpose of carefully drafted language is to clearly communicate what conditions, when fulfilled, are sufficient to reach given results, then relating conditions and results in a simple and recognizable manner can help achieve that purpose. On the other hand, failure to do so can often render a straightforward idea virtually unintelligible. [This] * * * example is a contractual provision that details the conditions under which a life insurance policy offered by the Company will be reinstated:

REINSTATEMENT: If any renewal premium be not paid within the time granted the Insured for payment, a subsequent acceptance of premium by the Company or by any agent duly authorized by the Company to accept such premium, without requiring in connection therewith an application for reinstatement, shall reinstate the policy; provided, however, that if the Company or such agent requires an application for reinstatement and issues a conditional receipt for the premium tendered, the policy will be reinstated upon approval of such application by the Company or, lacking such approval, upon the 45th day (30th day in New Mexico) following the date of such conditional receipt unless the Company has previously notified the Insured in writing of its disapproval of such application. The reinstated policy shall cover only loss resulting from such accidental injury as may be sustained after the date of reinstatement and loss due to such sickness as may begin more than 10 days after such date. In all other respects the Insured and the Company shall have the same rights thereunder as they had under the policy immediately before the due date of the defaulted premium, subject to any provisions endorsed hereon or attached hereto in connection with the reinstatement. Any premium accepted in connection with a reinstatement shall be applied to a period for which premium has not been previously paid, but not to any period more than 60 days prior to the date of reinstatement.

Consider this reinstatement provision with respect to a particular factual situation. Suppose that—

1. the insured fails to pay a premium within the required time, and

2. he later pays a premium by check which he mails to the Company, and

3. the Company normally requires an application for reinstatement in connection with such acceptance, and

4. the Company has not notified the insured in writing that the reinstatement is disapproved, and

5. two months have elapsed since the policyholder paid the premium.

According to the above provision, should the policy be reinstated? While it is possible to carefully read the present language and answer the question, the task would be easier if the provision were drafted in normalized form. Readers may wish to test this for themselves by answering the question on the basis of the provision as drafted above before reading the normalized version * * *.

* * *

If

1. any renewal premium is not paid within the time granted the Insured for payment, and

2. (A) there is a subsequent acceptance of premium by the Company or by any agent duly authorized by the Company to accept such premium, without requiring in connection therewith an application for reinstatement, or

    (B) 1. the Company or such agent

        • requires an application for reinstatement, and

        • issues a conditional receipt for the premium tendered, and

        2. (A) such application is approved by the Company, or

            (B) the Company has not before the 45th day (30th day in New Mexico) following the date of such conditional receipt notified the Insured in writing of its disapproval of such application,

then

3. the policy shall be reinstated, and

4. the reinstated policy shall cover only loss resulting from such accidental injury as may be sustained after the date of reinstatement and loss due to such sickness as may begin more than 10 days after such date, and

5. in all other respects the Insured and the Company shall have the same rights thereunder as they had under the policy immediately before the due date of the defaulted premium, subject to any provisions endorsed hereon or attached hereto in connection with the reinstatement, and

6. any premium accepted in connection with a reinstatement shall be applied to a period for which premium has not been previously paid, but not to any period more than 60 days prior to the date of reinstatement.

Normalization, as demonstrated by Allen and Engholm, is generally performed on material drafted by someone else. It is a redrafting technique to impose parallel (or "normal") structure on material that previously lacked such structure. Thus it is not exactly accurate to speak of drafting normalized material. However, it is certainly possible to compose a first draft of complex material in which (1) particular attention goes to expressing parallel concepts in parallel structures and (2) tabulated sentence structure avoids potential ambiguities. In fact, some degree of tabulation is the most common method of expressing complex material clearly.

IV. PROBLEMS

Test your understanding of the explication techniques on the following provisions.

A. Explicate each provision by the method you find best suited for it. Remember that for the purposes of explication, you need to work with language and constructions exactly as they are.

B. Redraft each provision to present it clearly to potential users. You are free to change language and constructions to aid clarity so long as you maintain the substantive content of the original version.

PROBLEM 1 (ELECTION STATUTE)

1   If no candidate has been elected to a nonpartisan office pursuant to
2   Section 6611 or if the number of candidates elected at the primary
3   election is less than the total number to be elected to that office, then
4   candidates for that office at the ensuing election shall be those candi-
5   dates not elected at the primary who received the next highest number
6   of votes cast for nomination to that office, equal in number to twice the
7   number remaining to be elected to that office, or less, if the total
8   number of candidates not elected is less.

PROBLEM 2 (STATUTORY EXEMPTION FROM LIABILITY FOR UNAUTHORIZED COMMERCIAL PUBLICATION)

1 No relief may be obtained under Section 540.08 or Section 540.09,
2 against any broadcaster, publisher or distributor broadcasting, publish-
3 ing or distributing paid advertising matter by radio or television or in a
4 newspaper, magazine or similar periodical without knowledge or notice
5 that any consent required by Section 540.08 or Section 540.09, in
6 connection with such advertising matter has not been obtained, except
7 an injunction against the presentation of such newspaper, magazine or
8 similar periodical.

PROBLEM 3 (OFFICIAL LEAFLET ON UNEMPLOYMENT BENEFITS)

1 *What is a seasonal worker's rate of unemployment benefit in his season?*
2 For the ordinary benefit claimant, full rate benefit requires 50
3 contributions to have been paid or credited in the preceding contribu-
4 tion year. Of these 39 must be in Class 1. Benefit, even at a reduced
5 rate, is not payable unless 26 Class 1 contributions have been paid or
6 credited in the contribution year. But if a seasonal worker has not less
7 than 13 Class 1 contributions paid or credited in a contribution year, he
8 may count as Class 1 contributions any other contributions paid or
9 credited in that year for the purpose of determining his rate of benefit
10 if he is unemployed during his season. Thus if he should become
11 unemployed in that part of the year when he is normally working for
12 an employer, he should be entitled to full rate benefit so long as he has
13 contributed according to his class of insurance throughout the preced-
14 ing contribution year.

PROBLEM 4 (EXEMPTION PROVISION IN EQUAL OPPORTUNITY LEGISLATION)

1 Nothing in division H of this section * shall bar any religious or
2 denominational institution or organization, or any charitable or educa-
3 tional organization that is operated, supervised, or controlled by or in
4 connection with a religious organization, or any bona fide private or
5 fraternal organization, from giving preference to persons of the same
6 religion or denomination, or to members of such private or fraternal
7 organization, or from making such selection as is calculated by such
8 organization to promote the religious principles or the aims, purposes,
9 or fraternal principles for which it is established or maintained.

PROBLEM 5 (RULE OF CIVIL PROCEDURE ON DEFENSES AND OBJECTIONS)

1 A party waives all defenses and objections which he does not
2 present either by motion as hereinbefore provided or if he has made no

* [This passage is an excerpt from a state's equal opportunity legislation. Division H bars certain forms of discrimination in the sale, transfer, assignment, rental, lease, sublease, and financing of housing accommodations and burial lots.]

3 motion, by responsive pleading or an amendment thereof made as a
4 matter of course under Rule 15(A), except (1) the defense of failure to
5 state a claim upon which relief can be granted, the defense of failure to
6 join an indispensable party, the defense of lack of jurisdiction of the
7 subject matter, and the objection of failure to state a legal defense to a
8 claim, may be made by a later pleading, if one is permitted, by motion
9 for judgment on the pleadings or at the trial on the merits; and except
10 (2) whenever it appears by suggestion of the parties or otherwise that
11 the court lacks jurisdiction of the subject matter, the court shall dismiss
12 the action.

PROBLEM 6 (MORTGAGE PROVISION ON PROTECTING SE-CURED INTEREST)

1 The Mortgagors have agreed and do hereby agree to pay promptly,
2 as the same become due and payable, to the proper officers chargeable
3 with the collection, all taxes, assessments and other public charges
4 levied or assessed against or payable in respect to the above described
5 premises or any part thereof including all taxes which may be levied or
6 assessed under any law, now or hereafter existing, against the interest
7 in said premises created by this mortgage; and to keep the buildings
8 and improvements now or hereafter erected on said premises insured
9 against loss or damage by war damage, fire, lightning, tornado, wind-
10 storm or cyclone, in such amounts and with such companies as may be
11 satisfactory to the holder of this mortgage, by a policy or policies to be
12 left in such holder's possession with loss, if any, payable to such holder
13 as such holder's interest may appear by a standard mortgage clause
14 attached thereto, and at least five (5) days before the expiration of any
15 such policy to deposit with such holder an approved renewal policy of
16 like amount; or at the option of the Mortgagee, to deposit with the
17 Mortgagee on each monthly payment day of the note herein referred to
18 a sum equal to one-twelfth ($\frac{1}{12}$th) of the amount of annual premiums on
19 said insurance required by the Mortgagee, plus one-twelfth ($\frac{1}{12}$th) of the
20 amount of the annual taxes and assessments levied, or to be levied on
21 the premises herein conveyed as estimated by the Mortgagee, which
22 payments shall be held by the Mortgagee in trust, without interest, and
23 used by it to pay such insurance premiums, taxes and assessments
24 before the same become delinquent.

Chapter 9

DEFINING TERMS

I. LEXICAL AND STIPULATIVE DEFINITIONS

Definitions are either lexical or stipulative. In other words, they either describe or prescribe. Dictionary definitions are usually lexical; they describe accepted current usage rather than prescribing rules for correct usage.

In legal drafting, one usually need not give lexical definitions. However, it sometimes helps, depending on the intended audience, to give lexical definitions of technical terms. Also, if a term has several different dictionary meanings, only one of which applies in the document, it is appropriate to specify it. In general, however, if a reader of a document is unfamiliar with the common meanings of a term, then that reader can consult a dictionary. Nonetheless, needless lexical definitions often do appear in legal documents. For example, here is part of the definition section of a zoning ordinance regulating commercial advertising.

(4) *Sign* shall mean any display of characters, letters, illustrations, or any ornamentation designed or used as an advertisement, announcement or to indicate direction.

(5) *Erect* shall mean to construct, build, rebuild (if more than fifty (50) per cent of the structure members involved), relocate, raise, assemble, place, affix, attach, paint, draw, or in any other manner bring into being or establish.

(6) *Temporary sign* shall mean signs to be erected on a temporary basis, such as signs advertising the sale or rental of the premises on which located; signs advertising a subdivision of property; signs advertising construction actually being done on premises on which the sign is located; signs advertising future construction to be done on the premises on which located, and special events such as public meetings, sporting events, political campaigns or events of a similar nature.

Note too that the definitions misuse "shall." They should say that the terms "mean" something, not that they "shall mean" something. The meanings have present, not merely future, effect. If "shall" is intended to indicate the imperative mood rather than the future tense, it is nonetheless erroneous because the drafter does not command the terms to have a certain meaning. These definitions illustrate the common drafting mistake called the "false imperative."

Stipulative definitions differ from lexical ones and serve a valuable function in some documents. When a document includes a stipulative definition or a whole section of them, that indicates to the reader that, for the purposes of this document, or this section, or whatever context is spelled out, given terms mean what this definition says they mean— and the meanings are different from ordinary dictionary meanings. That is the purpose of stipulative definitions.

When we stipulate, we demand that readers understand a term as we define it, but in return we must not waver from the usage we have stipulated. We are released from the lexical definitions, which merely describe common usage, but we dare not contradict ordinary use or strain ordinary connotations so much that the reader has trouble accepting the orders. For example, consider these definitions regarding coastal zone protection.

> (6)(a) "Major structure" means houses, mobile homes, apartment buildings, condominiums, motels, hotels, restaurants, towers, other types of residential, commercial, or public buildings, and other construction having the potential for substantial impact on coastal zones.

*　*　*

> (c) "Nonhabitable major structure" means swimming pools; parking garages; pipelines; piers; canals, lakes, ditches, drainage structures, and other water retention structures; water and sewage treatment plants; electrical power plants and all related structures or facilities, transmission lines, distribution lines, transformer pads, vaults, and substations; roads, bridges, streets, and highways; and underground storage tanks.

Section (6)(a) is consistent with common use and connotations. However, it may be difficult to accept the notion expressed in (6)(c) that lakes are structures, especially given the surrounding list of other structures, all of which are constructed by humans. It is true that some lakes are constructed by humans, but not all are. Thus it is difficult to conceive of lakes generically as structures. It may be a little easier to think of transmission lines as structures, but it is not clear why anyone would think it necessary to spell out that transmission lines are nonhabitable.

R. DICKERSON, LEGISLATIVE DRAFTING

90–91 (1954).*

Few principles of legal drafting call for more scrupulous adherence than the principle that a term should not be defined in a sense that

---

significantly conflicts with the way it would normally be understood in that context by the legislative audience to whom the law is primarily addressed.

The principle is rooted in human psychology. No matter how explicitly the drafter stipulates, a reader cannot easily substitute a new set of connotations for very different ones that automatically come to mind. Professor Dickerson illustrates by asking us to contemplate what would happen if a mathematics professor suddenly asked the class to assume that "two" meant "four" and "four" meant "eight." The student asked to recite multiplication tables would encounter terrible psychic contortions.[1] Drafters have no reason to impose such trouble on the users of documents.

Moreover, if a drafter tries to force a strained definition on a consumer in a standardized form contract, there is increasing danger that the courts will not honor it. This is in part the result of a new theory of contract, expressly adopted in several jurisdictions and implicitly accepted in others,[2] to the effect that "contract" means the parties' reasonable expectations regardless of what the piece of paper says that purports to manifest mutual assent. This theory is largely a response to the growing use of standardized forms. It assumes that the consumer does not read the document before becoming bound, which is probably true in many instances and certainly true in regard to insurance policies sent to the insured after they purchase insurance.[3]

If the meaning of the contract exists in spite of what the document says, then does it not matter what the drafter writes down? Yes, it does matter. The theory probably applies less strictly to contracts that are not standardized forms and to contracts between businesses rather than adhesion contracts. In any event, to the extent that the reasonable expectation doctrine applies at all, the drafter should be particularly careful not to attempt to impose strained definitions. Here is a case in point.

An insurance company issued a policy entitled, "BROAD FORM STOREKEEPERS POLICY" and "MERCANTILE BURGLARY AND ROBBERY POLICY." The policy defined "burglary" as meaning a felonious entry leaving "visible marks" on "the exterior of the premises at the place of such entry." Based on this definition the insurance company denied a claim for a burglary during which the burglar left visible marks of forcible entry on interior doors but not on exterior ones.[4] The Iowa Supreme Court refused to apply the policy's definition, finding that it contradicted common understanding of burglary and thus contradicted the reasonable expectations of the insured. The

---

1. R. Dickerson, Legislative Drafting 90 (1954).

2. See Slawson, The New Meaning of Contract: The Transformation of Contracts Law by Standard Forms, 46 U.Pa.L.Rev. 21, 30–31 (1984).

3. *Id.* at 26.

4. C & J Fertilizer, Inc. v. Allied Mutual Insurance Co., 227 N.W.2d 169, 171 (Iowa 1975).

policy had not been delivered until after the purchase, but the definition in it was nonetheless treated as unconscionable.[5]

II.　TYPES OF STIPULATIVE DEFINITIONS

For purposes of legal drafting, there are three essential types of stipulative definitions: restricting, enlarging, and confining.

A.　RESTRICTING DEFINITIONS

When a drafter stipulates a restricting definition, the common (lexical) meaning of the term does not change, but the definition restricts the number of particulars to which it applies. Restricting definitions use the verb "means." When used properly, they are a valuable form of shorthand. For example:

"Conveyance" *means* a conveyance made before May 4, 1970.

"Department" *means* the Department of Natural Resources.

If the only department mentioned in a document is the Department of Natural Resources, it is convenient to be able to refer to it throughout by the single word "Department." Sometimes restricting definitions can save us from constant and lengthy repetition.

H.　HURD, WRITING FOR LAWYERS
114 (1982).*

* * * Take a statute which regulates physicians, hospitals and nursing homes which provide health care and are reimbursed by the government with respect to needy patients. Obviously, the statute will be referring repeatedly to these regulated persons and entities. How convenient to create a defined term like "Service Provider—any physician, hospital or nursing home which provides health care to needy patients and is reimbursed for the cost of such care under a program of the U.S. Government." * * * [T]his definition * * * illustrat[es] the economy to be achieved by thereafter providing merely that, "A Service Provider shall . . ." and "A Service Provider shall not . . ." and "This section shall not apply to a Service Provider who . . ." throughout the body of the statute.

B.　ENLARGING DEFINITIONS

In an enlarging definition, the common meaning changes to add to the number of particulars to which the term applies. Enlarging defini-

---

5. *Id.* at 177, 178–79, 182. For a case in which judgment was for the insurance company on the same theory, see Farm Bureau Mutual Insurance Co. v. Sandbulte, 302 N.W.2d 104, 110–14 (Iowa 1981) (implied warranties, insured's reasonable expectations, and standard policy provisions found to be the same).

tions use the verb "includes." They also serve as a form of shorthand. For example:

"Mortgage" *includes* deed of trust.

"House" *includes* the lot on which the house stands.

If an enlarging definition goes too far, it strains the reader's willingness to accept the stipulation. For example, the Traffic and Parking Rules and Regulations for a university campus say that "Automobile—Includes all motor vehicles with four or more wheels," and "Bicycle—Includes every vehicle propelled solely by human power * * *." In other words, a tractor-trailer rig is an automobile, and a unicycle is a bicycle.

The Traffic and Parking definitions also illustrate a more common error in the use of "includes." The definitions do not just enlarge the lexical definition. They present lexical definition plus enlarged definition. The proper verb for such an all-encompassing definition is "means," not "includes." For example, a passenger car is commonly understood to be an automobile. That is lexical definition. There is no need in a legal document to give such a definition. Yet, as a motor vehicle with four wheels, the passenger car is made part of the Traffic and Parking definition.

However, if one wanted to enlarge the definition to include eight-passenger vans, or even tractor-trailers, the definition should state that "automobile" *includes* vans and tractor-trailers and not use language that conveys the lexical definition as well. Adding the lexical definition defeats the purpose of using the enlarging definition as a form of shorthand. On the other hand, "includes" is misused so often in legal documents, with both lexical and enlarged definitions given, that some people might argue that to leave lexical definitions out is to leave the door open to a reader in bad faith to insist that an unmentioned part of a definition is an excluded part.

C. CONFINING DEFINITIONS

Confining definitions expressly delete some of the particulars that are part of the common meaning. Confining definitions use the verb "does not include." For example:

"Faculty" does not include visiting professors.

"Writing" does not include typewriting.

Confining and restricting definitions may be regarded as different ways to accomplish the same result. Instead of saying, " 'Department' means the Department of Natural Resources," one could say, " 'Department' does not include departments other than the Department of Natural Resources." Likewise, instead of saying, " 'Faculty does not include visiting professors," one could say, " 'Faculty' means faculty other than visiting professors." The choice usually depends on which form produces the more concise sentence and the preferred emphasis.

D. PARTIAL AND TOTAL DEFINITIONS

One can distinguish among the three types of stipulative definition by characterizing enlarging and confining definitions as partial. The enlarging definition stipulates common meaning *plus* something; the confining definition stipulates common meaning *minus* something. The restricting definition is total rather than partial and stipulates something *instead of* common meaning.

III. METHODS OF DEFINING

Here are four methods that work well for stipulative definitions.[6]

A. MORE PARTICULAR OR FAMILIAR TERMS

Define by equating the term with a more particular or more familiar term. For example:

"Reserved Area" means the kitchen, club room, and sitting room in the clubhouse building.

"Rate card values" means rate card values published by Standard Rate and Data Service, Inc.

"Good faith" means honesty in the transaction concerned.

B. DIVISIONS

Define by analyzing the term's divisions or sub-divisions. For example:

"Rental agreement" means any written agreement, or oral agreement if for less duration than one year, providing for use and occupancy of premises.

"Condominium" means that form of ownership of condominium property under which units of improvements are subject to ownership by one or more owners, and there is appurtenant to each unit, as part thereof, an undivided share in the common elements.

C. LARGER CATEGORIES

Define by establishing the term's referent as part of some larger thing or category. For example:

"Common elements" means the portion of the condominium property not included in the units.

"Assessment" means a share of the funds required for the payment of common expenses which, from time to time, are assessed against the unit owner.

---

6. For a comprehensive discussion of the various methods of definition along with particular uses and misuses of stipulative definitions, see R. Dick, Legal Drafting 73–82 (2d ed. 1985). For an abbreviated version of the same discussion and additional examples of all methods, see Younger, The Definitive Word On Definitions, 72 ABA J. 98 (1986).

D. LIST OF REFERENTS

Define by listing the term's referents. For example:

"Institutional First Mortgagee" means a bank, savings and loan association, insurance company, mortgage company, real estate investment trust or other construction lender, or individual mortgage lender authorized to do business in the State of _____.

"Deposit money" means any money held by the landlord on behalf of the tenant, including, but not limited to, damage deposit, security deposit, advance rent deposit, pet deposit, or any contractual deposit agreed to between landlord and tenant either in writing or orally.

IV. DRAFTING PRINCIPLES FOR STIPULATIVE DEFINITIONS

A. NEEDLESS LEXICAL DEFINITIONS

Do not give lexical definitions as though they were stipulative, such as purporting to stipulate that an automobile is a four-wheeled motor vehicle. For another example:

A form is a piece of paper containing blank spaces, boxes or lines for the entry of dates, names, descriptive details or other items.

B. STRAINED DEFINITIONS

Avoid definitions that strain ordinary usage so much that they are difficult to accept. For example:

"Swimming Pool" includes the aprons and contiguous paved areas, and the Shuffleboard Court and the Playground.

The term "supplies" shall mean all property except land, and shall include public works, buildings, facilities, ships, floating equipment, and vessels of every character, type and description, aircraft, parts, accessories, equipment, machine tools and alteration or installation thereof.

It is reasonable to enlarge the definition of "swimming pool" to include its aprons and contiguous paved areas. It may be asking too much, however, to ask a reader to think of a shuffleboard court or a playground as part of a swimming pool. Likewise, it is easy to conceive of "supplies" as meaning the wide range of property listed, but alteration and installation are activities, not property; it is thus difficult to conceive of "supplies" as also including a process such as altering a building.

C. "MEANS AND INCLUDES"

Do not say "means and includes." The combination of restricting and enlarging terms is contradictory. For example, consider the following muddle, complete with a false imperative:

Expressway shall mean and include the Cross-Town Expressway passing through the City of _____, all of its facilities, related approaches, viaducts, bridges, interchange facilities and service roads now existing or as may be later constructed or designated.

Notice, however, that the following variation produces no trouble because it separates the restricting definition from the enlarging one:

> *Expressway* means the Cross-Town Expressway passing through the City of _____, including related approaches, viaducts, bridges, interchange facilities, and service roads now existing or as may be later constructed or designated.

What this version does is, first, to give a restricting definition of "Expressway" as the Cross-Town Expressway, and, second, to give an enlarging definition of "Cross-Town Expressway." In other words, there are no contradictory definitions of the same term. Also notice that in the second version, "includes" signals a technically correct enlarging definition since the definition does not contain language to refer to the roadway itself. It is thus free from any lexical component.

D. PARTIAL V. FULL DEFINITION

Remember that partial definitions, both enlarging and confining, can be valuable tools of shorthand, eliminating the obligation to set forth in exhaustive terms every particular that is included or excluded. In contrast, the restrictive definition that stipulates that X *means* Y carries a heavy obligation to be complete. If X means nothing else but Y, it also means every bit of Y. Furthermore, by implication, Y means nothing but X, and it also means every bit of X.

E. PLACEMENT OF DEFINITIONS

Avoid placing in an introductory definition section the definition of a term that is used only once in the rest of the document. If a definition is necessary, provide it when the term is used. Save the introductory definition section for definitions of terms used pervasively.

Often one does not know how often a term will appear in a document until the whole document has been drafted. For this reason, one should draft the definition section last. This can also prevent two embarrassing problems that do happen sometimes: (1) a term is defined one way in an introductory definition section but is used another way later in the document, and (2) a term is defined in a definition section and then never mentioned again in the rest of the document.

F. RULES BURIED IN DEFINITIONS

Do not let substantive rules creep into definitions. The rules usually do not help define terms, but the more serious problem is that the rules themselves become difficult to locate because they are out of their normal place. Consider the following purported definitions, for example. Note too that it is a sign of trouble when a new sentence begins in the midst of a definition.

1. Definition of "Wine"

(1) "Wine" means all beverages made from fresh fruits, berries, or grapes, either by natural fermentation or by natural fermentation with brandy added, in the manner required by the laws and regulations of the United States, and includes all sparkling wines, champagnes, combination of the aforesaid beverages, vermouths, and like products. Sugar, flavors, and coloring materials may be added to wine to make it conform to the consumer's taste, except that the ultimate flavor or the color of the product may not be altered to imitate a beverage other than wine or to change the character of the wine.

(2) "Fortified wine" means all wines containing more than 14 percent of alcohol by weight.

2. Definition of "Retail Sale"

(3)(a) "Retail sale" or a "sale at retail" means a sale to a consumer or to any person for any purpose other than for resale in the form of tangible personal property and includes all such transactions that may be made in lieu of retail sales or sales at retail. A resale must be in strict compliance with the rules and regulations, and any dealer making a sale for resale which is not in strict compliance with the rules and regulations shall himself be liable for and pay the tax. A dealer may, through the informal protest provided for in s. 213.21 and the rules of the Department of Revenue, provide the department with evidence of the exempt status of a sale. The department shall adopt rules to implement this act which shall provide that valid resale certificates and consumer certificates of exemption executed by those dealers or exempt entities which were registered with the department at the time of sales shall be accepted by the department when submitted during the protest period but shall not be accepted in any proceeding under chapter 120 or any circuit court action instituted under chapter 72.

V. DEFINITIONS AND CONCEPTS: A WARNING

Hollis T. Hurd warns of "the tendency of defined terms to take on a life of their own," by which he means the dangerous tendency of readers—and sometimes of drafters as well—to forget the stipulated definition and keep on thinking about the terms with their ordinary dictionary definitions.[7] This tendency is perhaps greater if the stipulated definition is excessively strained, but it can operate with any stipulated definition. It is not a problem of finding the right words to define a term. Rather it is a problem of finding the right term to use as a shorthand referent, the term that is stipulatively defined. This is a conceptual problem. Hurd uses the shorthand referent "employee" in the National Labor Relations Act to show what can go wrong.

7. H. Hurd, Writing for Lawyers 114–18 (1982).

H. HURD, WRITING FOR LAWYERS

115–17 (1982).*

* * * The Act protects various types of activity by employees, among them strikes. Clearly there is a recurring necessity to refer to these protected individuals, and the Act naturally refers to them as "employees," who are defined as including individuals whose work has ceased as a consequence of a current labor dispute. Now take a striker: the company is operating the plant and the striker refuses to come to work. Shouldn't that be regarded as a quit, just the same as when an employee voluntarily chooses to stay home for any other reason? Or, at the very least, shouldn't such absence justify the employer in discharging him and thus terminating the employer-employee relationship? You would think so, but the drafters of the NLRA have seduced all its readers by the choice of the defined term "employee".

As for a striker, the NLRA provides that he is entitled in some circumstances to receive his job back when the strike ends and in other circumstances merely to stand at the top of the list of applicants for future openings. That is the basic protection which the Act affords to a striker. However, this protected individual is always called an "employee" in the Act, and this has led to the startling conclusion, which is now widely held, that a company cannot discharge a striker, nor has a striker quit. We know this because strikers are "employees."

We wouldn't have this problem if the Act called these people "Protected Individuals." That title would make clear that such individuals have only the protection afforded by the Act and, while preferential re-hire may be one of them, continuous employment status is not. Or the defined term could be anything else, like "Martians" or "Yellow Vegetables." The whole point of defined terms is that, like symbols in algebra, they stand for something else; they have no intrinsic meaning. The NLRA intends only to say that people who can be described as members of this particular class with these characteristics (i.e., they used to be employees but went on strike) have certain rights. Any name would do, since it would serve only to incorporate the definition by reference.

But noooo! They had to choose the word "employee", and now most everyone thinks that strikers are still employees, as required by the Act. Strikers are "Protected Individuals"; they are not necessarily employees. Tempest in a teapot? Well, how about all the employee benefit plans of the company which, by their terms, cover "employees". Do strikers get continued free medical care, free life insurance, service credit toward pensions, and even vacations? And if they do, what incentive will there be to settle the strike? A poor choice of words can be very expensive indeed.

So, as a reader, always treat defined terms as merely incorporating their definitions by reference. In your mind, expand the document by adding back in all the redundancy which the defined terms removed. That is the only way to assure that you will not be seduced by the terms.

And as a writer, consider very carefully whether the obvious and natural choice for a defined term really fits in with your thesis in the document. If not, choose one that does. * * *

VI. PROBLEMS

PROBLEM 1

The following definition sections come from a variety of documents. Evaluate them according to the principles discussed in this chapter.

DOCUMENT 1. DECLARATION OF CONDOMINIUM

1 DEFINITIONS: As used in this Declaration of Condominium and
2 By-Laws and Exhibits attached hereto, and all Amendments thereof,
3 unless the context otherwise requires, the following definitions shall
4 prevail:

5   A. Declaration, or Declaration of Condominium, or Enabling Dec-
6 laration, means this instrument as it may be from time to time
7 amended.

8   B. Association, means the _____ non-profit corporation whose
9 name appears at the end of this Declaration as "Association", said
10 Association being the entity responsible for the operation of said
11 Condominium.

12   C. By-Laws, means the By-Laws of the Association specified above,
13 as they exist from time to time.

14   D. Common Elements, means the portion of the Condominium
15 property not included in the Units.

16   E. Limited Common Elements, means and includes those common
17 elements which are reserved for the use of a certain unit or units, to
18 the exclusion of all other units.

19   F. Condominium, means that form of ownership of condominium
20 property under which units of improvements are subject to ownership
21 by one or more owners, and there is appurtenant to each unit, as part
22 thereof, an undivided share in the common elements.

23   G. Condominium Act, means and refers to the Condominium Act
24 of the State of _____.

25   H. Common Expenses, mean the expenses for which the unit
26 owners are liable to the Association.

27   I. Common Surplus, means the excess of all receipts of the Associ-
28 ation from this condominium, including, but not limited to, assess-

29 ments, rents, profits, and revenues on account of the common elements,
30 over and above the amount of common expenses of this condominium.

31 J. Condominium property, means and includes the land in a
32 condominium, whether or not contiguous, and all improvements there-
33 on, and all easements and rights appurtenant thereto, intended for use
34 in connection with the condominium.

35 K. Assessment, means a share of the funds required for the
36 payment of common expenses which, from time to time, are assessed
37 against the unit owner.

38 L. Condominium Parcel or Parcel means a unit, together with the
39 undivided share in the common elements which are appurtenant to the
40 unit.

41 M. Condominium Unit, or Unit, is a unit as defined in the
42 Condominium Act, referring herein to each of the separate and identi-
43 fied units delineated in the survey attached to the Declaration as
44 Exhibit "1", and when the context permits, the condominium parcel
45 includes such unit, including its share of the common elements appurte-
46 nant thereto. The physical boundaries of each unit are as delineated in
47 the survey aforedescribed, and are as more particularly described in
48 Article III and Article XIX.B. of this Declaration.

49 N. Unit Owner, or Group of Unit Owners, or Owner of a Unit, or
50 Parcel Owner, means the owner or group of owners of a single condo-
51 minium parcel.

52 O. Developer, means the _____ corporation whose name appears
53 at the end of this Declaration as "Developer", its successors and
54 assigns.

55 P. Institutional First Mortgagee, means a bank, savings and loan
56 association, insurance company, mortgage company, a real estate in-
57 vestment trust or other construction lender, or individual mortgage
58 lender authorized to do business in the State of _____.

59 Q. Occupant, means the person or persons, other than the unit
60 owner, in possession of a unit.

61 R. Condominium Documents, means this Declaration, the By-
62 Laws and all Exhibits annexed hereto, as the same may be amended
63 from time to time.

64 S. Unless the context otherwise requires, all other terms used in
65 this declaration shall be assumed to have the meaning attributed to
66 said term by Section 3 of the Condominium Act as of the date of this
67 Declaration.

DOCUMENT 2. BY–LAWS OF CONDOMINIUM (SAME CONDO-MINIUM AS DOCUMENT 1)

ARTICLE I

GENERAL

* * *

Section 3. Definition: As used herein, the term "corporation" shall be the equivalent of "association" as defined in the Condominium Declaration, and the words "property", "Unit owner", and "condominium" are defined as set forth in the Condominium Declaration, etc., of the corporation, to which these By-Laws are attached.

* * *

ARTICLE IV

MEMBERSHIP

Section 1. Definition: Each parcel (apartment) owner shall be a member of the corporation, and membership in the corporation shall be limited to owners of condominium parcels.

* * *

ARTICLE VI

NOTICES

Section 1. Definition: Whenever under the provisions of the statutes or of the Certificate of Incorporation or of these By-Laws, notice is required to be given to any director or member, it shall not be construed to mean personal notice; but such notice may be given in writing by mail, by depositing the same in a post office or letter box in a postpaid, sealed envelope, addressed as appears on the books of the corporation.

DOCUMENT 3. RULES AND REGULATIONS OF CONDOMINI-UM ASSOCIATION

15. PARKING AND TRAFFIC CONTROL

a) Parking and traffic control shall at all times be subject to such rules and regulations as the Board of Governors may establish.

b) Definitions: For the purpose of these rules and regulations, a private passenger automobile is an operable, self-propelled vehicle which is designed primarily for the transportation of people, together with ancillary provision for their baggage and parcels. A private passenger automobile includes the vehicle known generally as the station wagon. The definition excludes trucks, commercial vehicles, vehicles carrying visible watercraft, or vehicles containing facilities for sleeping, cooking or waste disposal.

* * *

16. RECREATIONAL FACILITIES

    a) <u>Definitions:</u>

        i) "Recreational Facilities" as used herein means the entire area lying between the northwesterly side of the tennis court (projected) and the two creeks (_____ and _____), including structures and improvements thereon.

        ii) "Swimming Pool" includes the aprons and contiguous paved areas, and the Shuffleboard Court and the Playground.

        iii) "Clubhouse" means the building housing the club facilities and porches, balconies, patios and paved areas adjacent thereto (excluding the Swimming Pool).

        iv) "Reserved Area" means the kitchen, Club Room and the Sitting Room in the Clubhouse building. The Pool Room and the entire Health Club area are specifically excluded from the "Reserved Area".

        v) The arts and crafts facilities in Condominium Building No. II are not included in Recreational Facilities for the purpose of this Rule No. 16 only.

        vi) A "house guest" is an invitee to a condominium unit whose stay is temporary but includes staying overnight. A "party guest" is an invitee to a social or entertainment event in the Reserved Area. A "guest" is an invitee of a condominium unit resident who is not a party guest or a house guest.

        vii) For the purpose of these rules an "outside organization" or "outside organized group" is an aggregation of persons, a majority of whom are not residents of _____ Condominium, who associate together on specific occasions under a common name such as, but not limited to, "club", "association", "society", "fellowship", "auxiliary", "fraternity", "sorority" or word of similar import.

DOCUMENT 4. LAW SCHOOL FACULTY HANDBOOK

4.2   <u>Appointments, Faculty</u>

<u>Definitions</u>

For the purpose of participating in the governance of the College of Law by attending and voting at faculty meetings, "faculty" means those persons whose primary function is teaching and research and who hold the rank of professor, associate professor or assistant professor and includes the dean, associate dean, assistant dean and persons holding similar administrative positions if they also hold professorial rank but does not include the assistant to the dean, persons holding the rank of instructor or any interim rank or a member of the library staff, whether engaged in teaching or not, except that the law librarian by action of the faculty may be a member of the faculty. Persons serving in the College of Law with professorial rank as visitors, or holding an interim instructional rank, or otherwise directly engaged in the instructional program, are invited and encouraged to attend faculty meetings but are not eligible to vote.

COMMENT: The proposed definition is designed to identify those persons whose functions and responsibilities are at the heart of the educational process itself, as distinct from the personnel whose concern is centered in the necessary supporting services such as admissions, library, etc. The service of persons with interim status is from its inception usually intended to be of short duration. Therefore, these persons are not included within the fully participating faculty even though their duties may be exclusively in the teaching area. Visiting professors occupy a unique position. They are usually established teachers whose experiences constitute a valuable resource. On the other hand, their long range interest and commitment are usually elsewhere. Therefore, the proposal is that they participate in discussions but not directly in decisions.

In this definition, mention is made of eligibility to participate in the faculty's deliberative and decisional processes, because it is in connection with this type of action that the classification. of law school personnel is here important. It should be emphasized that regardless of classification, any person who engages in teaching is vested with a full measure of academic freedom and responsibility in his teaching role, even though for other purposes he is not included within the definition of "faculty."

Within the College of Law there have been examples of appointments to positions in which the title of the appointee has been determined solely or in part by the label on the budgetary item from which the appointee's compensation is paid. The philosophy of the definition is to posit faculty status on the duties assigned, and in the event of conflict between budgetary description and teaching function, the assigned duties should always prevail over budgetary or similar factors.

DOCUMENT 5. AUTOMOBILE RENTAL AGREEMENT

PAGE ONE (REVERSE SIDE)

——— RENTAL AGREEMENT

1. DEFINITIONS

This is an **Agreement** between you and the Company to rent to you a motor **Vehicle** ("car") (including tires, tools, accessories and equipment).

The **Vehicle** is described on Page 2 (front side).

The rent**or** (lessor) is called the **Company** and is identified in the upper lefthand corner on Page 2.

10   The renter (lessee) is you (sometimes called the **Customer**) and you
11 also are identified on Page 2. You must sign this Agreement.

12   An Authorized Driver is you (the Customer) and/or an additional
13 Authorized Driver who has been approved in writing by the Company
14 and has signed his or her name at the time of rental in Area 87 on page
15 2 of this agreement. The only other Authorized Driver is a person who
16 has your permission to use the Vehicle, but that person must have a
17 valid drivers license and be at least 18 years old. Some locations
18 require that he or she must be 21 or 25 years old (check this with the
19 location where you rent the car). In addition, such person must be a
20 member of your immediate family who permanently resides in your
21 household or must be your business associate (for example, partner,
22 employer, employee or fellow employee) and be driving the Vehicle for
23 customary business purposes. Customer agrees not to permit use of
24 Vehicle by any other person without obtaining the prior written con-
25 sent of Company.

DOCUMENT 6. RESIDENTIAL LEASE

1 G. Our office hours are from 10:00 A.M.–12:00 noon and 1:00–5:00
2   P.M. Monday thru Friday; after hours we will respond only to
3   emergencies.

4   The definition of an emergency is basically as follows:

5   "An emergency is one that if not followed thru promptly will
6   result in severe damage to your unit." We will also consider
7   as emergency calls those items which will make it prohibitive
8   for you to occupy your unit such as a heater breakdown in 35
9   degree weather, water leaks, power failure as a result of
10   components in your units, or any acts of God such as storm,
11   fire, etc.

PROBLEM 2

Reevaluate the definition section of Ordinance No. 82–19, the
swimming pool ordinance that is the subject of Problems C1–4 in
Chapter 5. (See pp. 152–55.) In light of your reevaluation, redraft the
ordinance.

PROBLEM 3

Reevaluate the definition section of Ordinance 84–10, the false
alarm ordinance that is the subject of Problems C5–8 in Chapter 5.
(See pp. 155–59.) In light of your reevaluation, redraft the ordinance.

Appendix A

BIBLIOGRAPHY

1. Books

There are many books on legal writing in general. The few listed below are especially helpful on legal drafting in particular.

Irwin Alterman, Plain and Accurate Style in Court Papers, American Law Institute—American Bar Association Committee on Continuing Professional Education, Philadelphia, Pa. (1987). This is a Plain English style manual for pleadings, motion practice, discovery, briefs, and other litigation documents.

Gertrude Block, Effective Legal Writing, Foundation Press, Mineola, N.Y. (3d ed. 1986). This book includes both practical advice on a wide range of stylistic matters and a useful review of grammar and punctuation.

Frank E. Cooper, Writing in Law Practice, Bobbs-Merril Co., Indianapolis, Ind. (1963). This book includes separate chapters on drafting each of the following: letters, pleadings, contracts, statutes, and wills.

Robert Dick, Legal Drafting, Carswell Co., Toronto, Canada (2d ed. 1985). This book includes detailed discussion of ambiguity, definitions, and style.

Reed Dickerson, The Fundamentals of Legal Drafting, Little, Brown and Co., Boston, Mass. (2d ed. 1985). In its first edition (1965), this was the first book to bring together the body of knowledge that is now known as "legal drafting." The second edition includes and updates most of the materials from Professor Dickerson's earlier book, Legislative Drafting (1954).

Carl Felsenfeld and Alan Siegel, Writing Contracts in Plain English, West Publishing Co., St. Paul, Minn. (1981). This is a definitive study of the Plain English Movement and how to apply its principles to drafting contracts.

Bryan A. Garner, A Dictionary of Modern Legal Usage, Oxford University Press, New York, N.Y. (1987). This book is more than a dictionary; it is a guide to style and usage. In one alphabetical list, it provides entries on specific points of word usage and grammar and includes short essays on special topics such as Latinisms and sexism. Garner does not merely record lexical definitions; he sets standards and views his own work as an instrument of reform.

Hollis T. Hurd, Writing for Lawyers, Journal Broadcasting and Communications, Pittsburgh, Pa. (1982). This book is not as scholarly as the others in this bibliography. It is written in an informal, often humorous style, with chapter headings that begin with "rules, tips and hints." Two chapters are loaded with practical drafting advice in terms not found in the more scholarly texts. One of these chapters is on style; the other is on drafting as such.

David Mellinkoff, Legal Writing: Sense and Nonsense, West Publishing Co., St. Paul, Minn. (1982). This book combines the legal scholar's knowledge and insight with informal style and brusk tone. The author shouts rules like "Beware the Twofer" and "Thou Shalt Not Never." This is not a convenient reference book in which to look up some particular drafting principle or kind of document. However, the person who reads it through can learn much from it about how to draft clearly, precisely, and concisely.

William P. Statsky, Legislative Analysis and Drafting, West Publishing Co., St. Paul, Minn. (2d ed. 1975). This book is as much about reading and construing statutes as about drafting them. However, it incorporates considerable detail on statute drafting and advice about style that is useful for any legal drafting.

Jule E. Stocker, Stocker on Drawing Wills, Practising Law Institute, New York, N.Y. (10th ed. 1987). This book focuses on drafting a typical will, discussing legacies, devises, trusts, and powers of appointment. It analyzes tax considerations, including estate tax under the Tax Reform Act of 1986. It also provides a sample will with trust provisions, selected alternative clauses, and codicil.

Richard C. Wydick, Plain English for Lawyers, Carolina Academic Press, Durham, N.C. (2d ed. 1985). This book uses copious examples to show how to achieve the major goals of writing in Plain English: omitting surplus words; using familiar, concrete words; using short sentences; using base verbs and the active voice; arranging words with care; and avoiding language quirks. The book also contains exercises on each of these matters and suggested answers to all of the exercises.

2. Articles

A great deal of helpful material about drafting is in periodicals. The list of sources below is not intended to be exhaustive but includes a broad sample of the kind of coverage available.

Allen, Symbolic Logic: A Razor-Edged Tool for Drafting and Interpreting Legal Documents, 66 Yale L.J. 833 (1957).

Allen and Engholm, The Need for Clear Structure in "Plain Language" Legal Drafting, 13 J.L. Reform 455 (1980).

Allen and Engholm, Normalized Legal Drafting and the Query Method, 29 J.Legal Educ. 380 (1978).

Alterman, Plain and Accurate Style in Lawsuit Papers, 62 Mich. B.J. 964 (1983).

Benson, The End of Legalese: The Game Is Over, 13 N.Y.U.Rev.L. & Soc.Change 519 (1984–85).

Benson, Plain English Comes to Court, 13 Litigation No. 1, 21 (1986).

Benson, Up a Statute with Gun and Camera: Isolating Linguistic and Logical Structures in the Analysis of Legislative Language, 8 Seton Hall Legis.J. 279 (1984).

Block, Plain Language Laws: Promise v Performance, 62 Mich.B.J. 950 (1983).

Browne, Development of the FNMA/FHLMC Plain Language Mortgage Documents—Some Useful Techniques, 14 Real Prop.Prob. & Tr.J. 696 (1979).

Christie, Vagueness and Legal Language, 48 Minn.L.Rev. 885 (1964).

Cusack, The Blue-Pencilled Will, August 1979 Tr. & Est. 33.

Cusack, The Plain English Will Revisited, July 1980 Tr. & Est. 42.

Davis, Protecting Consumers from Overdisclosure and Gobbledygook: An Empirical Look at the Simplification of Consumer-Credit Contracts, 63 Va.L.Rev. 841 (1977).

Dickerson, Legal Drafting: Writing as Thinking, or, Talk-back from Your Draft and How To Exploit It, 29 J.Legal Educ. 373 (1978).

Dickerson, Obscene Telephone Calls: An Introduction to the Reading of Statutes, 22 Harv.J. on Legis. 173 (1985).

Dickerson, Toward a Legal Dialectic, 61 Ind.L.J. 315 (1986).

Felsenfeld, The Future of Plain English, 62 Mich.B.J. 942 (1983).

Fitzgerald and Spratt, Rule Drafting—I, 119 (Part 2) New L.J. 991 (1969).

Fitzgerald and Spratt, Rule Drafting—III, 119 (Part 2) New L.J. 1052 (1969).

Kirk, Legal Drafting: Curing Unexpressive Language, 3 Tex.Tech L.Rev. 23 (1971).

Kirk, Legal Drafting: How Should a Document Begin? 3 Tex.Tech L.Rev. 233 (1972).

Kirk, Legal Drafting: Some Elements of Technique, 4 Tex.Tech L.Rev. 297 (1973).

Llewellyn, Remarks on the Theory of Appellate Decision and the Rules or Canons About How Statutes Are To Be Construed, 3 Vand.L. Rev. 395 (1950).

McCarty, That Hybrid "and/or," 39 Mich.St.B.J. 9 (No. 5, May 1960).

Robinson, Drafting—Its Substance and Teaching, 25 J.Legal Educ. 514 (1973).

Ross, On Legalities and Linguistics: Plain Language Legislation, 30 Buffalo L.Rev. 317 (1981).

Slawson, The New Meaning of Contract: The Transformation of Contracts Law by Standard Forms, 46 U.Pa.L.Rev. 21 (1984).

Trawick, Form as Well as Substance, 49 Fla.B.J. 437 (1975).

Wason, The Drafting of Rules, 118 (Part 1) New L.J. 548 (1968).

Word, A Brief for Plain English Wills and Trusts, 14 U.Rich.L.Rev. 471 (1980).

Wydick, Plain English for Lawyers, 66 Calif.L.Rev. 727 (1978).

3. *Comments*

Comment, Attorney Malpractice in California: The Liability of a Lawyer Who Drafts an Imprecise Contract or Will, 24 U.C.L.A.L.Rev. 422 (1976).

Comment, Sexism in the Statutes: Identifying and Solving the Problem of Ambiguous Gender Bias in Legal Writing, 32 Buffalo L.Rev. 559 (1983).

Appendix B

DOCUMENTS FOR DISCUSSION AND ADDITIONAL DRAFTING PRACTICE

Collected in Appendix B are miscellaneous additional documents illustrating both good and not so good drafting. With minor editing in some instances, all of these samples are real. None is a model of perfection. All are gathered here as a collection of raw materials for study, discussion, and redrafting practice. They are in alphabetical order according to title.

DOCUMENT 1

CONDITIONS OF ADMISSION

TO

_____ HOSPITAL

1. General Duty Nursing: The hospital provides only general duty nursing care. Under this system nurses are called to the bedside of the patient by a signal system. If the patient is in such condition as to need continuous or special duty nursing care, it is agreed that such must be arranged by the patient, or his legal representative, or his physicians, and the hospital shall in no way be responsible for failure to provide the same and is hereby released from any and all liability arising from the fact that said patient is not provided with such additional care.

2. Medical and Surgical Consent: The undersigned consents to any x-ray examination, laboratory procedures, anesthesia, medical or surgical treatment or hospital services rendered the patient under the general and special instructions of the physician. The undersigned recognizes that all doctors of medicine furnishing services to the patient, including the radiologist, pathologist, anesthetist and the like are independent contractors and are not employees or agents of the hospital.

3. Release of information: The hospital may disclose all or any part of the patient's record to any person or corporation which is or may be liable under a contract to the hospital or to the patient or to a family member or employer of the patient for all or part of the hospital's charge, including, but not limited to, hospital or medical service companies, insurance companies, workmen's compensation carriers, or welfare funds.

4. Personal Valuables: It is understood and agreed that the hospital maintains a safe for the safekeeping of money and valuables and the hospital shall not be liable for the loss or damage to any money, jewelry, glasses, dentures, documents, furs, fur coats and fur garments or other articles of unusual value and small compass, unless placed therein, and shall not be liable for loss or damage to any other personal property, unless deposited with the hospital for safekeeping.

5. Financial Agreement: The undersigned agrees, whether he signs as agent or as patient, that in consideration of the services to be rendered to the patient, he hereby individually obligates himself to pay the account of the hospital in accordance with the regular rates and terms of the hospital. Should the account be referred to an attorney for collection, the undersigned shall pay reasonable attorney's fees and collection expense. All delinquent accounts may bear interest at the legal rate.

The undersigned certifies that he has read the foregoing, receiving a copy thereof, and is the patient, or is duly authorized by the patient as patient's general agent to execute the above and accept its terms.

_____

PATIENT

_____

PATIENT'S AGENT OR
REPRESENTATIVE

_____

RELATIONSHIP TO PATIENT

A copy of this Document is to be delivered to the patient.

Time of signing _____ 19__, Hour _____ M _____

Witness _____

If Translation Required,
Individual Translating, Sign
Below:

_____

Child—Legal Drafting ACB—10

DOCUMENT 2

CUSTOMER AGREEMENT FOR ELECTRONIC FUND TRANSFER SERVICES

This Agreement governs the use of electronic fund transfer ("EFT") services offered in conjunction with your checking and/or savings accounts ("Account") with a _____ Bank. These services include preauthorized transfers to and from your Account such as automated deposits of Social Security checks, automated loan payments and all transactions resulting from a debit card made through an automated teller machine, a Point-of-Sale (POS) terminal or any other device whether electronic or not. In consideration of the EFT services made available to you, ("Customer") and any other person using the EFT services in conjunction with the Account (who, by such use, agrees to be bound hereby as though such user were the Customer) by signing, accepting, or using the EFT service, jointly and severally agree as follows:

1. **CUSTOMER LIABILITY:** If your statement which we will make available to you periodically shows transfers that you did not make, tell us at once. If you do not tell us within 60 days after the statement was mailed to you, you may not get back any money you lost after the 60 days if we can prove that we could have stopped someone from taking the money if you had told us in time.

    If a good reason kept you from telling us (such as a long trip or a hospital stay), the time period specified above will be extended to a reasonable time.

    If you believe that someone has transferred or may transfer money from your Account without your permission, contact us at the telephone number or address listed on this Agreement.

2. **BUSINESS DAYS:** Our business days are Monday through Friday. Holidays are not included.

3. **CHARGES:** Your Account(s) remain subject to the Bank's standard activity charges. No additional charges are assessed for the use of _____ Bank's automated teller machine or for the use of Point-of-Sale terminals or other preauthorized transfers, with **exception** to ATM withdrawals made at non-_____ automated teller machines.

    There is a 75¢ charge for each withdrawal made at non-_____ Automated Teller Machines.

4. **DISCLOSURE OF ACCOUNT INFORMATION TO THIRD PARTIES:** We will disclose information to third parties about your Account or the transfers you make:

    (a) where it is necessary for completing transfers, or

    (b) in order to verify the existence and condition of your Account for a third party, such as a credit bureau, merchant or financial institution, or

(c) in order to comply with government agency or court order, or

(d) if you give us your written permission, or

(e) if any of your accounts become delinquent or overdrawn, information may be released to attorneys, accounts collection bureaus, credit bureaus, financial institutions, and others involved in collection, adjustment, settlement, or reporting of accounts.

5. RECEIPTS AND STATEMENTS:

(a) Preauthorized credits. If you have arranged to have direct deposits made to your Account at least once every 60 days from the same person or company, you can call us at the telephone number on the reverse side to find out whether or not the deposit has been made.

(b) Periodic statement. You will get a monthly account statement unless there are not transfers in a particular month. In any case you will get the statement at least quarterly.

6. PREAUTHORIZED TRANSFERS:

(a) Right to stop payment and procedure for doing so. If you have told us in advance to make regular payments out of your Account, you can stop any of these payments. Here's how:

Contact us in time for us to receive your request 3 business days or more before the payment is scheduled to be made. If you call, we may also require you to put your request in writing and get it to us within 14 days after you call. We will charge you for each stop-payment order you give.

(b) Notice of varying amounts. If these regular payments may vary in amount, the person you are going to pay will tell you 10 days before each payment, when it will be made and how much it will be. You may choose instead to get this notice only when the payment would differ by more than a certain amount from the previous payment, or when the amount would fall outside certain limits that you set.

(c) Liability for failure to stop payment of preauthorized transfer. If you order us to stop one of these payments 3 business days or more before the transfer is scheduled, and we do not do so, we will be liable for your loss or damages.

7. LIABILITY FOR FAILURE TO MAKE TRANSFERS: If we do not complete a transfer to or from your Account on time or in the correct amount according to our agreement with you, we will be liable for your losses or damages. However, there are some exceptions. We will not be liable for instance:

(a) If, through no fault of ours, you do not have enough money in your account to make the transfer.

(b) If the transfer will go over the credit limit on your overdraft line.

(c) If circumstances beyond our control (such as fire or flood) prevent the transfer, despite reasonable precautions that we have taken.

(d) There may be other exceptions stated in our agreement with you.

8. **RESOLUTION OF ERRORS AND QUESTIONS ABOUT YOUR ELECTRONIC TRANSFERS:** Contact us as soon as you can, if you think your statement is wrong or if you need more information about a transfer listed on the statement or receipt. We must hear from you no later than 60 days after we sent you the FIRST statement on which the problem or error appeared.

(a) Tell us your name and account number.

(b) Describe the error or the transfer you are unsure about, and explain as clearly as you can why you believe it is an error or why you need more information.

(c) Tell us the dollar amount of the suspected error.

If you tell us orally, we may require that you send us your complaint or question in writing within 10 business days.

We will tell you the results of our investigation within 10 business days if the suspected transfer was initiated at an ATM within the United States or any of its territories, or within 20 business days if the suspected transfer was (1) outside the United States or any of its territories or (2) was made with a POS debit card. We will correct any error promptly. If we need more time, however, we may take up to 45 calendar days (90 calendar days if the suspected transfer was outside the United States or its territories or made with a POS debit card) to investigate your complaint or questions. If we decide to do this, we will recredit your Account within 10 business days (20 business days if the suspected transfer was outside the United States or its territories or made with a POS debit card) provided the account is not a margin account, for the amount you think is in error, so that you have the use of the money during the time it takes to complete our investigation.

If we decide that there was no error, we will send you a written explanation within three business days after we finish our investigation. You may ask for copies of the documents that we used in our investigation.

If we ask you to put your complaint or question in writing and we do not receive it within 10 business days, we may not recredit your Account.

9. **ADDRESS CHANGE:** You agree to immediately notify the Bank in writing at the Bank or at the address listed below of any address changes, and all notices mailed to your last known address will be effective as though received.

132 **10. APPLICABLE RULES AND LAWS:** All EFT transactions shall
133 be governed by this Agreement, the Bank's signature card agree-
134 ment and account contracts and the normal rules governing the
135 Account, and by the laws of the State of Florida.

136 **11. MODIFICATION OF AGREEMENT:** This Agreement may be
137 modified at any time by the Bank giving you notice of such change
138 at least 21 days prior to the effective date thereof. Notice will be
139 mailed to your address.

DOCUMENT 3

LEASE AGREEMENT

1 THIS AGREEMENT, made and entered into this _____ day of
2 _____, 19__, between _____, INC., party of the first part, here-in-
3 after called Carrier which term shall mean and include the party of the
4 first part, its successors and assigns and _____

5 _____
6 party of the second part, here-in-after called the Contractor.

7 WITNESSETH:

8 WHEREAS, Carrier is a common carrier of property by motor
9 vehicles operating under certificates of public convenience and necessi-
10 ty issued by the _____ Public Service Commission and certificates
11 issued by the Interstate Commerce Commission, as applicable.

12 WHEREAS, the Contractor is the owner of the motor vehicle
13 equipment hereinafter referred to, which said vehicle Carrier desires to
14 lease from the contractor and the Contractor desires to lease the
15 equipment to Carrier,

16 NOW, THEREFORE, in consideration of the covenants and agree-
17 ments herein contained, Carrier and the Contractor agree as follows:

18 1. The Contractor, as an independent contractor, hereby agrees to
19 lease to Carrier and Carrier agrees to lease from the Contractor the
20 motor vehicle equipment owned by the Contractor for the purpose of
21 supplying motive power to Carrier's trailers, which said motor vehicle
22 equipment is described as follows:

23 YEAR   MAKE   MODEL   SERIAL NO.   TAG NO.

24 2. The Contractor shall furnish, at its expense, a full complement
25 of experienced and qualified employees, which may include the Con-
26 tractor and shall maintain said equipment in such condition so as to
27 keep said equipment operating daily for the maximum number of hours
28 and the maximum number of miles consistent with proper and safe
29 operation in pulling the trailer of Carrier in intrastate and interstate
30 commerce in the business of Carrier.

31 3. The Contractor shall provide and continuously maintain the
32 said motor vehicle in good, safe, serviceable, and efficient operating
33 condition in all respects, at its expense, and shall pay all expenses of

34 operation of said vehicle, including by way of illustration, but not
35 limited to, the cost of all fuel, fuel taxes, lubricants, oil, parts, repairs,
36 and accessories, tires, tubes, safety equipment, vehicle licenses, taxes,
37 salaries of drivers or other employees, fines and tolls, and every other
38 expense not specifically mentioned of any nature whatsoever pertaining
39 to the operation of the leased motor vehicle equipment.

40   4. The Contractor shall furnish and maintain, at its expense, so-
41 called "bobtail" insurance, covering said equipment with minimum
42 limits as may be required by _____ law or regulation in the case of
43 intrastate operations or by Federal law or regulations of the Interstate
44 Commerce Commission in the event of interstate transportation, but in
45 no event shall such minimum limits be less that $100,000 for injury to
46 any one person and $300,000 for injury in any accident and coverage of
47 $50,000 for damage to property. The Contractor shall furnish Carrier
48 with a copy of such insurance which affords coverage for bodily injury
49 and property damage when Contractor's equipment isn't being operated
50 in conjunction with Carrier's equipment. The Contractor agrees that it
51 shall comply with any and all applicable laws, ordinances, regulations,
52 and requirements of Federal, State, County, and Municipalities gov-
53 erning the business of Carrier or the operation of the vehicle covered by
54 this agreement, and shall include, but shall not be limited to, the rules
55 and regulations of the United States Department of Transportation, the
56 Interstate Commerce Commission, the _____ Public Service Commis-
57 sion, as applicable, or any other regulatory body or agency.

58   5. The Contractor shall pay all compensation of every kind and
59 character of its employees and shall pay all taxes, charges, benefits,
60 claims, and liabilities of every kind which may arise by virtue of their
61 employment by the Contractor and their acts and duties hereunder.
62 The Contractor shall not operate the said equipment hereby leased to
63 Carrier in the business of Carrier until the Contractor has been
64 certified by Carrier, in writing, as qualified in meeting any and all of
65 the laws and requirements of the aforementioned governmental and
66 regulatory bodies, and the Contractor shall not cause or permit any one
67 of its drivers or employees to operate said leased equipment until its
68 employee or driver has been certified by the Contractor in writing to
69 Carrier and by Carrier in writing, to the Contractor, as being qualified
70 in meeting said laws and other requirements.

71   6. Carrier shall furnish and maintain, at its expense, bodily injury
72 and property damage liability insurance while the Contractor's equip-
73 ment is being operated in carrying out the transportation service
74 Carrier is authorized to perform under its certificates or permits issued
75 by the _____ Public Service Commission or the Interstate Commerce
76 Commission, as applicable. Carrier will not be responsible for provid-
77 ing or paying for any fire, theft, or collision insurance on the motor
78 vehicle equipment leased from the Contractor at any time, and Carrier
79 will not be responsible for any damage to or theft of the Contractor's
80 equipment.

81 7. The Contractor should furnish and maintain, at its expense,
82 insurance adequate for full fire, theft, and collision, covering the
83 equipment leased to Carrier for the mutual benefit of the parties hereto
84 and such policies shall contain a provision to the effect that no right of
85 subrogation shall arise against Carrier on the part of the Contractor's
86 insurance carrier. The Contractor agrees that Carrier shall not be
87 responsible for any loss, destruction or damage to said leased equip-
88 ment for any cause whatsoever, including any acts of negligence,
89 whether by omission or commission by Carrier, its agents, servants, or
90 employees, and Contractor hereby agrees to indemnify and save harm-
91 less, Carrier from any liability, actions, claims, or demands for any such
92 loss, destruction, or damage.

93 8. The Contractor's equipment hereby leased to Carrier shall be
94 operated in a manner to satisfactorily and safely effect the transporta-
95 tion of its authorized commodities in connection with the transporta-
96 tion service authorized to be performed by Carrier under its certificates
97 and permits as applicable, as a motor common carrier. Carrier shall
98 have exclusive possession, control, and use of equipment for the dura-
99 tion of this lease and accordingly, Carrier shall assume complete
100 responsibility for the operation of the equipment during the duration of
101 this lease and said equipment during the term hereof shall be used
102 exclusively in the transportation of authorized commodities under
103 Carrier's certificates and permits, as applicable.

104 9. Any and all identification plates required by the aforemen-
105 tioned governmental and regulatory bodies shall be displayed on Con-
106 tractor's equipment during the term of this Agreement, and upon
107 termination hereof, said plates shall be removed and be delivered to
108 Carrier. All lettering, decals, and paintings of said equipment which
109 Contractor desires to place upon the leased equipment shall be at
110 Contractor's expense. To the extent that lettering, decals, and paint-
111 ings placed upon the leased equipment indicates that the equipment is
112 performing service pursuant to certificates and permits issued to Carri-
113 er; such lettering, decals, and paintings shall be immediately removed
114 from said equipment upon termination of this agreement.

115 10. The compensation to be paid to the contractor by the Carrier
116 for the leasing of the said equipment and for the service of the driver
117 shall be at the rate of _____% of the gross revenue earned by the
118 Contractor less any applicable deductions. Settlement of compensation
119 shall be made by the Carrier to the Contractor on a weekly basis,
120 payable on Friday of each week for all trips or work performed by the
121 contractor under the terms of this agreement, covered by Bills of
122 Lading submitted by the end of business on Friday of the prior week.
123 All transactions of this paragraph shall be conducted at the _____,
124 _____, Terminal of the Carrier.

125 11. Contractor warrants that the equipment described herein is
126 not the subject of any other lease, memorandum, or agreement. Con-
127 tractor further warrants that the equipment herein described will be

128 used only for the performance of this Lease and for no other purpose.
129 It is the intention of the parties and acknowledged by the parties that
130 neither the Contractor nor any of its drivers, employees, or agents shall
131 be deemed to be agents, employees, or servants of the Carrier or his
132 agents for any purpose, but the Contractor is, and shall be, an indepen-
133 dent contractor and is subject to the direction by the Carrier merely as
134 to the results to be accomplished and not as to the means and methods
135 for accomplishing the results, but with each party recognizing the
136 requirements and responsibilities placed upon the Carrier by the
137 _____ Public Service Commission, the Interstate Commerce Commis-
138 sion, and other regulatory bodies, as applicable.

139   12. The Contractor will be responsible to the Carrier for physical
140 damage loss to Carrier's equipment up to $500 per unit owned or rented
141 by Carrier in tractor trailer combinations. Additionally, Contractor
142 will be responsible to the Carrier for physical damage loss to cargo up
143 to $500 per shipment.

144   13. The Contractor may assign all or any part of the rental
145 provided for herein; and Carrier may assign, sublet, interchange, or
146 otherwise designate the use of the motor vehicle as may best serve the
147 public as required by the Interstate Commerce Commission or the
148 _____ Public Service Commission, as applicable.

149   14. The parties agree that should the Contractor become involved
150 in a labor dispute with its employee, he will immediately notify Carrier.
151 If, in the opinion of Carrier, such labor dispute interferes, or tends to
152 interfere with the motor common carrier operations of the Carrier,
153 then in that event, said lease may be immediately cancelled by Carrier
154 without penalty to the shipping and receiving public.

155   15. The Contractor agrees and understands that he is not an
156 employee of Carrier as contemplated by any Workmen's Compensation
157 Act of the State of _____ or otherwise, and agrees, as here-in-before
158 stated, that if he hires employees to provide services under this con-
159 tract, he will provide the necessary workmen's compensation on such
160 employees as required by law and provide Carrier with a certificate of
161 insurance covering such employee.

162   16. This Agreement shall be effective for a term of at least sixty
163 (60) days from the date hereof and from month to month thereafter
164 unless cancelled by either party after giving ten (10) days notice of
165 intent to cancel. In the event of the breach of any provision of this
166 Agreement by either party, the other may forthwith cancel this Agree-
167 ment by written, telegraphic, or personal notice; and further provided
168 that the Contractor, as a condition precedent to cancelling this Agree-
169 ment, shall first pay to Carrier any and all indebtedness owing to
170 Carrier. Final settlement of compensation between Carrier and Con-
171 tractor will be no sooner than fourteen (14) and no later than twenty
172 one (21) days from the date of termination of this Lease Agreement.

173   17. Contractor agrees to a deduction from the first settlement of
174 compensation as herein provided in the amount of thirty (30) dollars to

175 help offset Carrier's costs of decals and paper work as required by
176 regulatory bodies. The said monies will be returned to the Contractor
177 after the initial term of this Agreement.

178   18. The Contractor agrees to indemnify the Carrier against any
179 loss resulting from the injury or death of any of the Contractor's drivers
180 or employees and the loss or damage resulting from the negligence,
181 incompetence or dishonesty of such drivers or employees.

182   19. In conducting operations under this agreement, the parties
183 hereto recognize that Contractor will gain access to and become aware
184 of confidential business relationships between Carrier and its custom-
185 ers. Accordingly, Contractor agrees that in the event of termination of
186 this Agreement, for any reason other than reduction in forces, the
187 Contractor shall not solicit transportation from any of Carrier's custom-
188 ers within an area of 100 miles from the Contractor's domicile point for
189 a period of one year from the date of termination of this agreement.

190   IN WITNESS WHEREOF, the parties hereto have executed this
191 Agreement in triplicate on the day and year first above written.

192 Signed, sealed and delivered in
193 the presence of:

194 _____   _____
195   Carrier

196 _____
197 As to Carrier

198 _____   _____
199   Contractor

200 _____
201 As to Contractor

DOCUMENT 4

MORTGAGE

1   **1. Mortgage.** In consideration of ten dollars and other valuable
2 considerations received by Mortgagor (named above), Mortgagor hereby,
3 on the date stated above, mortgages to Mortgagee (named above) the
4 mortgaged property described herein, for the purposes identified below.

5   **2. Secured indebtedness; future advances; maximum**
6 **amount and time.** This mortgage shall secure (a) the indebtedness of
7 Mortgagor (and each of them, if more than one) to Mortgagee, as
8 evidenced by a negotiable promissory note of even date herewith,
9 executed by Mortgagor and payable to Mortgagee, in the amount
10 specified on page one hereof, and (b) any future advances made by
11 Mortgagee to Mortgagor (or any of them, if more than one). The total
12 amount of indebtedness secured hereby may decrease or increase from
13 time to time, but the total unpaid balance so secured at any one time

14 shall not exceed the maximum principal amount specified on page one
15 hereof, plus interest thereon, and any disbursements made for the
16 payment of taxes, levies, or insurance on the mortgaged property, and
17 for maintenance, repair, protection, and preservation of the mortgaged
18 property, with interest on such disbursements, all as provided in this
19 mortgage. This mortgage shall not secure any future advances made
20 more than twenty years from the date hereof.

21 **3. Payment of secured indebtedness.** Mortgagor shall pay all
22 indebtedness and perform all obligations secured hereby promptly
23 when due.

24 **4. Title covenants.** Mortgagor covenants that the mortgaged
25 property is free from all encumbrances (other than this mortgage)
26 except as may be specifically stated herein, that lawful seisin of and
27 good right to encumber the mortgaged property are vested in Mortga-
28 gor, and that Mortgagor hereby fully warrants the title to the mort-
29 gaged property and will defend the same against the lawful claims of
30 all persons whomsoever.

31 **5. Improvements, fixtures, etc.** This mortgage extends to and
32 shall encumber all buildings, improvements, fixtures or appurtenances
33 now or hereafter erected or existing upon the mortgaged property,
34 including all elevators and all gas, steam, electric, water, cooking,
35 refrigerating, lighting, plumbing, heating, air conditioning, ventilation,
36 and power systems, machines, appliances, fixtures, and appurtenances,
37 even though they be detached or detachable, all of which shall be
38 deemed part of the mortgaged property.

39 **6. Maintenance and repair.** Mortgagor shall permit, commit, or
40 suffer no waste, impairment, or deterioration of the mortgaged proper-
41 ty. Mortgagor shall maintain the mortgaged property in good condi-
42 tion and repair. If Mortgagor fails to do so, then Mortgagee, without
43 waiving the option to foreclose, may take some or all measures that
44 Mortgagee reasonably deems necessary or desirable for the mainte-
45 nance, repair, preservation, or protection of the mortgaged property,
46 and any expenses reasonably incurred by Mortgagee in so doing shall
47 become part of the indebtedness secured hereby, shall become immedi-
48 ately due and payable, and shall bear interest at the highest lawful rate
49 specified in any note evidencing any indebtedness secured hereby.
50 Mortgagee shall have no obligation to care for and maintain the
51 mortgaged property, or, having taken some measures therefor, to con-
52 tinue the same or take other measures.

53 **7. Hazard insurance.** If any buildings now or hereafter consti-
54 tute part of the mortgaged property, Mortgagor shall keep the same
55 insured against loss or damage by fire, lightning, windstorm, and other
56 perils customarily insured against or as may be reasonably required by
57 Mortgagee, in the full insurable value thereof (or such lesser amount as
58 Mortgagee may authorize in writing), with an insurer of high financial
59 reputation and to which Mortgagee has no reasonable objection. The
60 policy or policies of insurance shall contain a standard mortgagee clause

in favor of Mortgagee and shall be delivered to Mortgagee. Mortgagor shall pay all premiums and charges for the maintenance and renewal of the insurance, and shall furnish Mortgagee with receipts and proofs thereof not less than ten days before the expiration thereof, without notice or demand from Mortgagee. If Mortgagor fails to do so, then Mortgagee, without waiving the option to foreclose, may obtain such insurance for the protection of Mortgagee, and any expenses reasonably incurred by Mortgagee in so doing shall become part of the indebtedness secured hereby, shall become immediately due and payable, and shall bear interest at the highest lawful rate specified in any note evidencing any indebtedness secured hereby. In the event of loss, the insurance proceeds shall be applied by Mortgagee to the reduction of the indebtedness secured hereby, or to the restoration and repair of the mortgaged property, at the option of Mortgagee. In the event of foreclosure of this mortgage or transfer of the mortgaged property in full or partial satisfaction of the indebtedness secured hereby, all interest of Mortgagor in the policy or policies of insurance (including any claim to proceeds attributable to losses theretofore occurring but not yet paid to Mortgagor) shall pass to the purchaser, grantee, or transferee.

8. Rents and profits. This mortgage shall extend to and encumber all rents, issues, profits, proceeds, and revenues derived from the mortgaged property, but Mortgagor may receive the same while this mortgage is not in default.

9. Receiver. If this mortgage falls into default, Mortgagee shall be entitled to the appointment of a receiver to take charge of the mortgaged property, and the rents, issues, profits, proceeds, and revenues arising therefrom, and hold the same subject to the direction of a court of competent jurisdiction, regardless of the solvency of Mortgagor or the adequacy of the security.

10. Taxes, assessments, and liens. Mortgagor shall pay all taxes, assessments, liens, and other charges upon or with respect to the mortgaged property before the same become delinquent, and shall furnish Mortgagee with receipts and proofs thereof at least ten days before the last day allowed for payment free from penalty, without notice or demand from Mortgagee. If Mortgagor fails to do so, then Mortgagee, without waiving the option to foreclose, may pay the same, and the amount so paid shall become part of the indebtedness secured hereby, shall become immediately due and payable, and shall bear interest at the highest lawful rate specified in any note evidencing any indebtedness secured hereby.

11. Inspection. Mortgagee and Mortgagee's representatives may enter upon the mortgaged property for inspection at all reasonable times and in a reasonable manner, both before and after default.

12. Eminent domain. This mortgage extends to and shall encumber any judgments, awards, damages, and settlements hereafter rendered or paid and resulting from condemnation proceedings with respect to the mortgaged property or the taking of the mortgaged

108 property or any part thereof under the power of eminent domain, and
109 Mortgagee may require that any sums payable to Mortgagor and
110 arising out of the power of eminent domain with respect to the property
111 shall be applied to the indebtedness secured hereby.

DOCUMENT 5

State of   **Mortgage**
FHA Case No.

This Mortgage, dated the   day of   , A.D.
by and between   hereinafter
called the Mortgagor, and

                       , a corporation organized and existing under the laws of the   of
                       hereinafter called the Mortgagee:

     Witnesseth, that for divers good and valuable considerations, and also in consideration of the aggregate sum named in the promissory note hereinafter described, the said Mortgagor does hereby grant, bargain, sell, alien, remise, release, convey, and confirm unto the said Mortgagee all that certain piece, parcel, or tract of land of which the said Mortgagor is now seized and possessed and in actual possession, situate in the county of
and state of   , described as follows:

     Together with all structures and improvements now and hereafter on said land, and fixtures attached thereto, and all rents, issues, proceeds, and profits accruing and to accrue from said premises, all of which are included within the foregoing description and the habendum thereof; also all gas, steam, electric, water, and other heating, cooking, refrigerating, lighting, plumbing, ventilating, irrigating, and power systems, machines, appliances, fixtures, and appurtenances, which now are or may hereafter pertain to, or be used with, in, or on said premises, even though they be detached or detachable.

This form is used in connection with mortgages insured under sections 203(b), (i) and (n) of the National Housing Act and provides for a One-Time Mortgage Insurance Premium payment in accordance with the regulations for those programs.

To Have And To Hold the same, together with all and singular the tenements, hereditaments and appurtenances thereunto belonging or in anywise appertaining, and the reversion and reversions, remainder or remainders, rents, issues and profits thereof; and also all the estate, right, title, interest, homestead, separate estate, possession, claim and demand whatsoever, as well in law as in equity, of the said Mortgagor in and to the same, and every part thereof, with the appurtenances of the said Mortgagor in and to the same, and every part and parcel thereof unto the said Mortgagee in fee simple.

And the Mortgagor hereby covenants with the Mortgagee that he is indefeasibly seized of said land in fee simple; that he has full power and lawful right to convey the same in fee simple as aforesaid; that it shall be lawful for the Mortgagee, at all times peaceably and quietly to enter upon, hold, occupy, and enjoy said land, and every part thereof; that the land is and will remain free from all encumbrances; that said Mortgagor will make such further assurances to prove the fee simple title to said land in said Mortgagee as may be reasonably required, and that said Mortgagor does hereby fully warrant the title to said land, and every part thereof, and will defend the same against the lawful claims of all persons whomsoever.

Provided always, and these presents are executed and delivered upon the following conditions, to wit:

The Mortgagor agrees to pay the Mortgagee, or order, the principal sum of

Dollars ($),

as evidenced by a note of even date herewith, with interest from date at the rate of

per centum (%), per annum on the unpaid balance until paid. The said principal and interest shall be payable at the office of

or at such other place as the holder of the note may designate in writing, in monthly installments of

Dollars ($),

commencing on the first day of   , and on the first day of each month thereafter until the

principal and interest are fully paid, except that the final payment of principal and interest, if not sooner paid, shall be due and payable on the first day of

And shall duly, promptly, and fully perform, discharge, execute, effect, complete, and comply with and abide by each and every the stipulations, agreements, conditions, and covenants of said promissory note and of this mortgage, then this mortgage and the estate hereby created shall cease and be null and void.

And the Mortgagor further covenants as follows:

1. That he will pay the indebtedness as hereinbefore provided. Privilege is reserved to pay the debt, in whole or in part, on any installment due date.

2. That, in order more fully to protect the security of this mortgage, the Mortgagor, together with, and in addition to, the monthly payments under the terms of the note secured hereby, on the first day of each month until the said note is fully paid, will pay to the Mortgagee the following sums:

(a) A sum equal to the ground rents, if any, next due, plus the premiums that will next become due and payable on policies of fire and other hazard insurance covering the mortgaged property, plus taxes and assessments next due on the mortgaged property (all as estimated by the Mortgagee) less all sums already paid therefor divided by the number of months to elapse before one month prior to the date when such ground rents, premiums, taxes, and assessments will become delinquent, such sums to be held by Mortgagee in trust to pay said ground rents, premiums, taxes, and special assessments; and

(b) All payments mentioned in the preceding subsection of this paragraph and all payments to be made under the note secured hereby shall be added together and the aggregate amount thereof shall be paid by the Mortgagor each month in a single payment to be applied by the Mortgagee to the following items in the order set forth:
(i) ground rents, taxes, assessments, fire and other hazard insurance premiums;
(ii) interest on the note secured hereby;
(iii) amortization of the principal of said note;
(iv) late charges

Any deficiency in the amount of such aggregate monthly payment shall, unless made good by the Mortgagor prior to the due date of the next such payment, constitute an event of default under this mortgage. The Mortgagee may collect a "late charge" not to exceed four cents (4¢) for each dollar ($1) of each payment more than fifteen (15) days in arrears to cover the expense involved in handling delinquent payments.

3. That if the total of the payments made by the Mortgagor under (a) of paragraph 2 preceding shall exceed the amount of payments actually made by the Mortgagee for ground rents, taxes and assessments and insurance premiums, as the case may be, such excess, if the loan is current, at the option of the Mortgagor, shall be credited on subsequent payments to be made by the Mortgagor, or refunded to the Mortgagor. If, however, the monthly payments made by the Mortgagor under (a) of paragraph 2 preceding shall not be sufficient to pay ground rents, taxes and assessments and insurance premiums, as the case may be, when the same shall become due and payable, then the Mortgagor shall pay to the Mortgagee any amount necessary to make up the deficiency, on or before the date when payment of such ground rents, taxes, assessments, or insurance premiums shall be due. If at any time the Mortgagor shall tender to the Mortgagee, in accordance with the provisions of the note secured hereby, full payment of the entire indebtedness represented thereby, the Mortgagee shall, in computing the amount of such indebtedness, credit to the account of the Mortgagor any balance remaining in the funds accumulated under the provisions of (a) of said paragraph 2. If there shall be a default under any of the provisions of this mortgage resulting in a public sale of the premises covered hereby, or if the Mortgagee acquires the property otherwise after default, the Mortgagee shall apply, at the time of the commencement of such proceedings, or at the same time the property is otherwise acquired, the balance then remaining in the funds accumulated under (a) of paragraph 2 preceding as a credit against the amount of principal then remaining unpaid under said note.

4. That he will pay all taxes, assessments, water rates, and other governmental or municipal charges, fines, or impositions, for which provision has not been made hereinbefore, and in default thereof the Mortgagee may pay the same; and that he will promptly deliver the official receipts therefor to the Mortgagee.

[E2807]

5. That he will permit, commit, or suffer no waste, impairment, or deterioration of said property or any part thereof; and in the event of the failure of the Mortgagor to keep the buildings on said premises and those to be erected on said premises, or improvements thereon, in good repair, the Mortgagee may make such repairs as in its discretion it may deem necessary for the proper preservation thereof, and the full amount of each and every such payment shall be immediately due and payable, and shall be secured by the lien of this Mortgagee.

6. That he will pay all and singular the costs, charges, and expenses, including reasonable lawyer's fees, and costs of abstracts of title, incurred or paid at any time by the Mortgagee because of the failure on the part of the Mortgagor promptly and fully to perform the agreements and covenants of said promissory note and this mortgage, and said costs, charges, and expenses shall be immediately due and payable and shall be secured by the lien of this mortgage.

7. That he will keep the improvements now existing or hereafter erected on the mortgaged property insured as may be required from time to time by the Mortgagee against loss by fire and other hazards, casualties, and contingencies, in such amounts and for such periods as may be required by Mortgagee, and will pay promptly, when due, any premiums on such insurance for payment of which provision has not been made hereinbefore. All insurance shall be carried in companies approved by Mortgagee and the policies and renewals thereof shall be held by Mortgagee and have attached thereto loss payable clauses in favor of and in form acceptable to the Mortgagee. In event of loss he will give immediate notice by mail to Mortgagee, and Mortgagee may make proof of loss if not made promptly by Mortgagor, and each insurance company concerned is hereby authorized and directed to make payment for such loss directly to the Mortgagee instead of to the Mortgagor and the Mortgagee jointly, and the insurance proceeds, or any part thereof, may be applied by the Mortgagee at its option, either to the reduction of the indebtedness hereby secured or to the restoration or repair of the property damaged. In event of foreclosure of this mortgage and other transfer of title to the mortgaged property in extinguishment of the indebtedness secured hereby, all right, title and interest of the Mortgagor in and to any insurance policies then in force shall pass to the purchaser or grantee.

8. That if the premises, or any part thereof, be condemned under any power of eminent domain, or acquired for a public use, the damages, proceeds, and in consideration for such acquisition, to the extent of the full amount of indebtedness upon this Mortgage, and the Note secured hereby remaining unpaid, are hereby assigned by the Mortgagor to the Mortgagee and shall be paid forthwith to the Mortgagee to be applied by it on account of the indebtedness secured hereby, whether due or not.

9. That the Mortgagee may, at any time pending a suit upon this mortgage, apply to the court having jurisdiction thereof for the appointment of a receiver, and such court shall forthwith appoint a receiver of the premises covered hereby all and singular, including all and singular the income, profits, issues, and revenues from whatever source derived, each and every of which, it being expressly understood, is hereby mortgaged as if specifically set forth and described in the granting and habendum clauses hereof, and such receiver shall have all the broad and effective functions and powers in anywise entrusted by a court to a receiver, and such appointment shall be made by such court as an admitted equity and a matter of absolute right to said Mortgagee, and without reference to the adequacy or inadequacy of the value of the property mortgaged or the solvency of said Mortgagor or the defendants, and that such rents, profits, income, issues, and revenues shall be applied by such receiver according to the lien of this mortgage and

the practice of such court. In the event of any default on the part of the Mortgagor hereunder, the Mortgagor agrees to pay to the Mortgagee on demand as a reasonable monthly rental for the premises an amount at least equivalent to one-twelfth (1/12) of the aggregate of the twelve monthly installments payable in the then current year plus the actual amount of the annual taxes, assessments, water rates, and insurance premiums for such year not covered by the aforesaid monthly payments.

10. That (a) in the event of any breach of this mortgage or default on the part of the Mortgagor, or (b) in the event that any of said sums of money herein referred to be not promptly and fully paid without demand or notice, or (c) in the event that each and every the stipulations, agreements, conditions, and covenants of said note and this mortgage, are not duly, promptly, and fully performed; then in either or any such event, the said aggregate sum mentioned in said note then remaining unpaid, with interest accrued to that time, and all moneys secured hereby, shall become due and payable forthwith, or thereafter, at the option of said Mortgagee, as fully and completely as if all of the said sums of money were originally stipulated to be paid on such day, anything in said note or in this mortgage to the contrary notwithstanding; and thereupon or thereafter, at the option of said Mortgagee, without notice or demand, suit at law or in equity, may be prosecuted as if all moneys secured hereby had matured prior to its institution. The Mortgagee may foreclose this mortgage, as to the amount so declared due and payable, and the said premises shall be sold to satisfy and pay the same together with costs, expenses, and allowances. In case of partial foreclosure of this mortgage, the mortgaged premises shall be sold subject to the continuing lien of this mortgage for the amount of the debt not then due and unpaid. In such case the provisions of this paragraph may again be availed of thereafter from time to time by the Mortgagee.

11. That he will give immediate notice by mail to the Mortgagee of any conveyance, transfer, or change of ownership of the premises.

12. That no waiver of any covenant herein or of the obligation secured hereby shall at any time thereafter be held to be a waiver of the terms hereof or of the note secured hereby.

13. That if the Mortgagor default in any of the covenants or agreements contained herein, or in said note, than the Mortgagee may perform the same, and all expenditures (including reasonable attorney's fees) made by the Mortgagee in so doing shall draw interest at the rate set forth in the note secured hereby, and shall be repayable immediately and without demand by the Mortgagor to the Mortgagee, and, together with interest and costs accruing thereon, shall be secured by this mortgage.

14. That the mailing of a written notice or demand addressed to the owner of record of the mortgaged premises, or directed to the said owner at the last address actually furnished to the Mortgagee, or directed to said owner at said mortgaged premises, and mailed by the United States mails, shall be sufficient notice and demand in any case arising under this instrument and required by the provisions hereof or by law.

15. The Mortgagor further covenants that should this mortgage and the note secured hereby not be eligible for insurance under the National Housing Act within _____ days from the date (written statement of any officer of the Department of Housing and Urban Development or authorized agent of the Secretary of Housing and Urban Development date subsequent to the _____ days' time from the date of this mortgage, declining to insure said note and this mortgage, being deemed conclusive proof of such inelegibility), the Mortgagee or

the holder of the note may, at its option, declare all sums secured hereby immediately due and payable. Notwithstanding the foregoing, this option may not be exercised by the Mortgagee when the ineligibility for insurance under the National Housing Act is due to the Mortgagee's failure to remit the mortgage insurance premium to the Department of Housing and Urban Development.

16. Attorney's fees, as used in this Mortgage and in the Note, "Attorney's Fees" shall include attorney's fees, if any, which shall be awarded by an Appellate Court.

The covenants herein contained shall bind, and the benefits and advantages shall inure to, the respective heirs, executors, administrators, successors, and assigns of the parties hereto. Whenever used, the singular number shall include the plural, the plural the singular, and the use of any gender shall include all genders.

In witness whereof the Mortgagor has hereunto set his hand and seal the day and year first aforesaid.

Signed, sealed, and delivered in the presence of—

_____   _____ [Seal]

_____   _____ [Seal]

                                    _____ [Seal]

                                    _____ [Seal]

State of   )
)   *ss:*

County of   )

Before me personally appeared   and

his wife, to me well known to be the individuals described in and who executed the foregoing instrument, and acknowledged before me that they executed the same for the purposes therein expressed.

Witness my hand and official seal this   day of   . 19

_____

(Notary Public in and for the County and State aforesaid)

My Commission expires: _____

State of   )
)   *ss:*

County of   )

Before me personally appeared   , to me well known and known to me to be the individual described in and who executed the foregoing instrument, and acknowledged before me that he executed the same for the purposes therein expressed.

Witness my hand and official seal this   day of   . 19

_____

(Notary Public in and for the County and State aforesaid)

My Commission expires: _____

[E2809]

DOCUMENT 6

NOTE

This Note is payable in _____ equal monthly payments of $_____ each, except that the final payment is equal to the unpaid balance of the Amount Financed and the unpaid Finance Charge thereon.

Amount Financed $_____

FINANCE CHARGE $_____

Documentary stamp tax $_____

Total of Payments $_____

ANNUAL PERCENTAGE RATE _____ %

PLAIN LANGUAGE NOTE. We've written this Note in simple and easy-to-read language because we want you to understand the terms of your loan. Please read this Note carefully and feel free to contact us if you have any questions. We use the words **you** and **your** to mean the Borrowers. In the Insurance Statement, **I** means the one of you who is the principal wage earner. The words **we, us** and **our** refer to the Lender.

YOUR PROMISE TO PAY AND THE TERMS OF REPAYMENT. To repay your loan, you promise to pay us the Amount Financed shown above together with finance charge at the Agreed Rate of Finance Charge until paid. You agree to pay this sum to us at our office in

---

Credit Life Insurance Cost: $_____

Accident and Health Insurance Cost: $_____

INSURANCE STATEMENT. Credit life insurance and accident and health insurance are available at the cost shown above, for the term of the loan. Neither type of insurance is required by us in order for you to obtain this loan. The principal wage earner is the person to be insured and the person who must sign this statement if insurance is desired.

You authorize us to retain from the loan proceeds the cost of any insurance checked below.

1. **Check One:** ☐ I desire credit life and accident and health insurance.

                ☐ I desire credit life insurance only.

                ☐ I do not wish to purchase any insurance.

2. **Sign Here:** _____
                          (principal wage earner)

3. **Date Here:** _____/_____/_____

You have the option of assigning any other life insurance policy or policies which you own or may obtain for the purpose of covering your loan.

[E2810]

monthly payments according to the terms of repayment shown above. Each payment will be applied first to the finance charge due on the date of payment and then to the Amount Financed. The date of this Note is the date we mail or give you the loan proceeds and your first payment is due one month later. Your remaining payments are due on the same day of each following month until the loan is paid. You can prepay your loan any time.

RATE OF CHARGE. The Agreed Rate of Finance Charge per year on your loan is the Annual Percentage Rate shown on this Note computed on the Amount Financed as computed from time to time; however, at the end of 12 months following the last contractual payment date, the finance charge on any balance still unpaid will not exceed 10% per year. The monthly rate is one-twelfth of this yearly rate for each full month. The rate for each day in a fraction of a month, when the period for which the charge is computed is more or less than one month, is 1/365th of the annual rate.

DEFAULT — ENTIRE BALANCE DUE. If you don't make a payment on time, you'll be in default. When that happens, you agree that without giving you any advance notice, we can require you to pay the outstanding balance of this loan at once (including any unpaid finance charge).

LOAN LICENSE. We are licensed by the State of Florida to make loans in sums of $25,000 or less pursuant to Chapter 516, Florida Statutes, as amended.

SIGNATURES. If you agree to be bound by the terms of this Note, please sign your name below. All persons signing this Note will be fully responsible for paying it in full.

_____

1st Signature (principal wage earner)

_____

Social Security Number   Phone Number

         /   /

_____

2nd Signature (if two persons named above)   Date

Lender:

[E2811]

DOCUMENT 7

NOTIFICATION OF SUBSCRIBER RIGHTS UNDER THE CABLE FRANCHISE POLICY AND COMMUNICATIONS ACT OF 1984

Dear Subscriber:

In connection with your subscription to _____ Cable _____, herein "_____ Cable," personally identifiable information will be collected and maintained, such as your name, service, billing address, home telephone, other telephone, social security number or driver's license number, employer, premium service subscription information, marketing information and subscriber complaints. This information is collected for use by _____ Cable in rendering certain cable service and other services to you, such as billing, and in monitoring unauthorized reception of cable communications, and _____ Cable may disclose this information if the disclosure is necessary to render, or conduct legitimate business activity related to, a cable service or other service provided to you. _____ Cable will not otherwise use this information without your prior written or electronic consent. _____ Cable will not maintain this information after it is no longer necessary for carrying on our business.

The specific restrictions and prohibitions regarding the acquisition and use of personally identifiable subscriber information are as follows:

1. _____ Cable may not use any electronic device to record, transmit or observe any events or listen to, record or monitor any conversations which take place inside your residence, work place or place of business, without obtaining your express written or electronic consent.

2. Except as provided herein, _____ Cable may not collect or disclose personally identifiable information regarding any of its subscribers without the subscriber's express written consent.

3. Personally identifiable information shall be made available for your examination within 30 days of the receipt of a request from you. You shall be responsible for all costs of copying of documents supplied. Upon a reasonable showing, a cable television operator is required to correct any inaccurate information. All personally identifiable information will be made available between 8:30 a.m.–5:00 p.m., Monday–Friday at _____, _____, _____.

4. _____ Cable shall not make personally identifiable information available to government agencies in the absence of legal compulsion, and shall promptly notify you of any such request prior to responding. At the court proceeding, the agency must offer clear and convincing evidence that the subject of the information is reasonably suspected of engaging in criminal activity and that the information sought would be material evidence in the case. The subject of the information must be

43
44 afforded that opportunity to appear and contest the agency's claim.

45
46
47 5. In the event that any person receives personally identifiable information from _____ Cable, that person shall likewise be subject to these provisions.

48
49
50
51 6. Violation of these provisions may lead to certain criminal and civil liabilities. A person aggrieved by a violation of these provisions may bring a civil action for damages in United States District Court.

52
53
54
55
56
57 The law does not prohibit _____ Cable from compiling, maintaining and distributing non-cable service related mailing lists containing the names and addresses of its subscribers. However, you have the right to elect not to be included on such a list. If you do not desire to be included on any such list, you must notify _____ Cable of your election to be excluded in writing at _____, _____, _____, _____.

DOCUMENT 8

POWER OF ATTORNEY REGARDING MEDICAL CARE AND TREATMENT

1
2
3
4
5
6
7
8
9
10
11
12
13
14
15 KNOW ALL PERSONS BY THESE PRESENTS that I, _____, as principal, currently residing at _____, hereby constitute and appoint my friend _____, currently residing at _____, as my true and lawful attorney, to act for me, and in my name, in the event that I am ill, incapacitated, or injured, and cannot make decisions on my own regarding the course of my medical care and treatment. In such circumstance, I authorize my said attorney to make all decisions relating to my medical care and treatment, including but not limited to X-rays, tests, examinations, anesthetic, medical, surgical or other treatments or procedures which are carried out under the supervision of and upon the advice of a duly licensed physician. I further authorize my said attorney to consult with any physicians and/or other medical personnel who are treating me or who may treat me and I instruct that my medical records be made available to my said attorney as part of said consultation.

16
17
18
19 I grant my said attorney the powers and rights set forth hereinabove as fully and in place of any powers and rights that would otherwise accrue to any parent, spouse or other relative in the event that I had not executed this instrument.

20
21 This power of attorney shall not be affected by the principal's subsequent disability or incompetence.

22 This instrument may not be changed orally.

23
24 IN WITNESS WHEREOF, I have set my hand hereto this _____ day of _____, 19__.

25

26 STATE OF _____ ⎫
27 COUNTY OF _____ ⎬ ss.:
⎭

28   On the _____ day of _____, 19__, before me personally appeared
29 _____, to me known and known to be the individual described in, and
30 who executed the foregoing instrument, and he acknowledged that he
31 knows the contents thereof and he executed the same.

32   _____

DOCUMENT 9

QUIT–CLAIM DEED

1   Know all Men by these Presents That, _____, the Grantor, for
2 divers good causes and considerations thereunto moving, and especially
3 for the sum of _____ Dollars ($_____) received to full satisfaction of
4 _____, the Grantee, have Given, Granted, Remised, Released and
5 Forever Quit-Claimed, and do by these presents absolutely give, grant,
6 remise, release and forever quit-claim unto the said grantee, _____
7 heirs and assigns forever, all such right and title as _____, the said
8 grantor, have or ought to have in and to the following described piece
9 or parcel of land, situated in the _____ of _____ County of _____
10 and State of _____:

11   To Have and to Hold the premises aforesaid, with the appurte-
12 nances thereunto belonging to the said grantee _____, heirs and
13 assigns, so that neither the said grantor _____, nor _____ heirs, nor
14 any other persons claiming title through or under _____, shall or will
15 hereafter claim or demand any right or title to the premises, or any
16 part thereof; but they and every one of them shall by these presents be
17 excluded and forever barred.

18   In Witness Whereof, _____ have hereunto set _____
19 hand _____, the _____ day of _____, in the year of our Lord one
20 thousand nine hundred and _____.

21 Signed and acknowledged in presence of _____ ss.

22 _____   _____

23 _____   _____

24 _____   _____

25 _____   _____

26 _____   _____

27 _____   _____

28 _____   _____

29 The State of _____ ⎫
30 County of _____ ⎬ SS.
31 ⎭

Before me, a notary public, in and for said County and State, personally appeared the above named

32 who acknowledged that _____ did sign the foregoing instrument and
33 that the same is _____ free act and deed.

34 In Testimony Whereof, I have hereunto set my hand and official seal, at
35 _____ this _____ day of _____ A.D. 19__.

36 This instrument prepared by

37 _____
38 Notary Public

DOCUMENT 10

RESTRICTIVE COVENANTS

1 KNOW ALL PERSONS BY THESE PRESENTS that:

2 WHEREAS, _____ and _____, his wife, hereinafter called "Own-
3 ers", are desirous of placing certain restrictive covenants on the use of
4 said property, which said property is more particularly described as
5 follows:

6 NOW, THEREFORE, THESE PRESENTS WITNESSETH: That
7 the Owners, for and in consideration of the covenants herein contained,
8 and for other good and valuable considerations, do herein and hereby
9 covenant and agree, for their successors and assigns, that the following
10 covenants and restrictions are hereby placed upon the said property
11 above described:

12 1. All building sites shall be used solely and only for residential
13 purposes and no structures, permanent or temporary, shall be erected,
14 altered, placed or permitted to remain on any lot other than one
15 detached, single-family dwelling, not to exceed two and one-half (2½)
16 stories in height.

17 2. There shall be no detached or accessory buildings except ca-
18 banas which are permissible when erected adjacent to and used in
19 conjunction with a swimming pool.

20 3. No building shall be erected, placed or altered on any premises
21 until the building plans, specifications, and plot plan showing the
22 location of such building have been approved as to conformity and
23 harmony of external design with the existing structures in the develop-
24 ment, and as to location of the building with respect to topography and
25 finished ground elevation, by an architectural committee as outlined in
26 paragraph number 17.

27 4. No building shall be located on any lot except within the
28 setback and easement lines indicated on the recorded plat, however,
29 said structures are to be at least 25 feet from the front of said property

line and at least 12½ feet from the side of the property line and at least 20 feet from the back of the property line.

5. No lots shall be resubdivided into parcels smaller than that recorded in Plat Book _____, Page _____, of the Public Records of _____ County, _____.

6. No noxious or offensive trade or activity shall be carried on upon any building site, nor shall anything be done thereon which may be or become an annoyance or nuisance to the neighborhood.

7. No trailer, tent, shack, garage, barn or other out building erected on a building site covered by these covenants shall at any time be used for human habitation, temporarily or permanently, nor shall any structure of a temporary character be used for human habitation.

8. The keeping of a mobile home, either with or without wheels, on any parcel of property covered by these covenants is prohibited. Any motor boat, house boat, boat trailer or other similar water borne vehicle may be maintained, stored, or kept on any parcel of residential property covered by these covenants only if housed completely within a structure which has been architecturally approved by provisions of paragraph number 3 hereof.

9. Self propelled motor homes may be kept on the property, but only if they are placed in the back yard of the property and cannot be seen from the side boundary or the front side of the property.

10. No dwelling shall be permitted on any building site covered by these covenants, the habitable floor area of which, exclusive of basements, porches, and garages, is less than 1800 square feet.

11. Easements are hereby reserved for utility installation and maintenance as indicated on the recorded plat, and no structures of any kind shall be erected in the area of such easements. Nothing may be placed within area of the drainage easements indicated on the recorded plat to impede or alter the flow of water within such drainage easements.

12. No animals or poultry of any kind other than house pets shall be kept or maintained on any part of said property.

13. When any building site shall be for sale, only one "For Sale" sign will be permitted for each lot, and this sign shall be no larger than 6 square feet; except that a sign of up to 32 square feet may be used by a builder or real estate broker to advertise a new property for sale during the construction and sales period, the sales period to extend for no more that 3 months from the date of the issuance of the building permit.

14. No fence, wall or hedge shall be permitted to extend beyond the minimum building set back lines established herein except upon approval by the architectural committee as provided in paragraph 17 hereof.

74 15. It is prohibited for any garage or carport to face the front of
75 the property. All garages and carports must have side entrances with
76 the front portion of the garage or carport being of the same type and
77 design as the remainder of the dwelling.

78 16. All driveways and parking areas must be paved with either
79 asphaltic concrete or Portland Cement concrete. Drives must be paved
80 to the curb line and shall be continuously paved in any area meant for
81 driving or automobile storage. There shall be garages, carports or
82 paved area on each building site for the parking of at least four
83 automobiles. No car shall be parked, stored or otherwise left on any
84 unpaved area. At no time shall there be any repairing, dismantling, or
85 other mechanical work done on any automobiles or other vehicles,
86 except in a closed carport or garage.

87 17. An architectural control committee is hereby established.
88 This committee is composed of _____ and _____, his wife. The
89 committee may designate a representative to act for it. In the event of
90 death or resignation of any member of the committee, the remaining
91 member shall have full authority to designate a successor. Should the
92 membership of such committee be changed, notice of this change shall
93 be recorded in the Office of the Clerk of the Circuit Court of _____
94 County, _____.

95 The architectural control committee shall approve or disapprove
96 any design within 15 days from the date of the submission of these
97 plans, and such approval or disapproval shall be in writing. In the
98 event the committee, or its designated representative, fails to approve
99 or disapprove within said 15 days, then approval is deemed to have
100 been granted and the related covenants shall be deemed to have been
101 fully complied with.

102 These covenants are to run with the land and shall be binding on
103 all parties and all persons claiming under them until January 1, 2005,
104 at which time said covenants shall be automatically extended for
105 successive periods of ten (10) years, unless by vote of a majority of the
106 then owners of the lots, it is agreed to change said covenants in whole
107 or in part.

108 If the parties hereto, or any of them, or their heirs or assigns, shall
109 violate or attempt to violate any of the covenants herein, it shall be
110 lawful for any other person or persons owning any real property
111 situated in said subdivision to prosecute any proceedings at law or in
112 equity against the person or persons violating or attempting to violate
113 any such covenant, and either to prevent him or them from so doing, or
114 to recover damages for such violation.

115 Invalidation of any one of these covenants, or any part thereof, by
116 judgment or court order shall in no wise affect any of the other
117 provisions, which shall remain in full force and effect.

118 IN WITNESS WHEREOF, the Owners have hereunto affixed their
119 signatures this _____ day of _____, A.D., 19__.

120 Signed in the presence of:

121 _____   _____

122 _____   _____

123 STATE OF _____
124 COUNTY OF _____

125   BEFORE ME personally appeared _____ and _____, his wife,
126 well known and known to me to be the individuals described in and
127 who executed the foregoing instrument as "Owners" of the above
128 named real property and severally acknowledged to and before me that
129 they executed such instrument as their own free act and deed and for
130 the reasons therein expressed.

131   WITNESS my hand and official seal this _____ day of _____,
132 A.D., 19__.

133

134   _____
135   Notary Public, State at Large
                                      My Commission Expires:

DOCUMENT 11

WAIVER OF LIEN

1 State of: _____
2 County of: _____

3   To All Whom It May Concern,

4   Whereas we the undersigned _____, have been employed by
5 _____ to furnish, supply, and install a _____ _____, for the
6 building known as _____ _____, County of _____, State of _____.

7   Now, therefore, know ye, that _____ the undersigned for, and in
8 consideration for the sum of _____, and other good and valuable
9 considerations the receipt whereof, is hereby acknowledged, do hereby
10 waive and release any and all lien, or claim or right to lien on said
11 above described building and premises under the statutes of the state of
12 _____ relating to mechanics liens, on account of labor or materials, or
13 both, furnished or which may be furnished, by the undersigned to or on
14 account of the said _____ and/or _____ for said building or prem-
15 ises.

16 Given Under _____ Hand _____ and Seal _____ This _____ Day
17 of _____ A.D., 19__.

18   _____ Seal

19   _____ Seal

Index of Subjects

[References are to pages.]
[See also, Index of Documents.]

Index of Documents

[References are to pages.]
[See also, Index of Subjects.]

†